BATMAN

ARKHAM UNHINGED

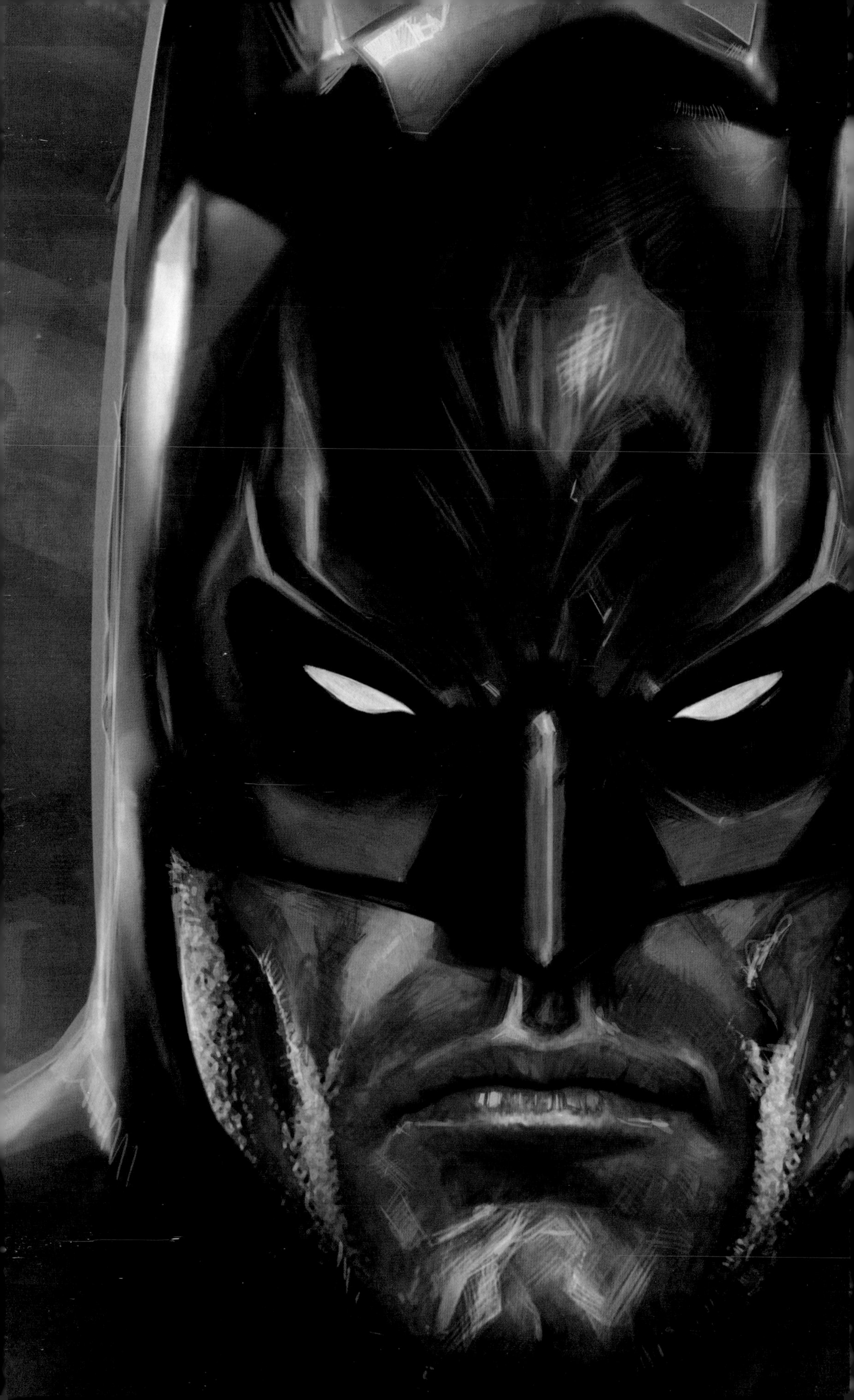

DEREK FRIDOLFS
PAUL DINI   MARLY HALPERN-GRASER
PAUL CROCKER   SEFTON HILL writers

MIKE S. MILLER   BRIAN CHING   JUAN RYP
SIMON COLEBY   BRUNO REDONDO   PETE WOODS
AL BARRIONUEVO   JIMBO SALGADO   LIVESAY
SANTI CASAS   CLIFF RATHBURN
MICHEL LACOMBE   JEFFREY HUET artists

GABE ELTAEB   TONY AVIÑA
ANDREW ELDER   RANDY MAYOR colorists

TRAVIS LANHAM letterer

DAVE WILKINS collection cover

BATMAN CREATED BY BOB KANE

Jim Chadwick Editor – Original Series
Sarah Gaydos and Chynna Clugston Flores Assistant Editors – Original Series
Robin Wildman Editor
Robbin Brosterman Design Director – Books
Louis Prandi Publication Design

Bob Harras Senior VP – Editor-in-Chief, DC Comics

Diane Nelson President
Dan DiDio and Jim Lee Co-Publishers
Geoff Johns Chief Creative Officer
John Rood Executive VP – Sales, Marketing and Business Development
Amy Genkins Senior VP – Business and Legal Affairs
Nairi Gardiner Senior VP – Finance
Jeff Boison VP – Publishing Planning
Mark Chiarello VP – Art Direction and Design
John Cunningham VP – Marketing
Terri Cunningham VP – Editorial Administration
Alison Gill Senior VP – Manufacturing and Operations
Hank Kanalz Senior VP – Vertigo & Integrated Publishing
Jay Kogan VP – Business and Legal Affairs, Publishing
Jack Mahan VP – Business Affairs, Talent
Nick Napolitano VP – Manufacturing Administration
Sue Pohja VP – Book Sales
Courtney Simmons Senior VP – Publicity
Bob Wayne Senior VP – Sales

DC Comics, 1700 Broadway, New York, NY 10019
A Warner Bros. Entertainment Company.
Printed by RR Donnelley, Salem, VA, USA. 7/5/13. First Printing.
ISBN: 978-1-4012-4018-9

Library of Congress Cataloging-in-Publication Data

Batman : Arkham unhinged / [Derek Fridolfs, Dave Wilkens].
   p. cm.
   "Originally published online in Batman: Arkham Unhinged Chapters 1-13 and Batman: Arkham City
Digital Chapters 6-7."
   ISBN 978-1-4012-3749-3
   1. Graphic novels. I. Fridolfs, Derek. II. Wilkens, Dave.
   PN6728.B36B3776 2012
   741.5'973—dc23
                        2012033191

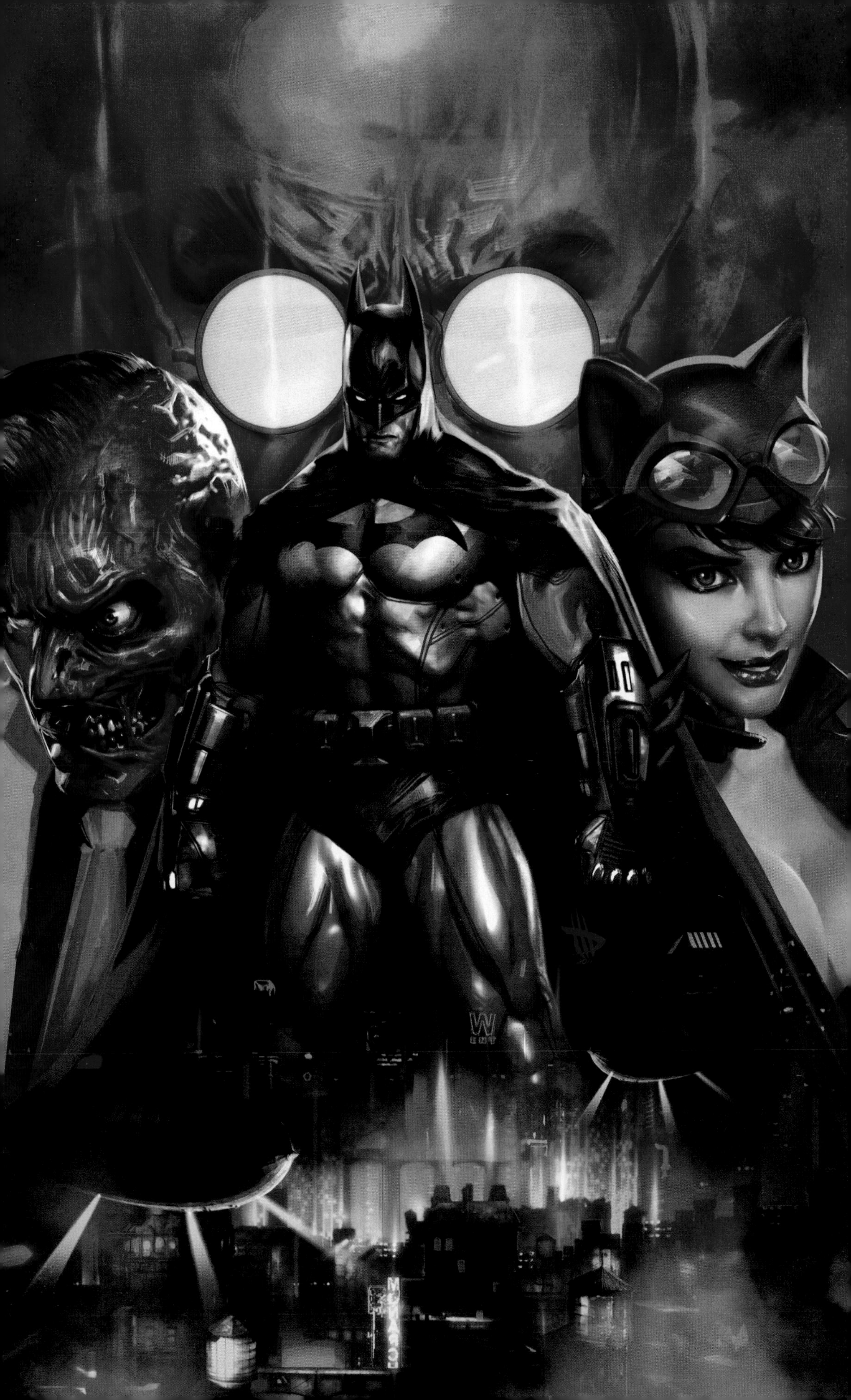

INSIDE JOB

WRITTEN BY: **DEREK FRIDOLFS**

BASED ON A TELEPLAY BY: **MARLY HALPERN-GRASER**

STORY BY: **MARLY HALPERN-GRASER**
PAUL CROCKER
SEFTON HILL

ART BY: **MIKE S. MILLER**

COLORS BY: **GABE ELTAEB**

LETTERS BY: **TRAVIS LANHAM**

COVER: **DAVE WILKINS**

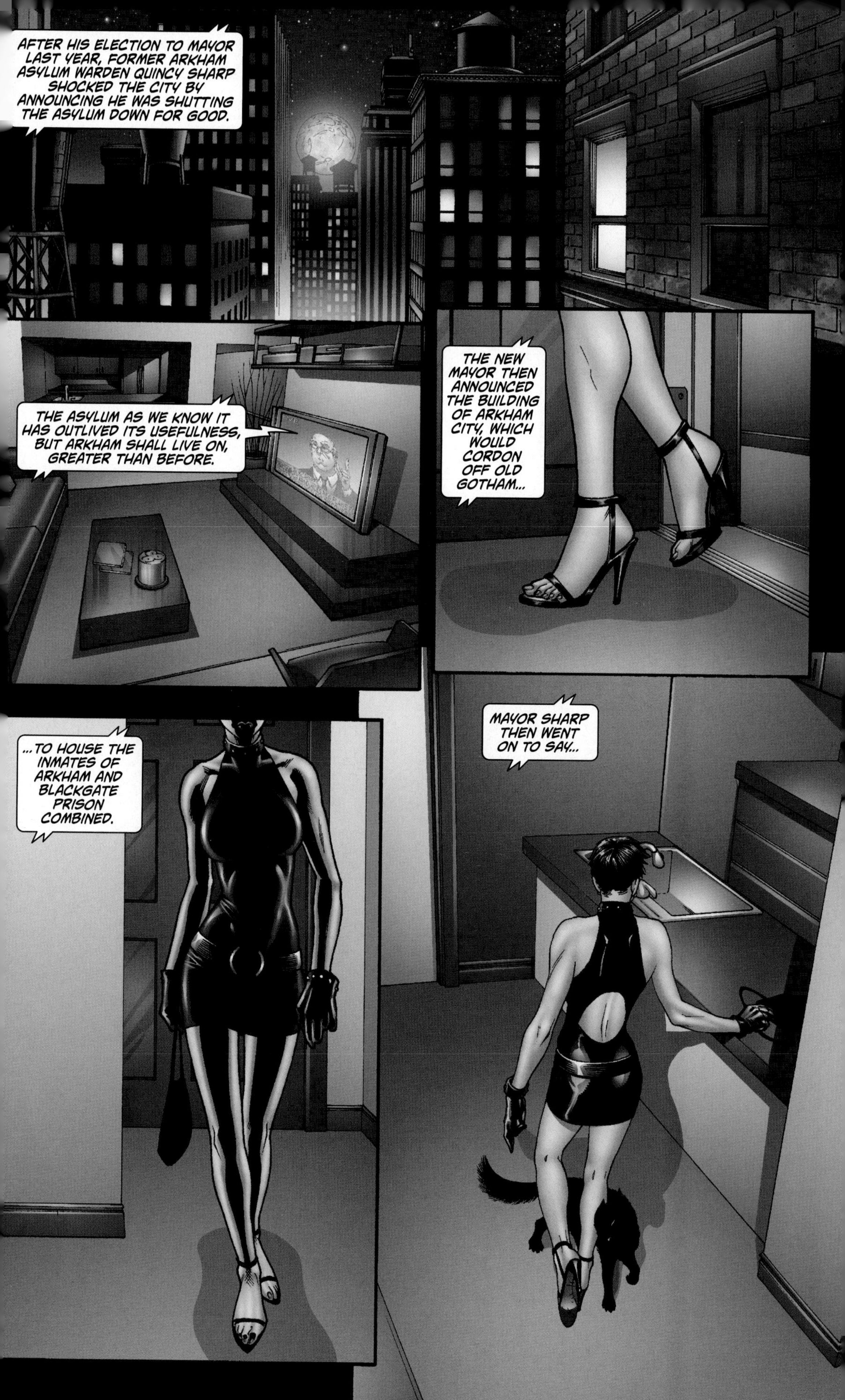
AFTER HIS ELECTION TO MAYOR LAST YEAR, FORMER ARKHAM ASYLUM WARDEN QUINCY SHARP SHOCKED THE CITY BY ANNOUNCING HE WAS SHUTTING THE ASYLUM DOWN FOR GOOD.
THE ASYLUM AS WE KNOW IT HAS OUTLIVED ITS USEFULNESS, BUT ARKHAM SHALL LIVE ON, GREATER THAN BEFORE.
THE NEW MAYOR THEN ANNOUNCED THE BUILDING OF ARKHAM CITY, WHICH WOULD CORDON OFF OLD GOTHAM...
...TO HOUSE THE INMATES OF ARKHAM AND BLACKGATE PRISON COMBINED.
MAYOR SHARP THEN WENT ON TO SAY...

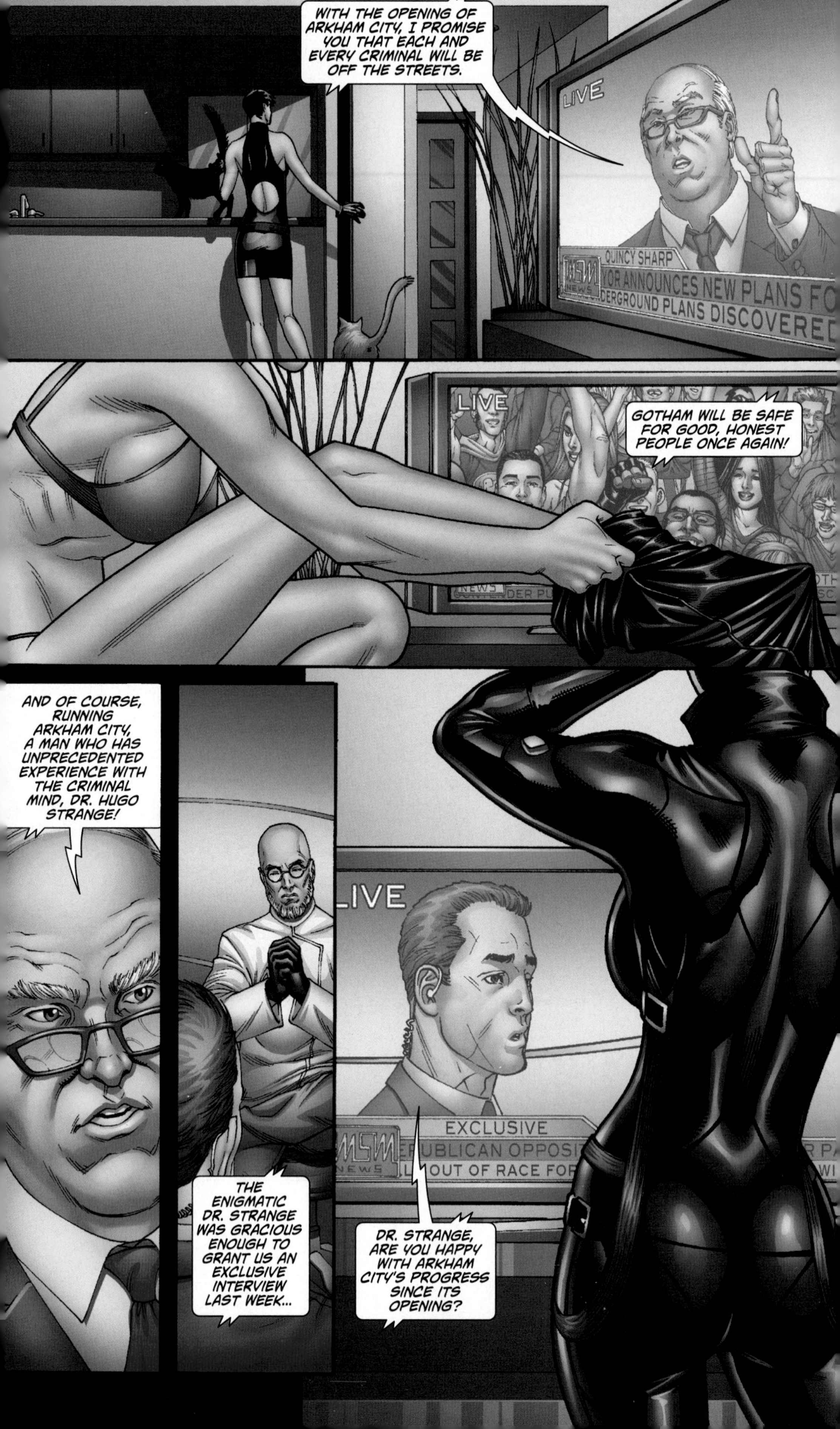

WITH THE OPENING OF ARKHAM CITY, I PROMISE YOU THAT EACH AND EVERY CRIMINAL WILL BE OFF THE STREETS.
LIVE
QUINCY SHARP
LIVE
GOTHAM WILL BE SAFE FOR GOOD, HONEST PEOPLE ONCE AGAIN!
AND OF COURSE, RUNNING ARKHAM CITY, A MAN WHO HAS UNPRECEDENTED EXPERIENCE WITH THE CRIMINAL MIND, DR. HUGO STRANGE!
THE ENIGMATIC DR. STRANGE WAS GRACIOUS ENOUGH TO GRANT US AN EXCLUSIVE INTERVIEW LAST WEEK...
LIVE
EXCLUSIVE
DR. STRANGE, ARE YOU HAPPY WITH ARKHAM CITY'S PROGRESS SINCE ITS OPENING?

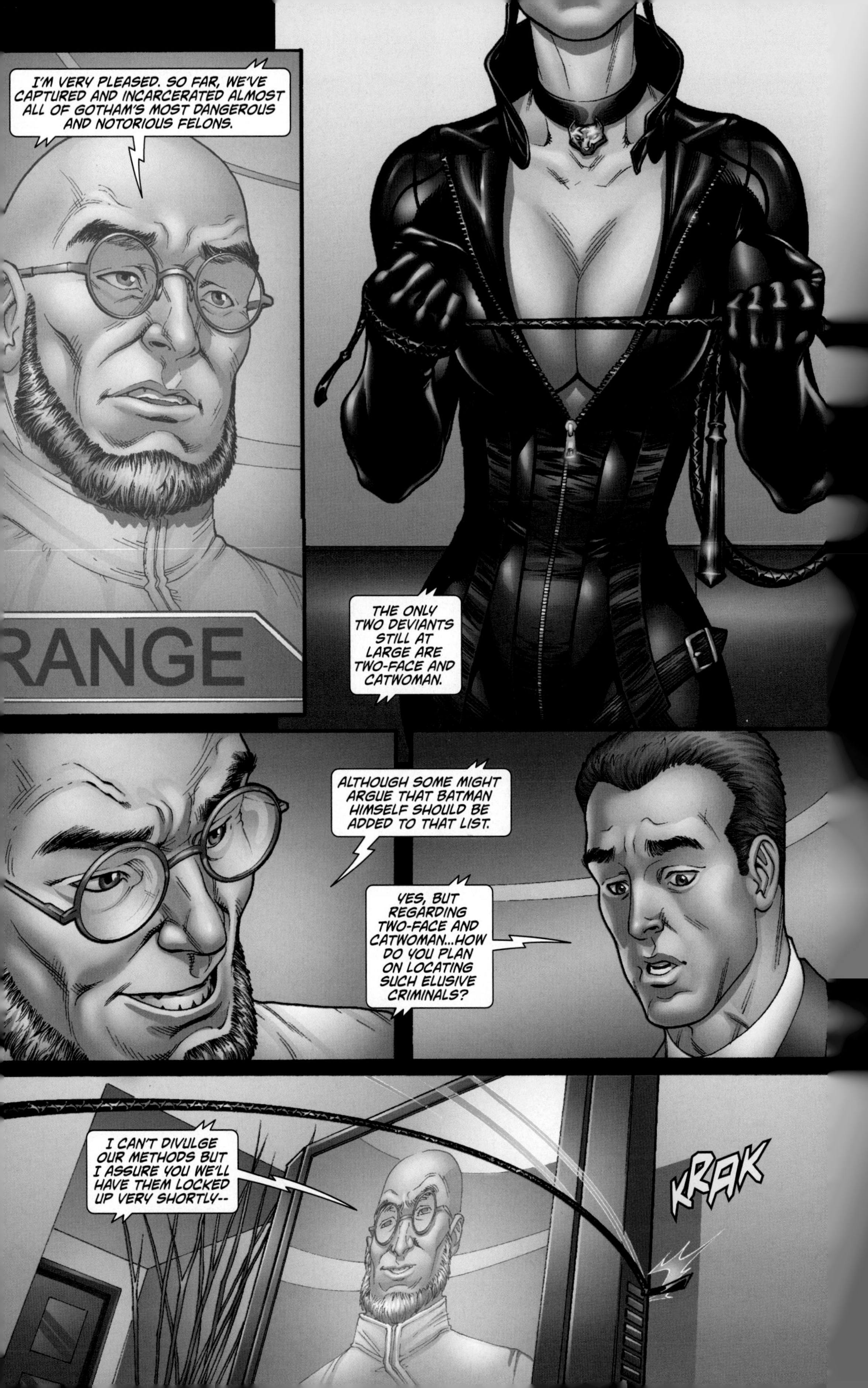
I'M VERY PLEASED. SO FAR, WE'VE CAPTURED AND INCARCERATED ALMOST ALL OF GOTHAM'S MOST DANGEROUS AND NOTORIOUS FELONS.
RANGE
THE ONLY TWO DEVIANTS STILL AT LARGE ARE TWO-FACE AND CATWOMAN.
ALTHOUGH SOME MIGHT ARGUE THAT BATMAN HIMSELF SHOULD BE ADDED TO THAT LIST.
YES, BUT REGARDING TWO-FACE AND CATWOMAN...HOW DO YOU PLAN ON LOCATING SUCH ELUSIVE CRIMINALS?
I CAN'T DIVULGE OUR METHODS BUT I ASSURE YOU WE'LL HAVE THEM LOCKED UP VERY SHORTLY--
KRAK

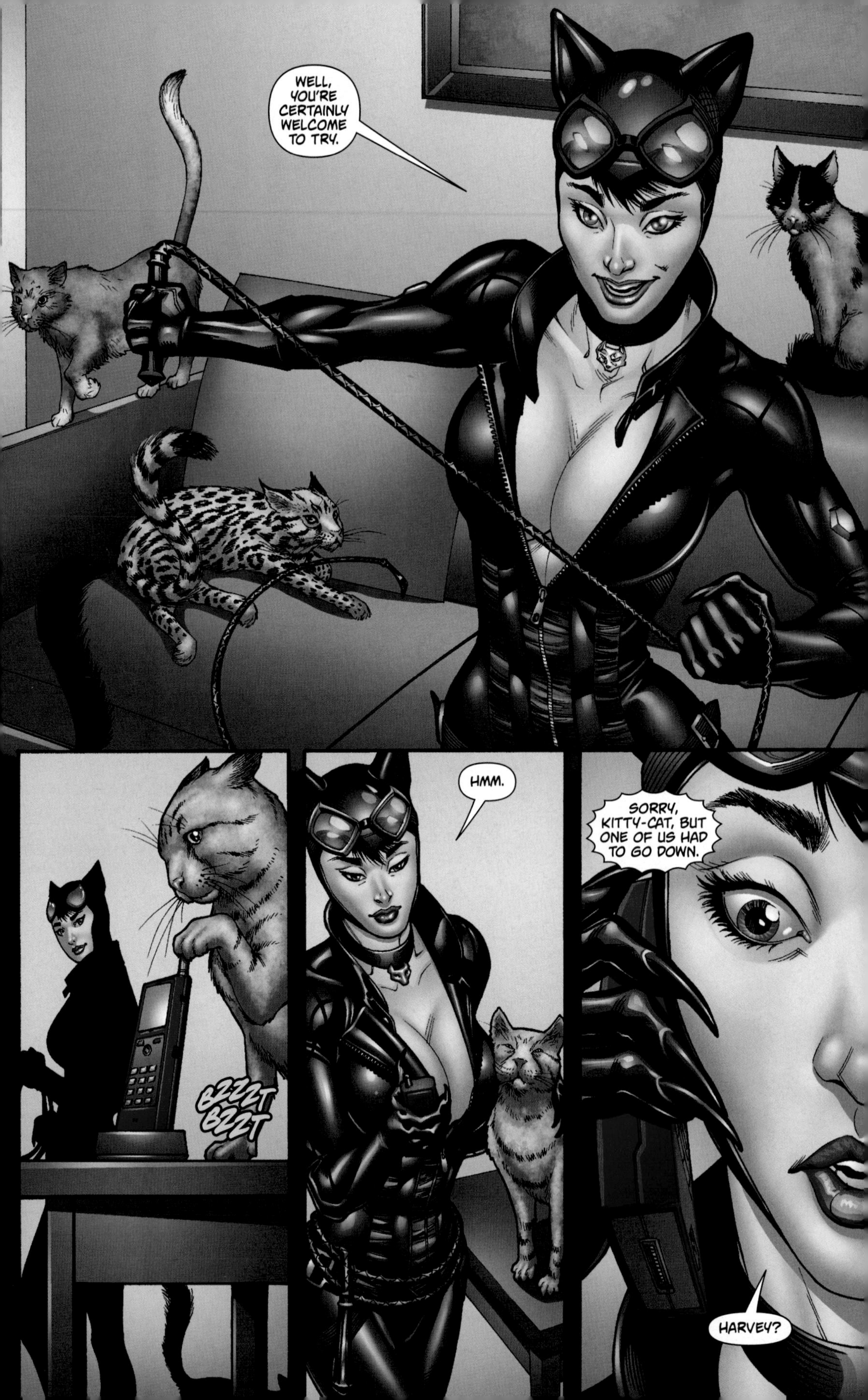
WELL, YOU'RE CERTAINLY WELCOME TO TRY.
BZZZT BZZT
HMM.
SORRY, KITTY-CAT, BUT ONE OF US HAD TO GO DOWN.
HARVEY?

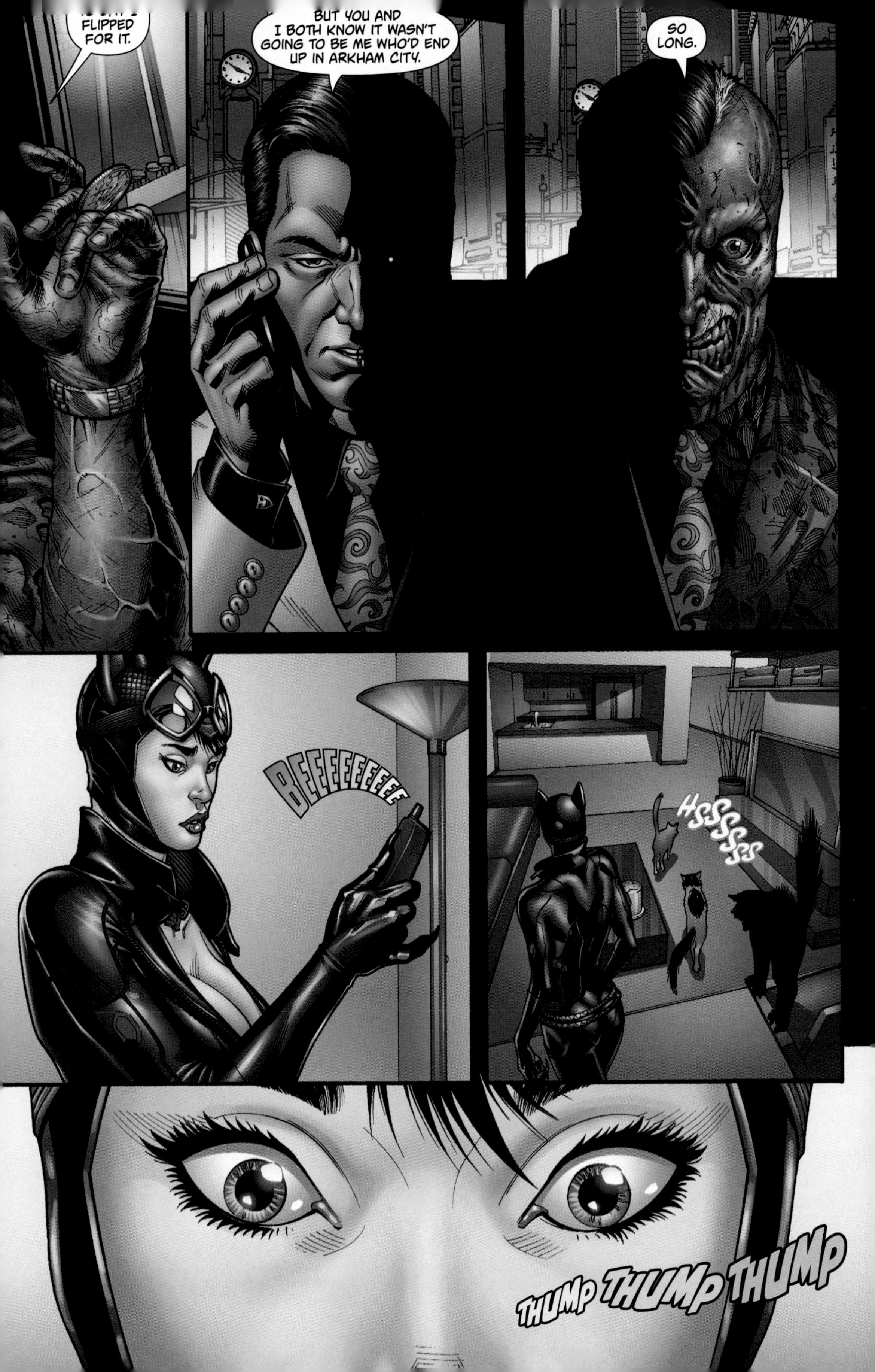
FLIPPED FOR IT.
BUT YOU AND I BOTH KNOW IT WASN'T GOING TO BE ME WHO'D END UP IN ARKHAM CITY.
SO LONG.
BEEEEEEEEEE
HSSSSSS
THUMP THUMP THUMP

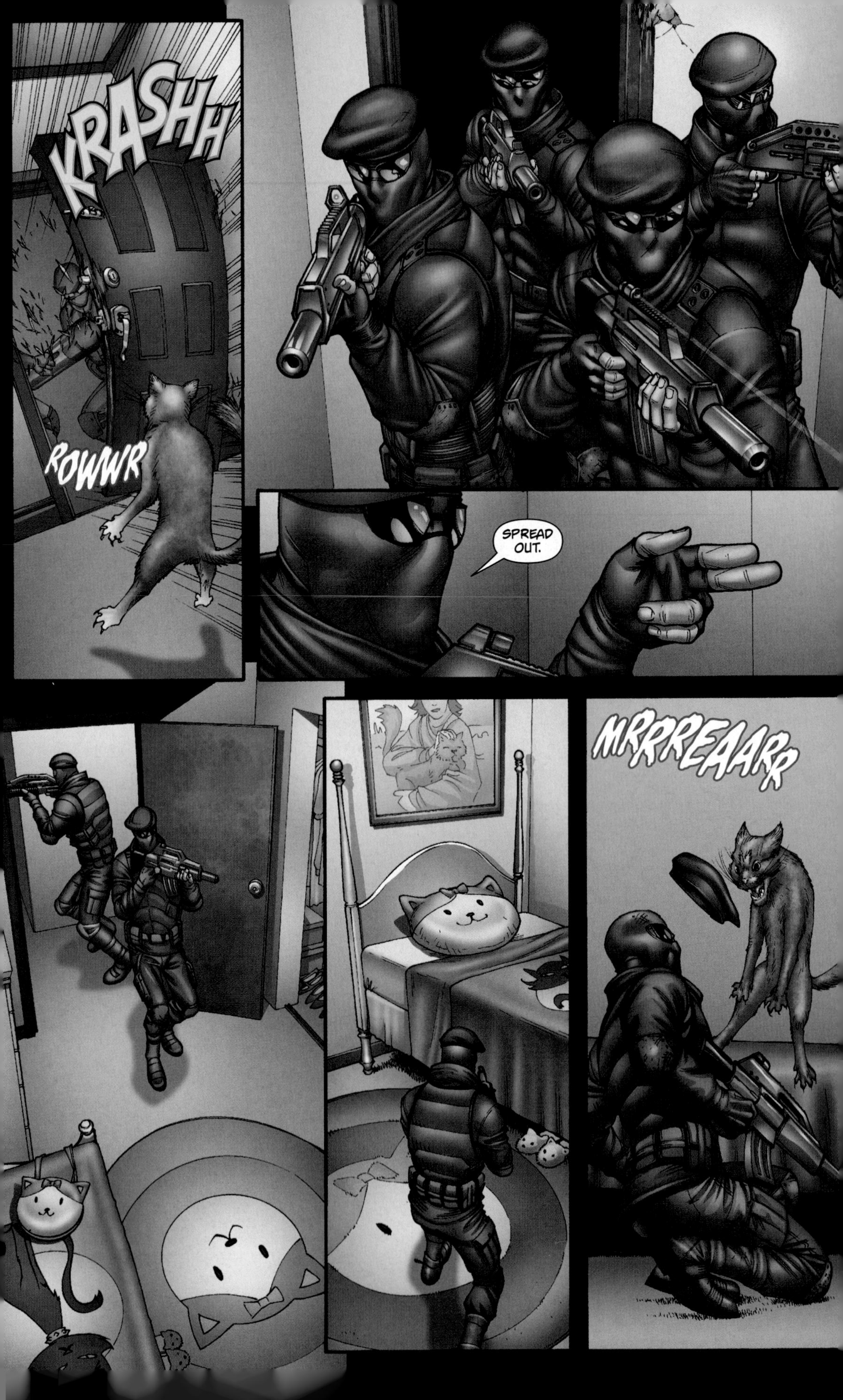
KRASHH
ROWWR
SPREAD OUT.
MRRREAARR

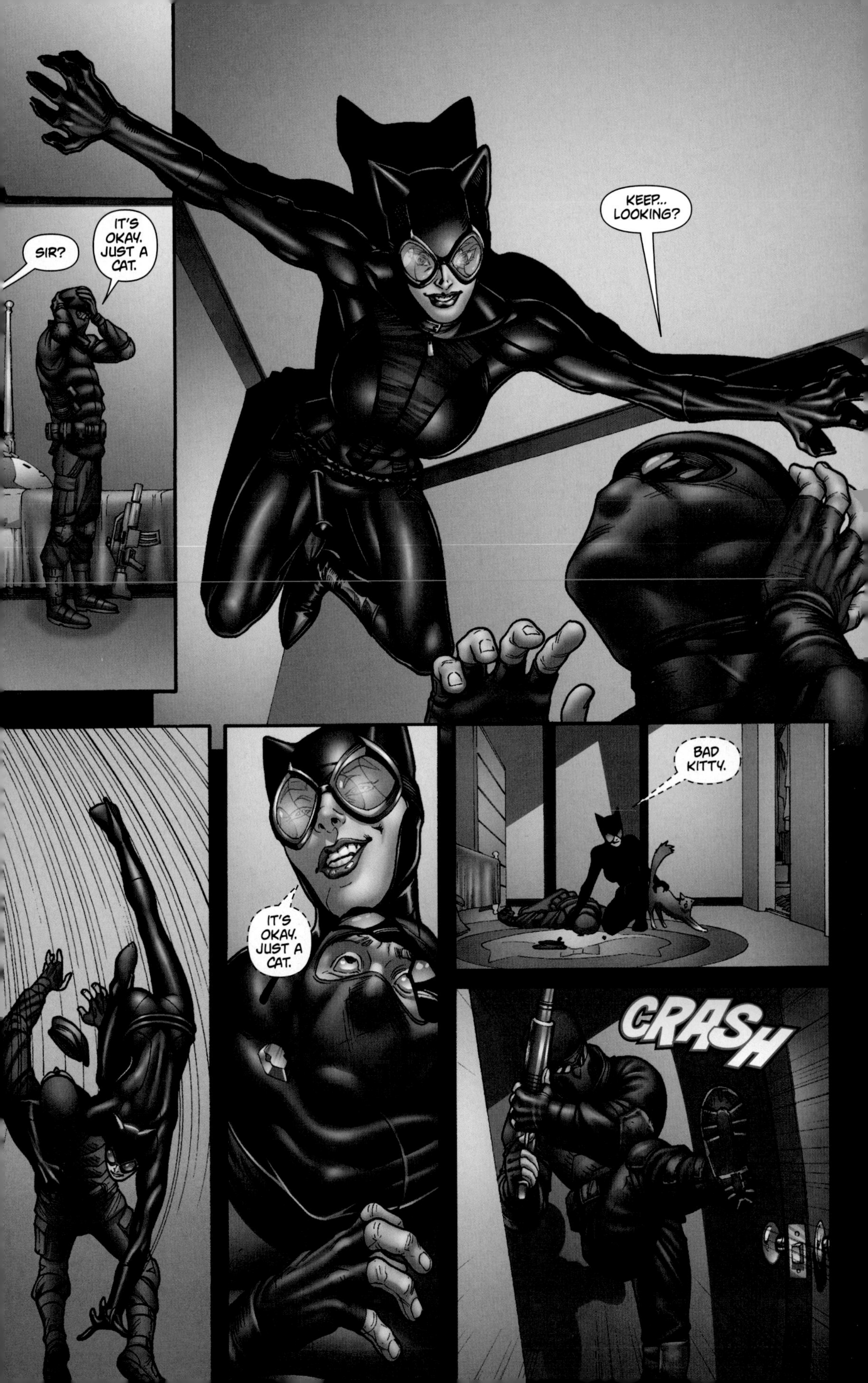
SIR?
IT'S OKAY. JUST A CAT.
KEEP... LOOKING?
IT'S OKAY. JUST A CAT.
BAD KITTY.
CRASH

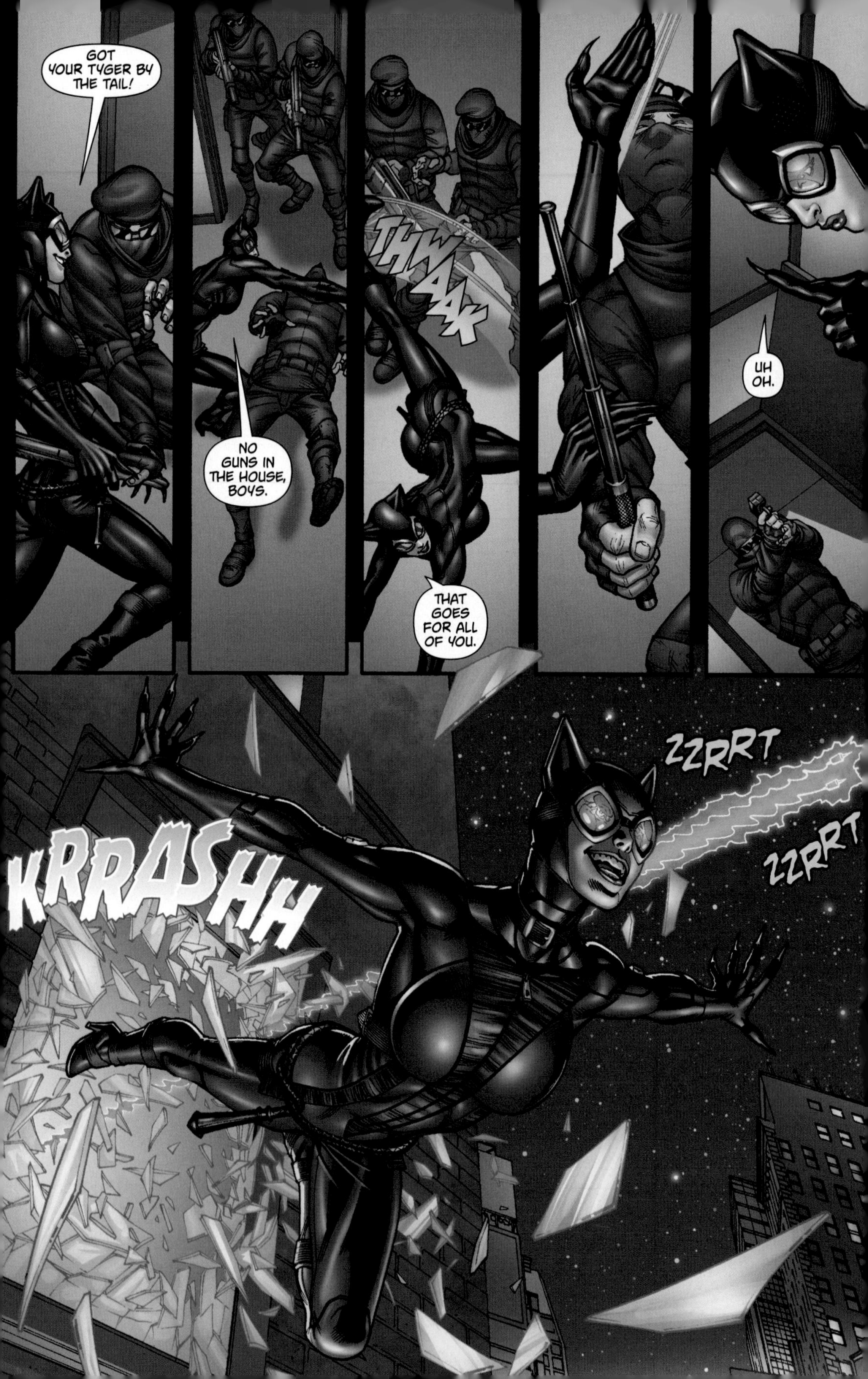
GOT YOUR TYGER BY THE TAIL!
NO GUNS IN THE HOUSE, BOYS.
THWAAK
THAT GOES FOR ALL OF YOU.
UH OH.
KRRASHH
ZZRRT
ZZRRT

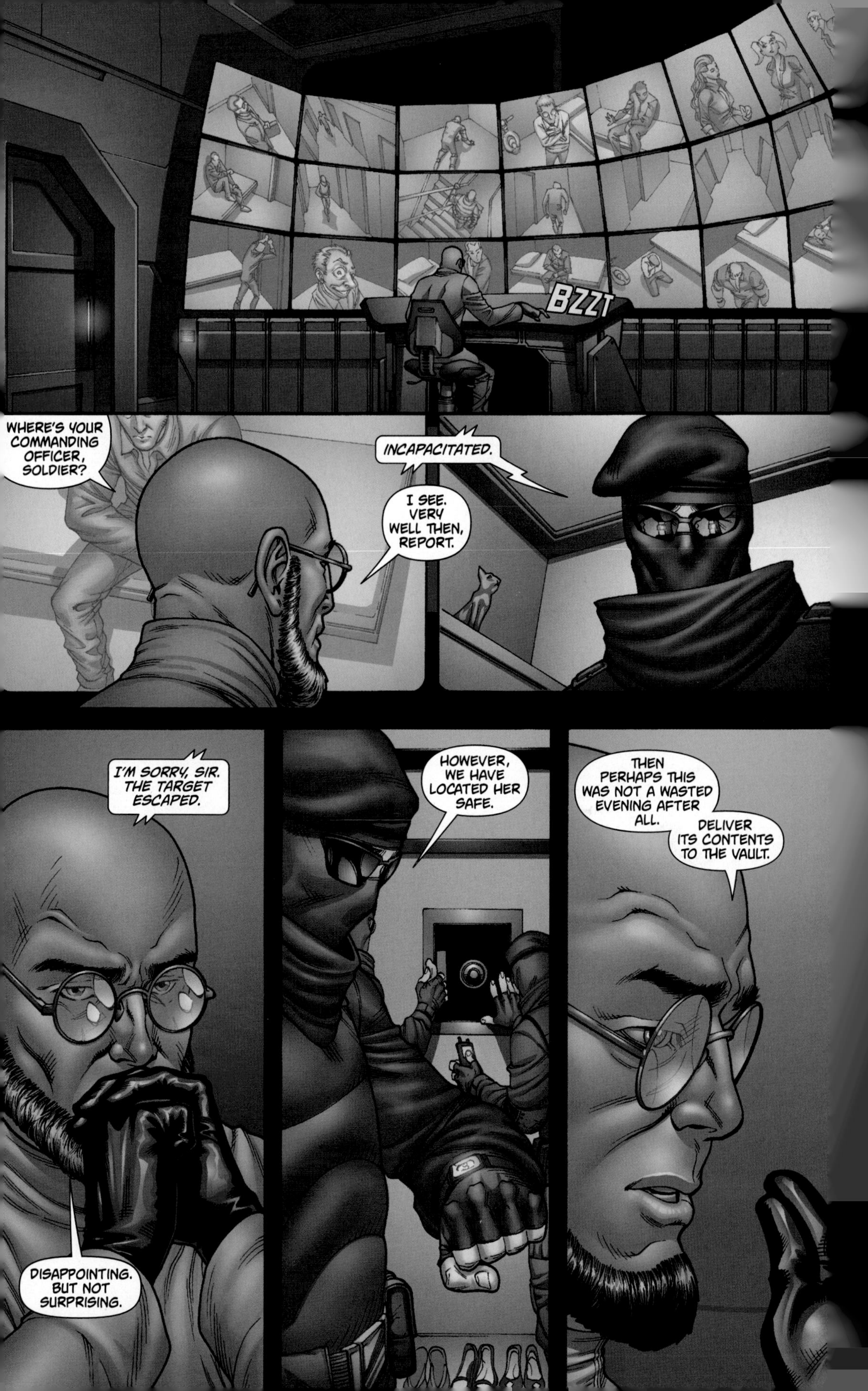
BZZT
WHERE'S YOUR COMMANDING OFFICER, SOLDIER?
INCAPACITATED.
I SEE. VERY WELL THEN, REPORT.
I'M SORRY, SIR. THE TARGET ESCAPED.
DISAPPOINTING. BUT NOT SURPRISING.
HOWEVER, WE HAVE LOCATED HER SAFE.
THEN PERHAPS THIS WAS NOT A WASTED EVENING AFTER ALL.
DELIVER ITS CONTENTS TO THE VAULT.

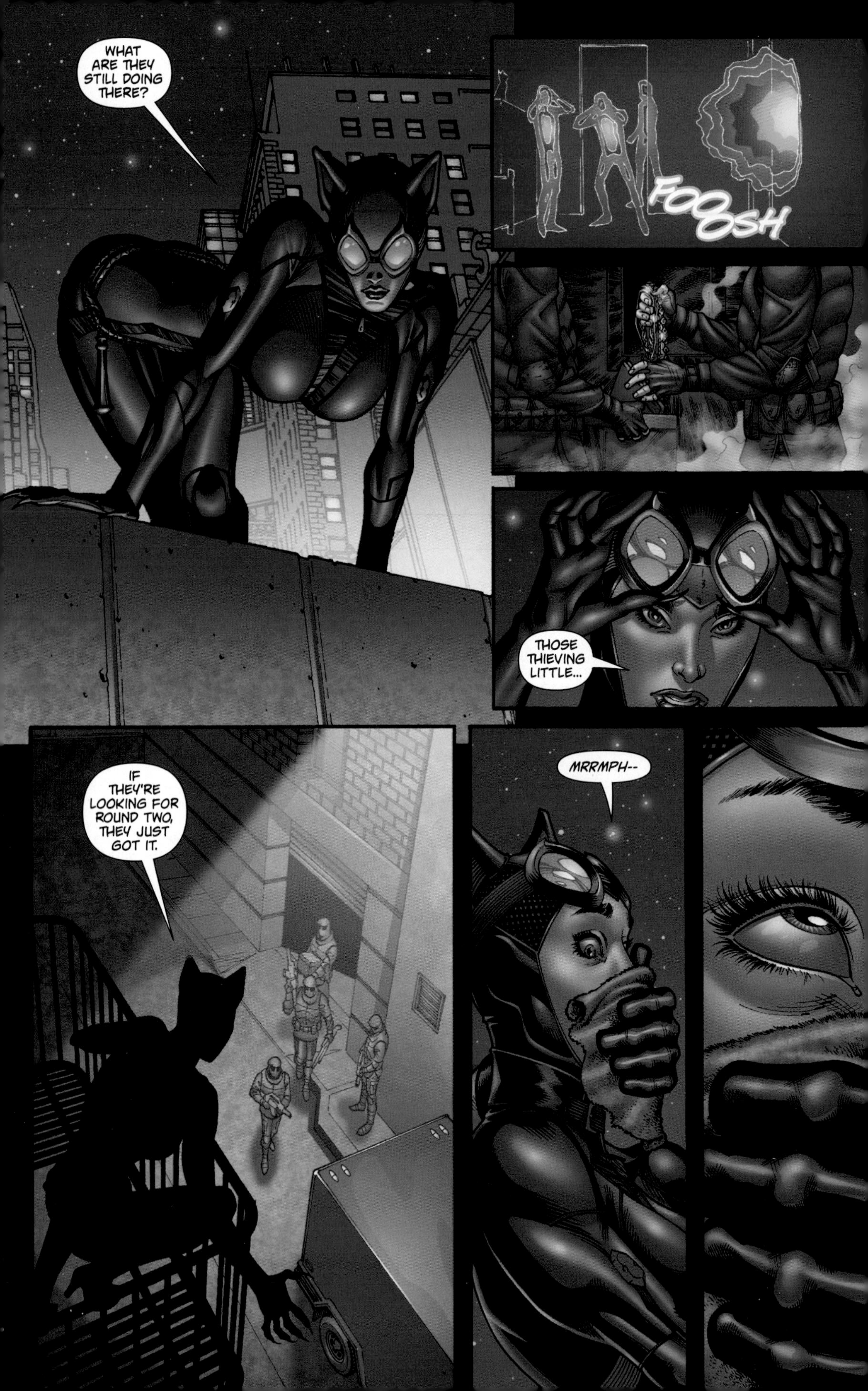
WHAT ARE THEY STILL DOING THERE?
FOOOSH
THOSE THIEVING LITTLE...
IF THEY'RE LOOKING FOR ROUND TWO, THEY JUST GOT IT.
MRRMPH--

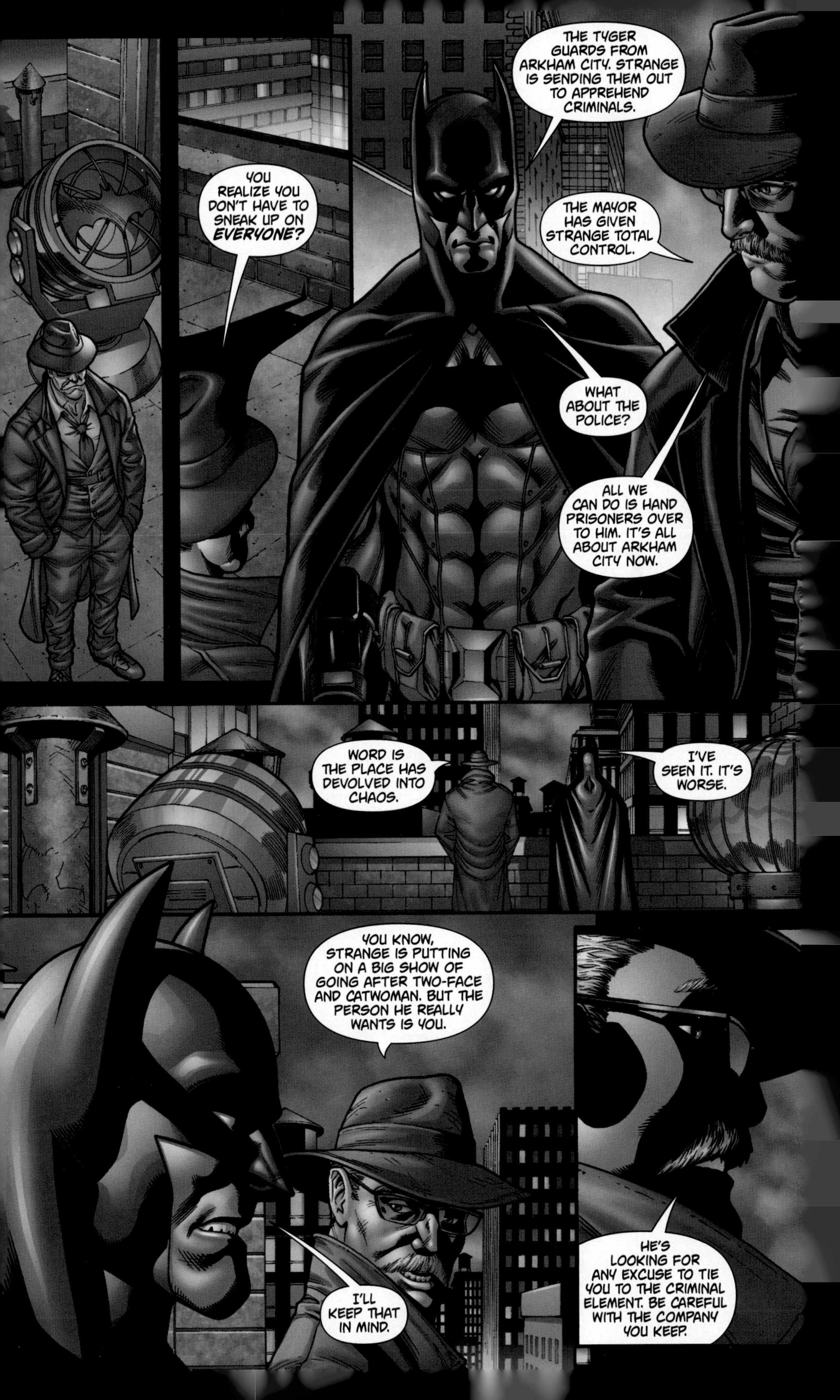

YOU REALIZE YOU DON'T HAVE TO SNEAK UP ON EVERYONE?
THE TYGER GUARDS FROM ARKHAM CITY. STRANGE IS SENDING THEM OUT TO APPREHEND CRIMINALS.
THE MAYOR HAS GIVEN STRANGE TOTAL CONTROL.
WHAT ABOUT THE POLICE?
ALL WE CAN DO IS HAND PRISONERS OVER TO HIM. IT'S ALL ABOUT ARKHAM CITY NOW.
WORD IS THE PLACE HAS DEVOLVED INTO CHAOS.
I'VE SEEN IT. IT'S WORSE.
YOU KNOW, STRANGE IS PUTTING ON A BIG SHOW OF GOING AFTER TWO-FACE AND CATWOMAN. BUT THE PERSON HE REALLY WANTS IS YOU.
I'LL KEEP THAT IN MIND.
HE'S LOOKING FOR ANY EXCUSE TO TIE YOU TO THE CRIMINAL ELEMENT. BE CAREFUL WITH THE COMPANY YOU KEEP.

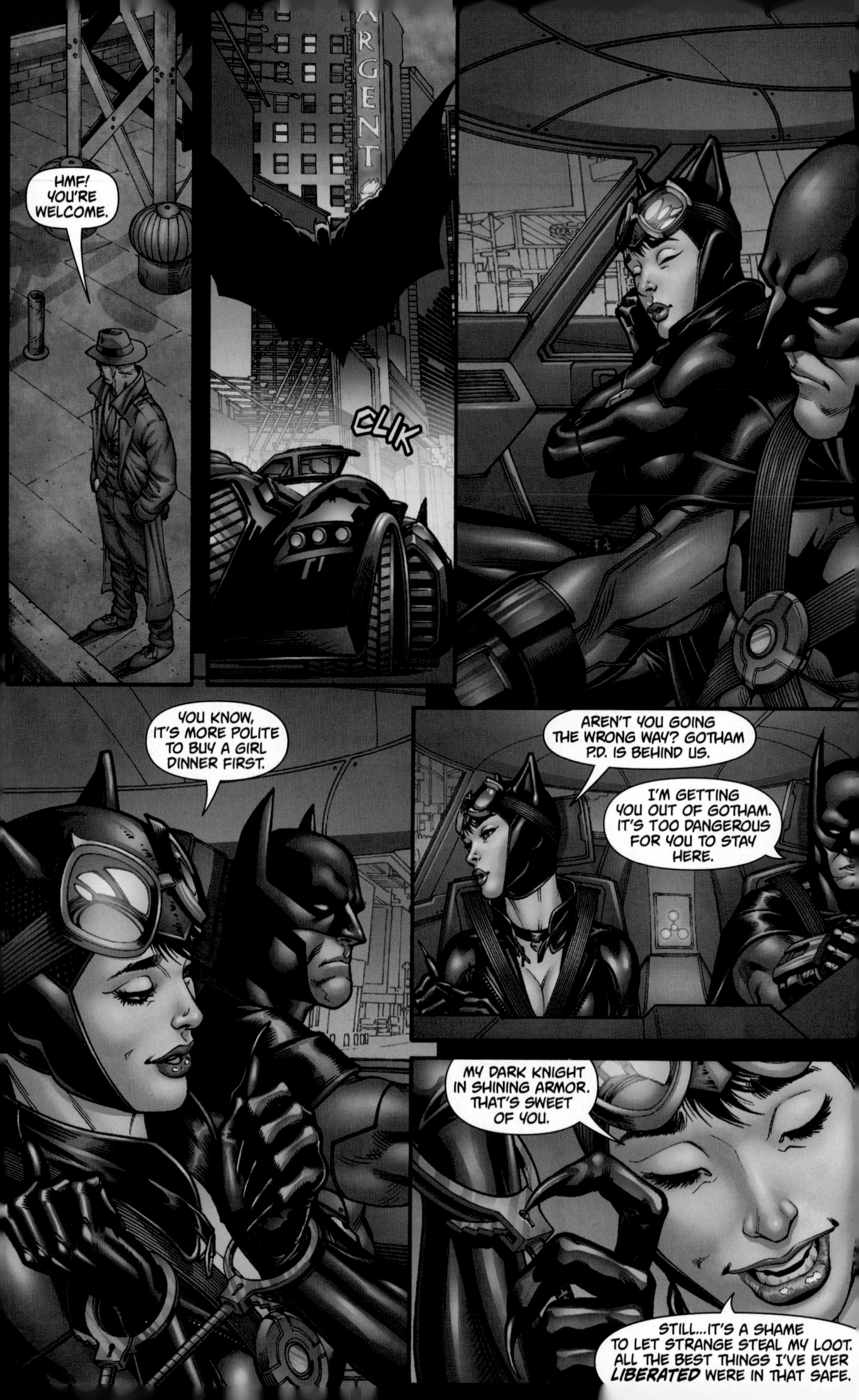
HMF! YOU'RE WELCOME.
ARGENT
CLIK
YOU KNOW, IT'S MORE POLITE TO BUY A GIRL DINNER FIRST.
AREN'T YOU GOING THE WRONG WAY? GOTHAM P.D. IS BEHIND US.
I'M GETTING YOU OUT OF GOTHAM. IT'S TOO DANGEROUS FOR YOU TO STAY HERE.
MY DARK KNIGHT IN SHINING ARMOR. THAT'S SWEET OF YOU.
STILL...IT'S A SHAME TO LET STRANGE STEAL MY LOOT. ALL THE BEST THINGS I'VE EVER *LIBERATED* WERE IN THAT SAFE.

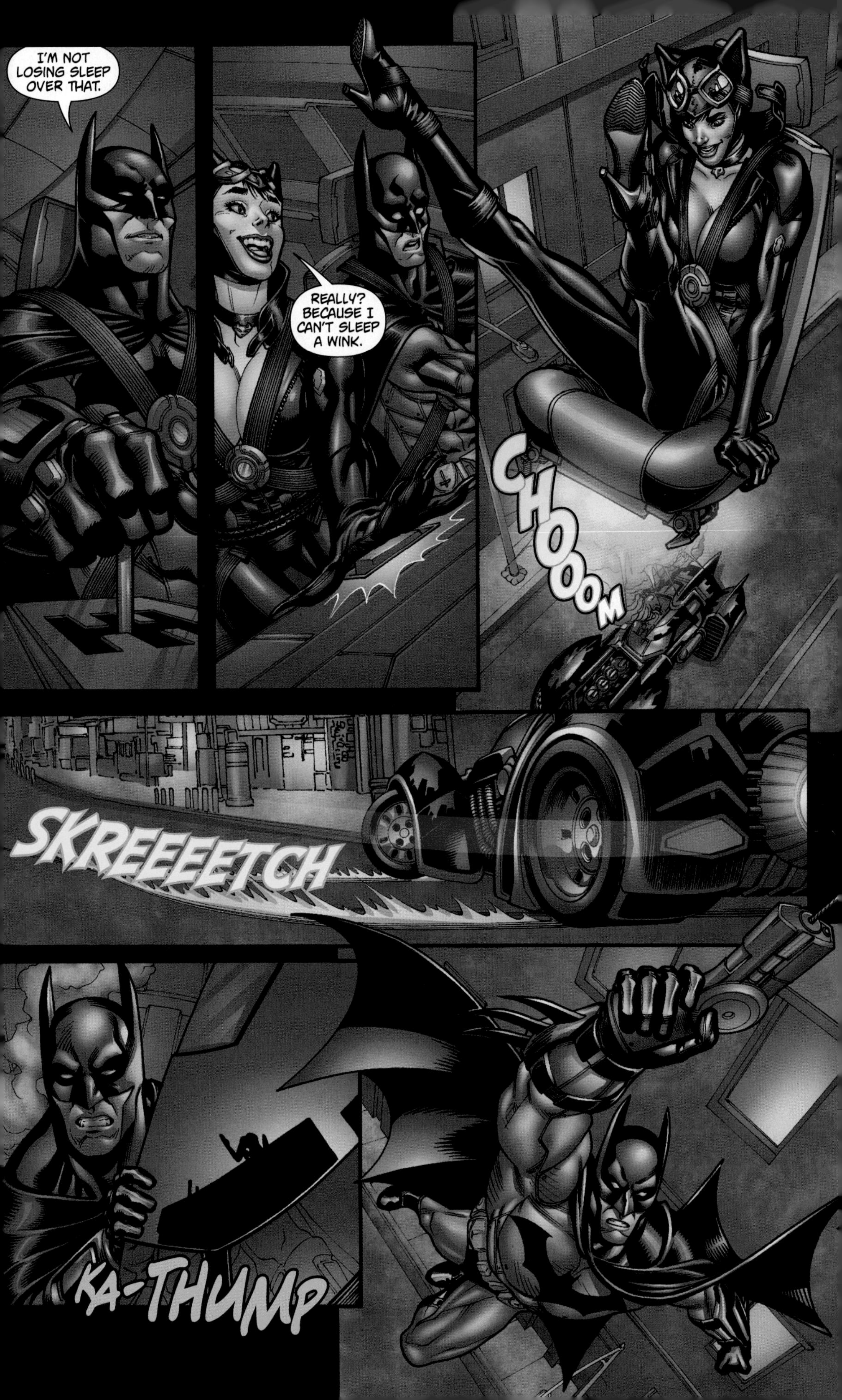
I'M NOT LOSING SLEEP OVER THAT.
REALLY? BECAUSE I CAN'T SLEEP A WINK.
CHOOOOM
SKREEEEETCH
KA-THUMP

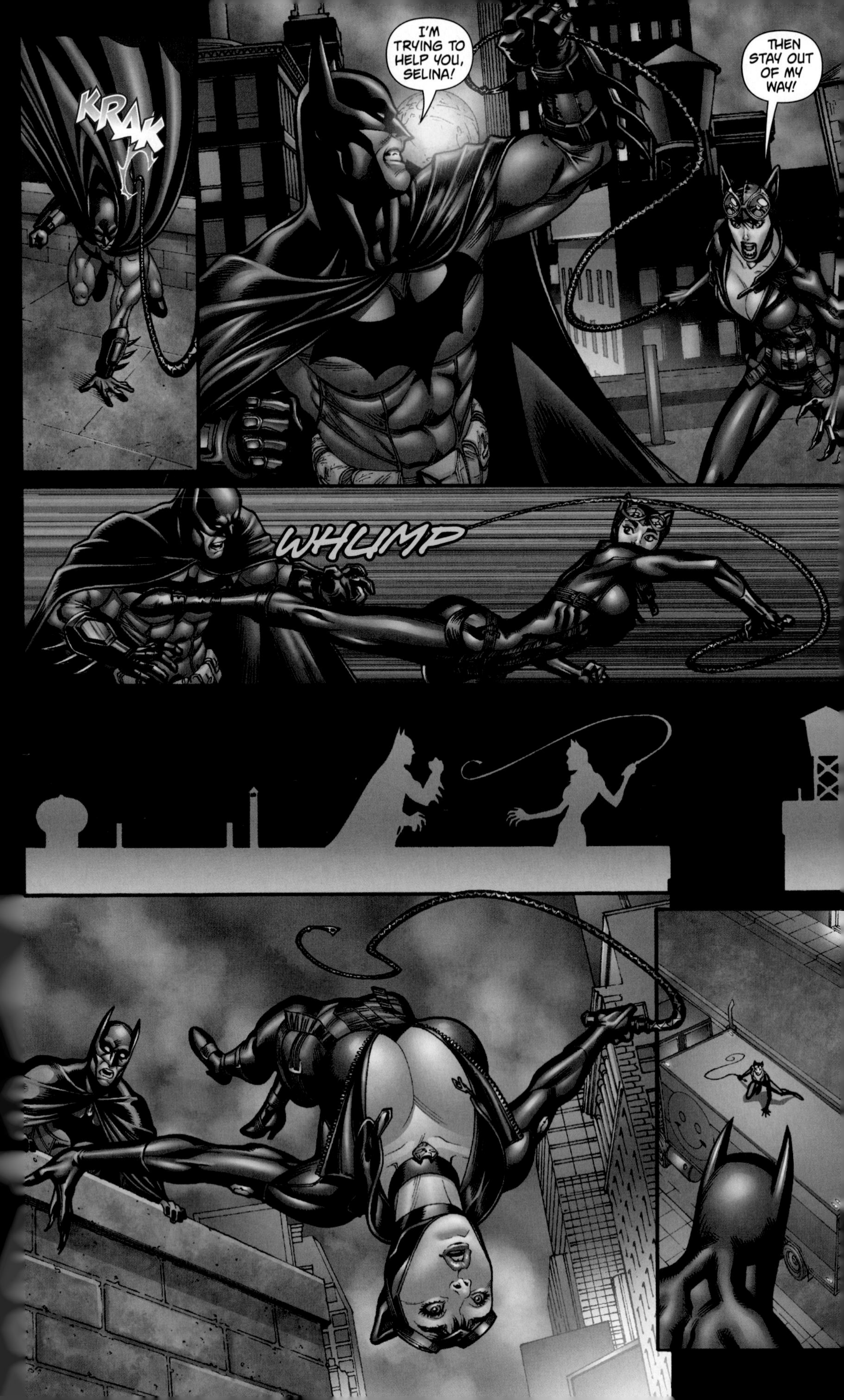
KRAK
I'M TRYING TO HELP YOU, SELINA!
THEN STAY OUT OF MY WAY!
WHUMP

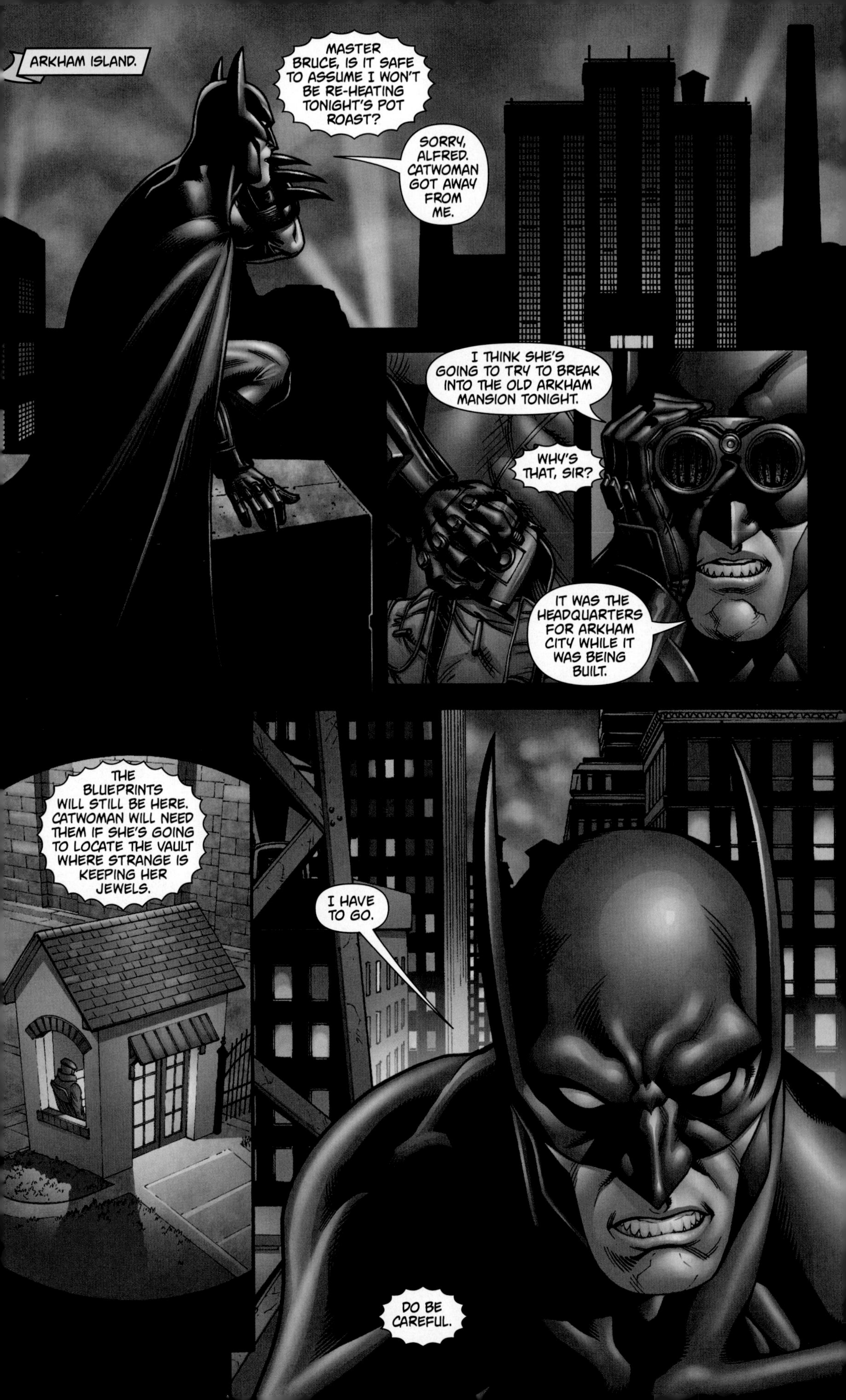
ARKHAM ISLAND.
MASTER BRUCE, IS IT SAFE TO ASSUME I WON'T BE RE-HEATING TONIGHT'S POT ROAST?
SORRY, ALFRED. CATWOMAN GOT AWAY FROM ME.
I THINK SHE'S GOING TO TRY TO BREAK INTO THE OLD ARKHAM MANSION TONIGHT.
WHY'S THAT, SIR?
IT WAS THE HEADQUARTERS FOR ARKHAM CITY WHILE IT WAS BEING BUILT.
THE BLUEPRINTS WILL STILL BE HERE. CATWOMAN WILL NEED THEM IF SHE'S GOING TO LOCATE THE VAULT WHERE STRANGE IS KEEPING HER JEWELS.
I HAVE TO GO.
DO BE CAREFUL.

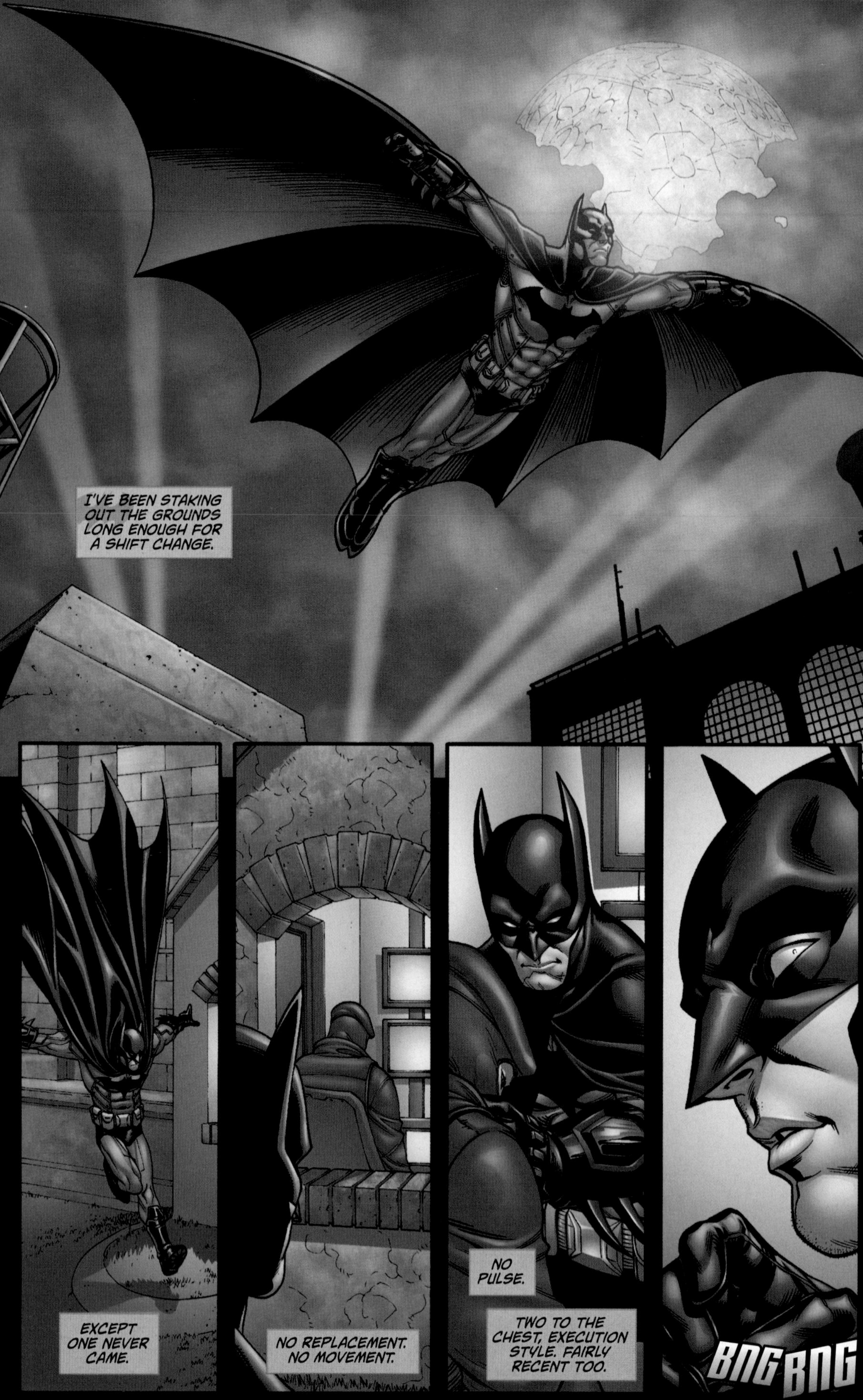
I'VE BEEN STAKING OUT THE GROUNDS LONG ENOUGH FOR A SHIFT CHANGE.
EXCEPT ONE NEVER CAME.
NO REPLACEMENT. NO MOVEMENT.
NO PULSE.
TWO TO THE CHEST, EXECUTION STYLE. FAIRLY RECENT TOO.
BNG BNG

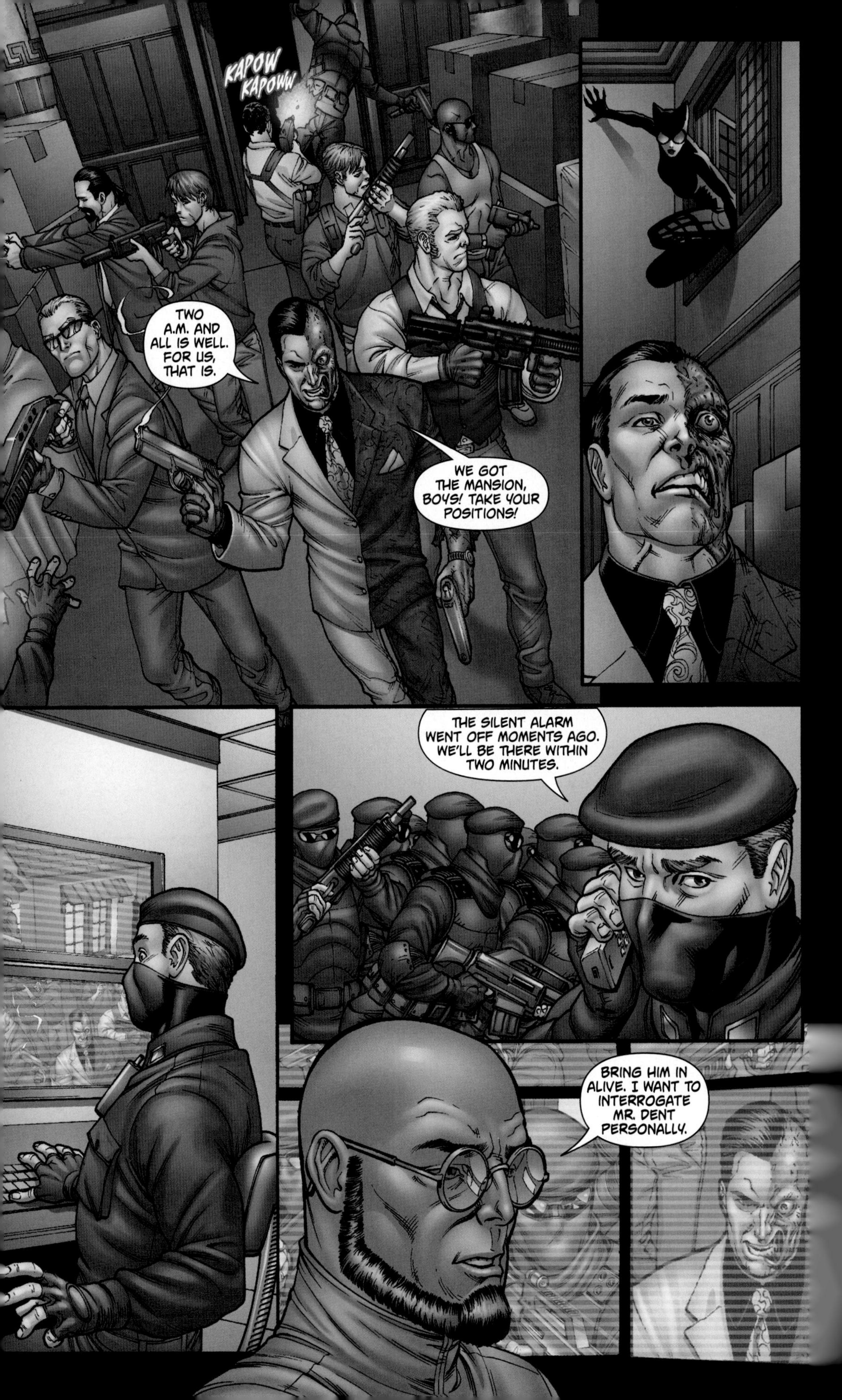
KAPOW
KAPOWW
TWO A.M. AND ALL IS WELL. FOR US, THAT IS.
WE GOT THE MANSION, BOYS! TAKE YOUR POSITIONS!
THE SILENT ALARM WENT OFF MOMENTS AGO. WE'LL BE THERE WITHIN TWO MINUTES.
BRING HIM IN ALIVE. I WANT TO INTERROGATE MR. DENT PERSONALLY.

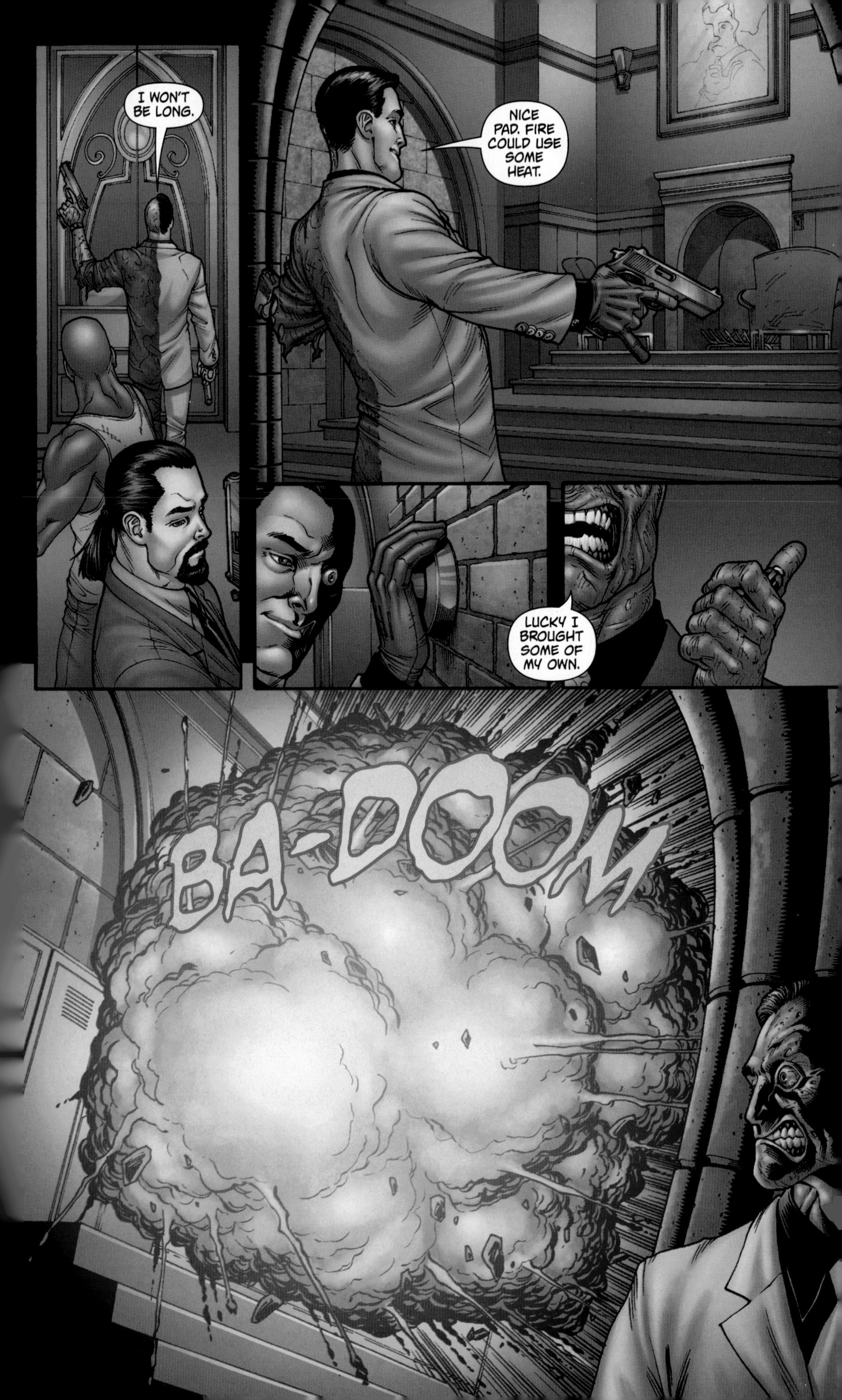
I WON'T BE LONG.
NICE PAD. FIRE COULD USE SOME HEAT.
LUCKY I BROUGHT SOME OF MY OWN.
BA-DOOM

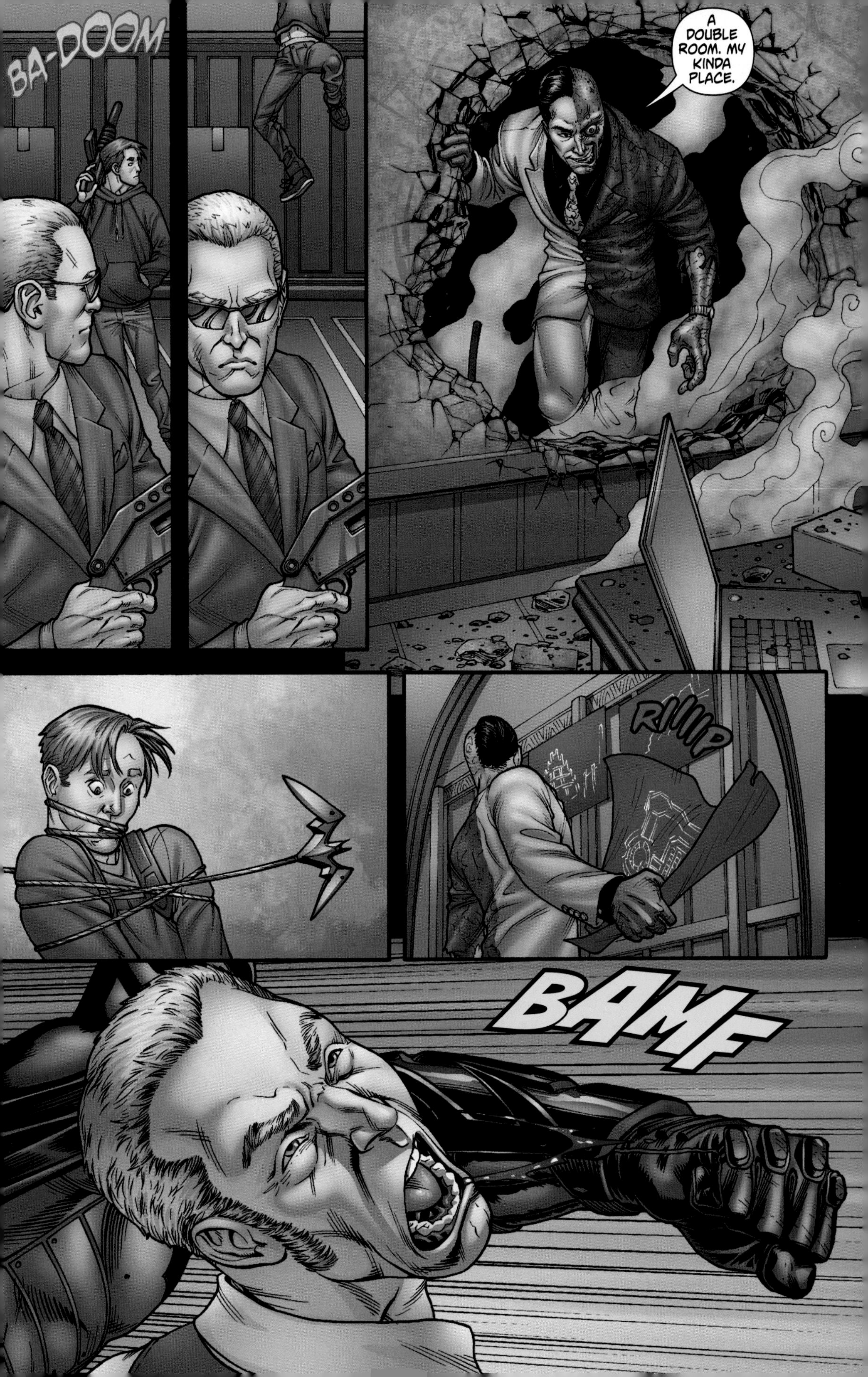
BA-DOOM
A DOUBLE ROOM. MY KINDA PLACE.
RIIIIP
BAMF

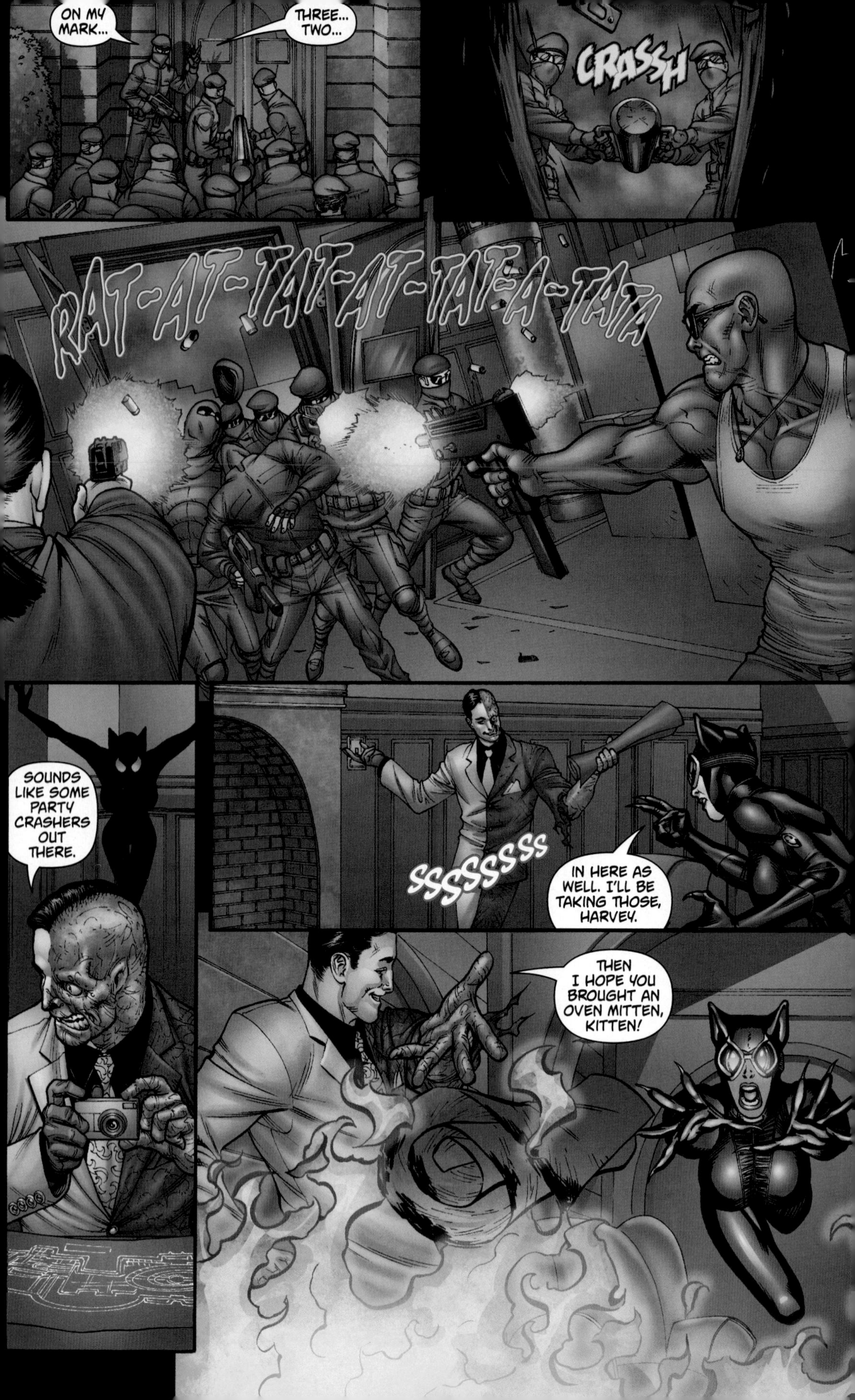
ON MY MARK...
THREE... TWO...
CRASSH
RAT-AT-TAT-AT-TAT-A-TATA
SOUNDS LIKE SOME PARTY CRASHERS OUT THERE.
SSSSSSSS
IN HERE AS WELL. I'LL BE TAKING THOSE, HARVEY.
THEN I HOPE YOU BROUGHT AN OVEN MITTEN, KITTEN!

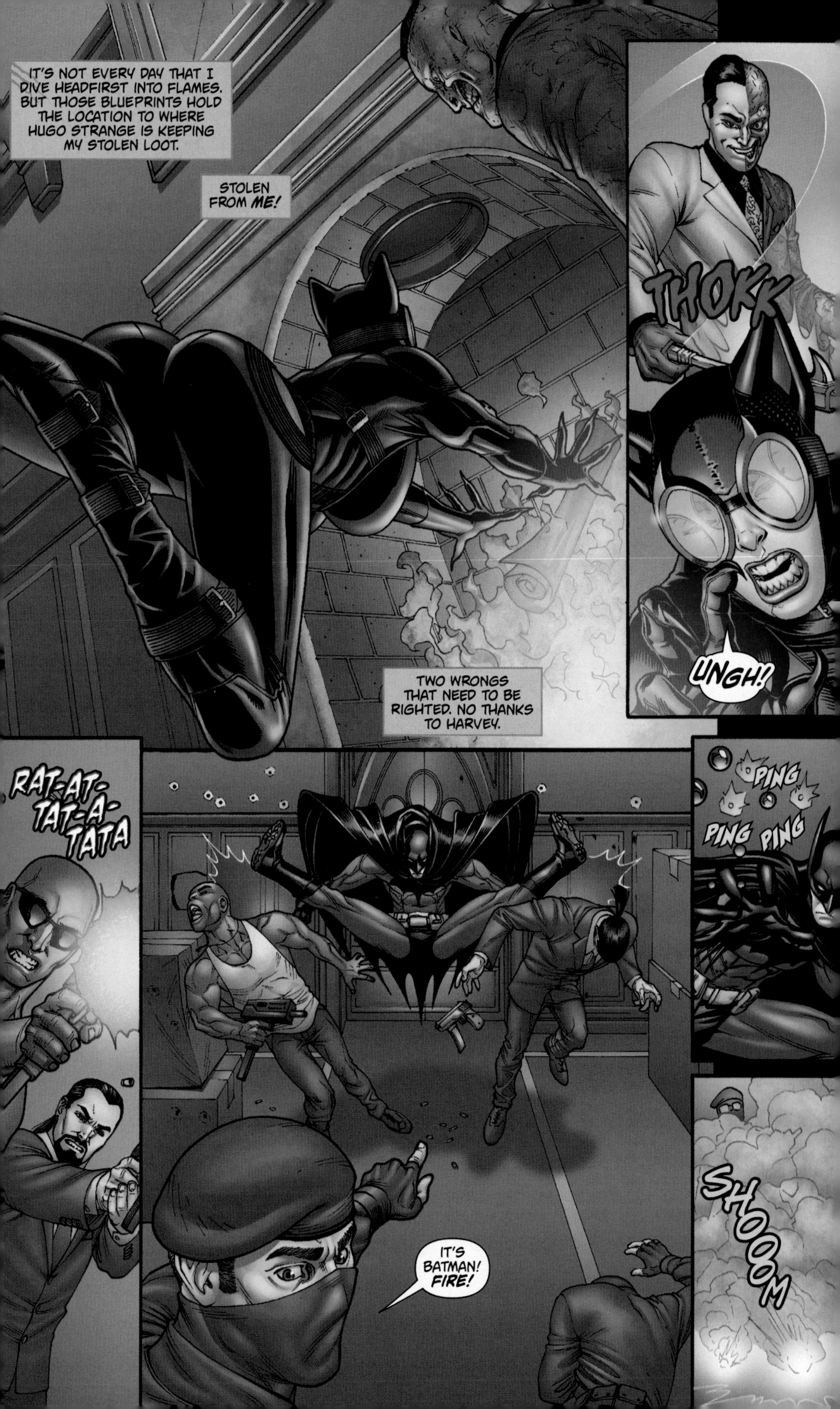

IT'S NOT EVERY DAY THAT I DIVE HEADFIRST INTO FLAMES. BUT THOSE BLUEPRINTS HOLD THE LOCATION TO WHERE HUGO STRANGE IS KEEPING MY STOLEN LOOT.
STOLEN FROM *ME!*
TWO WRONGS THAT NEED TO BE RIGHTED. NO THANKS TO HARVEY.
THOKK
UNGH!
RAT-AT-TAT-A-TATA
PING PING PING PING
IT'S BATMAN! *FIRE!*
SHOOOM

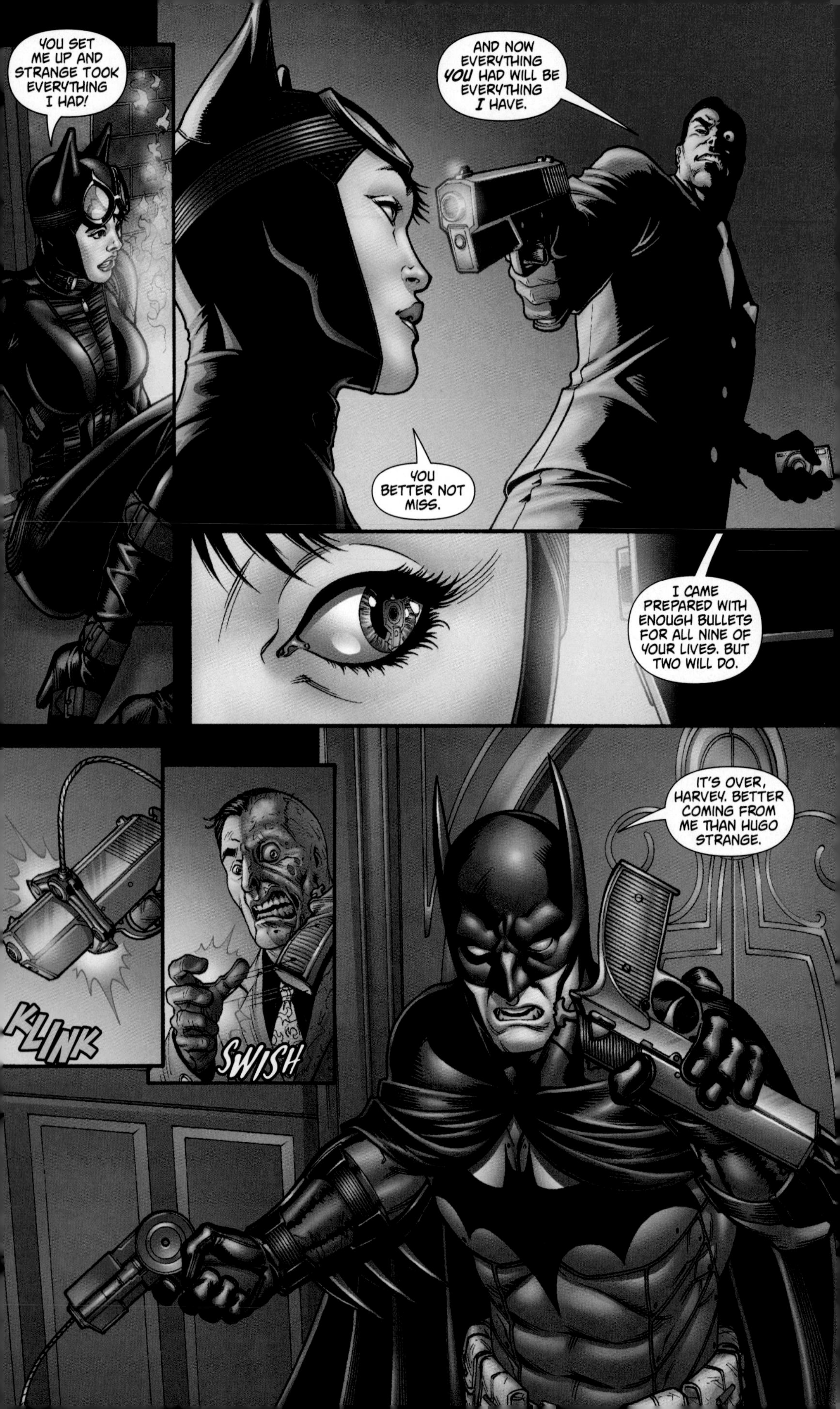

YOU SET ME UP AND STRANGE TOOK EVERYTHING I HAD!
AND NOW EVERYTHING *YOU* HAD WILL BE EVERYTHING *I* HAVE.
YOU BETTER NOT MISS.
I CAME PREPARED WITH ENOUGH BULLETS FOR ALL NINE OF YOUR LIVES. BUT TWO WILL DO.
KLINK
SWISH
IT'S OVER, HARVEY. BETTER COMING FROM ME THAN HUGO STRANGE.

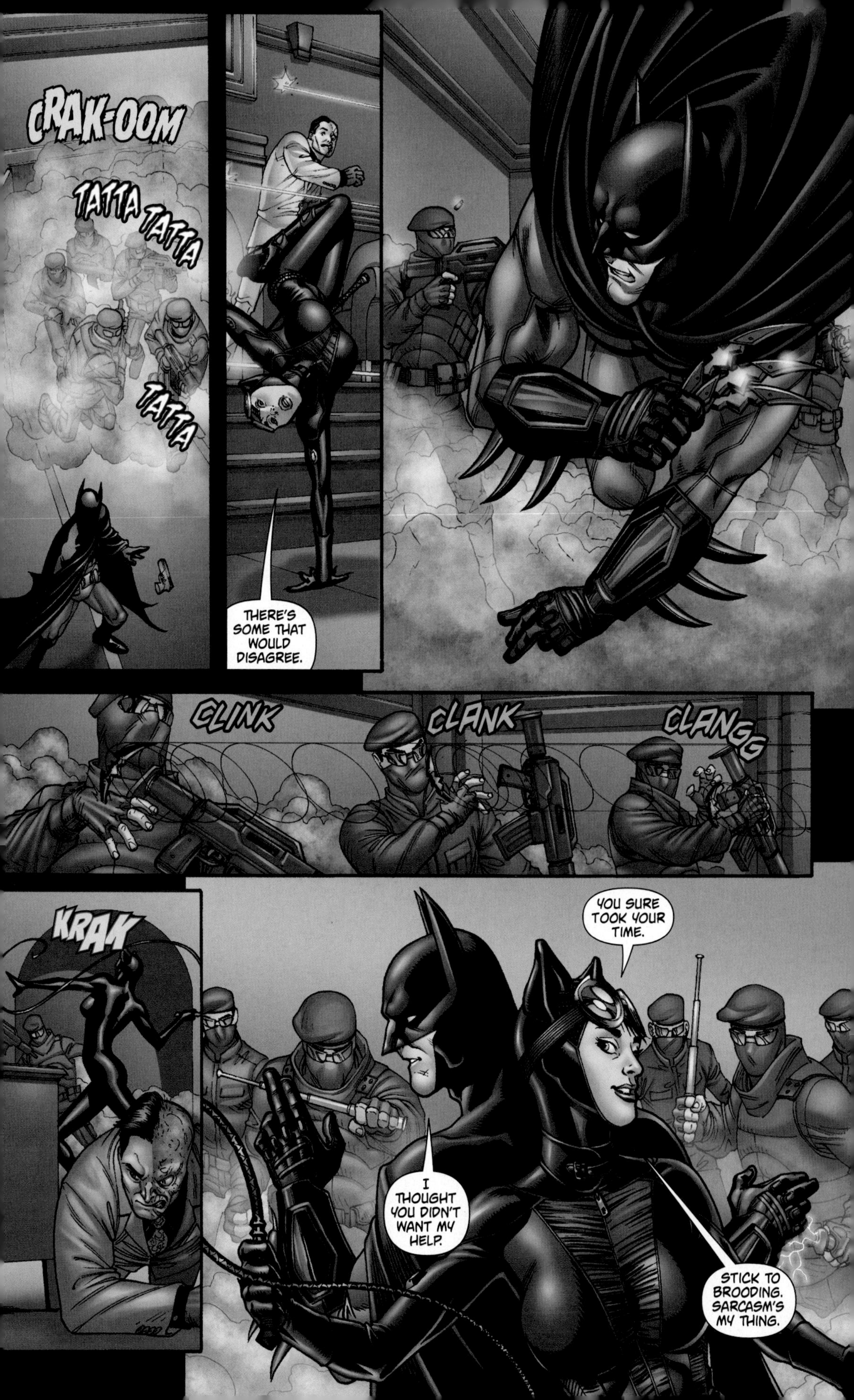
CRAK-OOM
TATTA TATTA
TATTA
THERE'S SOME THAT WOULD DISAGREE.
CLINK
CLANK
CLANGG
KRAK
YOU SURE TOOK YOUR TIME.
I THOUGHT YOU DIDN'T WANT MY HELP.
STICK TO BROODING. SARCASM'S MY THING.

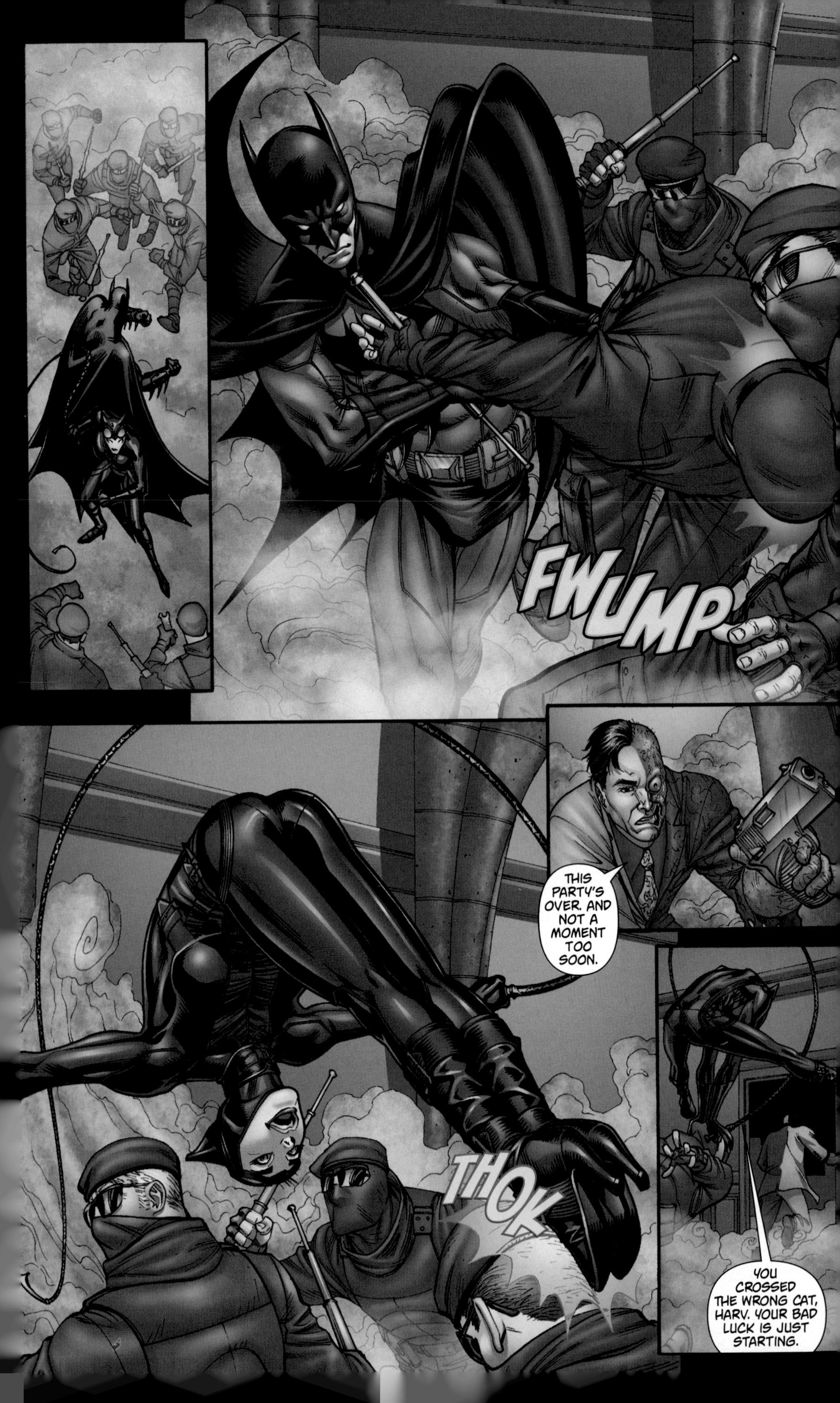
FWUMP
THIS PARTY'S OVER. AND NOT A MOMENT TOO SOON.
THOK
YOU CROSSED THE WRONG CAT, HARV. YOUR BAD LUCK IS JUST STARTING.

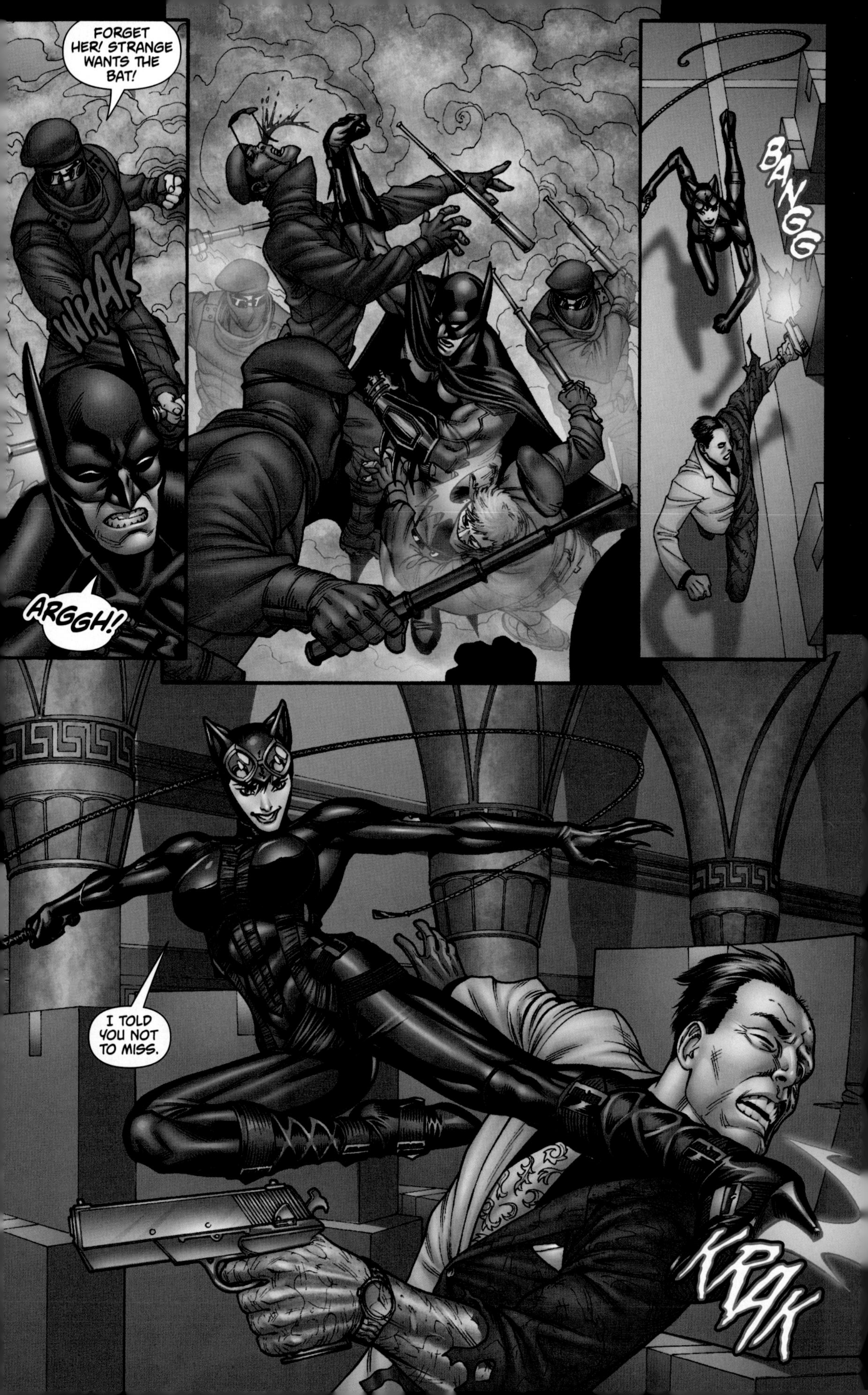
FORGET HER! STRANGE WANTS THE BAT!
WHAK
ARGGH!
BANGG
I TOLD YOU NOT TO MISS.
KRAK

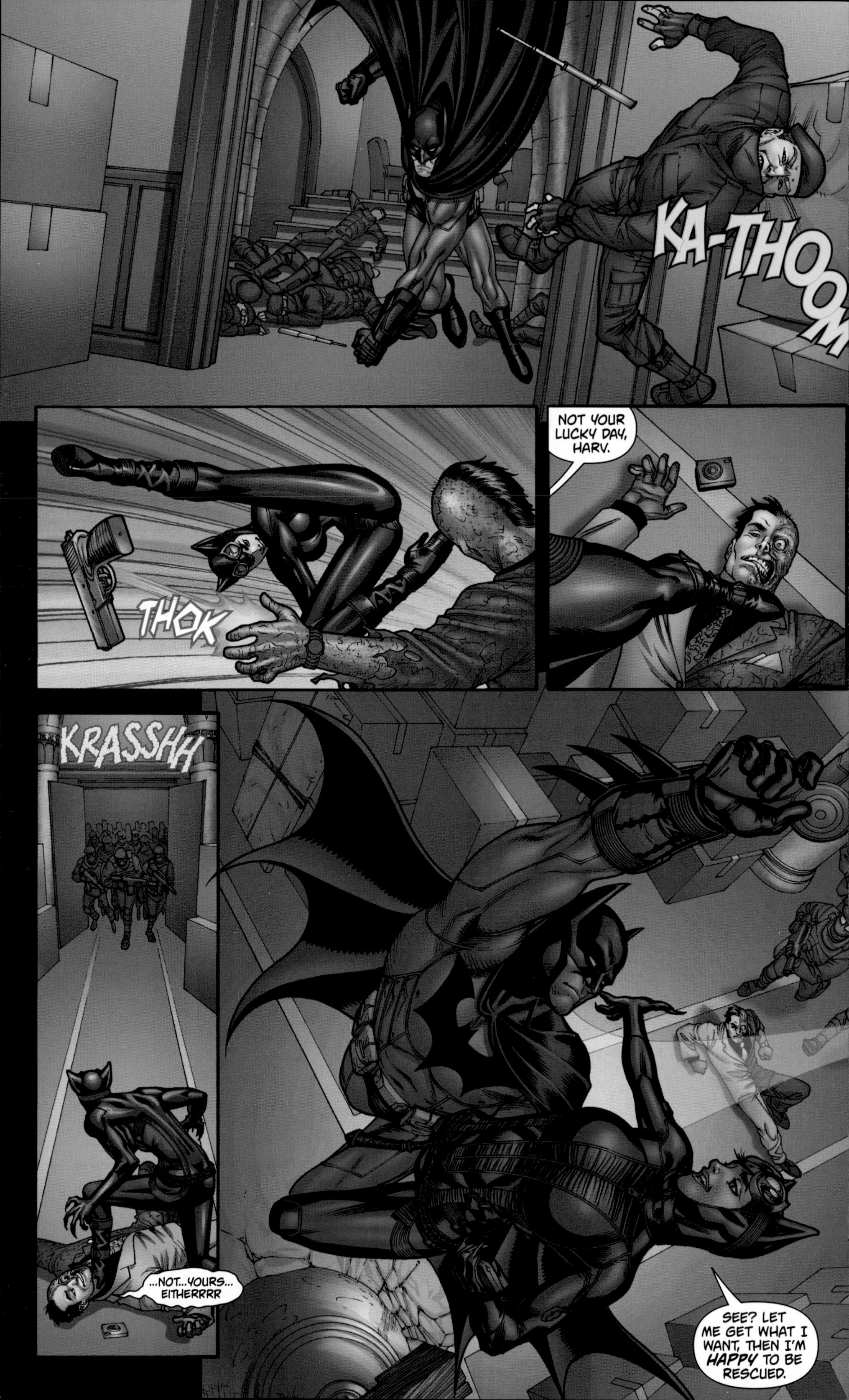
KA-THOOM
THOK
NOT YOUR LUCKY DAY, HARV.
KRASSHH
...NOT...YOURS... EITHERRRR
SEE? LET ME GET WHAT I WANT, THEN I'M HAPPY TO BE RESCUED.

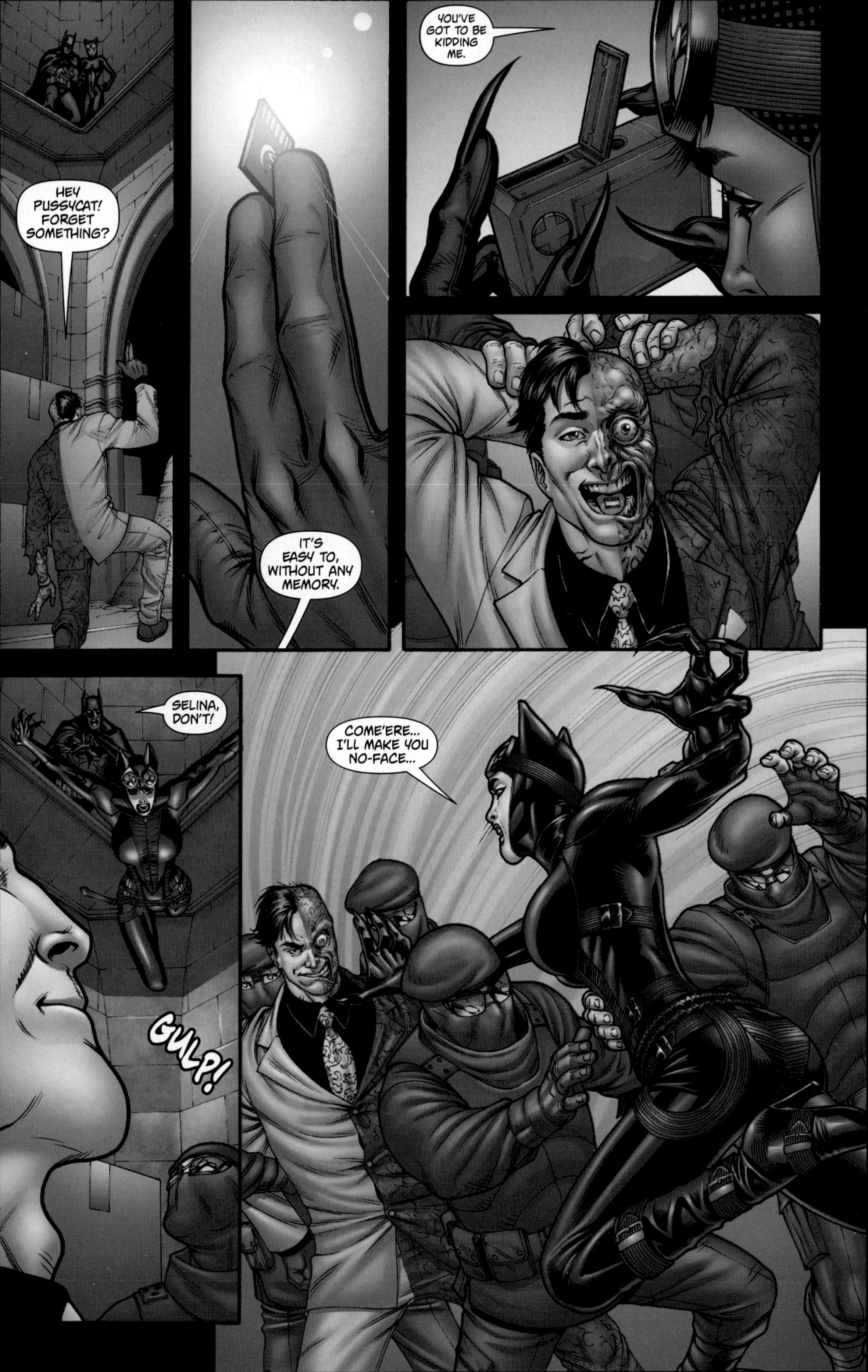
HEY PUSSYCAT! FORGET SOMETHING?
IT'S EASY TO, WITHOUT ANY MEMORY.
YOU'VE GOT TO BE KIDDING ME.
SELINA, DON'T!
COME'ERE... I'LL MAKE YOU NO-FACE...
GULP!

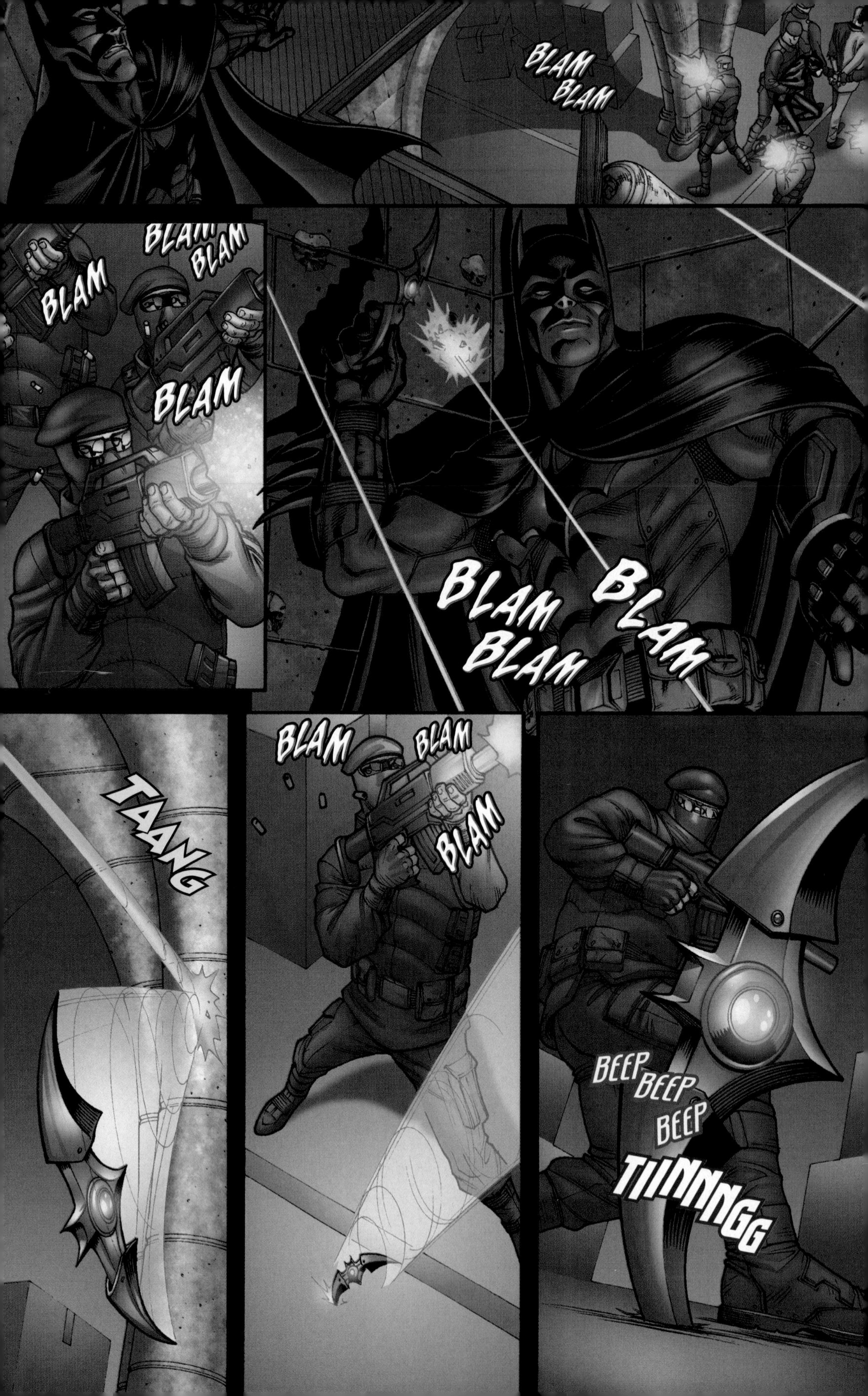
BLAM
BLAM
BLAM
BLAM
BLAM
BLAM
BLAM
BLAM
BLAM
BLAM
TAANG
BLAM
BLAM
BLAM
BEEP
BEEP
BEEP
TIINNNGG

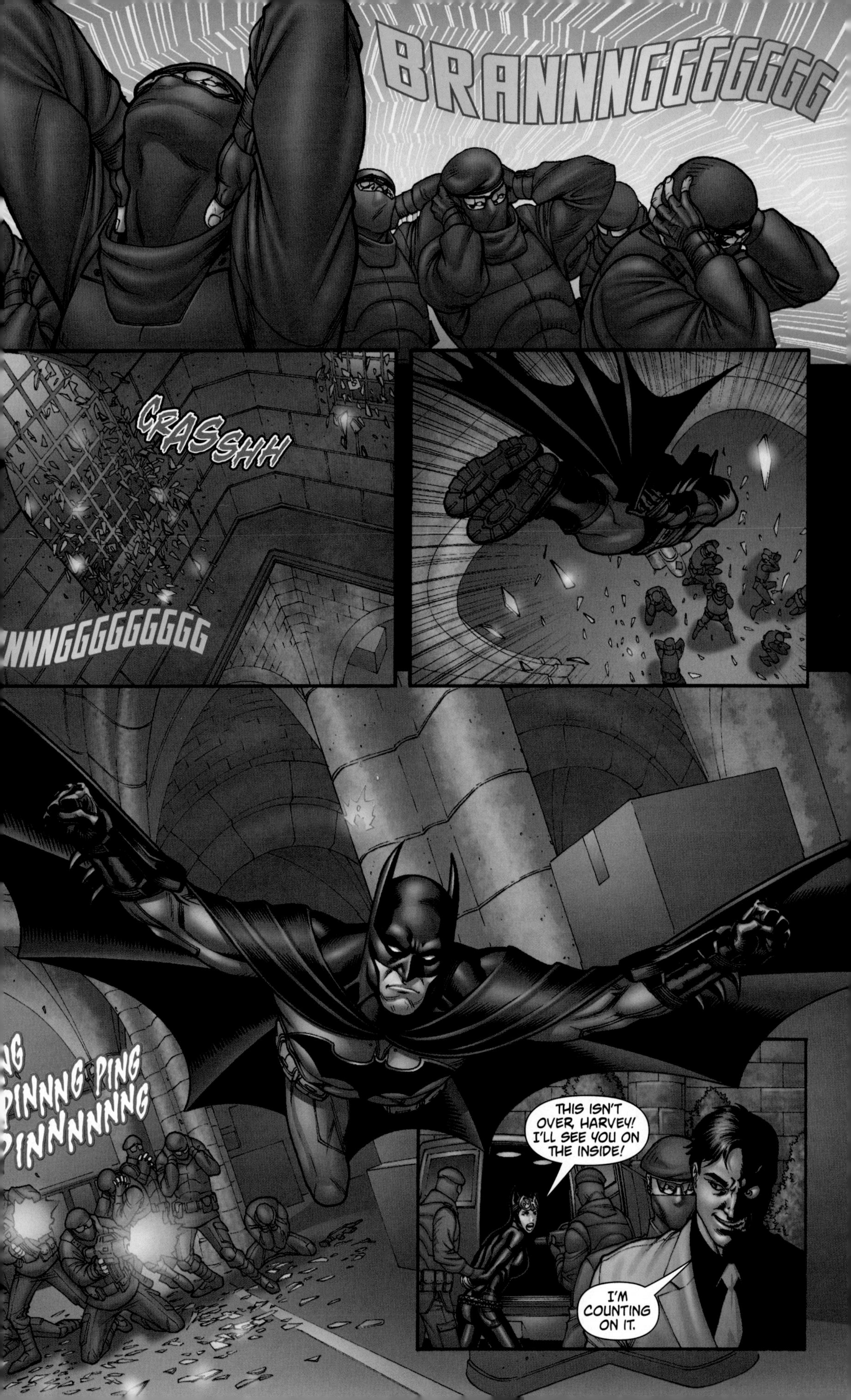
BRANNNGGGGGGG
CRASSHH
NNNGGGGGGGGGG
NG
PINNNG PING
PINNNNNNG
THIS ISN'T OVER, HARVEY! I'LL SEE YOU ON THE INSIDE!
I'M COUNTING ON IT.

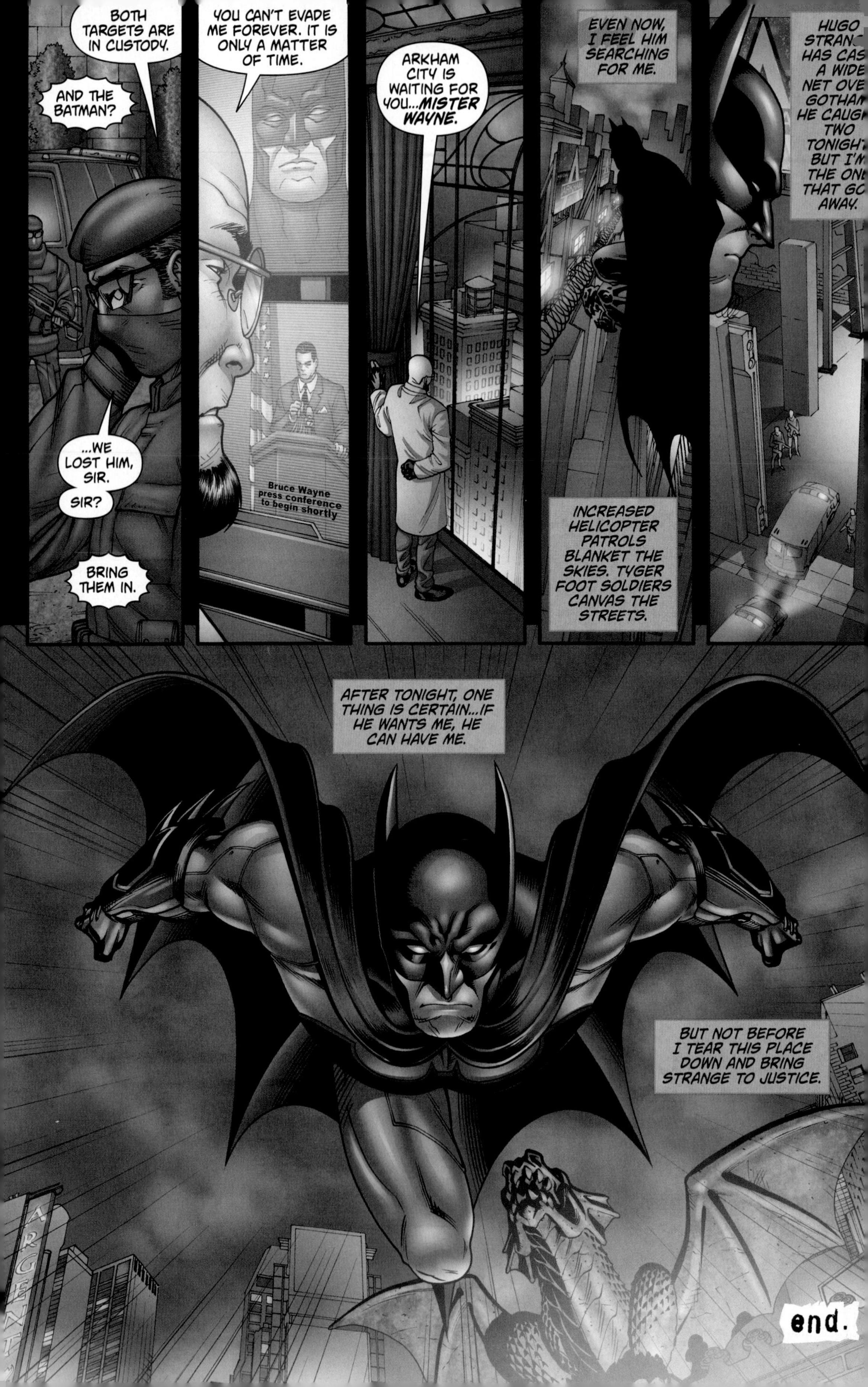

BOTH TARGETS ARE IN CUSTODY.
AND THE BATMAN?
...WE LOST HIM, SIR.
SIR?
BRING THEM IN.
YOU CAN'T EVADE ME FOREVER. IT IS ONLY A MATTER OF TIME.
Bruce Wayne press conference to begin shortly
ARKHAM CITY IS WAITING FOR YOU...MISTER WAYNE.
EVEN NOW, I FEEL HIM SEARCHING FOR ME.
INCREASED HELICOPTER PATROLS BLANKET THE SKIES. TYGER FOOT SOLDIERS CANVAS THE STREETS.
AFTER TONIGHT, ONE THING IS CERTAIN...IF HE WANTS ME, HE CAN HAVE ME.
BUT NOT BEFORE I TEAR THIS PLACE DOWN AND BRING STRANGE TO JUSTICE.
end.

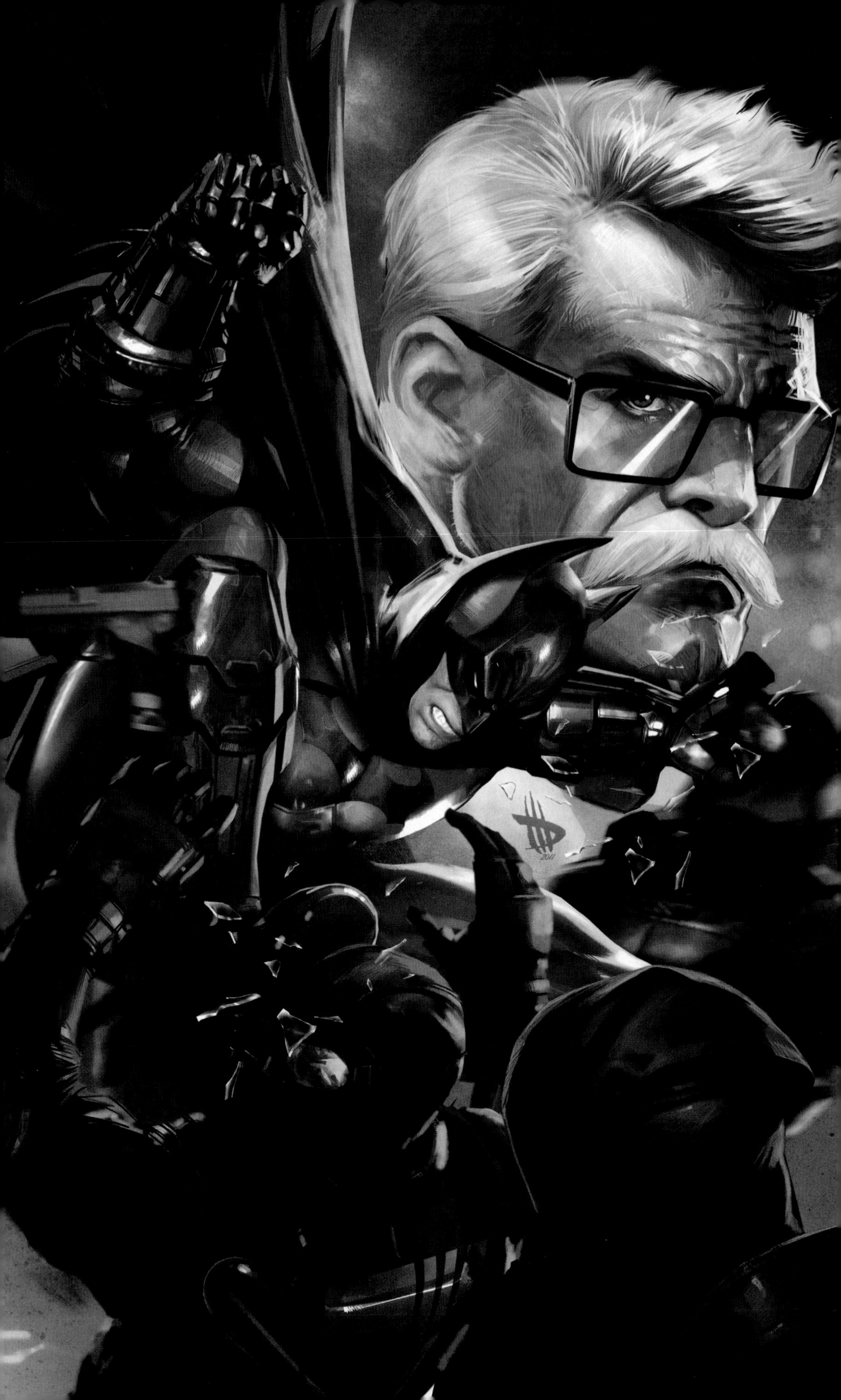

OBSERVATIONS

WRITTEN BY: **DEREK FRIDOLFS**

PENCILS BY: **BRIAN CHING**

INKS BY: **LIVESAY**

COLORS: **TONY AVIÑA**

LETTERS: **TRAVIS LANHAM**

COVER BY: **DAVE WILKINS**

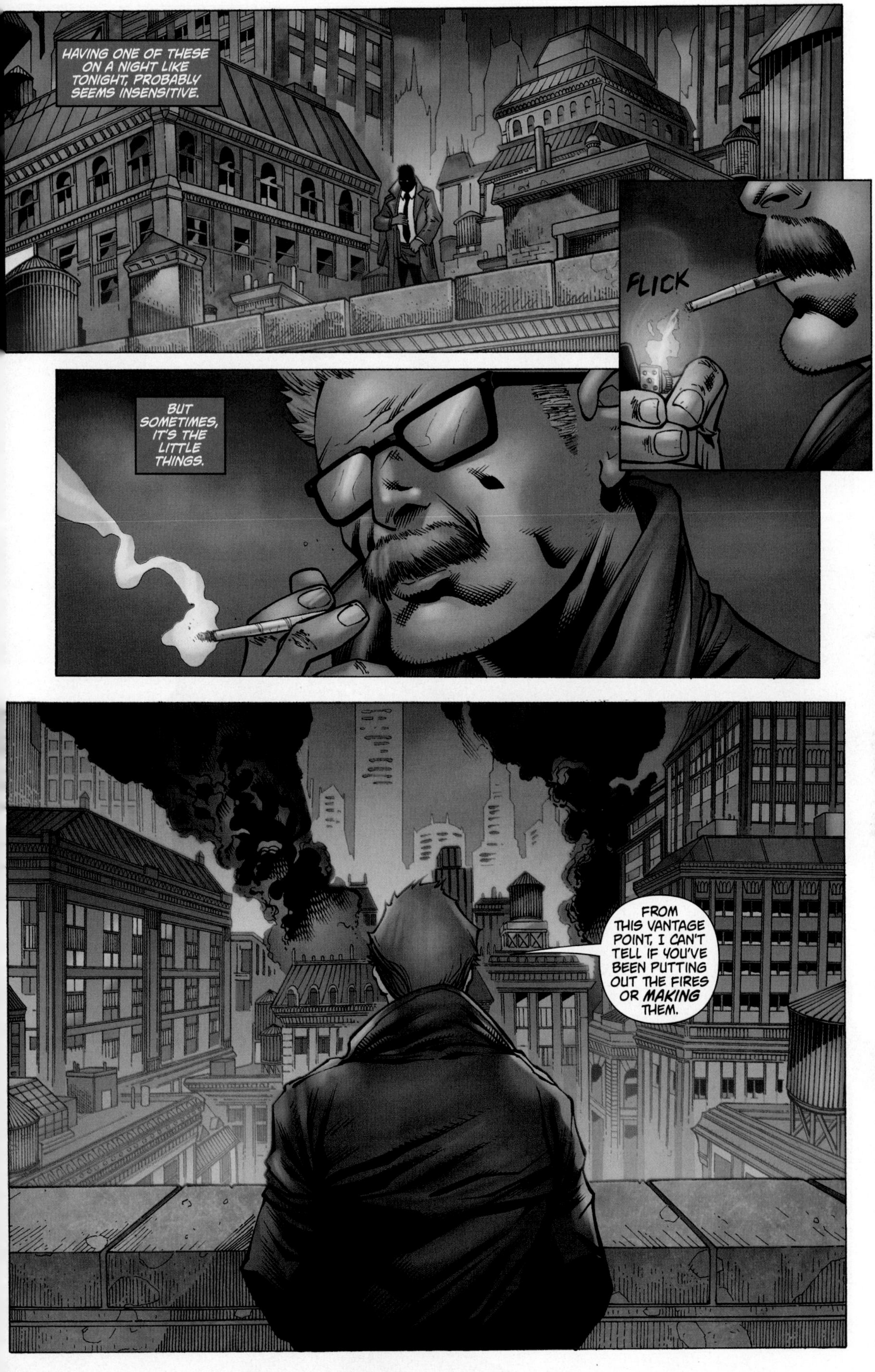

HAVING ONE OF THESE ON A NIGHT LIKE TONIGHT, PROBABLY SEEMS INSENSITIVE.
FLICK
BUT SOMETIMES, IT'S THE LITTLE THINGS.
FROM THIS VANTAGE POINT, I CAN'T TELL IF YOU'VE BEEN PUTTING OUT THE FIRES OR MAKING THEM.

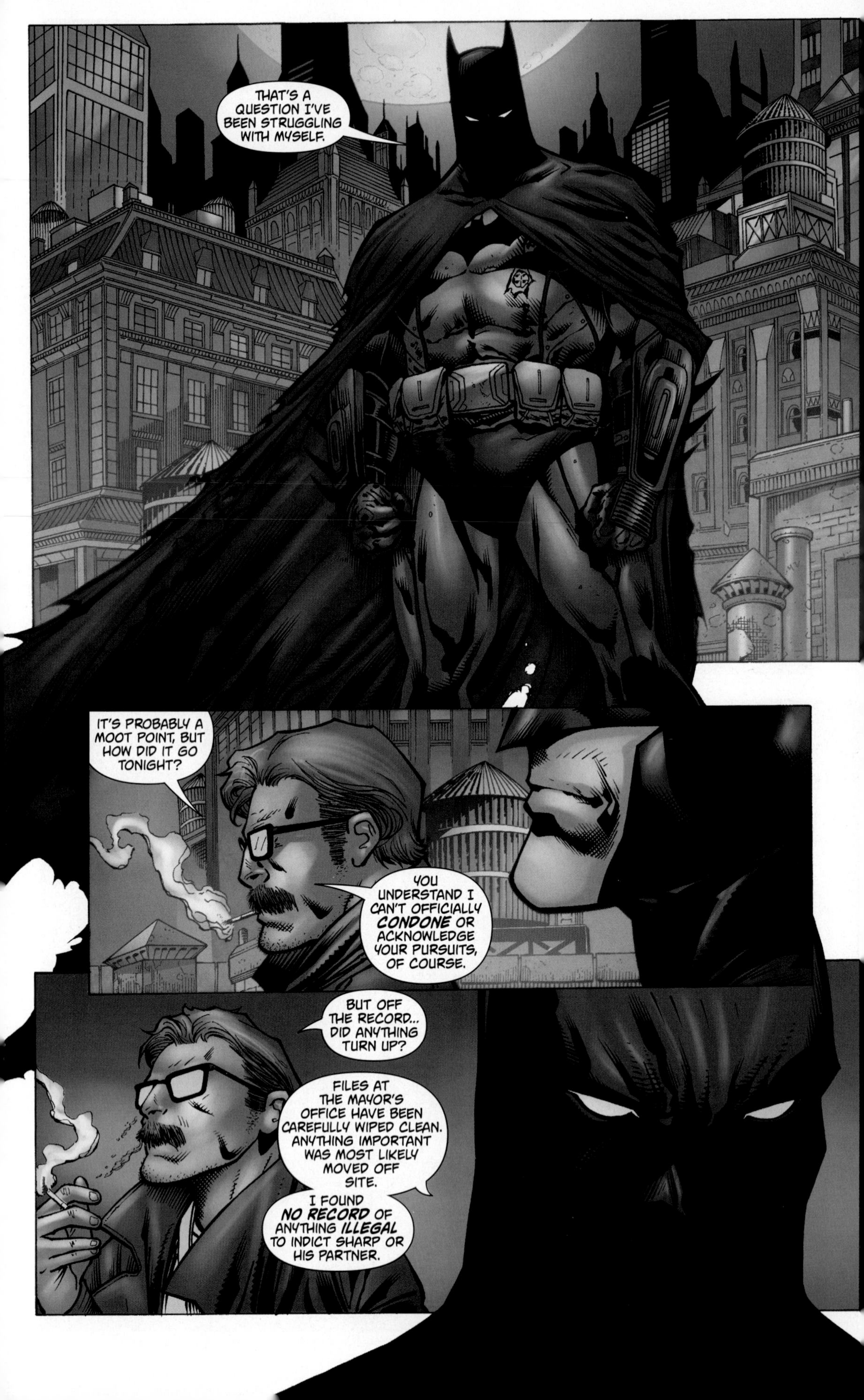
THAT'S A QUESTION I'VE BEEN STRUGGLING WITH MYSELF.
IT'S PROBABLY A MOOT POINT, BUT HOW DID IT GO TONIGHT?
YOU UNDERSTAND I CAN'T OFFICIALLY CONDONE OR ACKNOWLEDGE YOUR PURSUITS, OF COURSE.
BUT OFF THE RECORD... DID ANYTHING TURN UP?
FILES AT THE MAYOR'S OFFICE HAVE BEEN CAREFULLY WIPED CLEAN. ANYTHING IMPORTANT WAS MOST LIKELY MOVED OFF SITE.
I FOUND NO RECORD OF ANYTHING ILLEGAL TO INDICT SHARP OR HIS PARTNER.

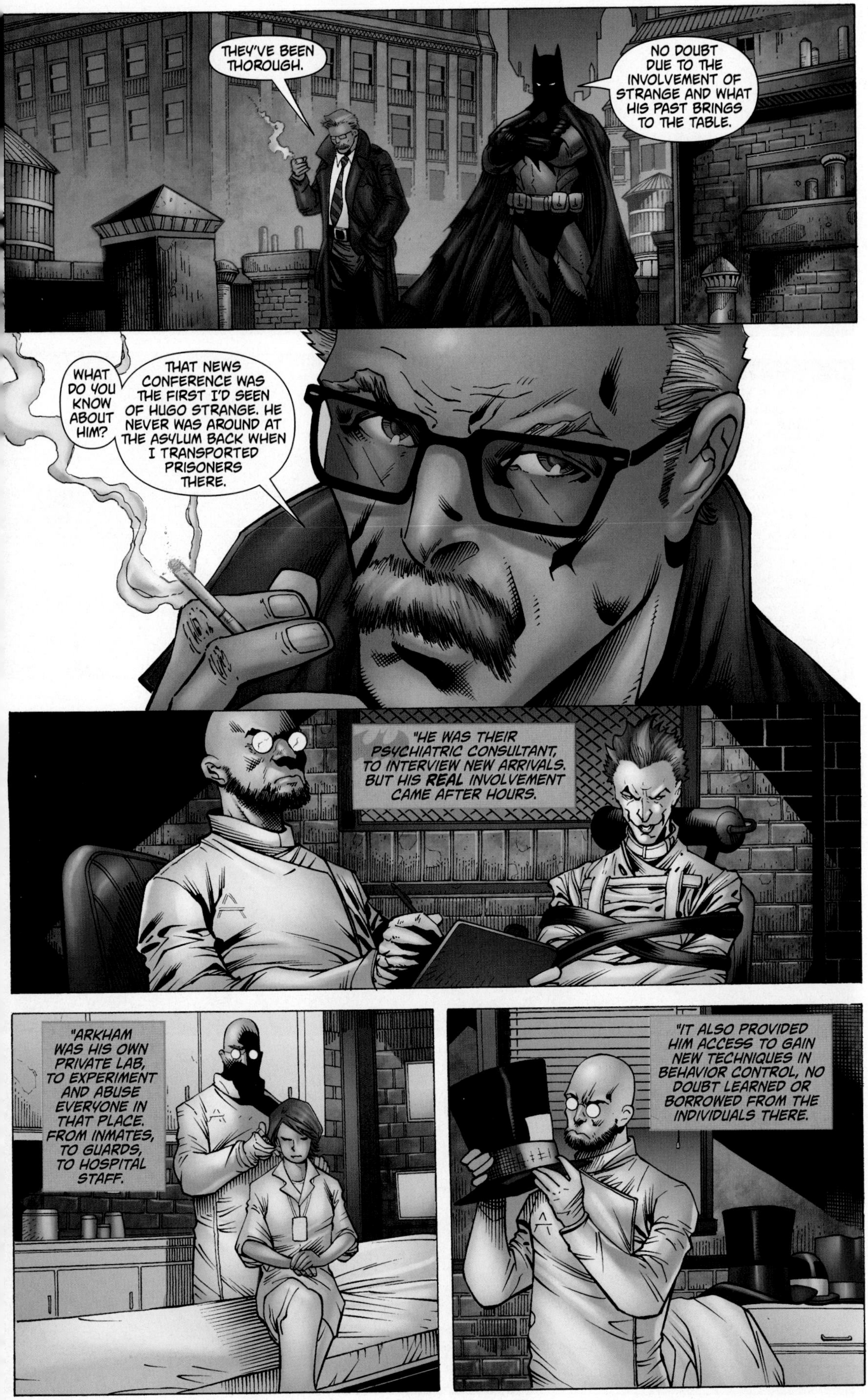
THEY'VE BEEN THOROUGH.
NO DOUBT DUE TO THE INVOLVEMENT OF STRANGE AND WHAT HIS PAST BRINGS TO THE TABLE.
WHAT DO YOU KNOW ABOUT HIM?
THAT NEWS CONFERENCE WAS THE FIRST I'D SEEN OF HUGO STRANGE. HE NEVER WAS AROUND AT THE ASYLUM BACK WHEN I TRANSPORTED PRISONERS THERE.
"HE WAS THEIR PSYCHIATRIC CONSULTANT, TO INTERVIEW NEW ARRIVALS. BUT HIS REAL INVOLVEMENT CAME AFTER HOURS.
"ARKHAM WAS HIS OWN PRIVATE LAB, TO EXPERIMENT AND ABUSE EVERYONE IN THAT PLACE. FROM INMATES, TO GUARDS, TO HOSPITAL STAFF.
"IT ALSO PROVIDED HIM ACCESS TO GAIN NEW TECHNIQUES IN BEHAVIOR CONTROL, NO DOUBT LEARNED OR BORROWED FROM THE INDIVIDUALS THERE.

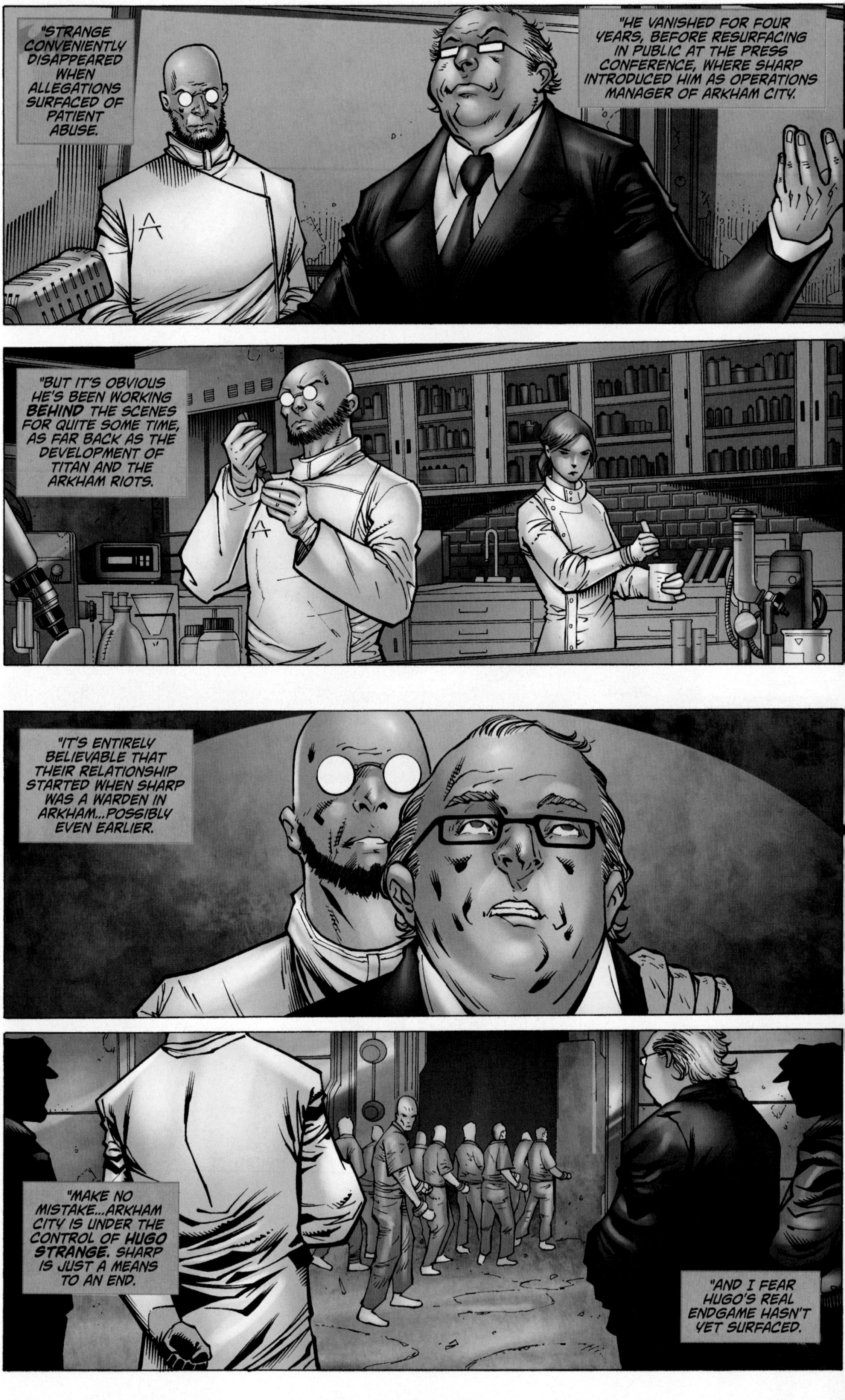
"STRANGE CONVENIENTLY DISAPPEARED WHEN ALLEGATIONS SURFACED OF PATIENT ABUSE.
"HE VANISHED FOR FOUR YEARS, BEFORE RESURFACING IN PUBLIC AT THE PRESS CONFERENCE, WHERE SHARP INTRODUCED HIM AS OPERATIONS MANAGER OF ARKHAM CITY.
"BUT IT'S OBVIOUS HE'S BEEN WORKING BEHIND THE SCENES FOR QUITE SOME TIME, AS FAR BACK AS THE DEVELOPMENT OF TITAN AND THE ARKHAM RIOTS.
"IT'S ENTIRELY BELIEVABLE THAT THEIR RELATIONSHIP STARTED WHEN SHARP WAS A WARDEN IN ARKHAM...POSSIBLY EVEN EARLIER.
"MAKE NO MISTAKE...ARKHAM CITY IS UNDER THE CONTROL OF HUGO STRANGE. SHARP IS JUST A MEANS TO AN END.
"AND I FEAR HUGO'S REAL ENDGAME HASN'T YET SURFACED.

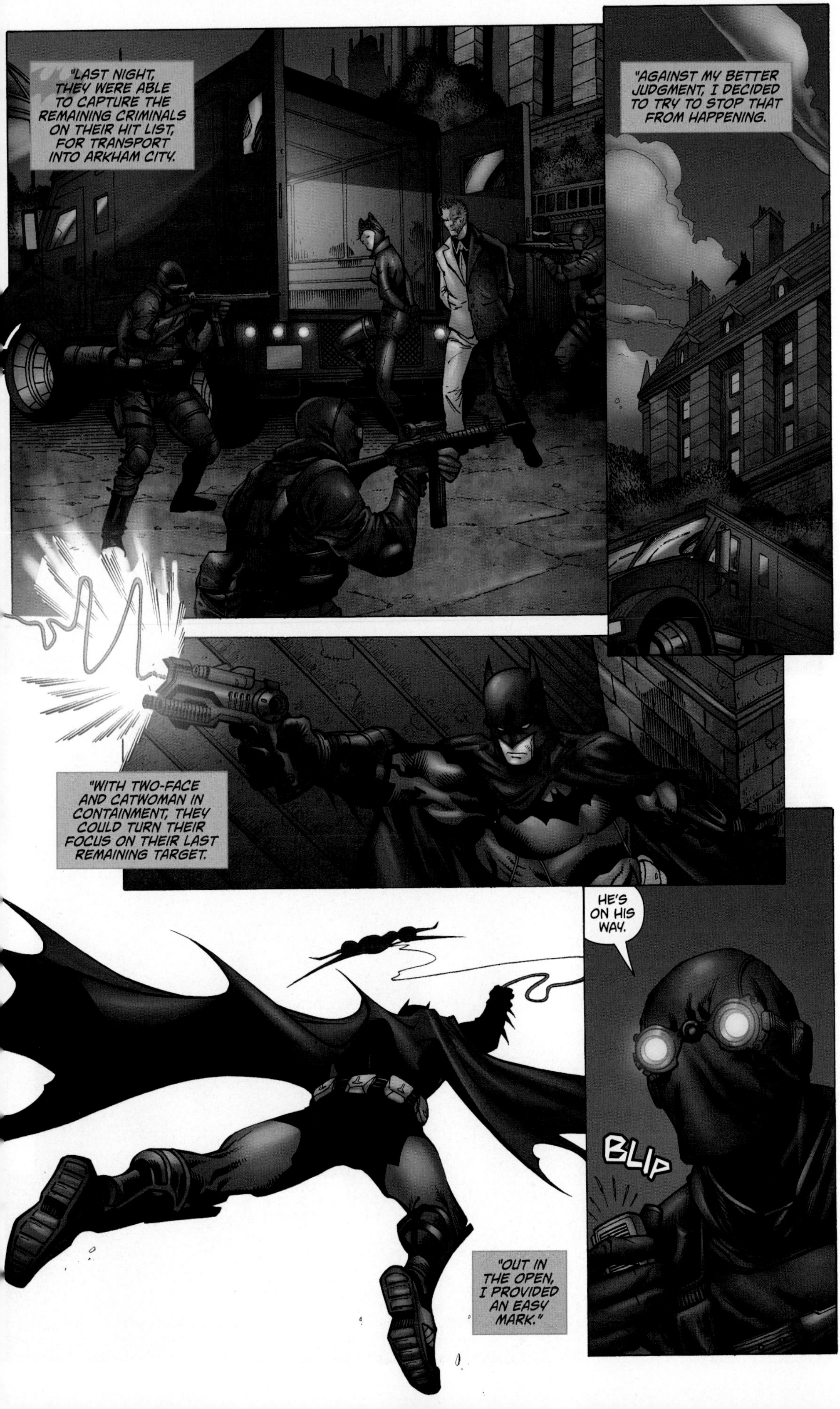
"LAST NIGHT, THEY WERE ABLE TO CAPTURE THE REMAINING CRIMINALS ON THEIR HIT LIST, FOR TRANSPORT INTO ARKHAM CITY.
"AGAINST MY BETTER JUDGMENT, I DECIDED TO TRY TO STOP THAT FROM HAPPENING.
"WITH TWO-FACE AND CATWOMAN IN CONTAINMENT, THEY COULD TURN THEIR FOCUS ON THEIR LAST REMAINING TARGET.
HE'S ON HIS WAY.
BLIP
"OUT IN THE OPEN, I PROVIDED AN EASY MARK."

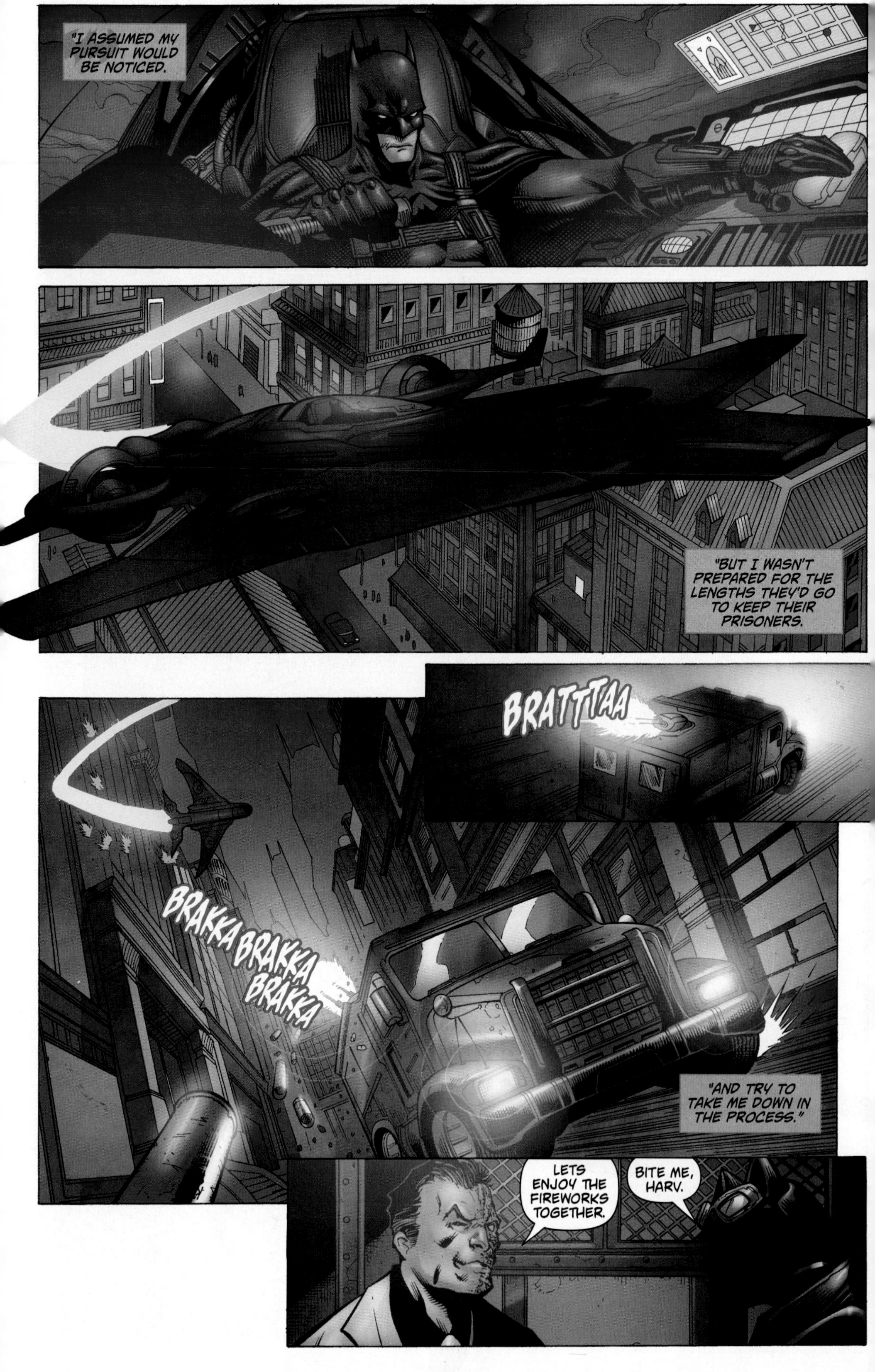
"I ASSUMED MY PURSUIT WOULD BE NOTICED.
"BUT I WASN'T PREPARED FOR THE LENGTHS THEY'D GO TO KEEP THEIR PRISONERS.
BRATTTAA
BRAKKA BRAKKA BRAKKA
"AND TRY TO TAKE ME DOWN IN THE PROCESS."
LETS ENJOY THE FIREWORKS TOGETHER.
BITE ME, HARV.

BOOM

BOOM

"WITH THE AMOUNT OF WEAPONRY ON DISPLAY, I MAKE A MENTAL NOTE.

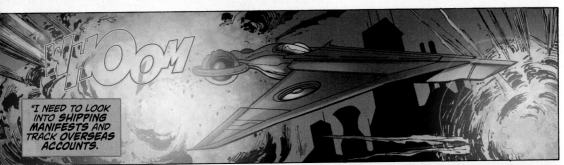

WHOOM

"I NEED TO LOOK INTO SHIPPING MANIFESTS AND TRACK OVERSEAS ACCOUNTS.

"THEY APPEAR TO HAVE A FOREIGN ARMS DEALER NOW INVOLVED.

SKREEEEE

FOOOSH

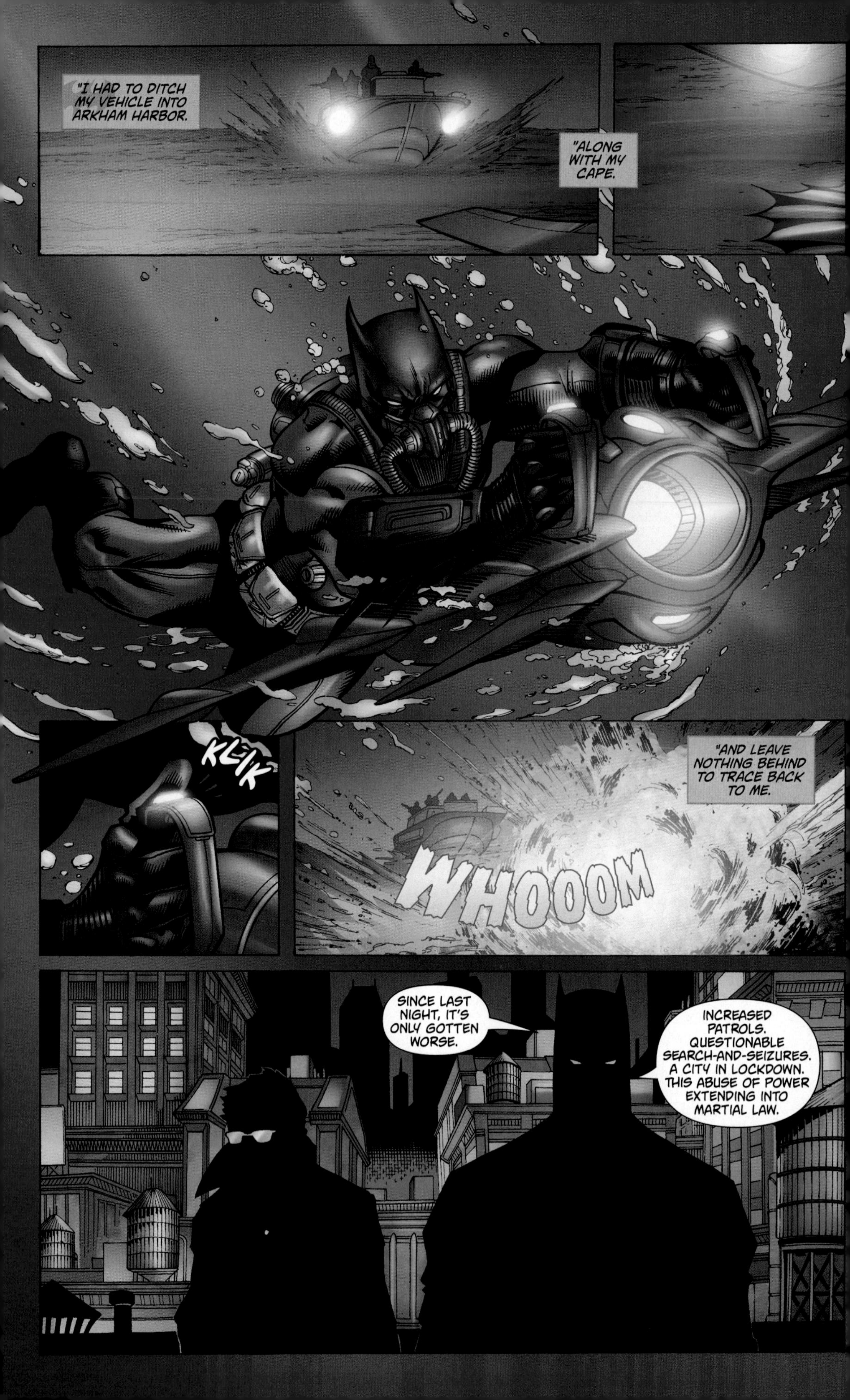
"I HAD TO DITCH MY VEHICLE INTO ARKHAM HARBOR.
"ALONG WITH MY CAPE.
KLIK
"AND LEAVE NOTHING BEHIND TO TRACE BACK TO ME.
WHOOOM
SINCE LAST NIGHT, IT'S ONLY GOTTEN WORSE.
INCREASED PATROLS. QUESTIONABLE SEARCH-AND-SEIZURES. A CITY IN LOCKDOWN. THIS ABUSE OF POWER EXTENDING INTO MARTIAL LAW.

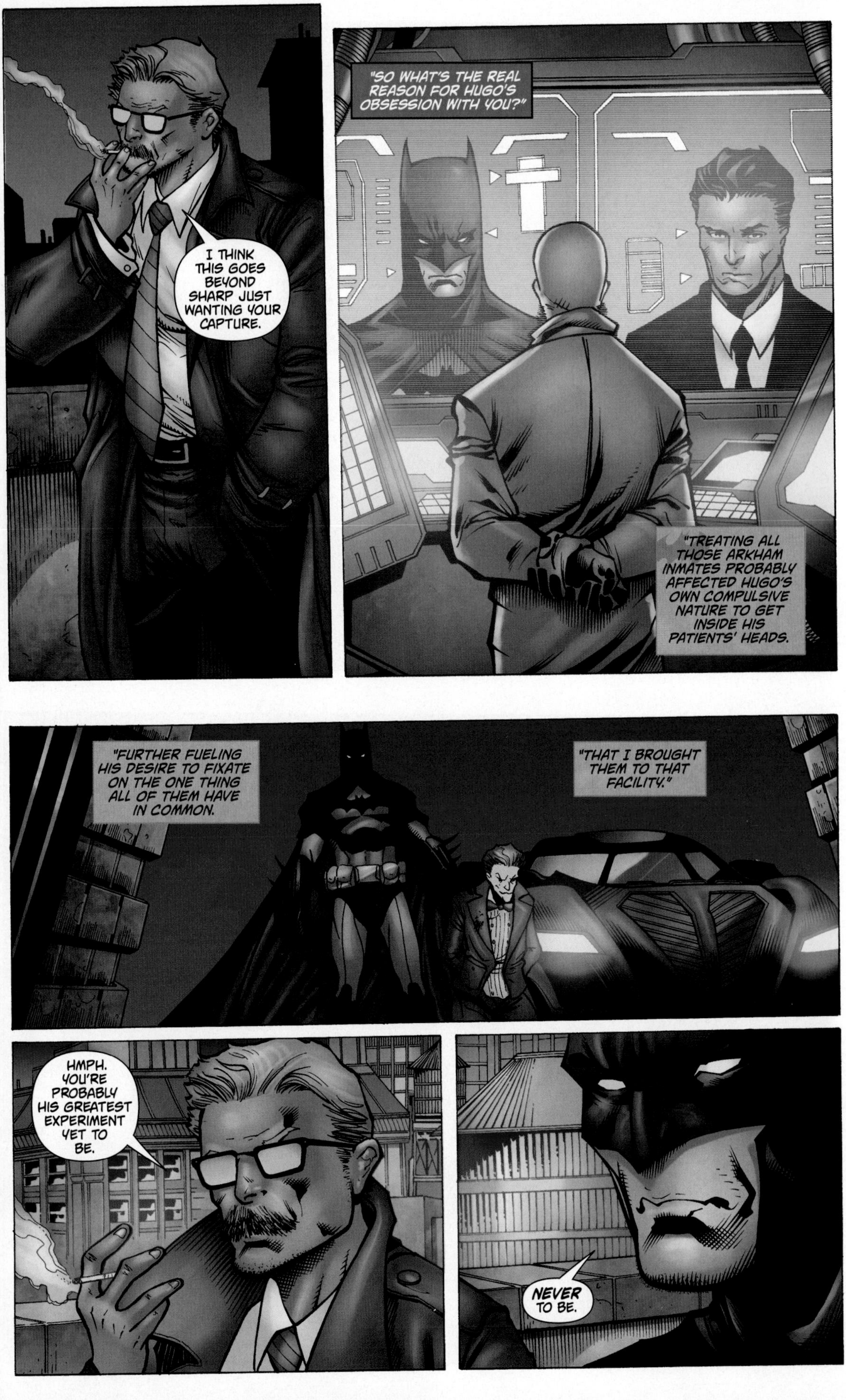
I THINK THIS GOES BEYOND SHARP JUST WANTING YOUR CAPTURE.
"SO WHAT'S THE REAL REASON FOR HUGO'S OBSESSION WITH YOU?"
"TREATING ALL THOSE ARKHAM INMATES PROBABLY AFFECTED HUGO'S OWN COMPULSIVE NATURE TO GET INSIDE HIS PATIENTS' HEADS.
"FURTHER FUELING HIS DESIRE TO FIXATE ON THE ONE THING ALL OF THEM HAVE IN COMMON.
"THAT I BROUGHT THEM TO THAT FACILITY."
HMPH. YOU'RE PROBABLY HIS GREATEST EXPERIMENT YET TO BE.
NEVER TO BE.

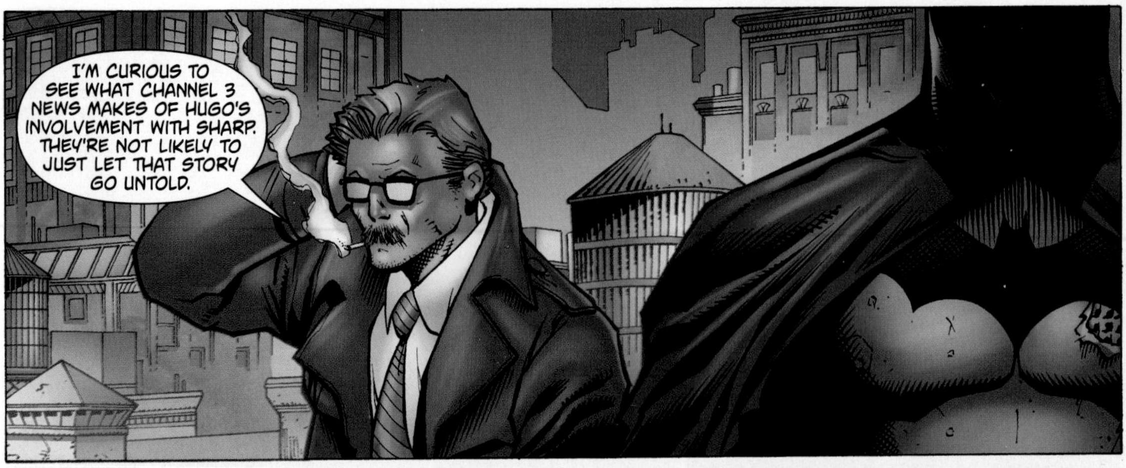
I'M CURIOUS TO SEE WHAT CHANNEL 3 NEWS MAKES OF HUGO'S INVOLVEMENT WITH SHARP. THEY'RE NOT LIKELY TO JUST LET THAT STORY GO UNTOLD.

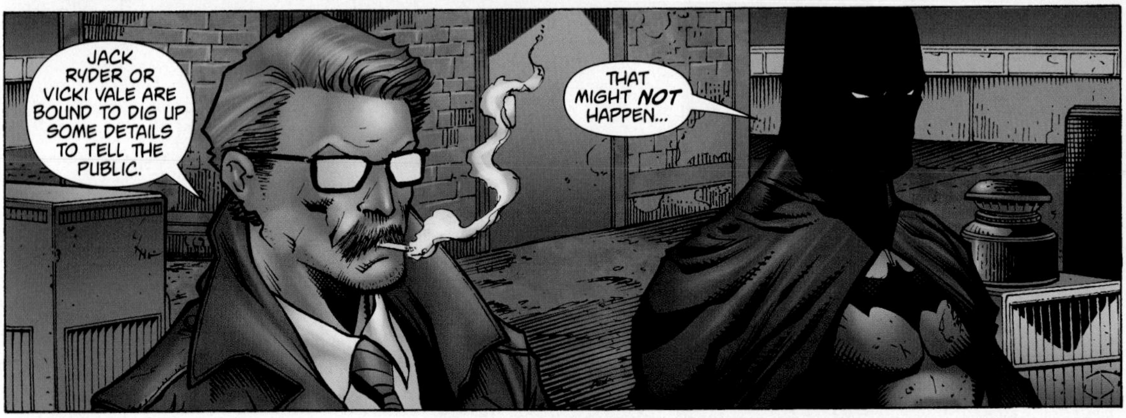
JACK RYDER OR VICKI VALE ARE BOUND TO DIG UP SOME DETAILS TO TELL THE PUBLIC.
THAT MIGHT NOT HAPPEN...

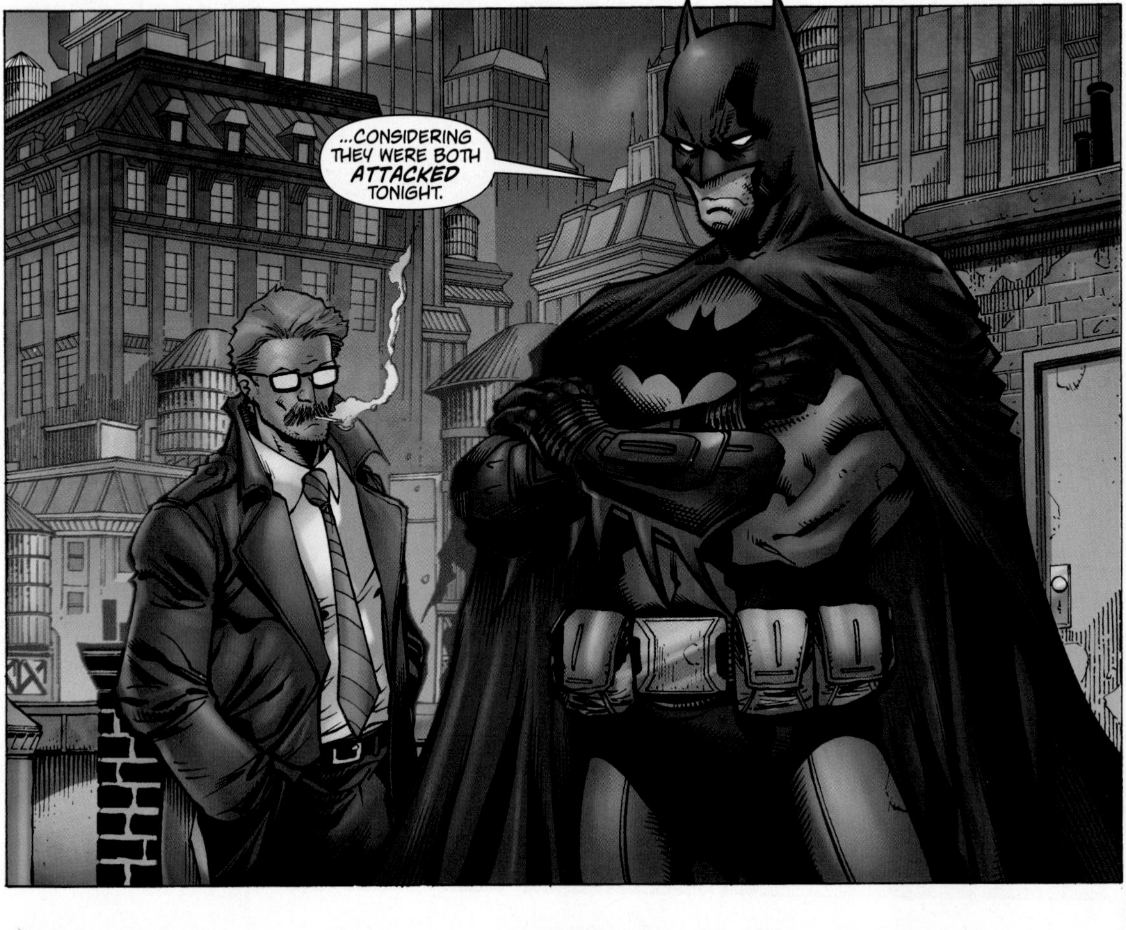
...CONSIDERING THEY WERE BOTH ATTACKED TONIGHT.

"AFTER MY INVESTIGATION AT THE MAYOR'S OFFICE, THE TYGERS MANAGED TO TRACK AND PURSUE ME FOR MOST OF THE NIGHT.

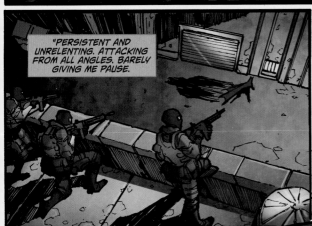

"PERSISTENT AND UNRELENTING. ATTACKING FROM ALL ANGLES. BARELY GIVING ME PAUSE.

FWOOSH!

THWAK
THWAK

THOK

"I TOOK COVER IN A NEARBY ELECTRONICS STORE. ANOTHER VICTIM OF FORECLOSURE AND BANKRUPTCY PROCEEDINGS.

"IT WAS VACANT AND GAVE ME A BRIEF MOMENT TO PLAN MY NEXT MOVE.

CLICK

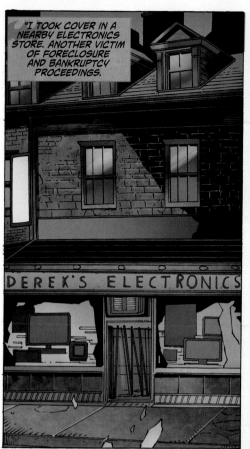

DEREK'S ELECTRONICS

"BUT ONE VISITOR WAS ALREADY WAITING FOR ME."

IT WAS VERY BOLD OF YOU TO RAID THE MAYOR'S OFFICE. UNFORTUNATELY, NOTHING OF PERTINENCE WAS AVAILABLE FOR YOU.

OH... THE SILENT TREATMENT? NO MATTER. I'VE BEEN LISTENING TO YOUR HIDDEN ALLIES ALL ALONG.

SALE
CLEARANCE

YOU HAVE BEEN A MOST INTERESTING SUBJECT TO WATCH, BATMAN. BUT WE BOTH KNOW WHO YOU REALLY ARE.

YES. I'M THE ONE WHO IS GOING TO BRING YOU DOWN.

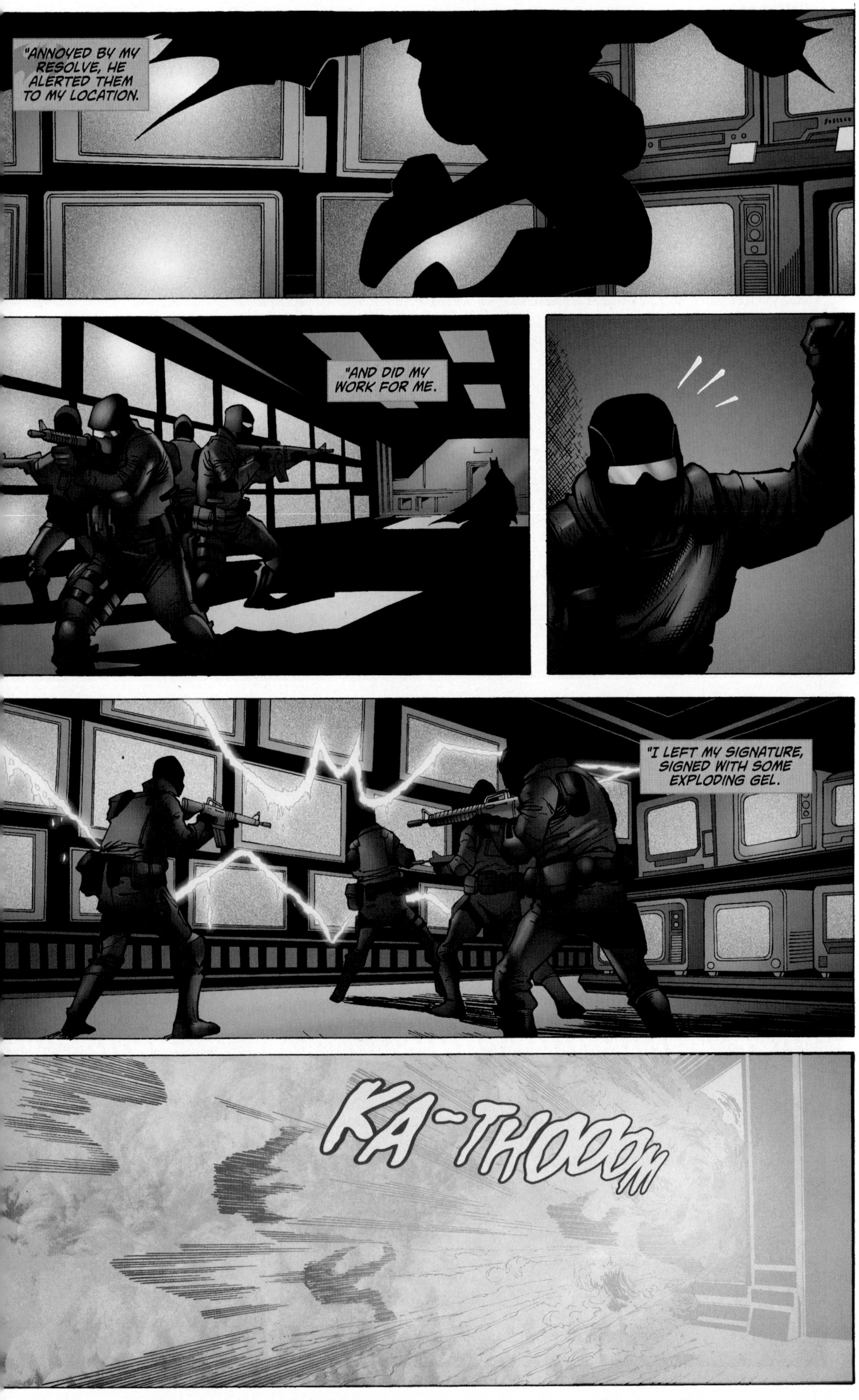
"ANNOYED BY MY RESOLVE, HE ALERTED THEM TO MY LOCATION.
"AND DID MY WORK FOR ME.
"I LEFT MY SIGNATURE, SIGNED WITH SOME EXPLODING GEL.
KA-THOOOM

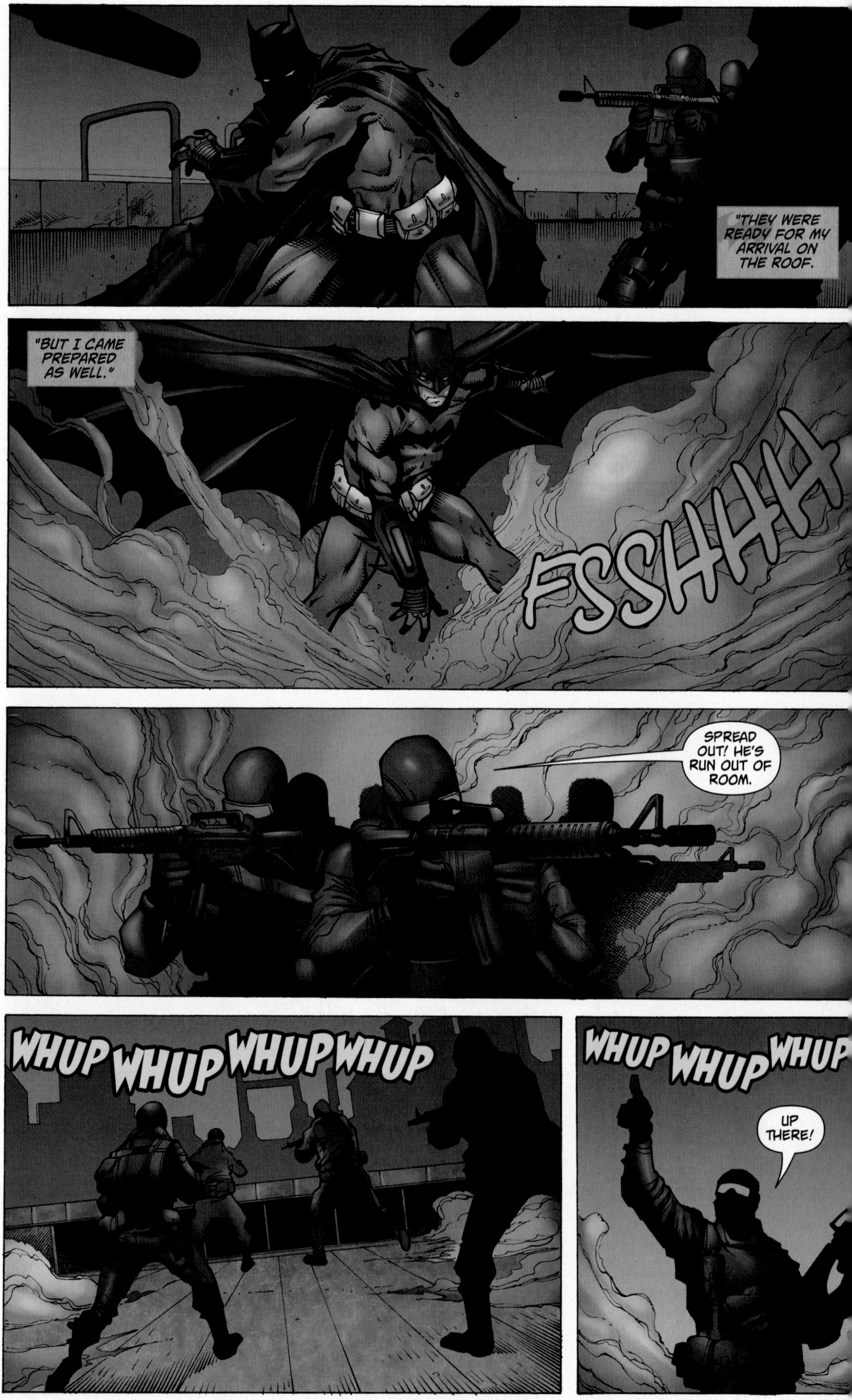
"THEY WERE READY FOR MY ARRIVAL ON THE ROOF.
"BUT I CAME PREPARED AS WELL."
FSSHHH
SPREAD OUT! HE'S RUN OUT OF ROOM.
WHUP WHUP WHUP WHUP
WHUP WHUP WHUP
UP THERE!

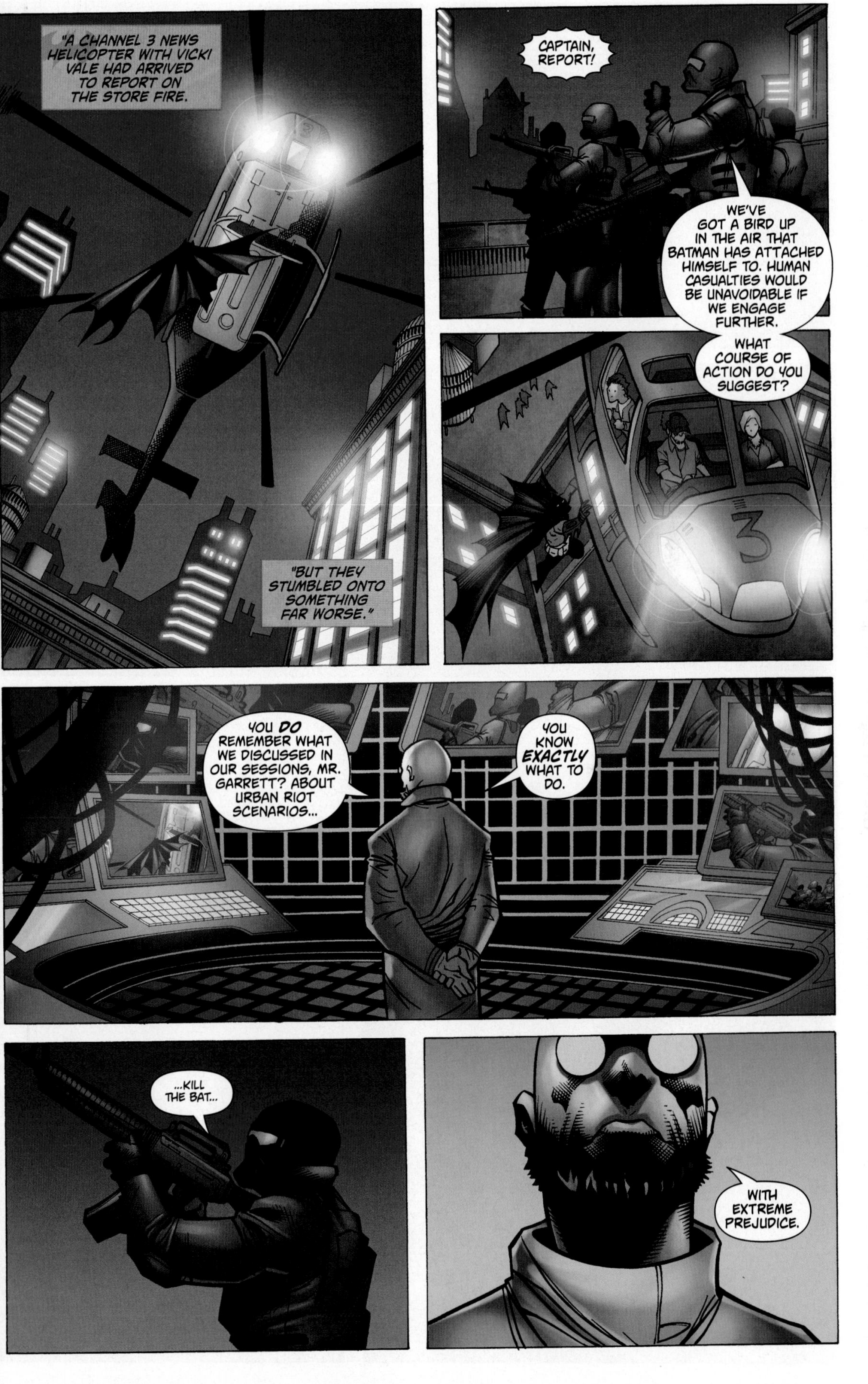
"A CHANNEL 3 NEWS HELICOPTER WITH VICKI VALE HAD ARRIVED TO REPORT ON THE STORE FIRE.
"BUT THEY STUMBLED ONTO SOMETHING FAR WORSE."
CAPTAIN, REPORT!
WE'VE GOT A BIRD UP IN THE AIR THAT BATMAN HAS ATTACHED HIMSELF TO. HUMAN CASUALTIES WOULD BE UNAVOIDABLE IF WE ENGAGE FURTHER.
WHAT COURSE OF ACTION DO YOU SUGGEST?
YOU DO REMEMBER WHAT WE DISCUSSED IN OUR SESSIONS, MR. GARRETT? ABOUT URBAN RIOT SCENARIOS...
YOU KNOW EXACTLY WHAT TO DO.
...KILL THE BAT...
WITH EXTREME PREJUDICE.

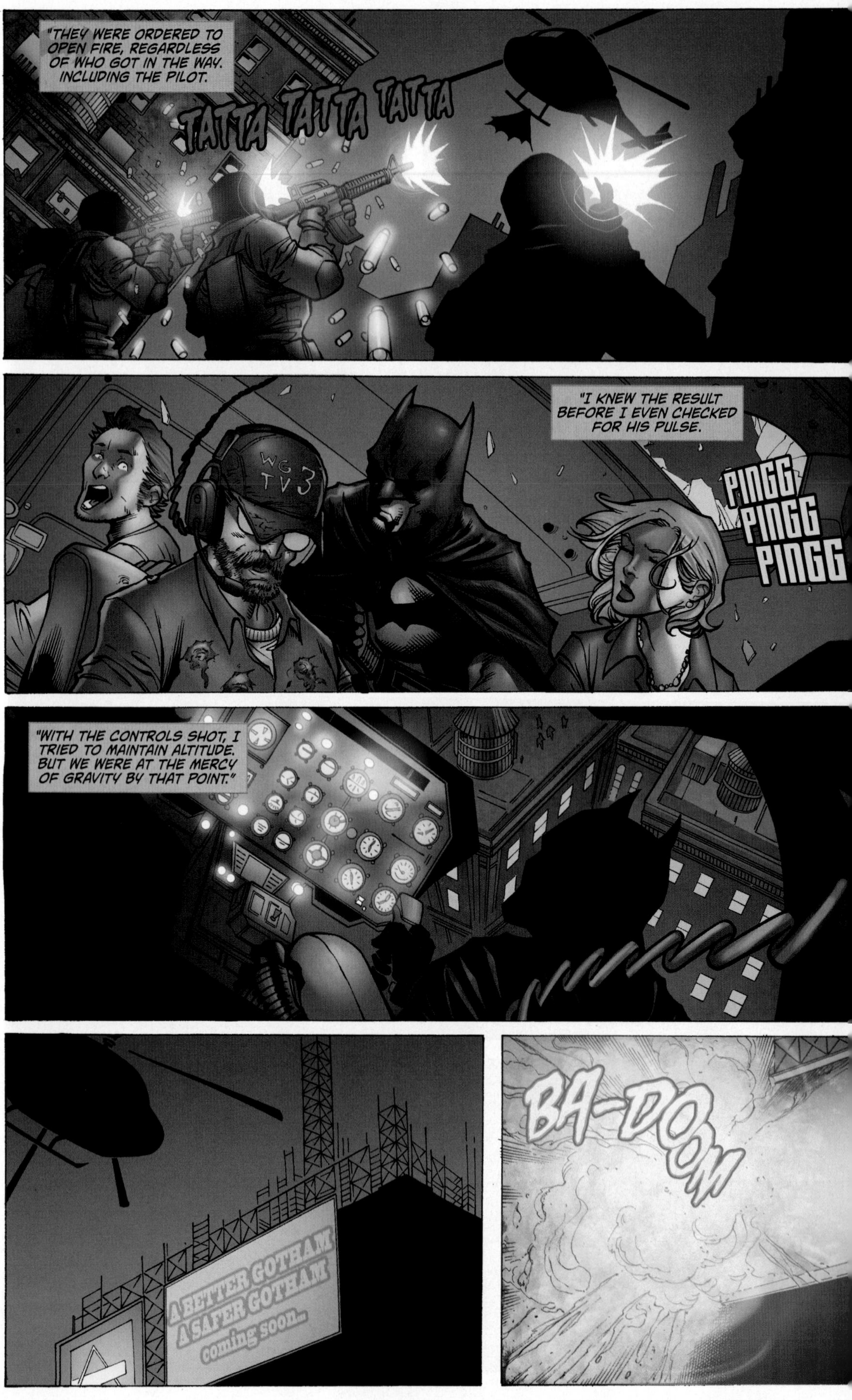
"THEY WERE ORDERED TO OPEN FIRE, REGARDLESS OF WHO GOT IN THE WAY. INCLUDING THE PILOT.
TATTA TATTA TATTA
"I KNEW THE RESULT BEFORE I EVEN CHECKED FOR HIS PULSE.
WG TV3
PINGG PINGG PINGG
"WITH THE CONTROLS SHOT, I TRIED TO MAINTAIN ALTITUDE. BUT WE WERE AT THE MERCY OF GRAVITY BY THAT POINT."
A BETTER GOTHAM
A SAFER GOTHAM
coming soon...
BA-DOOM

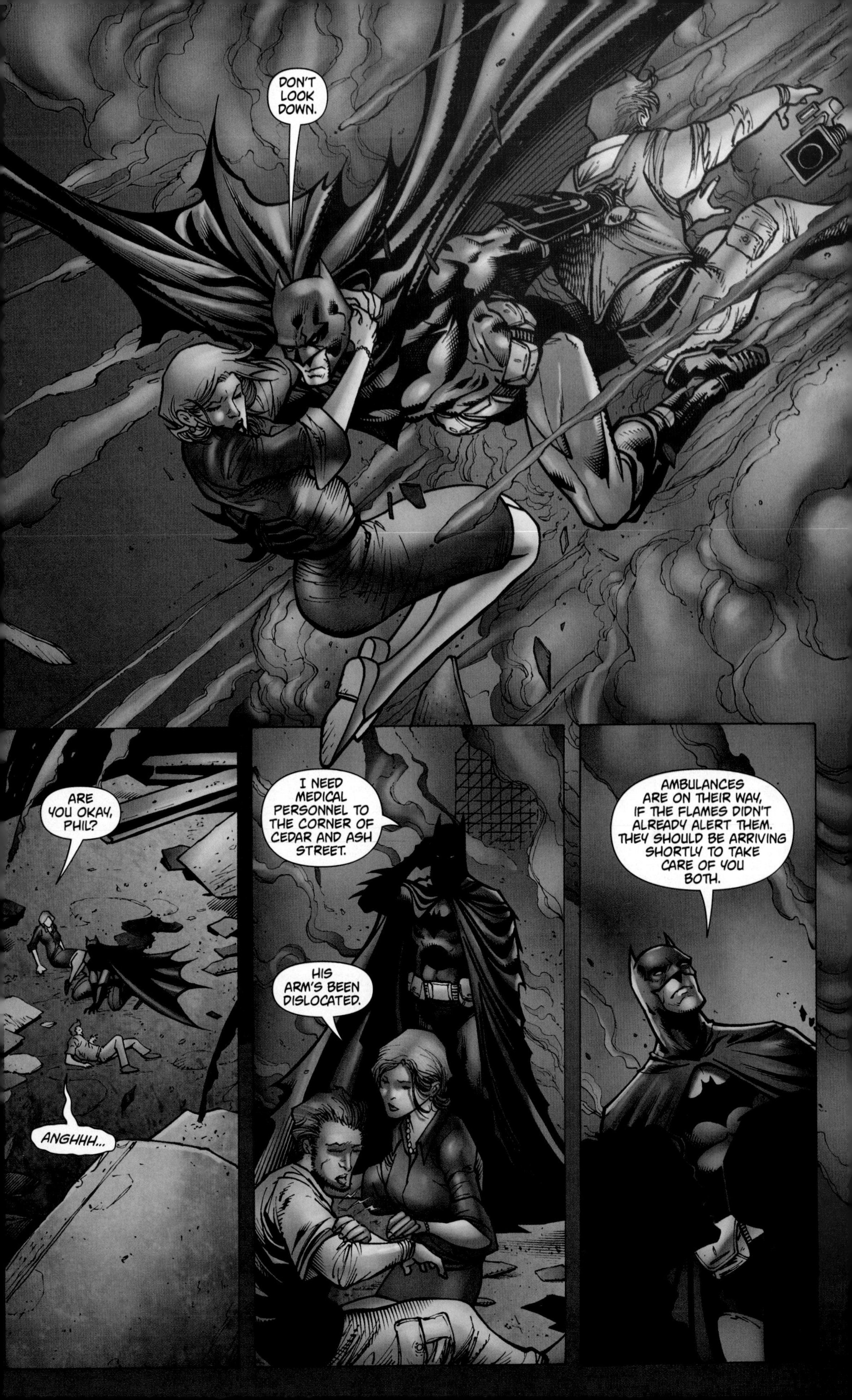
DON'T LOOK DOWN.
ARE YOU OKAY, PHIL?
ANGHHH...
I NEED MEDICAL PERSONNEL TO THE CORNER OF CEDAR AND ASH STREET.
HIS ARM'S BEEN DISLOCATED.
AMBULANCES ARE ON THEIR WAY, IF THE FLAMES DIDN'T ALREADY ALERT THEM. THEY SHOULD BE ARRIVING SHORTLY TO TAKE CARE OF YOU BOTH.

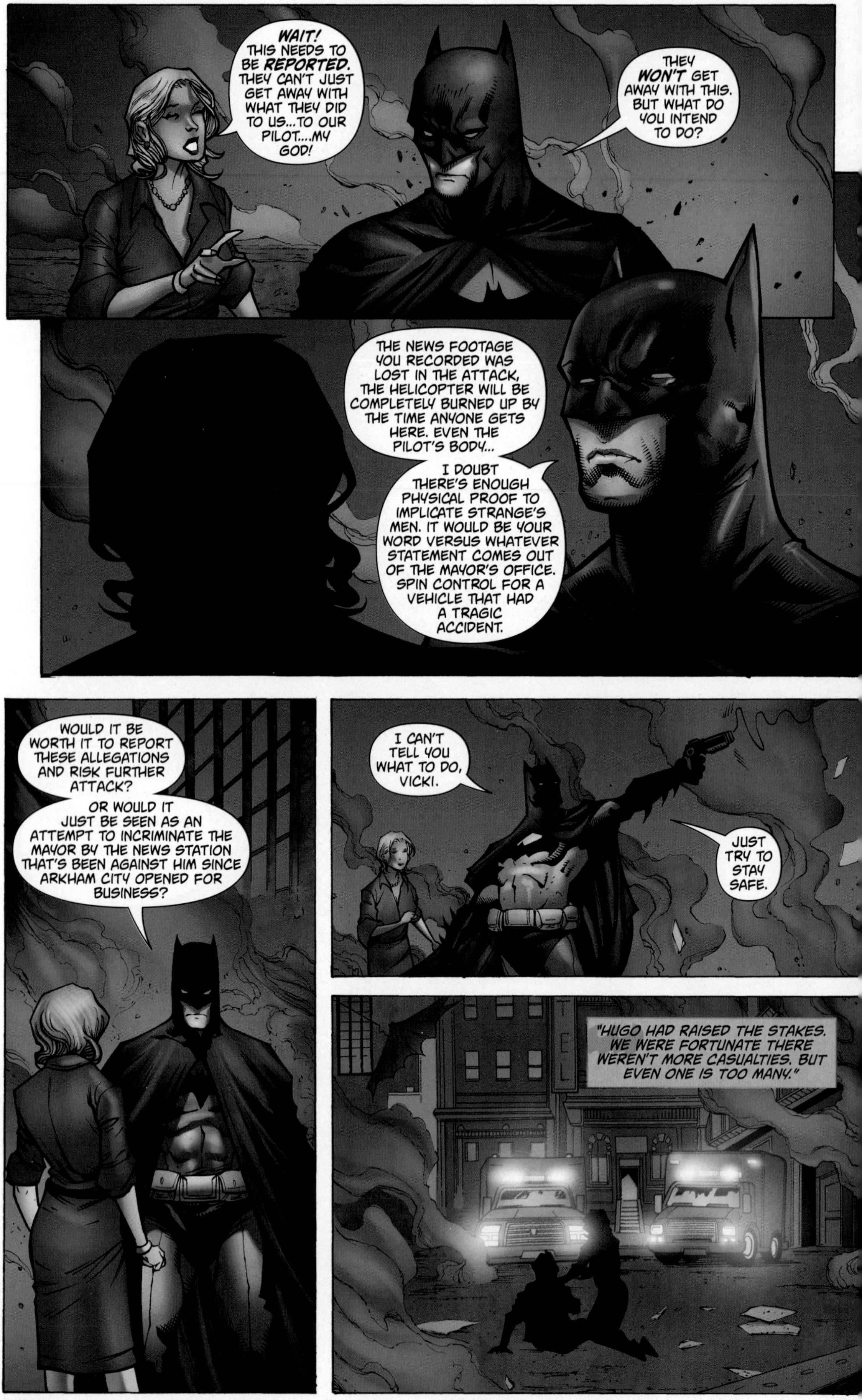

WAIT! THIS NEEDS TO BE REPORTED. THEY CAN'T JUST GET AWAY WITH WHAT THEY DID TO US...TO OUR PILOT....MY GOD!
THEY WON'T GET AWAY WITH THIS. BUT WHAT DO YOU INTEND TO DO?
THE NEWS FOOTAGE YOU RECORDED WAS LOST IN THE ATTACK, THE HELICOPTER WILL BE COMPLETELY BURNED UP BY THE TIME ANYONE GETS HERE. EVEN THE PILOT'S BODY...
I DOUBT THERE'S ENOUGH PHYSICAL PROOF TO IMPLICATE STRANGE'S MEN. IT WOULD BE YOUR WORD VERSUS WHATEVER STATEMENT COMES OUT OF THE MAYOR'S OFFICE. SPIN CONTROL FOR A VEHICLE THAT HAD A TRAGIC ACCIDENT.
WOULD IT BE WORTH IT TO REPORT THESE ALLEGATIONS AND RISK FURTHER ATTACK?
OR WOULD IT JUST BE SEEN AS AN ATTEMPT TO INCRIMINATE THE MAYOR BY THE NEWS STATION THAT'S BEEN AGAINST HIM SINCE ARKHAM CITY OPENED FOR BUSINESS?
I CAN'T TELL YOU WHAT TO DO, VICKI.
JUST TRY TO STAY SAFE.
"HUGO HAD RAISED THE STAKES. WE WERE FORTUNATE THERE WEREN'T MORE CASUALTIES. BUT EVEN ONE IS TOO MANY."

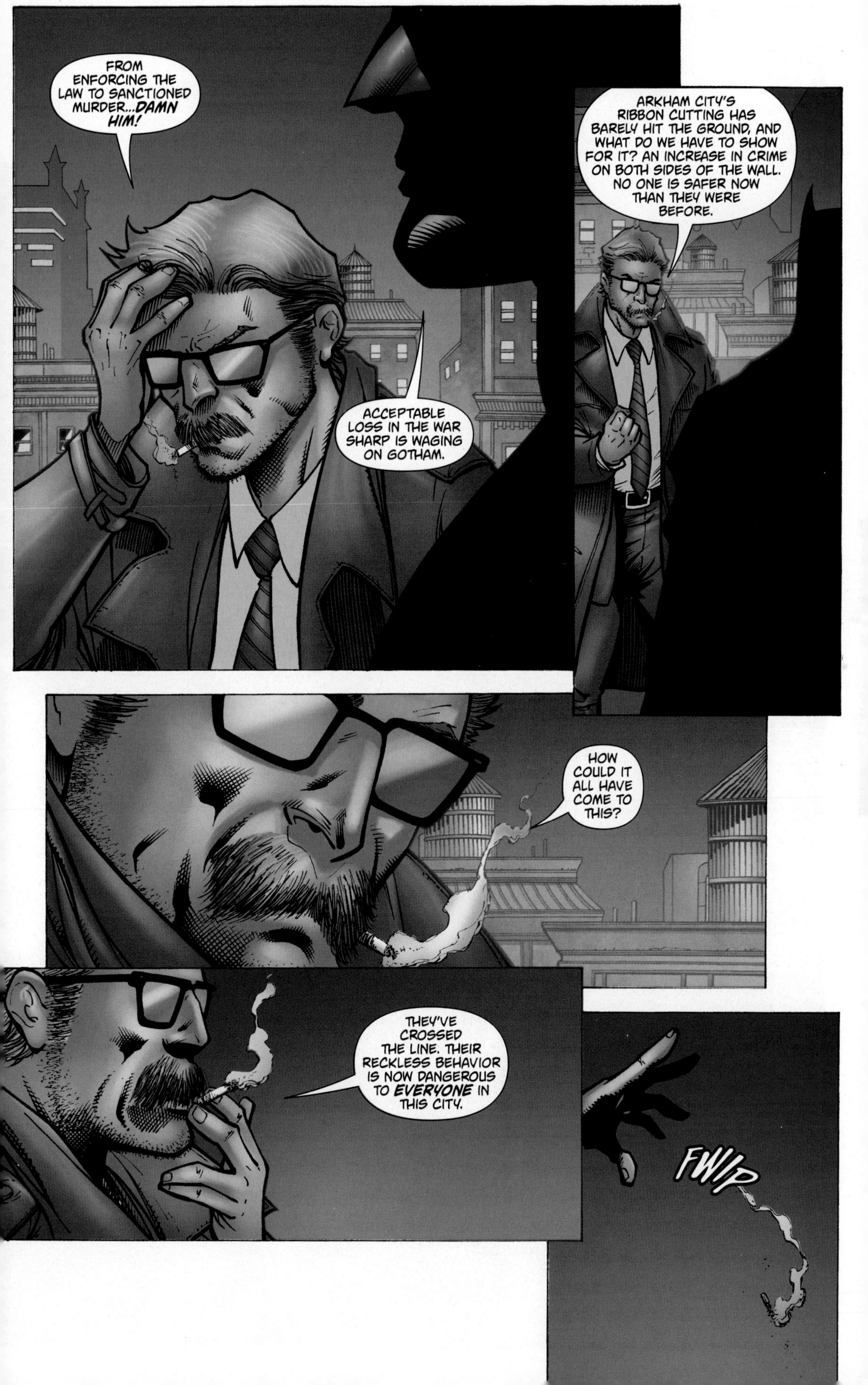
FROM ENFORCING THE LAW TO SANCTIONED MURDER...DAMN HIM!
ACCEPTABLE LOSS IN THE WAR SHARP IS WAGING ON GOTHAM.
ARKHAM CITY'S RIBBON CUTTING HAS BARELY HIT THE GROUND, AND WHAT DO WE HAVE TO SHOW FOR IT? AN INCREASE IN CRIME ON BOTH SIDES OF THE WALL. NO ONE IS SAFER NOW THAN THEY WERE BEFORE.
HOW COULD IT ALL HAVE COME TO THIS?
THEY'VE CROSSED THE LINE. THEIR RECKLESS BEHAVIOR IS NOW DANGEROUS TO EVERYONE IN THIS CITY.
FWIP

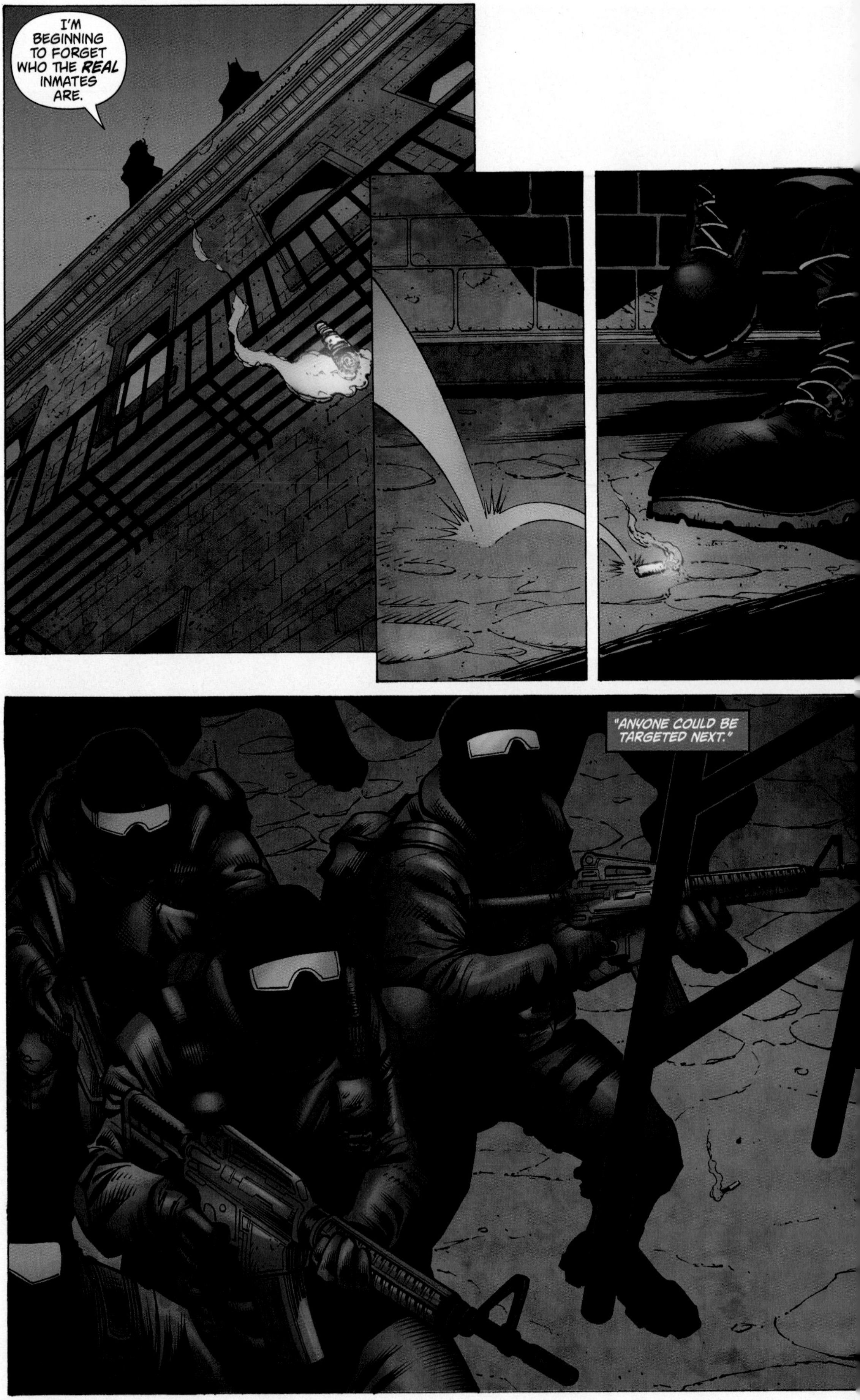

I'M BEGINNING TO FORGET WHO THE *REAL* INMATES ARE.
"ANYONE COULD BE TARGETED NEXT."

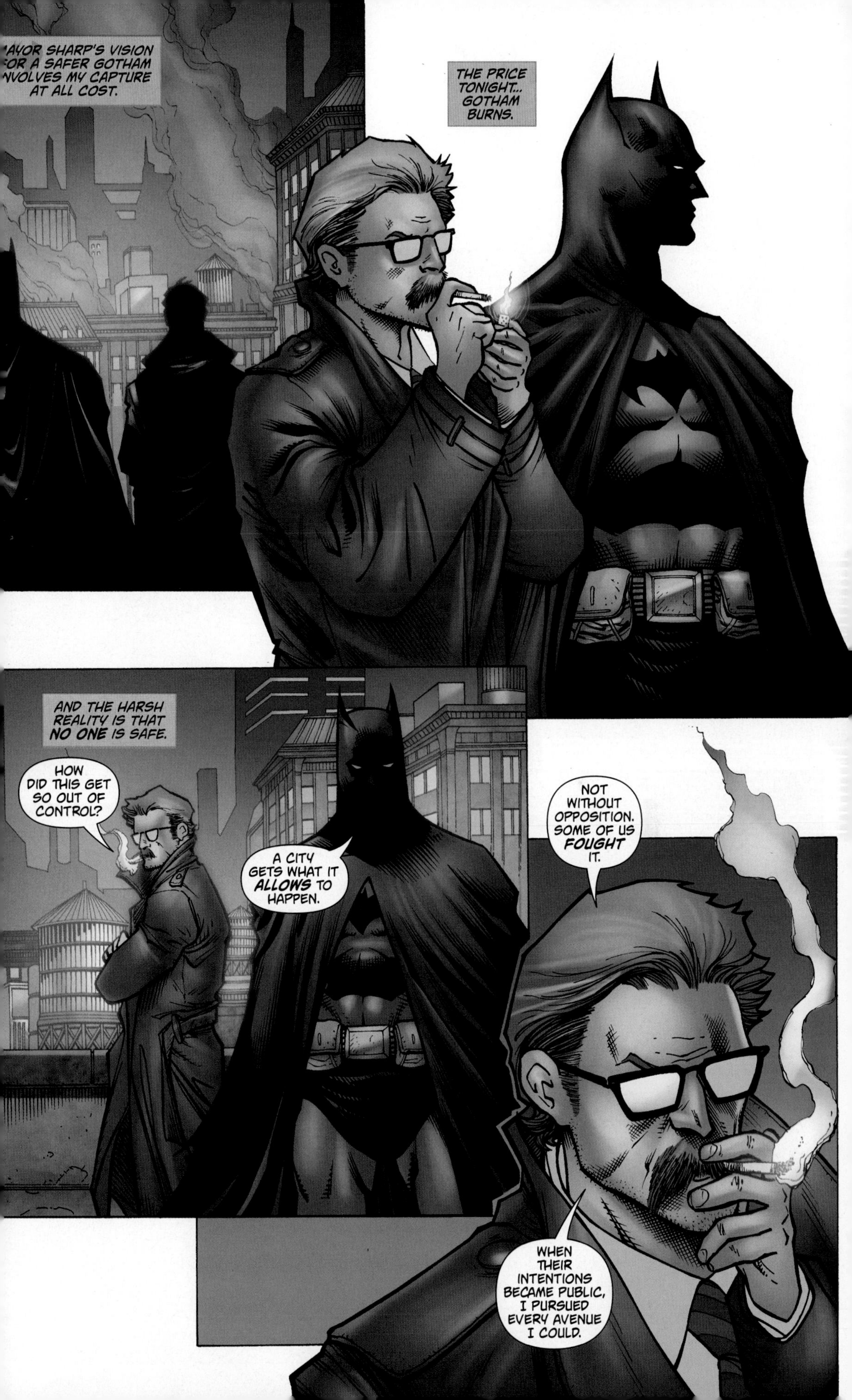

MAYOR SHARP'S VISION FOR A SAFER GOTHAM INVOLVES MY CAPTURE AT ALL COST.
THE PRICE TONIGHT... GOTHAM BURNS.
AND THE HARSH REALITY IS THAT NO ONE IS SAFE.
HOW DID THIS GET SO OUT OF CONTROL?
A CITY GETS WHAT IT ALLOWS TO HAPPEN.
NOT WITHOUT OPPOSITION. SOME OF US FOUGHT IT.
WHEN THEIR INTENTIONS BECAME PUBLIC, I PURSUED EVERY AVENUE I COULD.

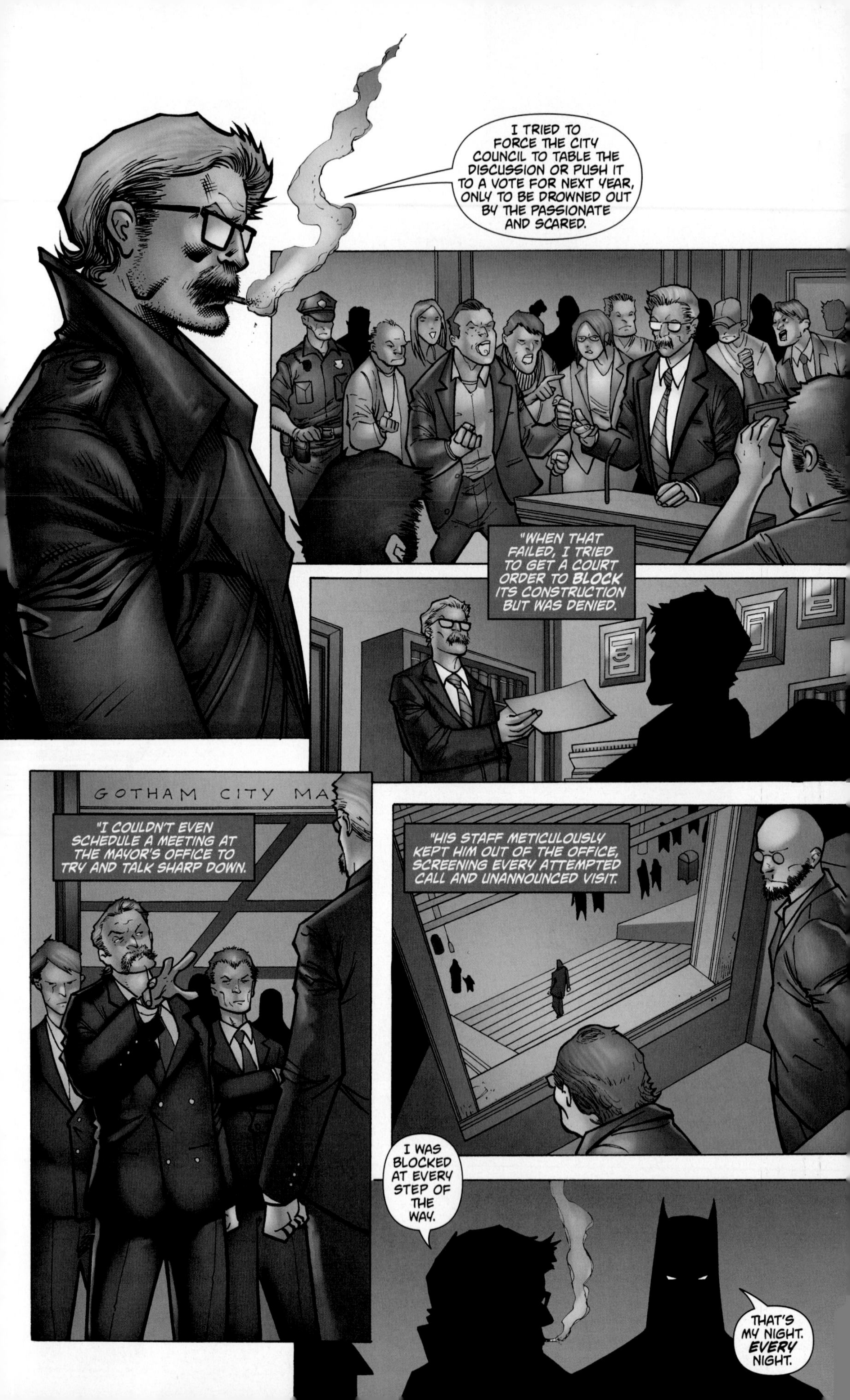
I TRIED TO FORCE THE CITY COUNCIL TO TABLE THE DISCUSSION OR PUSH IT TO A VOTE FOR NEXT YEAR, ONLY TO BE DROWNED OUT BY THE PASSIONATE AND SCARED.
"WHEN THAT FAILED, I TRIED TO GET A COURT ORDER TO BLOCK ITS CONSTRUCTION BUT WAS DENIED.
GOTHAM CITY MA
"I COULDN'T EVEN SCHEDULE A MEETING AT THE MAYOR'S OFFICE TO TRY AND TALK SHARP DOWN.
"HIS STAFF METICULOUSLY KEPT HIM OUT OF THE OFFICE, SCREENING EVERY ATTEMPTED CALL AND UNANNOUNCED VISIT.
I WAS BLOCKED AT EVERY STEP OF THE WAY.
THAT'S MY NIGHT. EVERY NIGHT.

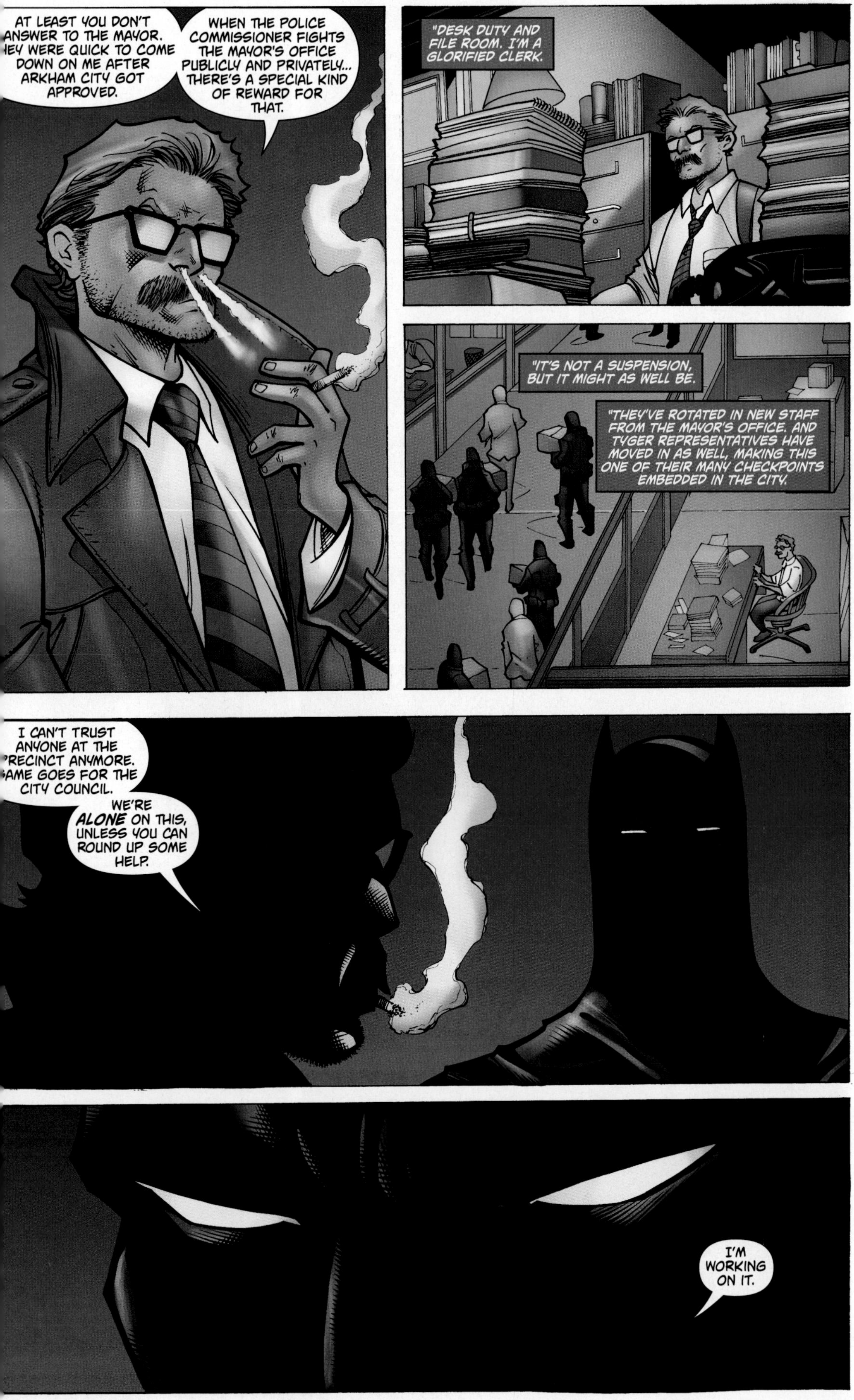

AT LEAST YOU DON'T ANSWER TO THE MAYOR. EY WERE QUICK TO COME DOWN ON ME AFTER ARKHAM CITY GOT APPROVED.
WHEN THE POLICE COMMISSIONER FIGHTS THE MAYOR'S OFFICE PUBLICLY AND PRIVATELY... THERE'S A SPECIAL KIND OF REWARD FOR THAT.
"DESK DUTY AND FILE ROOM. I'M A GLORIFIED CLERK.
"IT'S NOT A SUSPENSION, BUT IT MIGHT AS WELL BE.
"THEY'VE ROTATED IN NEW STAFF FROM THE MAYOR'S OFFICE. AND TYGER REPRESENTATIVES HAVE MOVED IN AS WELL, MAKING THIS ONE OF THEIR MANY CHECKPOINTS EMBEDDED IN THE CITY.
I CAN'T TRUST ANYONE AT THE RECINCT ANYMORE. AME GOES FOR THE CITY COUNCIL.
WE'RE *ALONE* ON THIS, UNLESS YOU CAN ROUND UP SOME HELP.
I'M WORKING ON IT.

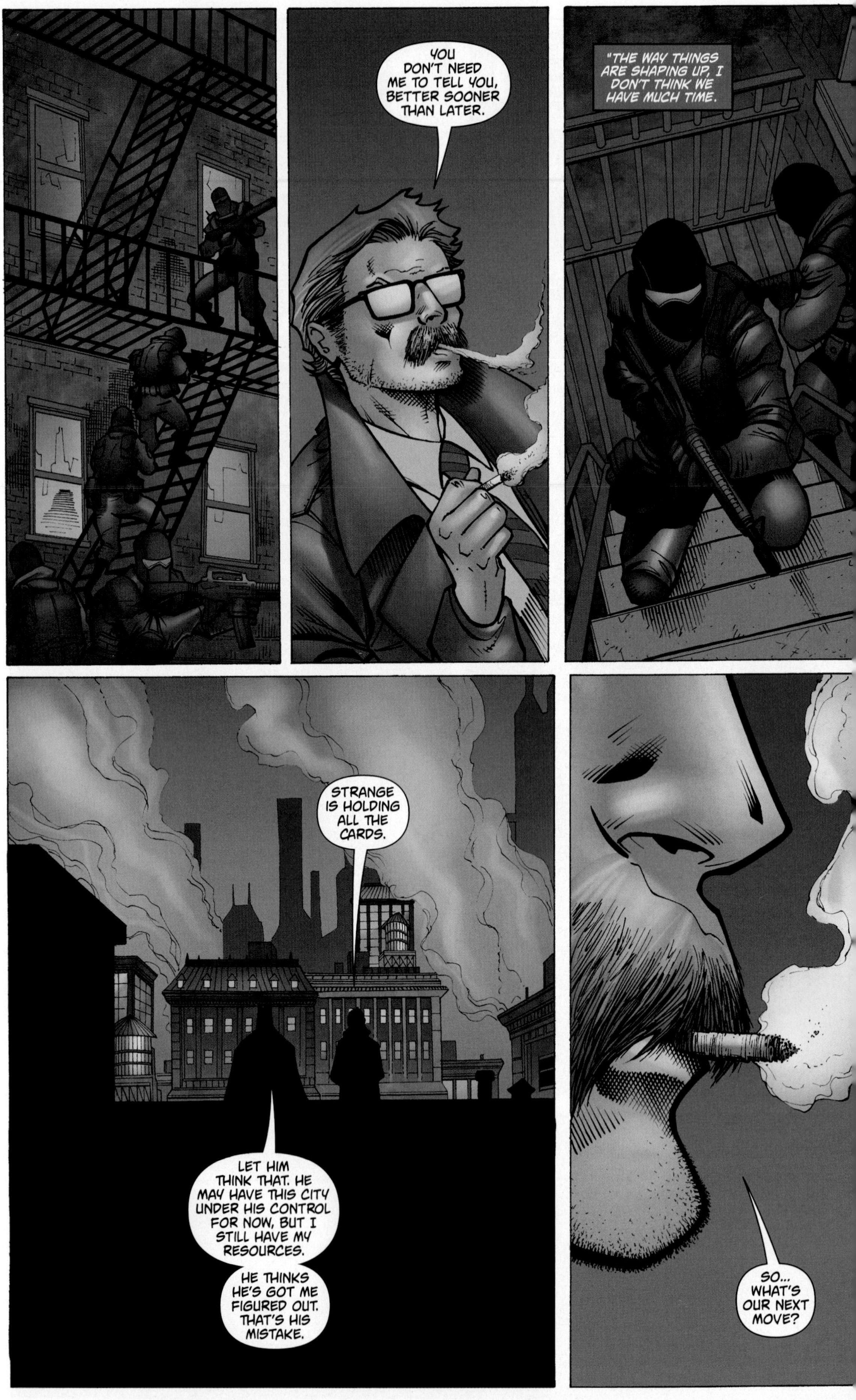
YOU DON'T NEED ME TO TELL YOU, BETTER SOONER THAN LATER.
"THE WAY THINGS ARE SHAPING UP, I DON'T THINK WE HAVE MUCH TIME.
STRANGE IS HOLDING ALL THE CARDS.
LET HIM THINK THAT. HE MAY HAVE THIS CITY UNDER HIS CONTROL FOR NOW, BUT I STILL HAVE MY RESOURCES.
HE THINKS HE'S GOT ME FIGURED OUT. THAT'S HIS MISTAKE.
SO... WHAT'S OUR NEXT MOVE?

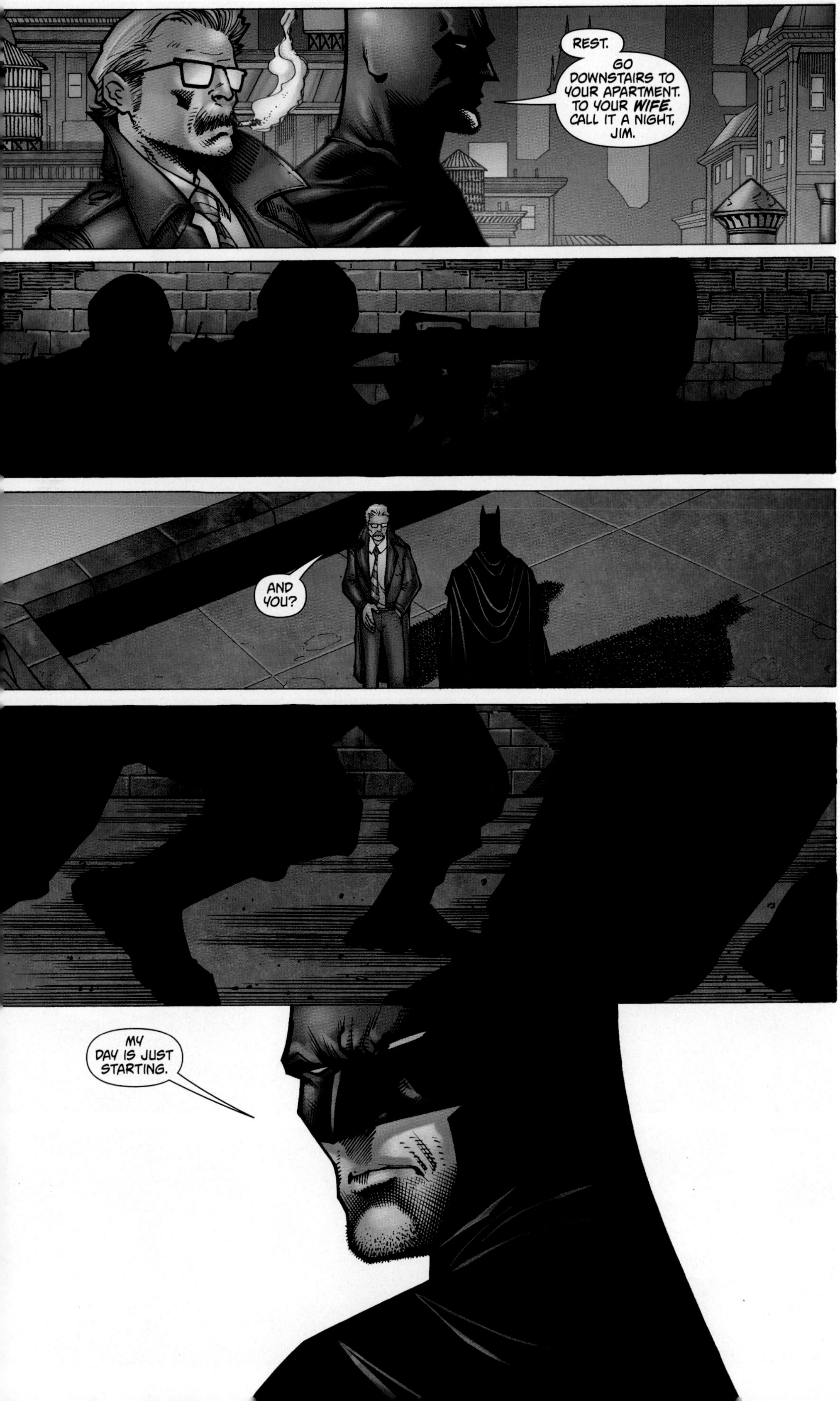
REST.
GO DOWNSTAIRS TO YOUR APARTMENT. TO YOUR WIFE. CALL IT A NIGHT, JIM.
AND YOU?
MY DAY IS JUST STARTING.

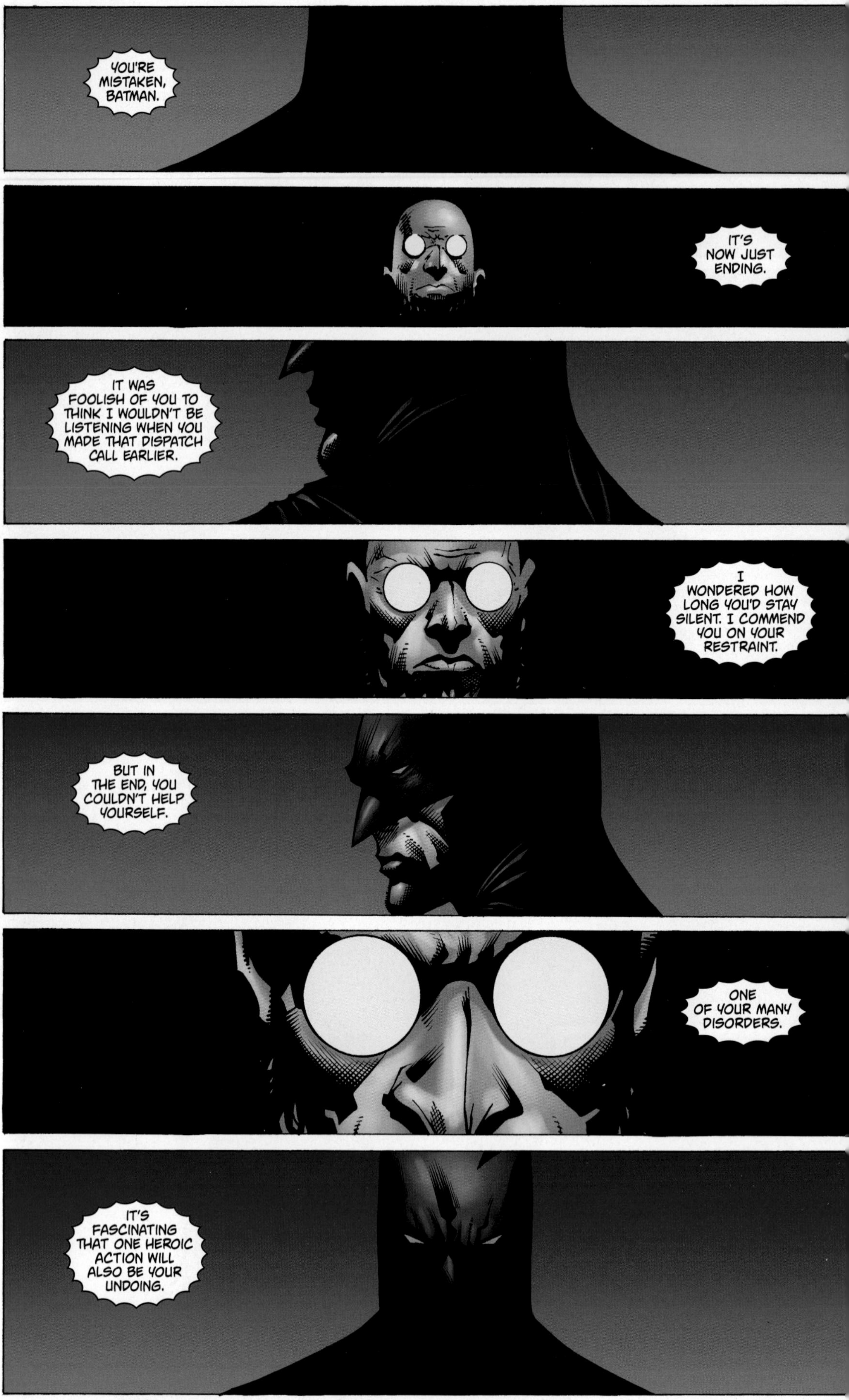
YOU'RE MISTAKEN, BATMAN.
IT'S NOW JUST ENDING.
IT WAS FOOLISH OF YOU TO THINK I WOULDN'T BE LISTENING WHEN YOU MADE THAT DISPATCH CALL EARLIER.
I WONDERED HOW LONG YOU'D STAY SILENT. I COMMEND YOU ON YOUR RESTRAINT.
BUT IN THE END, YOU COULDN'T HELP YOURSELF.
ONE OF YOUR MANY DISORDERS.
IT'S FASCINATING THAT ONE HEROIC ACTION WILL ALSO BE YOUR UNDOING.

CH-CHIK

WHERE IS HE, COMMISSIONER?

WHERE IS HE?!

DID MY WIFE SEND YOU UP HERE?

SMOKING IS A NASTY HABIT, BUT LAST I CHECKED, IT'S NOT AGAINST THE LAW IN THIS CITY.

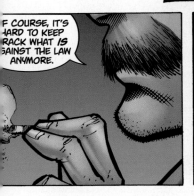

F COURSE, IT'S HARD TO KEEP RACK WHAT **IS** AINST THE LAW ANYMORE.

GOOD NIGHT, GENTLEMEN.

THE IMMEDIATE AREA IS CLEAR. LOCKED DOWN THE CITY BLOCK AND CHECKED NEARBY ROOFTOPS.

HE'S NOT HERE. AT LEAST NOT ANYMORE.

THAT'S WHAT HAPPENS WHEN YOU ARRIVE TO THE PARTY *LATE.*

WHO IS THIS?!

DON'T BOTHER LOOKING. THE PARTY ENDED A WHILE AGO.

OR HAVEN'T YOU HEARD OF TAPE DELAY?

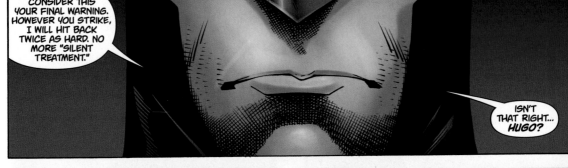

CONSIDER THIS YOUR FINAL WARNING. HOWEVER YOU STRIKE, I WILL HIT BACK TWICE AS HARD. NO MORE "SILENT TREATMENT."

ISN'T THAT RIGHT... *HUGO?*

...

CAPTAIN, *RADIO SILENCE* ON ALL FREQUENCIES AND RETURN TO BASE. *IMMEDIATELY!*

≥KLIK≤

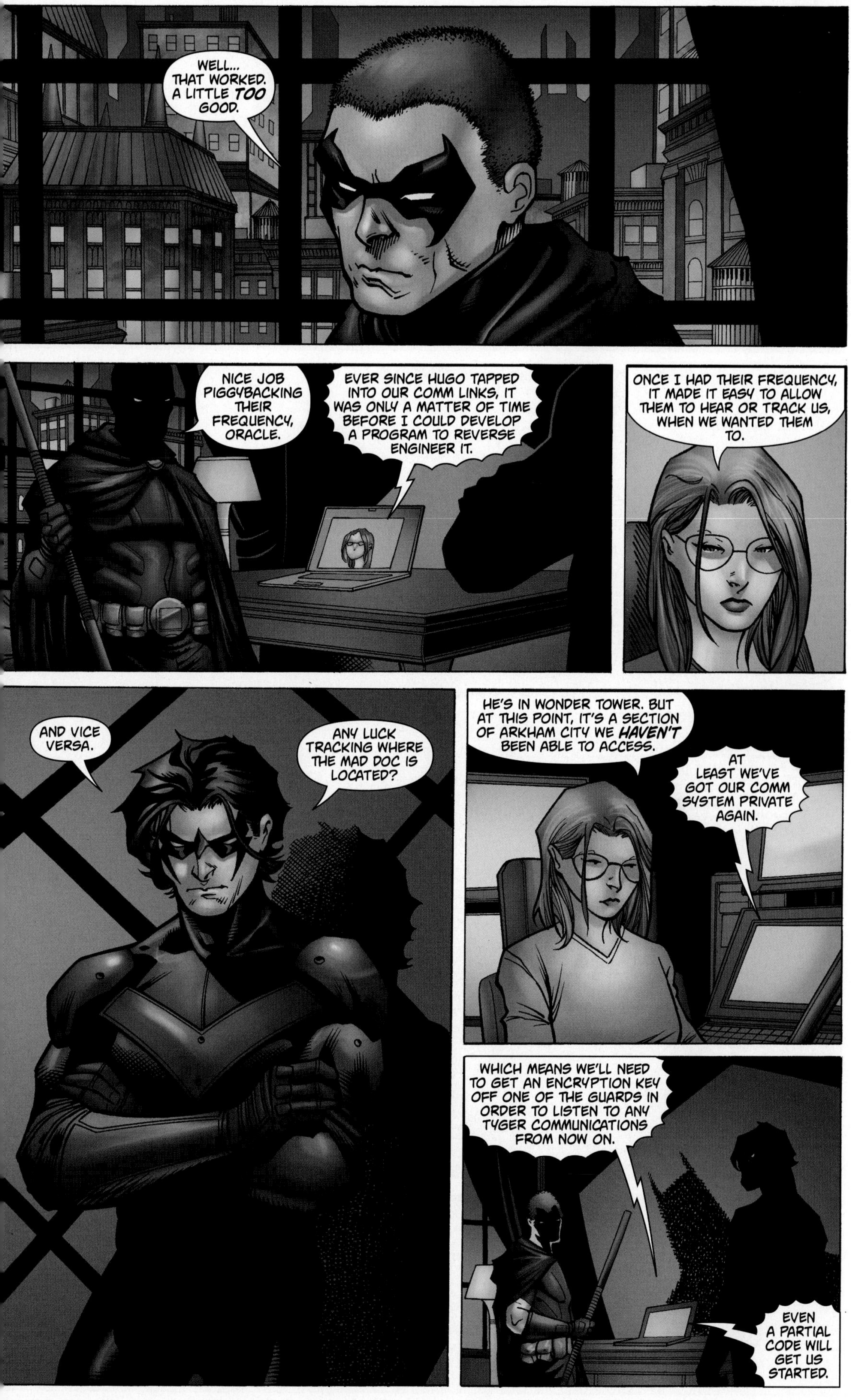
WELL... THAT WORKED. A LITTLE *TOO* GOOD.
NICE JOB PIGGYBACKING THEIR FREQUENCY, ORACLE.
EVER SINCE HUGO TAPPED INTO OUR COMM LINKS, IT WAS ONLY A MATTER OF TIME BEFORE I COULD DEVELOP A PROGRAM TO REVERSE ENGINEER IT.
ONCE I HAD THEIR FREQUENCY, IT MADE IT EASY TO ALLOW THEM TO HEAR OR TRACK US, WHEN WE WANTED THEM TO.
AND VICE VERSA.
ANY LUCK TRACKING WHERE THE MAD DOC IS LOCATED?
HE'S IN WONDER TOWER. BUT AT THIS POINT, IT'S A SECTION OF ARKHAM CITY WE *HAVEN'T* BEEN ABLE TO ACCESS.
AT LEAST WE'VE GOT OUR COMM SYSTEM PRIVATE AGAIN.
WHICH MEANS WE'LL NEED TO GET AN ENCRYPTION KEY OFF ONE OF THE GUARDS IN ORDER TO LISTEN TO ANY TYGER COMMUNICATIONS FROM NOW ON.
EVEN A PARTIAL CODE WILL GET US STARTED.

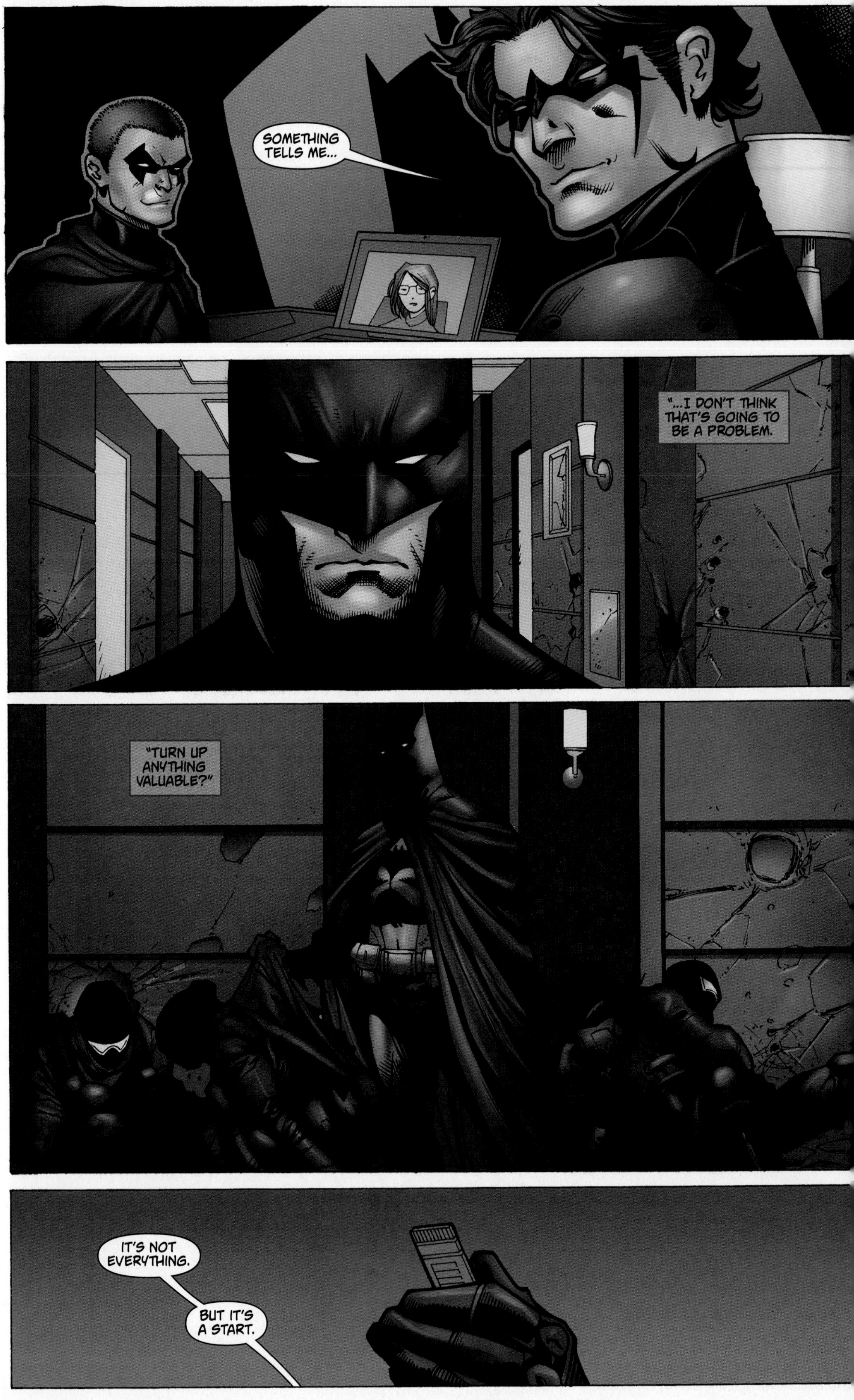
SOMETHING TELLS ME...
"...I DON'T THINK THAT'S GOING TO BE A PROBLEM.
"TURN UP ANYTHING VALUABLE?"
IT'S NOT EVERYTHING.
BUT IT'S A START.

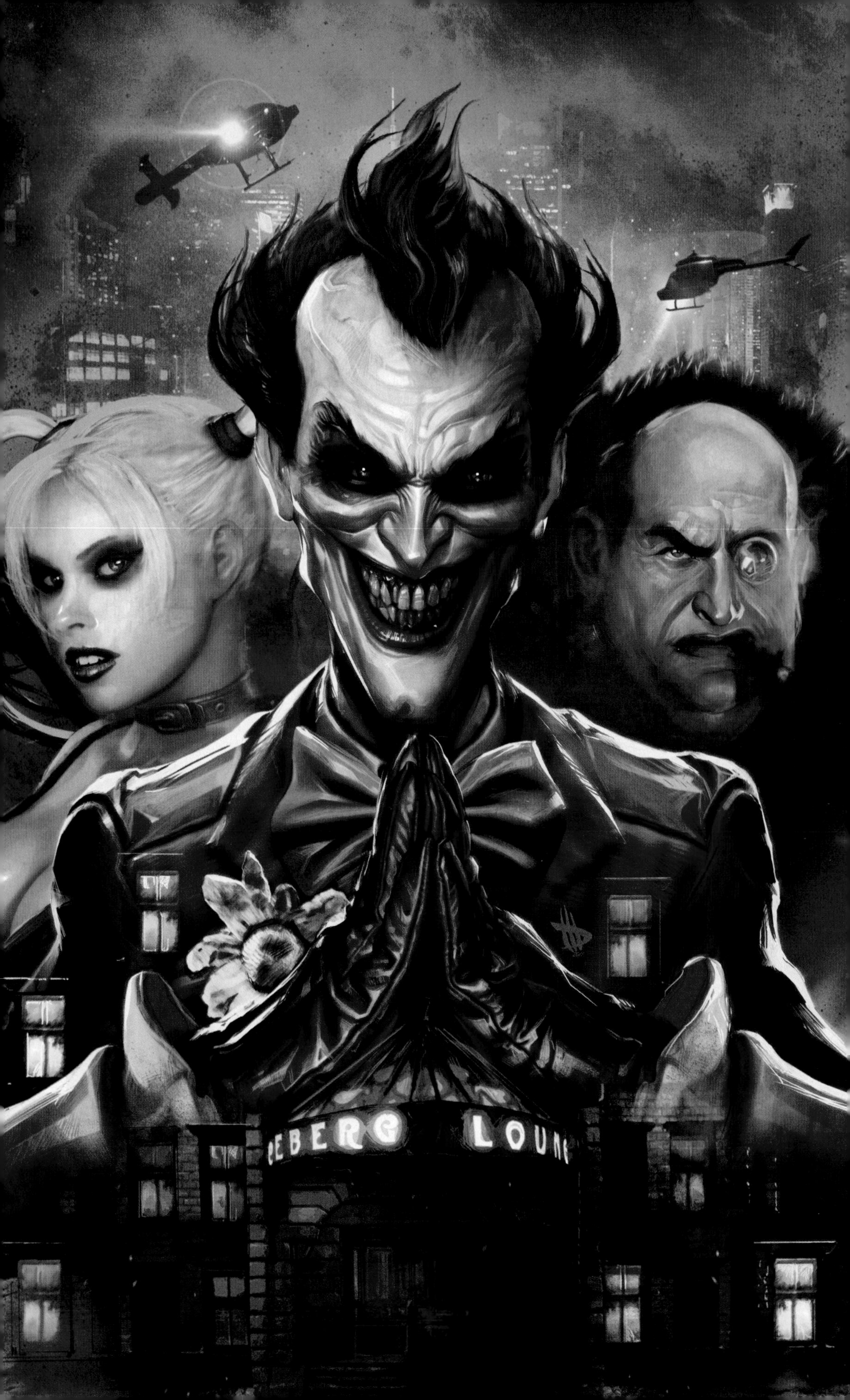
EBERG LOUNG

RUFFLED FEATHERS

WRITTEN BY: **DEREK FRIDOLFS**

PENCILS BY: **SIMON COLEBY**
BRUNO REDONDO

INKS BY: **SIMON COLEBY**
SANTI CASAS
CLIFF RATHBURN

COLORS BY: **GABE ELTAEB**

LETTERS BY: **TRAVIS LANHAM**

COVER BY: **DAVE WILKINS**

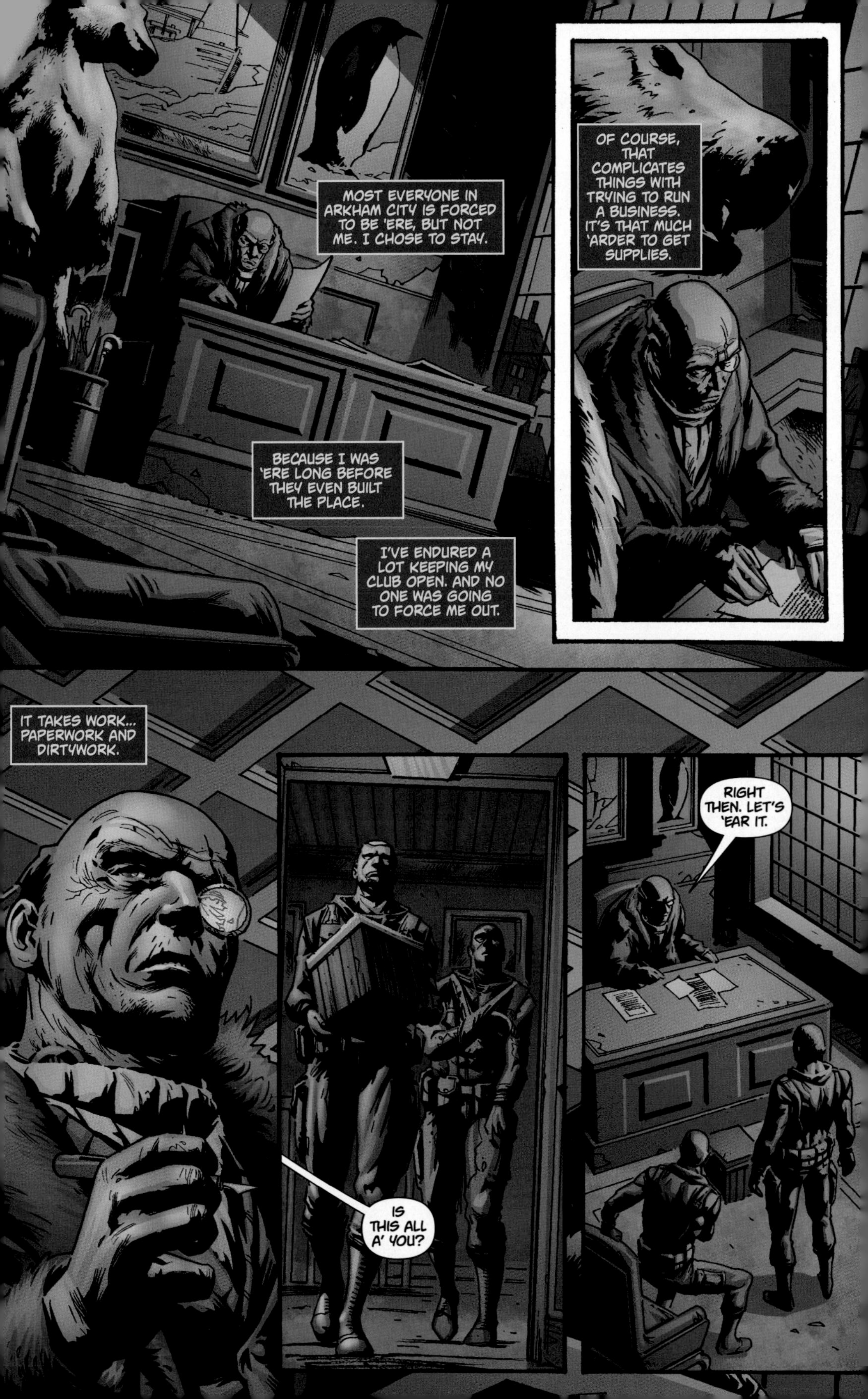
MOST EVERYONE IN ARKHAM CITY IS FORCED TO BE 'ERE, BUT NOT ME. I CHOSE TO STAY.
BECAUSE I WAS 'ERE LONG BEFORE THEY EVEN BUILT THE PLACE.
I'VE ENDURED A LOT KEEPING MY CLUB OPEN. AND NO ONE WAS GOING TO FORCE ME OUT.
OF COURSE, THAT COMPLICATES THINGS WITH TRYING TO RUN A BUSINESS. IT'S THAT MUCH 'ARDER TO GET SUPPLIES.
IT TAKES WORK... PAPERWORK AND DIRTYWORK.
IS THIS ALL A' YOU?
RIGHT THEN. LET'S 'EAR IT.

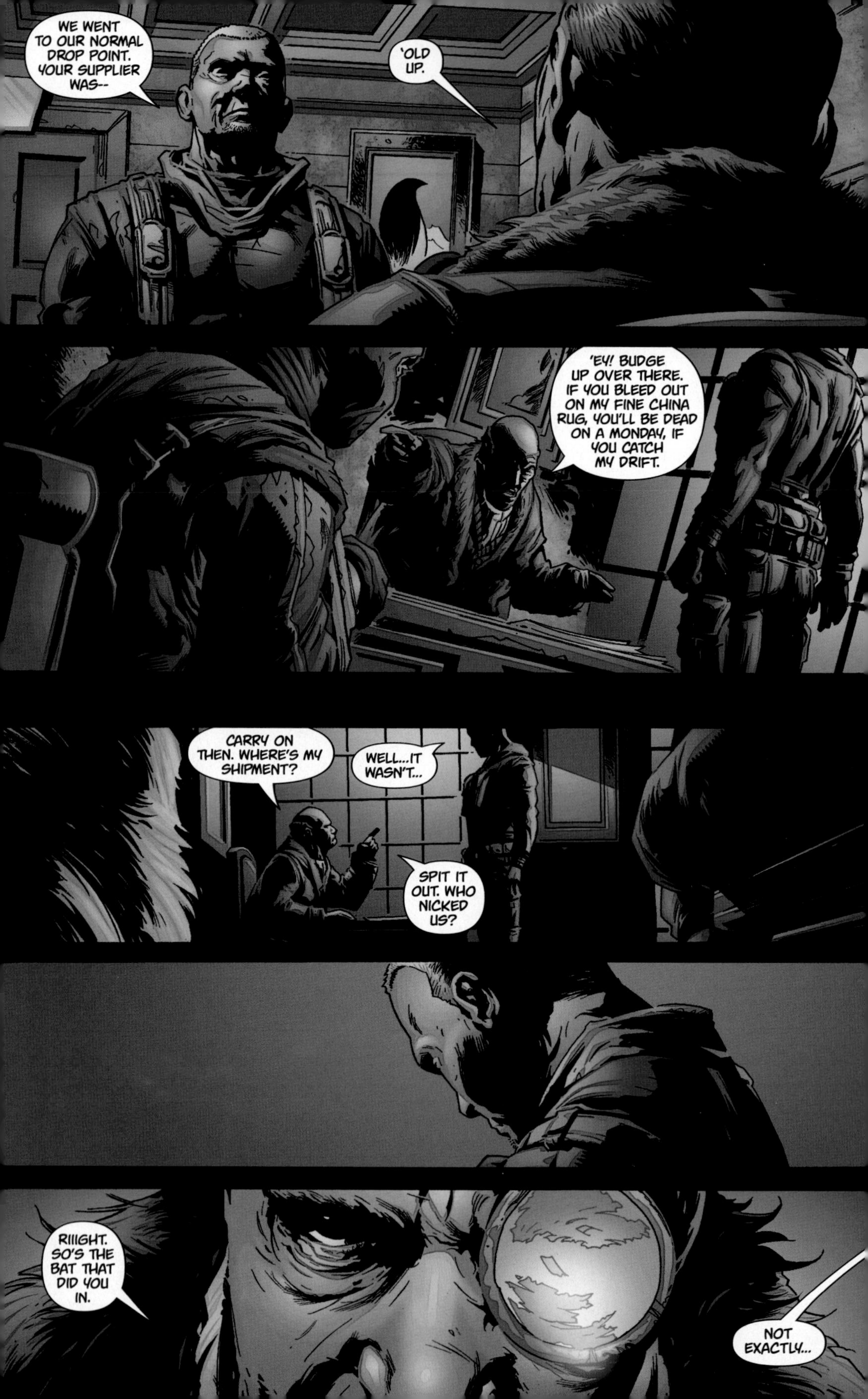

WE WENT TO OUR NORMAL DROP POINT. YOUR SUPPLIER WAS--
'OLD UP.
'EY! BUDGE UP OVER THERE. IF YOU BLEED OUT ON MY FINE CHINA RUG, YOU'LL BE DEAD ON A MONDAY, IF YOU CATCH MY DRIFT.
CARRY ON THEN. WHERE'S MY SHIPMENT?
WELL...IT WASN'T...
SPIT IT OUT. WHO NICKED US?
RIIIGHT. SO'S THE BAT THAT DID YOU IN.
NOT EXACTLY...

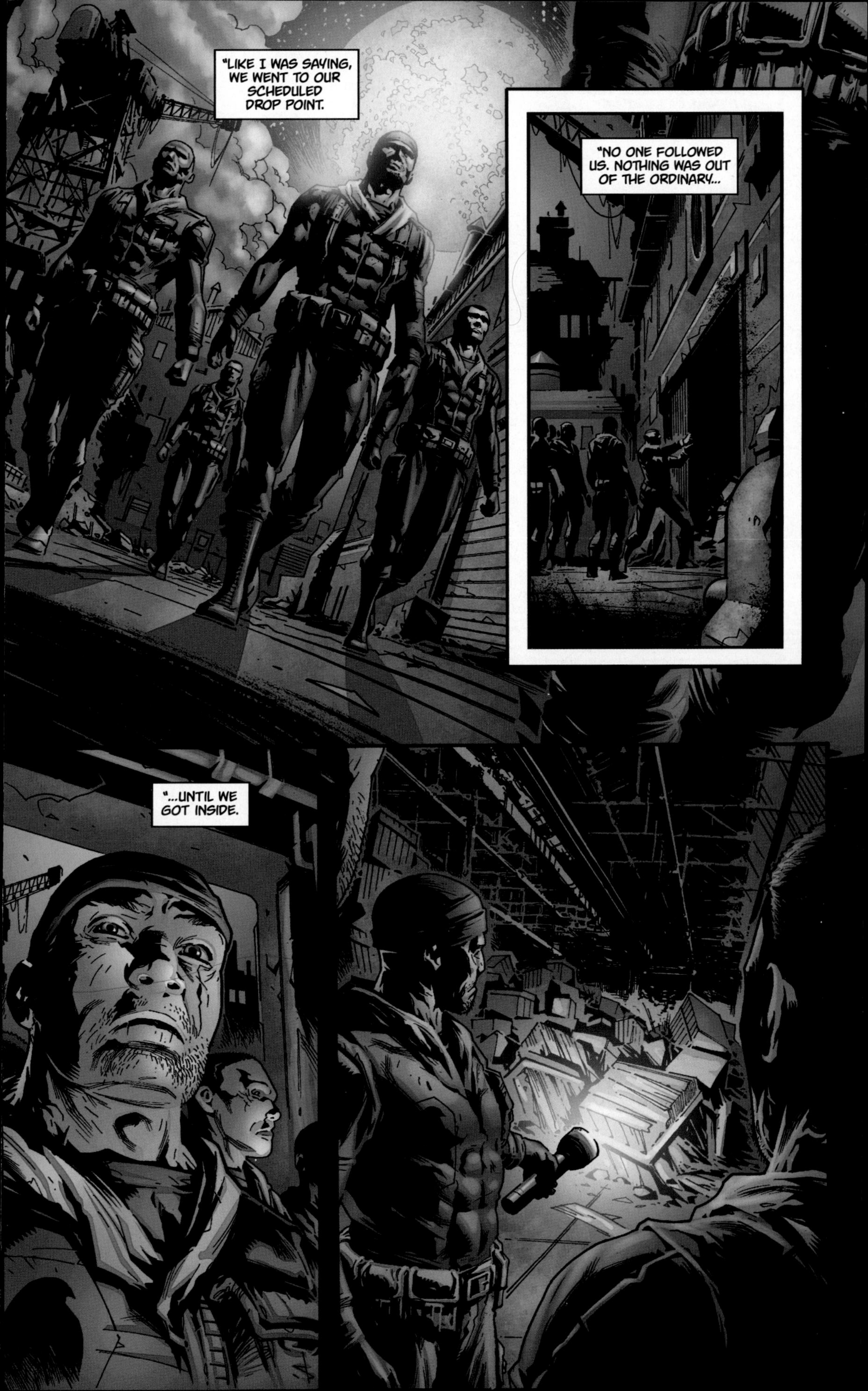
"LIKE I WAS SAYING, WE WENT TO OUR SCHEDULED DROP POINT.
"NO ONE FOLLOWED US. NOTHING WAS OUT OF THE ORDINARY...
"...UNTIL WE GOT INSIDE.

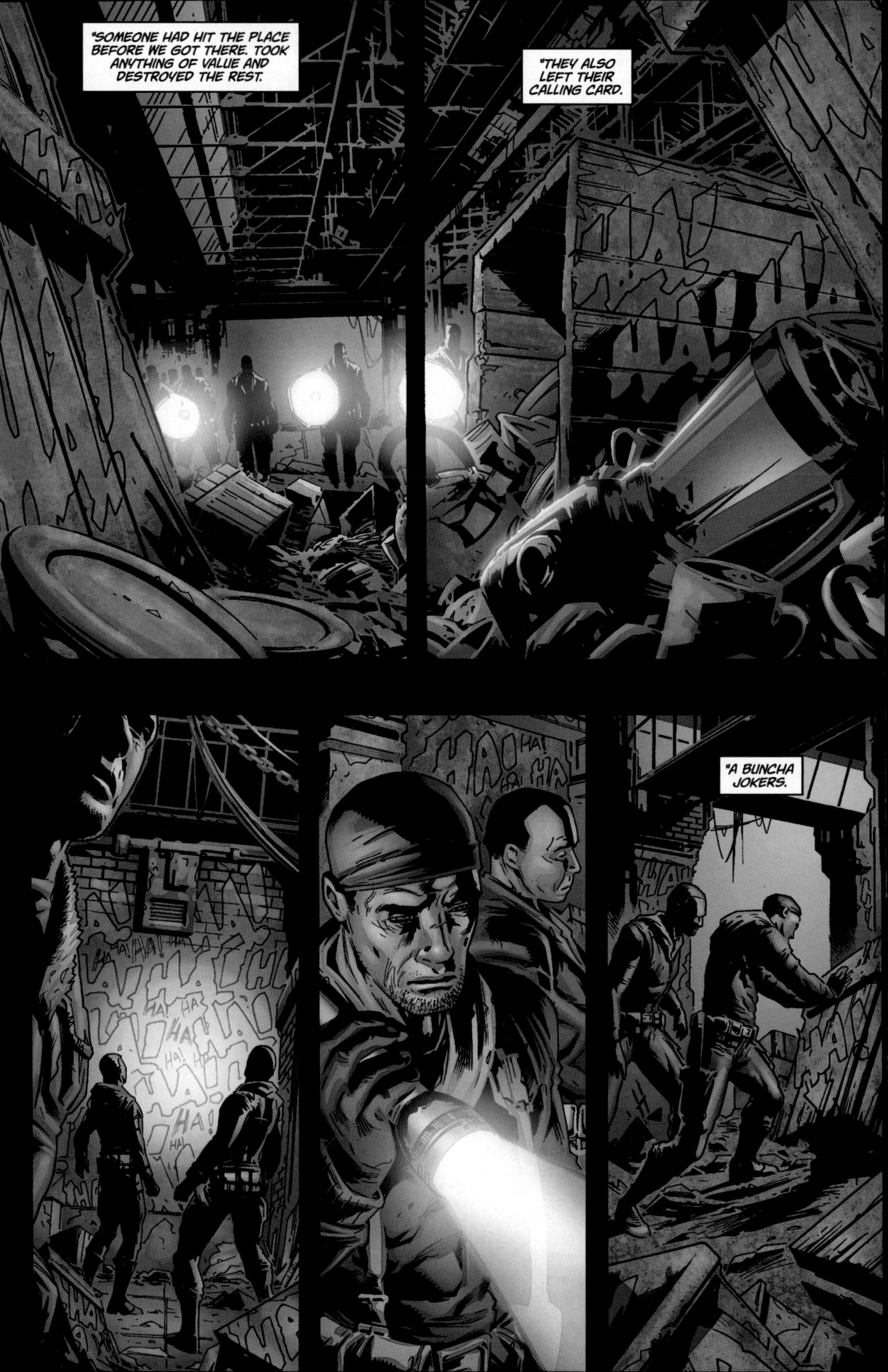
"SOMEONE HAD HIT THE PLACE BEFORE WE GOT THERE. TOOK ANYTHING OF VALUE AND DESTROYED THE REST.
"THEY ALSO LEFT THEIR CALLING CARD.
HA! HA!
HA! HA!
HA! HA!
HA!
HA!
"A BUNCHA JOKERS.

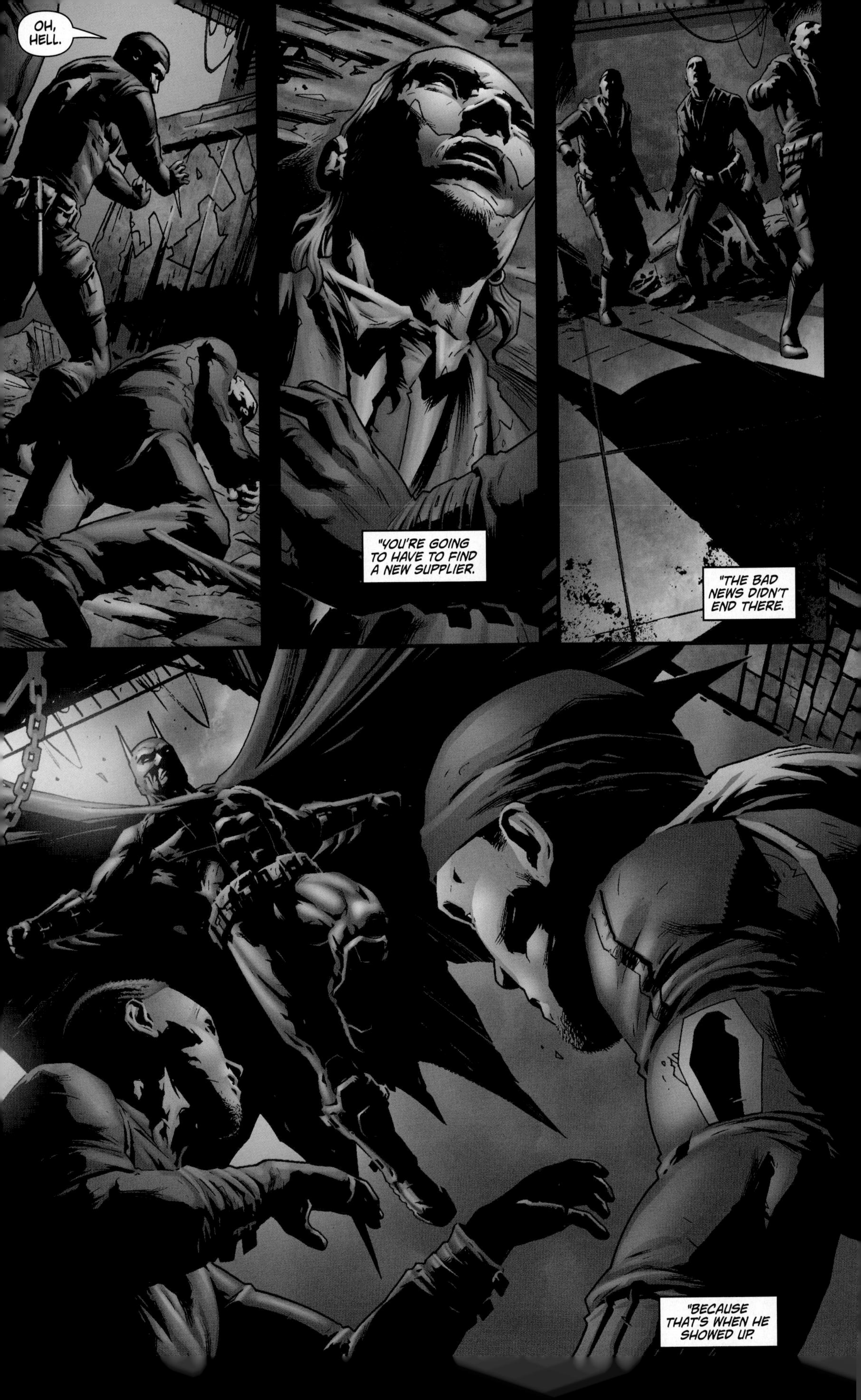
OH, HELL.
"YOU'RE GOING TO HAVE TO FIND A NEW SUPPLIER.
"THE BAD NEWS DIDN'T END THERE.
"BECAUSE THAT'S WHEN HE SHOWED UP.

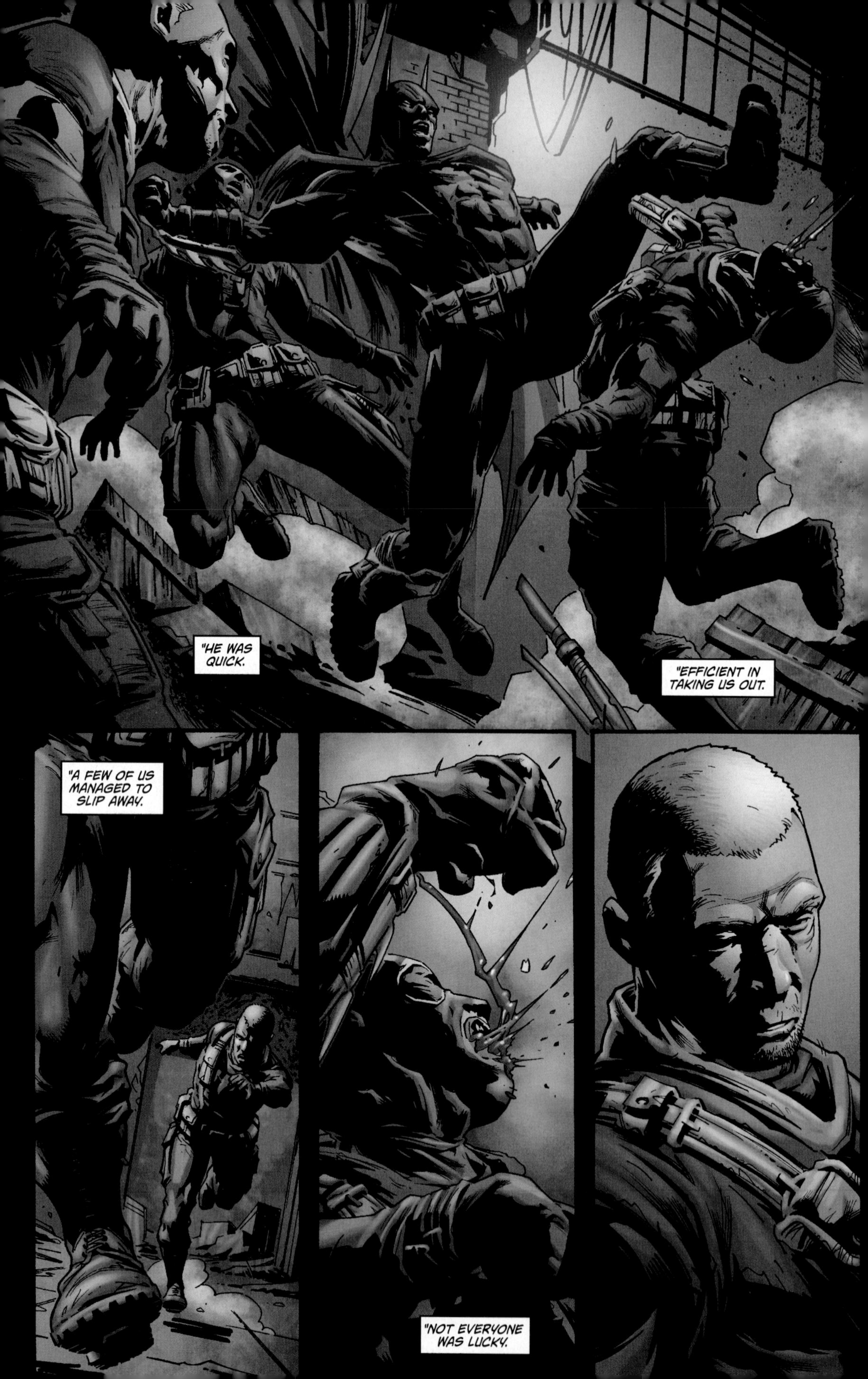
"HE WAS QUICK.
"EFFICIENT IN TAKING US OUT.
"A FEW OF US MANAGED TO SLIP AWAY.
"NOT EVERYONE WAS LUCKY.

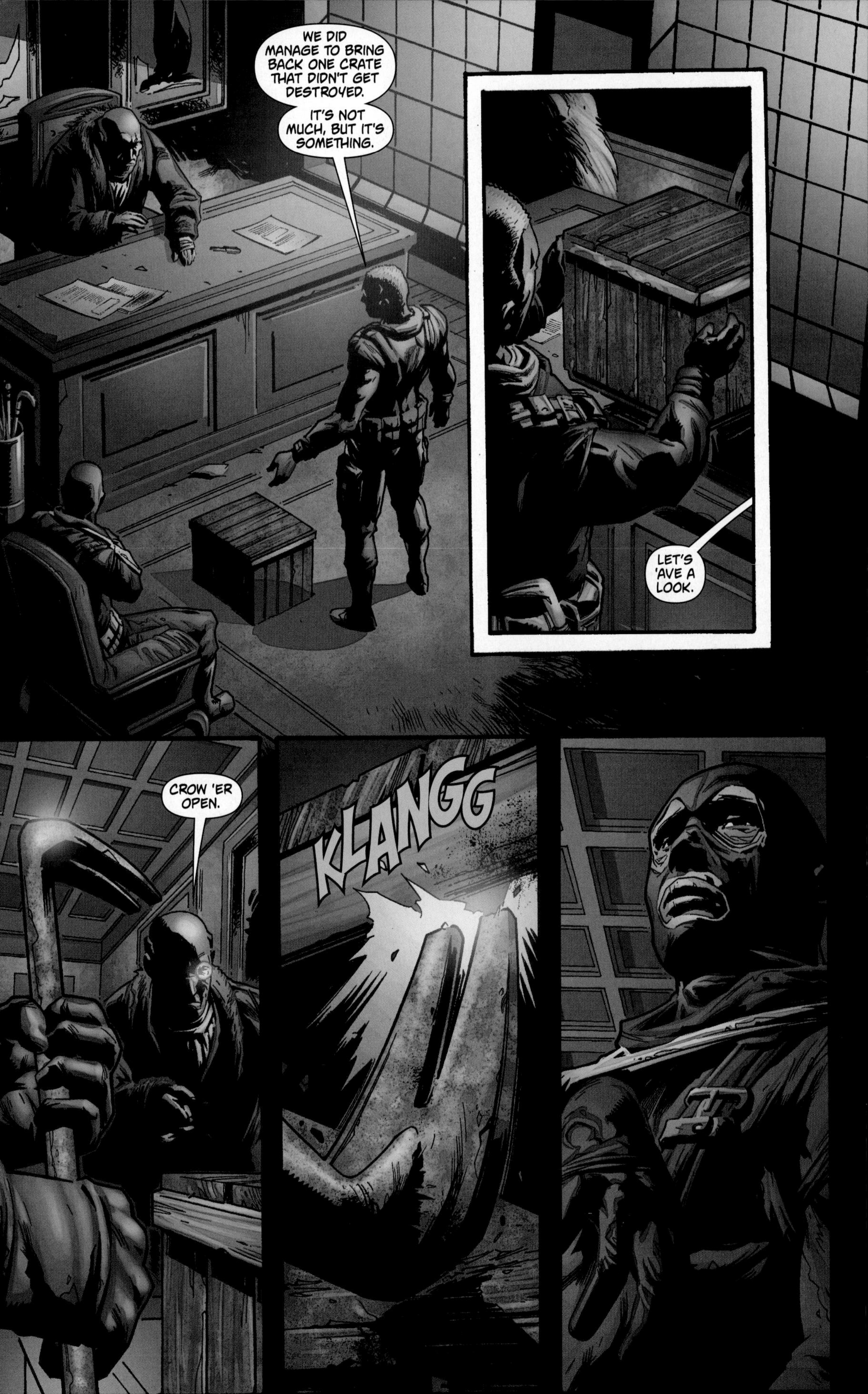
WE DID MANAGE TO BRING BACK ONE CRATE THAT DIDN'T GET DESTROYED.
IT'S NOT MUCH, BUT IT'S SOMETHING.
LET'S 'AVE A LOOK.
CROW 'ER OPEN.
KLANGG

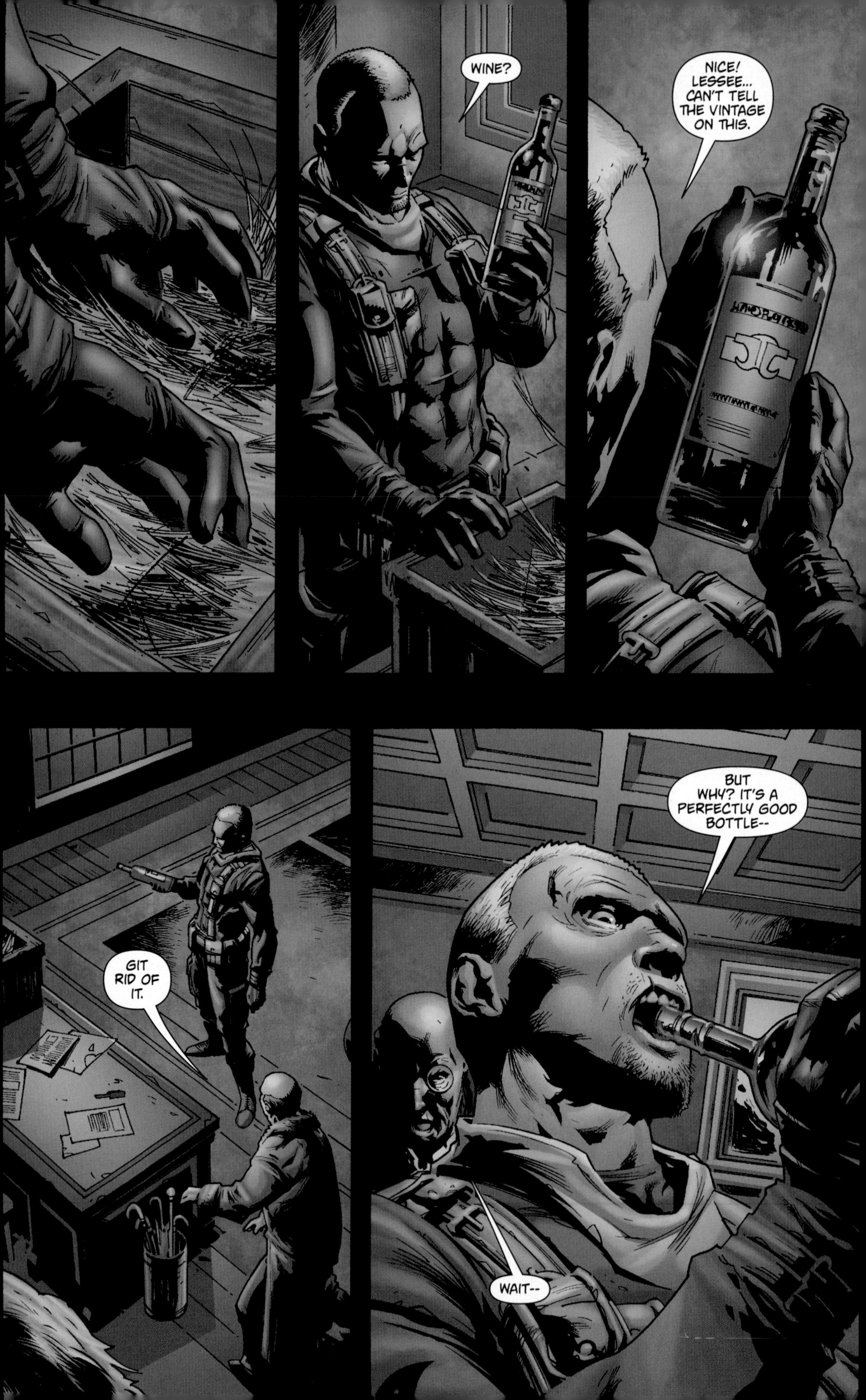
WINE?
NICE! LESSEE... CAN'T TELL THE VINTAGE ON THIS.
GIT RID OF IT.
BUT WHY? IT'S A PERFECTLY GOOD BOTTLE--
WAIT--

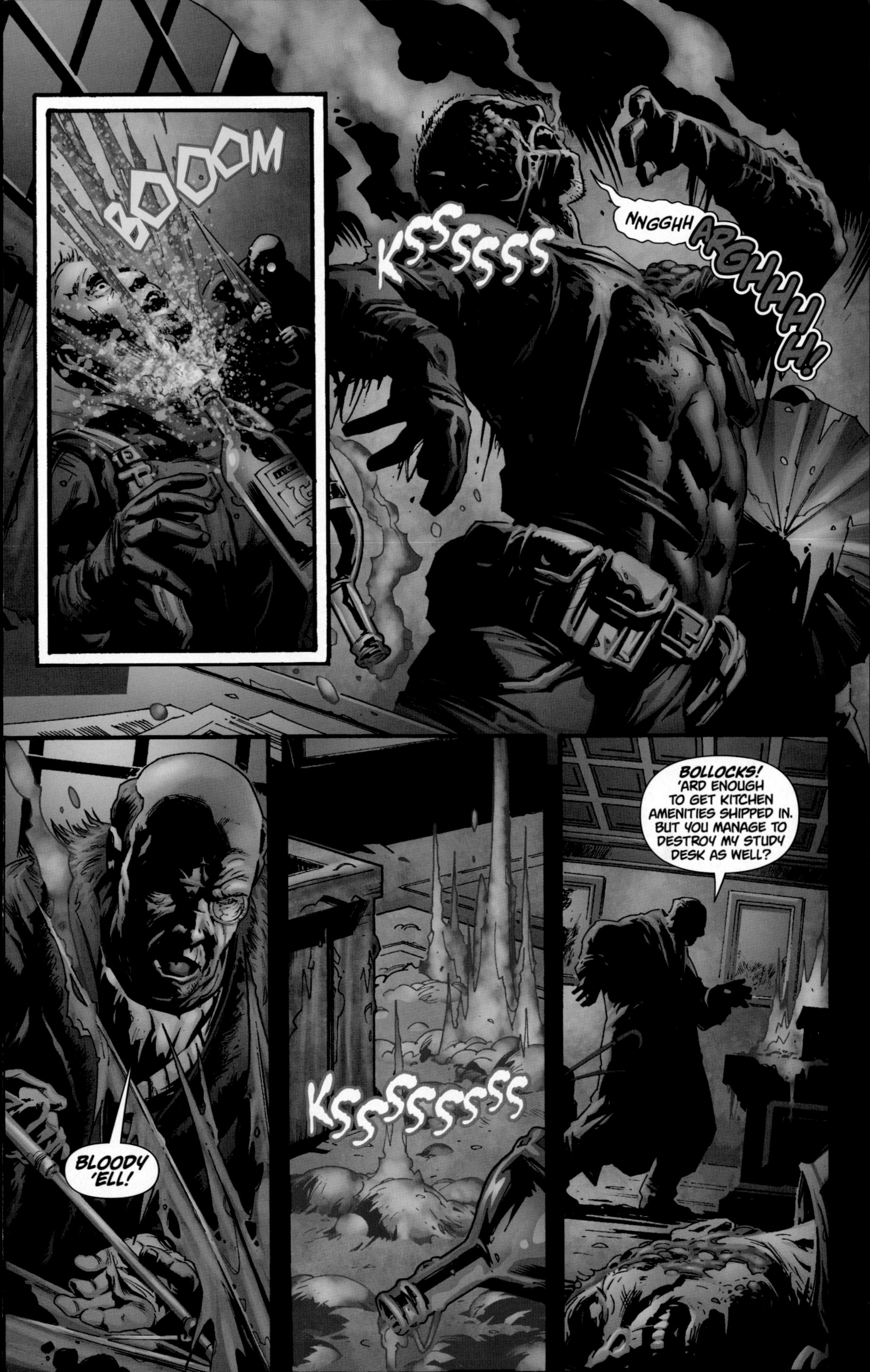
BOOOOM
KSSSSSSS
NNGGHH ARGHHHHH!
BLOODY 'ELL!
KSSSSSSSS
BOLLOCKS! 'ARD ENOUGH TO GET KITCHEN AMENITIES SHIPPED IN. BUT YOU MANAGE TO DESTROY MY STUDY DESK AS WELL?

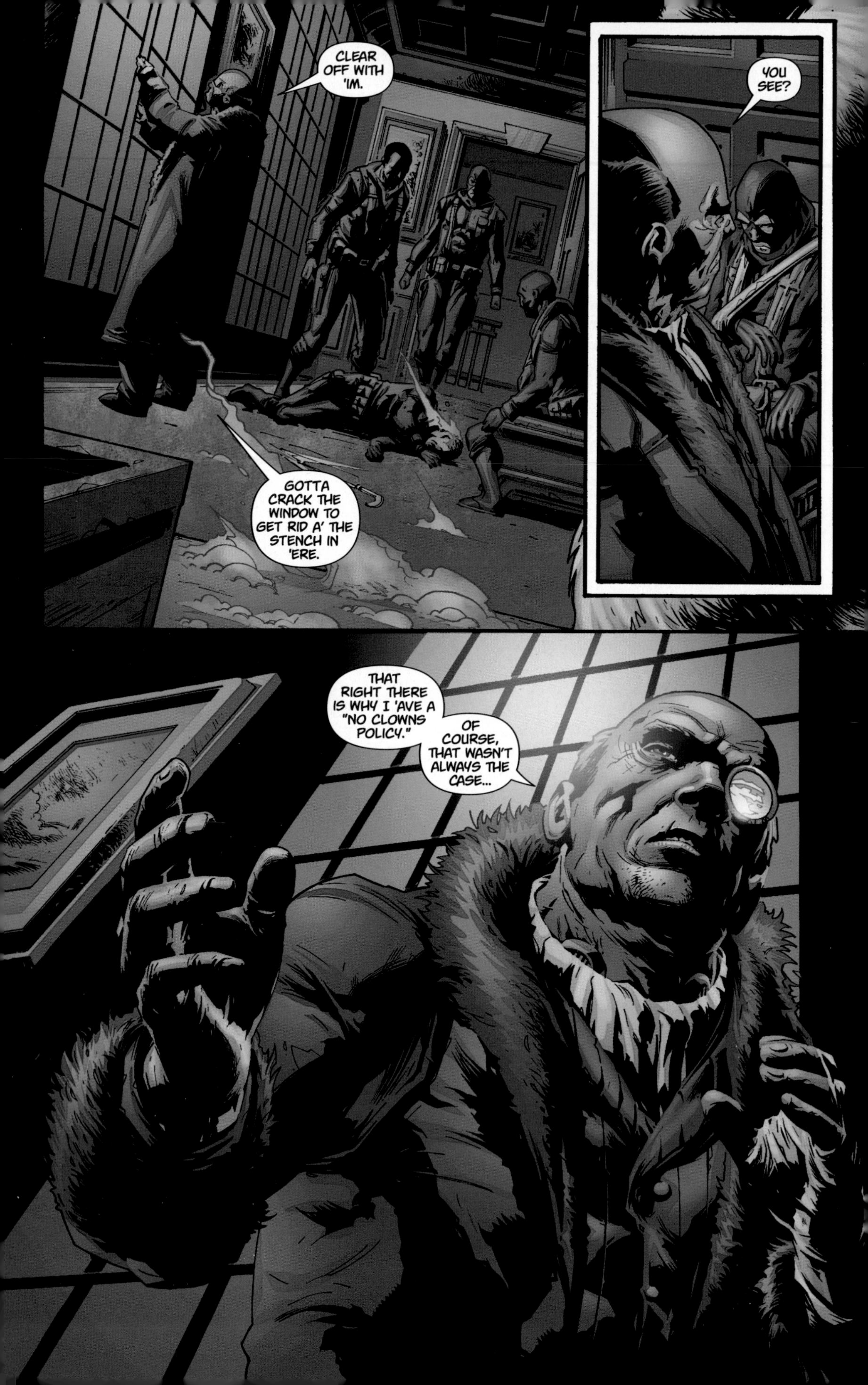
CLEAR OFF WITH 'IM.
GOTTA CRACK THE WINDOW TO GET RID A' THE STENCH IN 'ERE.
YOU SEE?
THAT RIGHT THERE IS WHY I 'AVE A "NO CLOWNS POLICY."
OF COURSE, THAT WASN'T ALWAYS THE CASE...

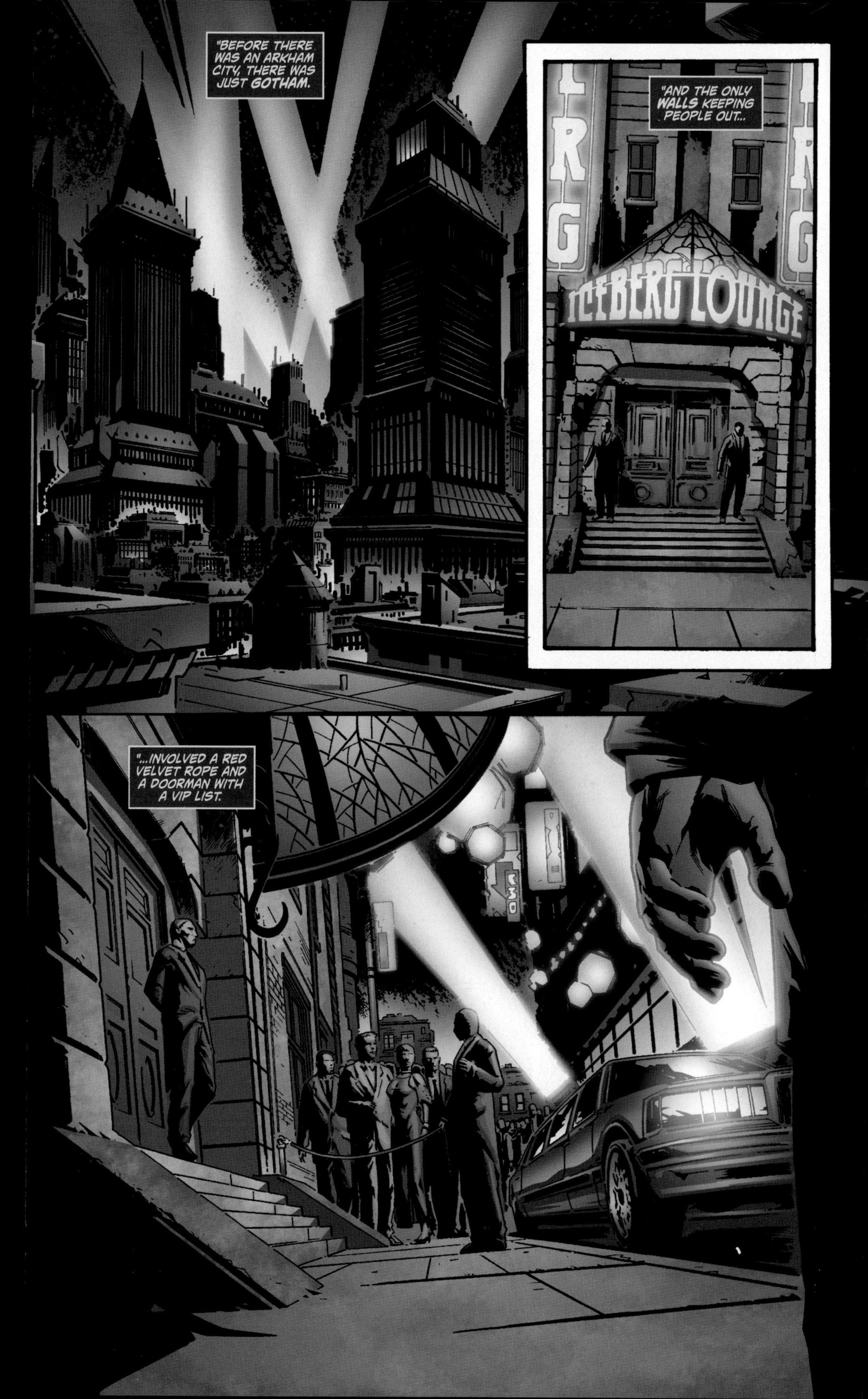
"BEFORE THERE WAS AN ARKHAM CITY, THERE WAS JUST GOTHAM.
"AND THE ONLY WALLS KEEPING PEOPLE OUT...
ICEBERG LOUNGE
"...INVOLVED A RED VELVET ROPE AND A DOORMAN WITH A VIP LIST.

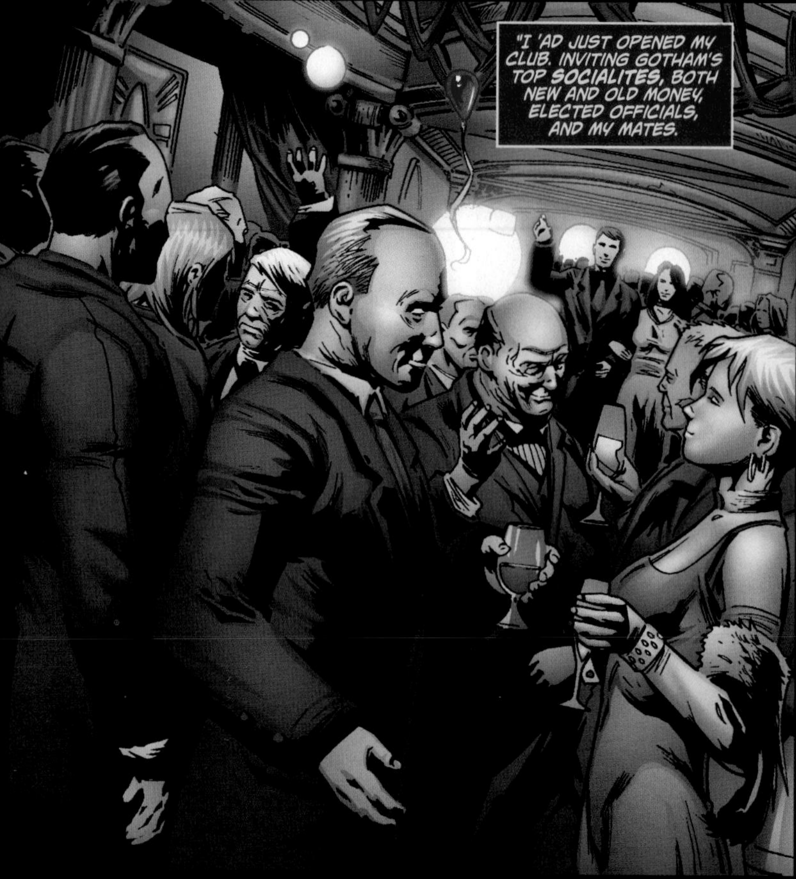
"I 'AD JUST OPENED MY CLUB, INVITING GOTHAM'S TOP SOCIALITES, BOTH NEW AND OLD MONEY, ELECTED OFFICIALS, AND MY MATES.
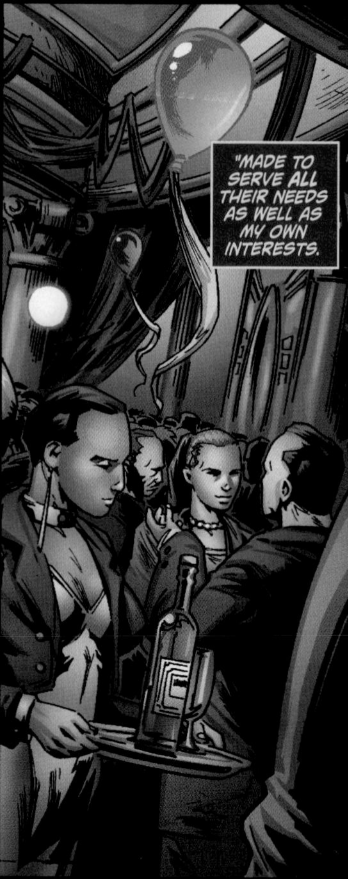
"MADE TO SERVE ALL THEIR NEEDS AS WELL AS MY OWN INTERESTS.
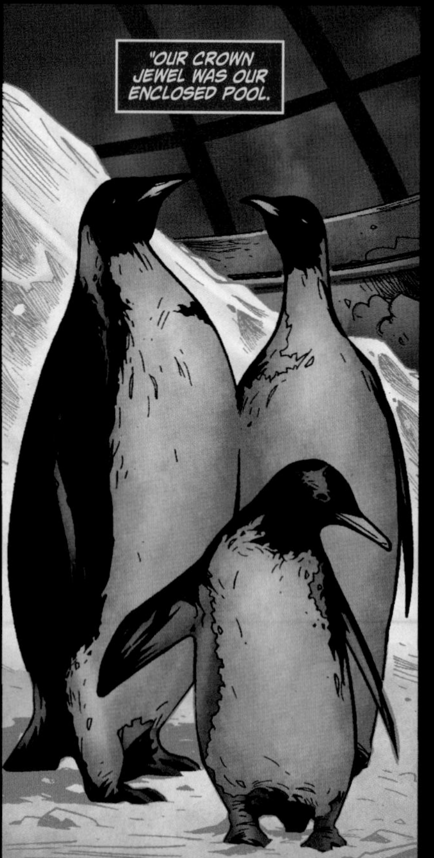
"OUR CROWN JEWEL WAS OUR ENCLOSED POOL.
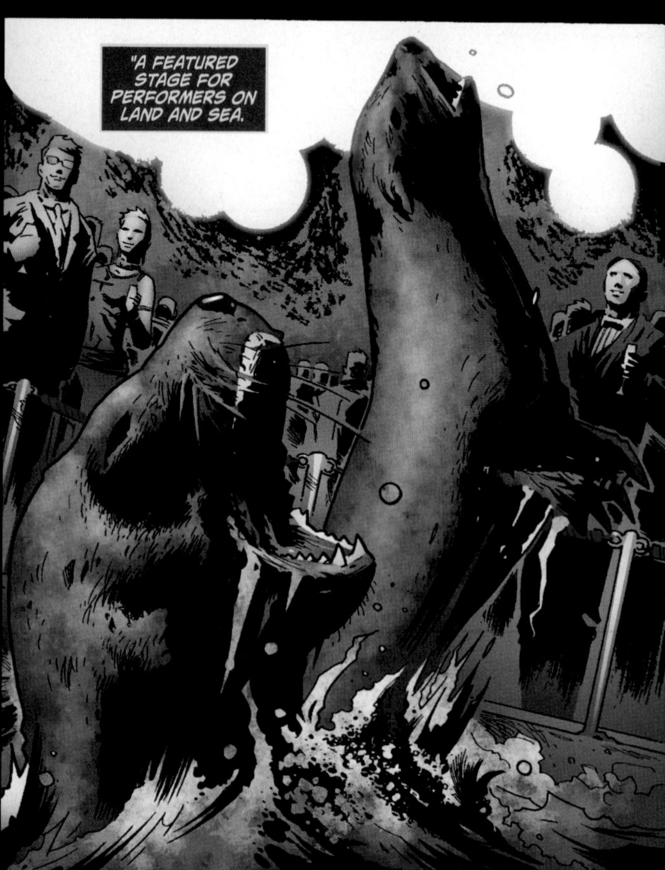
"A FEATURED STAGE FOR PERFORMERS ON LAND AND SEA.

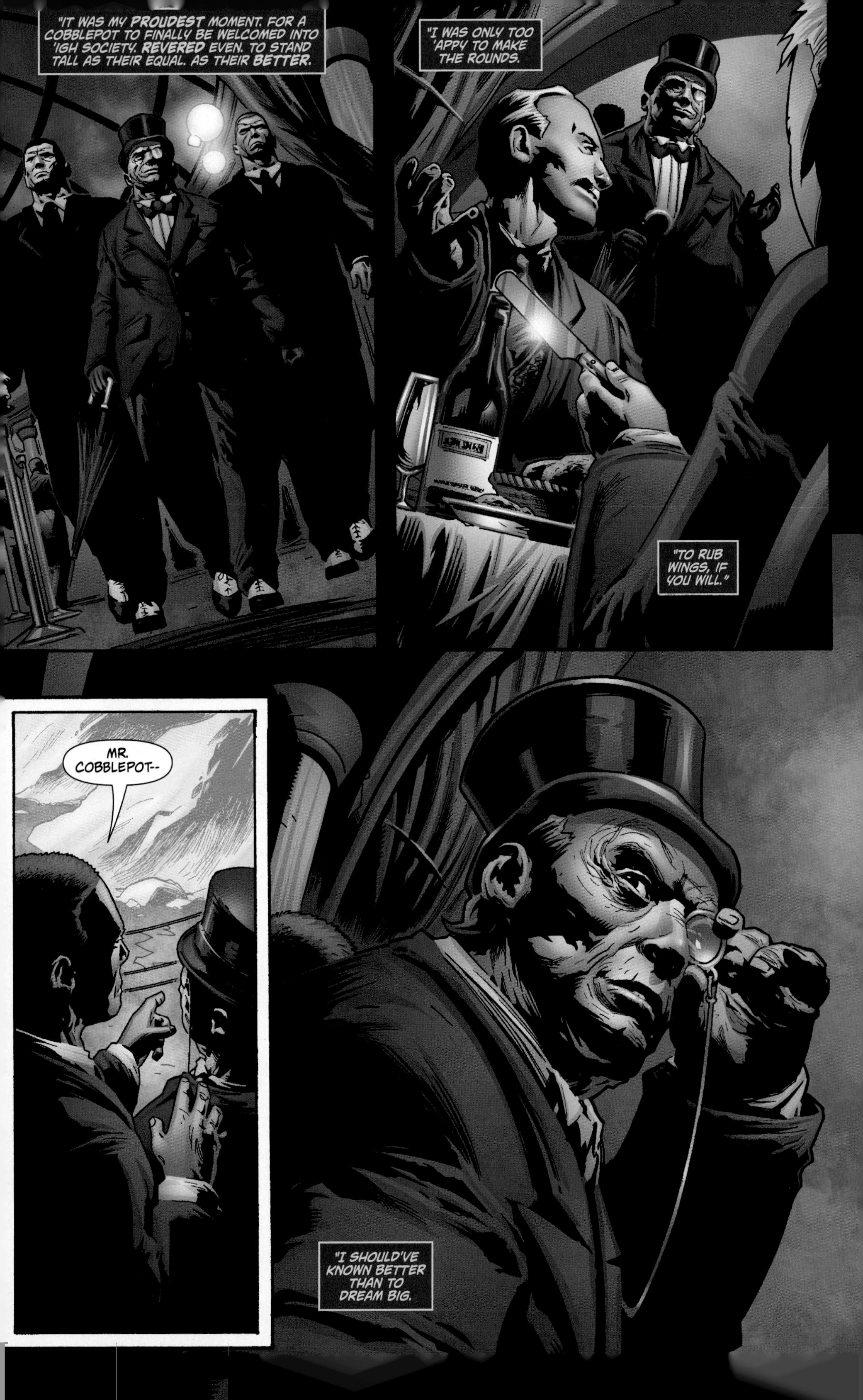
"IT WAS MY PROUDEST MOMENT. FOR A COBBLEPOT TO FINALLY BE WELCOMED INTO 'IGH SOCIETY. REVERED EVEN. TO STAND TALL AS THEIR EQUAL. AS THEIR BETTER.
"I WAS ONLY TOO 'APPY TO MAKE THE ROUNDS.
"TO RUB WINGS, IF YOU WILL."
MR. COBBLEPOT--
"I SHOULD'VE KNOWN BETTER THAN TO DREAM BIG.

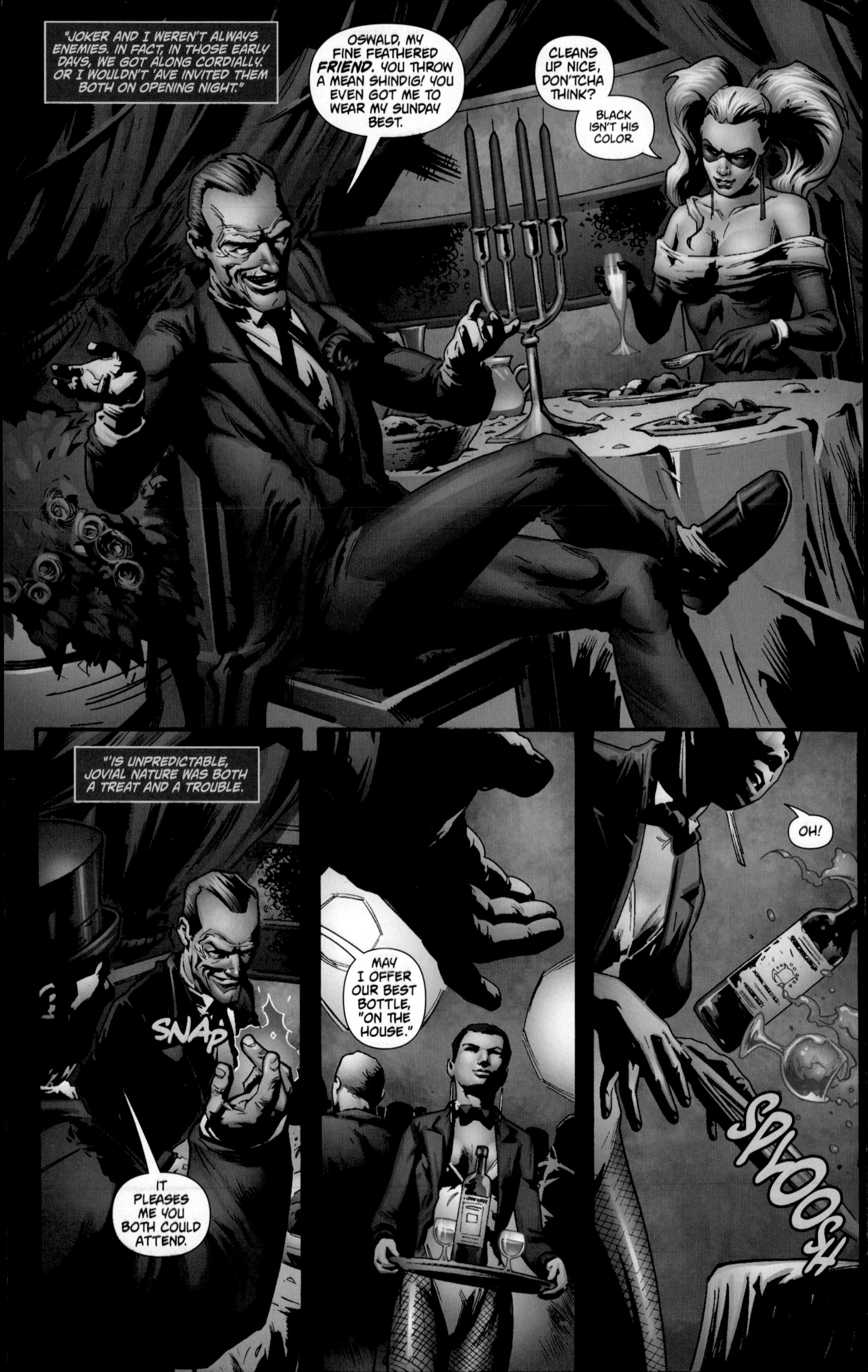
"JOKER AND I WEREN'T ALWAYS ENEMIES. IN FACT, IN THOSE EARLY DAYS, WE GOT ALONG CORDIALLY. OR I WOULDN'T 'AVE INVITED THEM BOTH ON OPENING NIGHT."
OSWALD, MY FINE FEATHERED FRIEND. YOU THROW A MEAN SHINDIG! YOU EVEN GOT ME TO WEAR MY SUNDAY BEST.
CLEANS UP NICE, DON'TCHA THINK?
BLACK ISN'T HIS COLOR.
"'IS UNPREDICTABLE, JOVIAL NATURE WAS BOTH A TREAT AND A TROUBLE.
SNAP
IT PLEASES ME YOU BOTH COULD ATTEND.
MAY I OFFER OUR BEST BOTTLE, "ON THE HOUSE."
OH!
SWOOSH

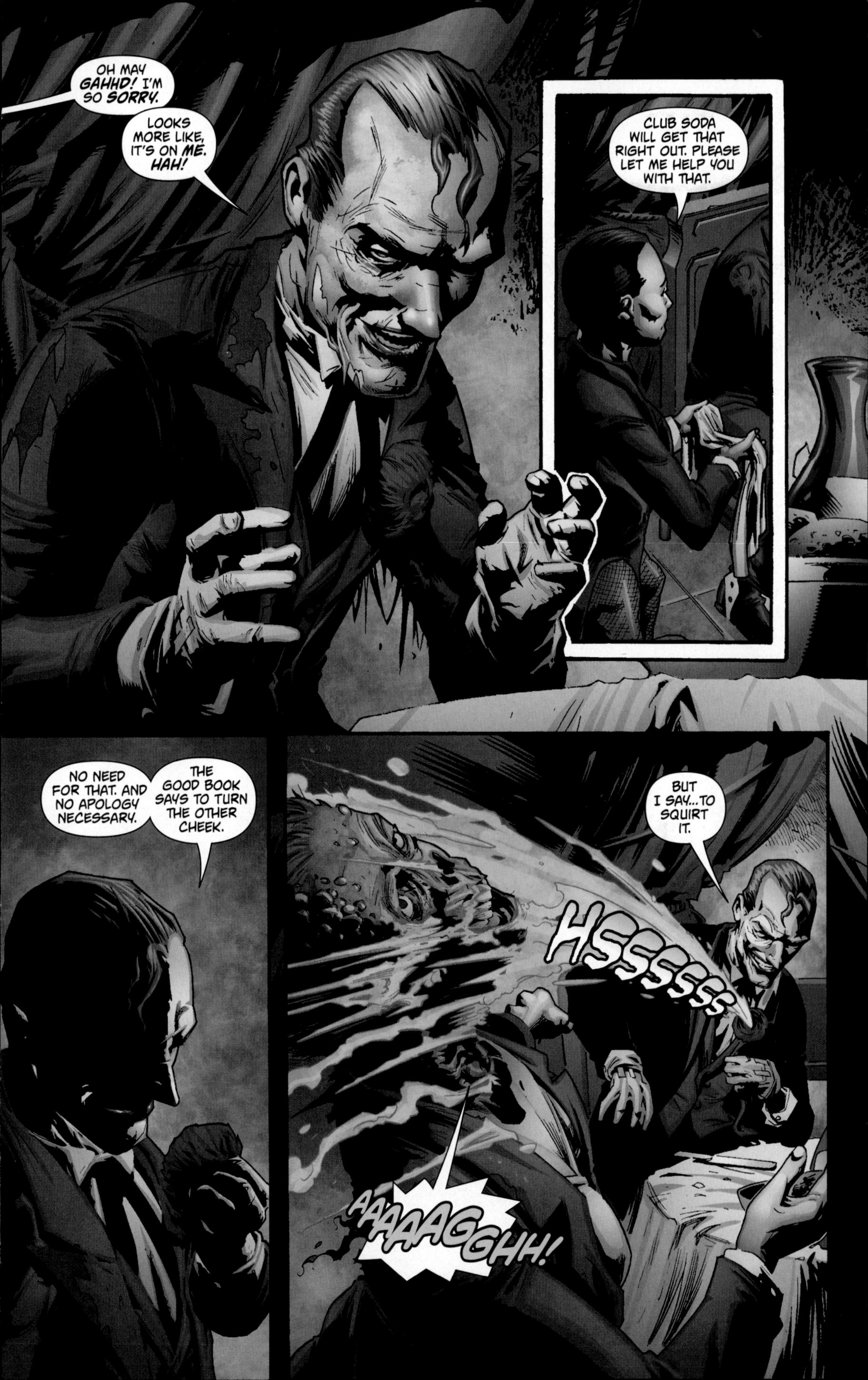

OH MAY GAHHD! I'M SO SORRY.
LOOKS MORE LIKE, IT'S ON ME. HAH!
CLUB SODA WILL GET THAT RIGHT OUT. PLEASE LET ME HELP YOU WITH THAT.
NO NEED FOR THAT. AND NO APOLOGY NECESSARY.
THE GOOD BOOK SAYS TO TURN THE OTHER CHEEK.
BUT I SAY...TO SQUIRT IT.
HSSSSSS
AAAAAGGHH!

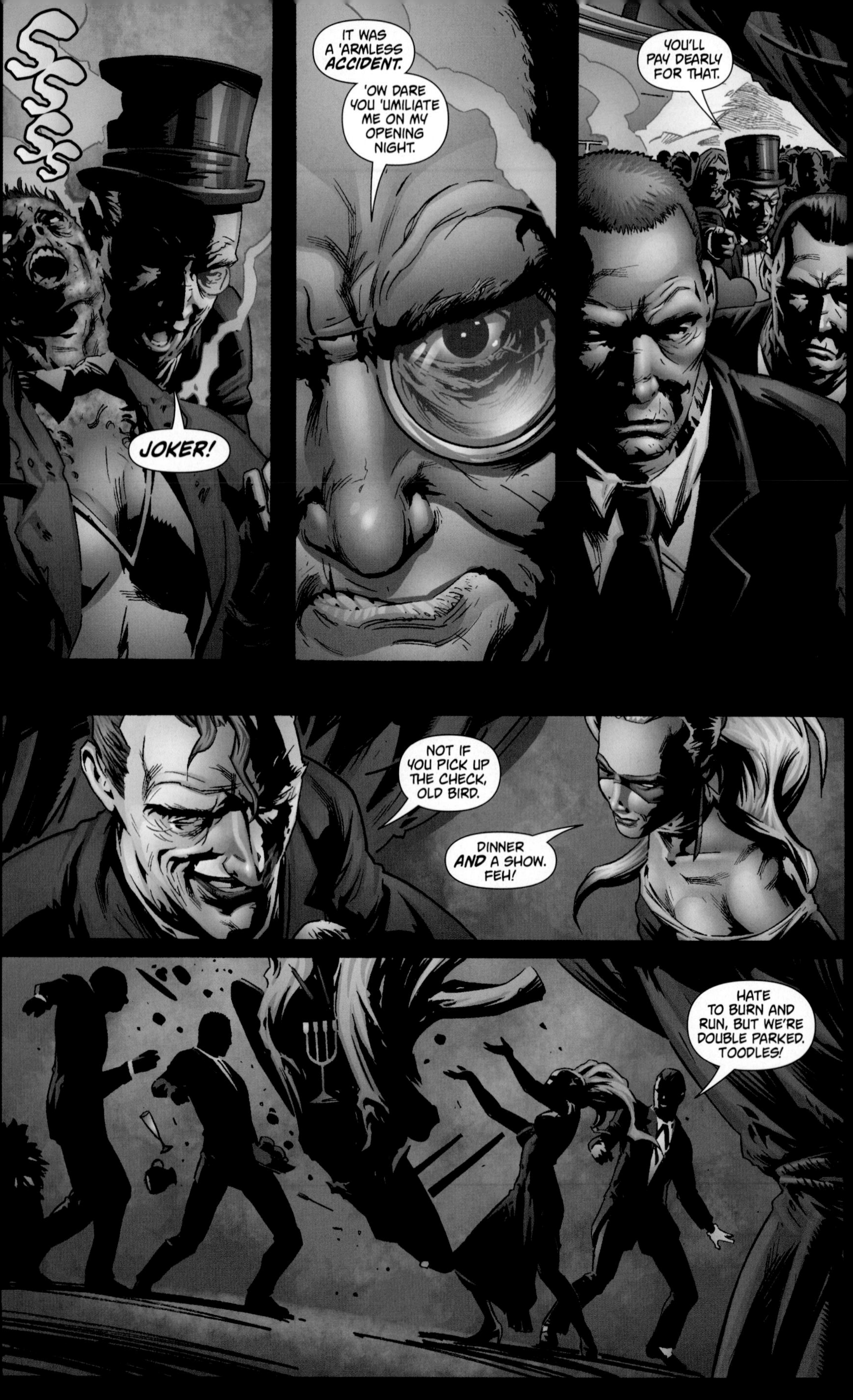
SSSSS
JOKER!
IT WAS A 'ARMLESS ACCIDENT.
'OW DARE YOU 'UMILIATE ME ON MY OPENING NIGHT.
YOU'LL PAY DEARLY FOR THAT.
NOT IF YOU PICK UP THE CHECK, OLD BIRD.
DINNER AND A SHOW. FEH!
HATE TO BURN AND RUN, BUT WE'RE DOUBLE PARKED. TOODLES!

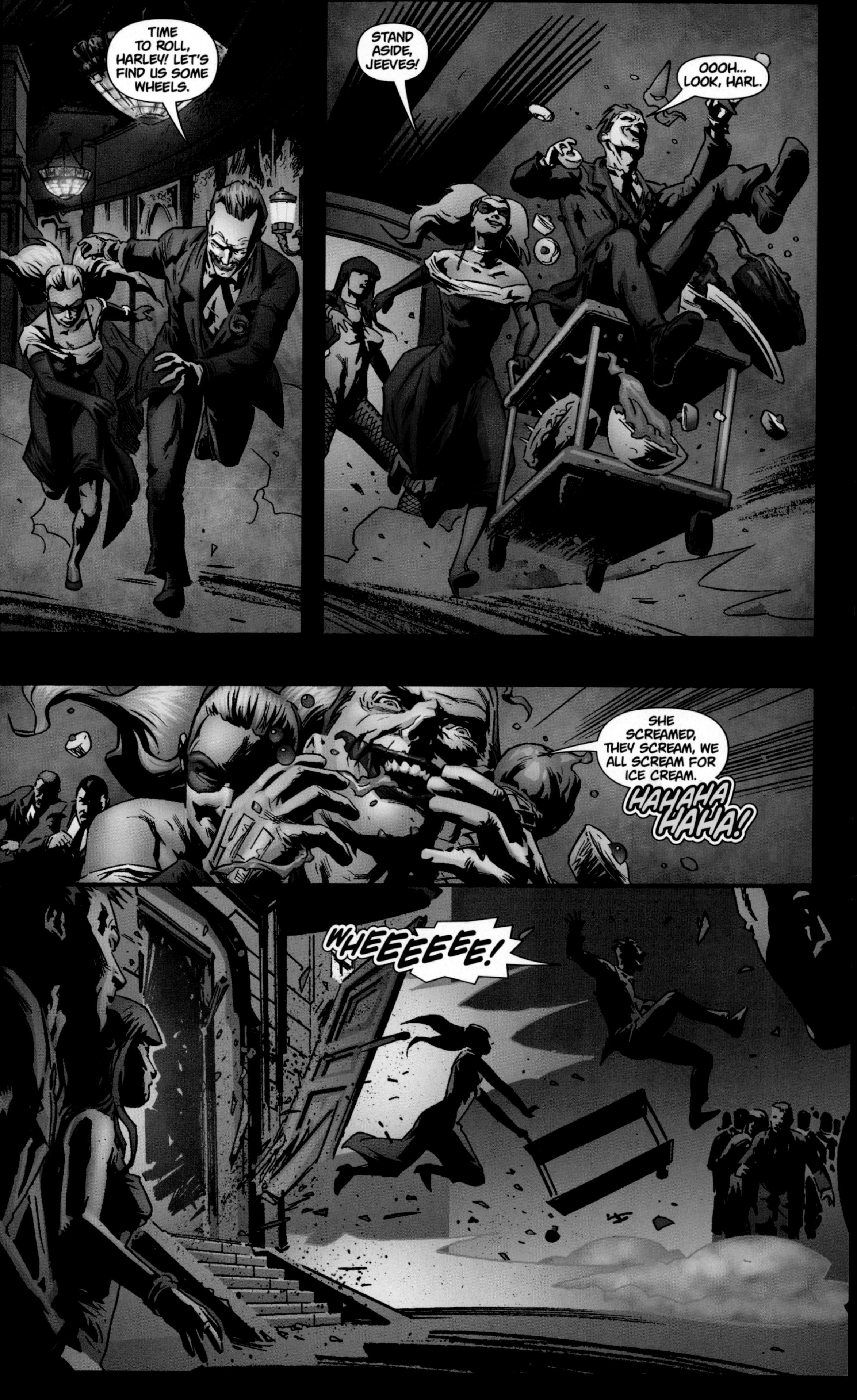
TIME TO ROLL, HARLEY! LET'S FIND US SOME WHEELS.
STAND ASIDE, JEEVES!
OOOH... LOOK, HARL.
SHE SCREAMED, THEY SCREAM, WE ALL SCREAM FOR ICE CREAM.
HAHAHA HAHA!
WHEEEEEEE!

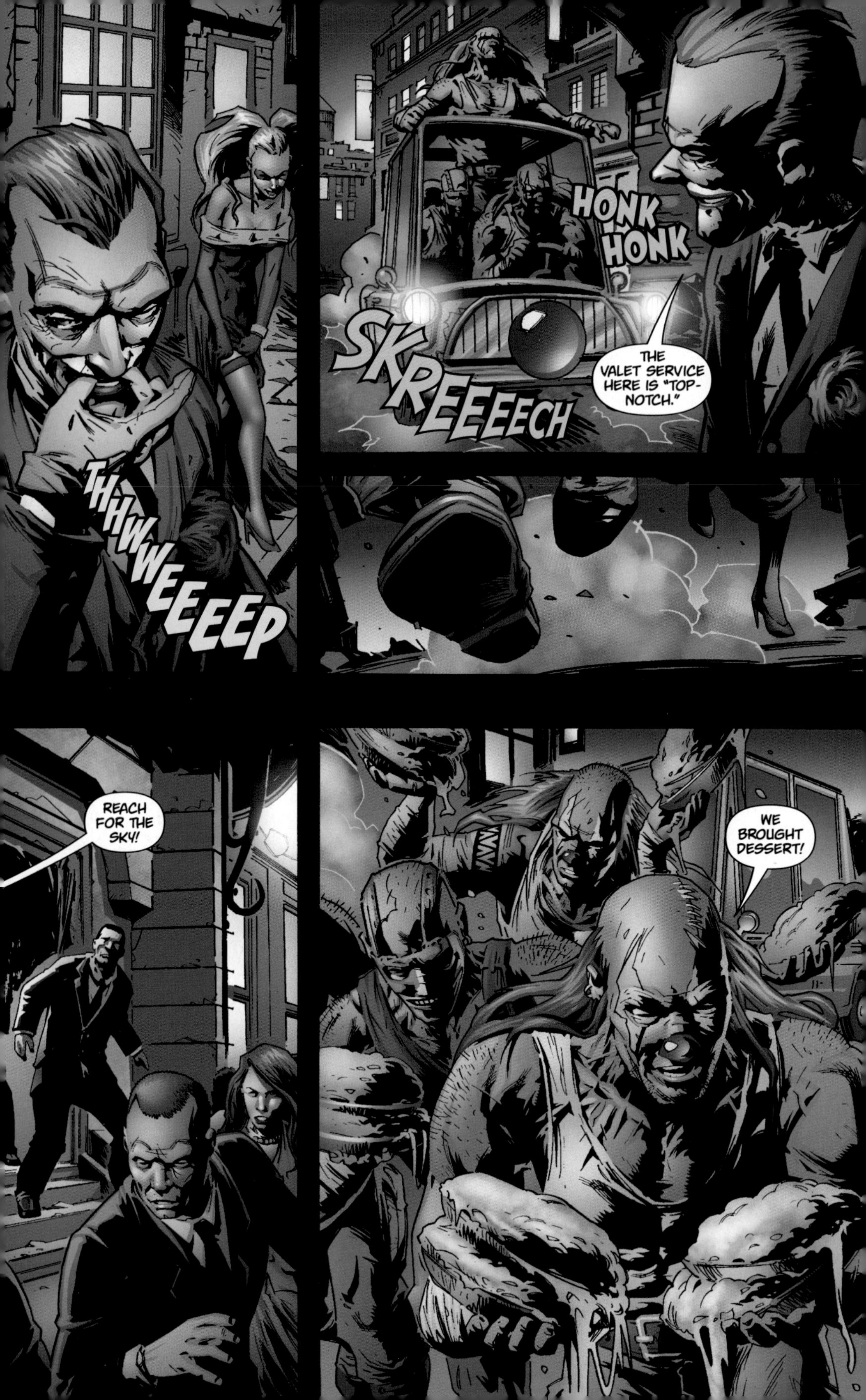
THHWWEEEEEP
HONK HONK
SKREEEEECH
THE VALET SERVICE HERE IS "TOP-NOTCH."
REACH FOR THE SKY!
WE BROUGHT DESSERT!

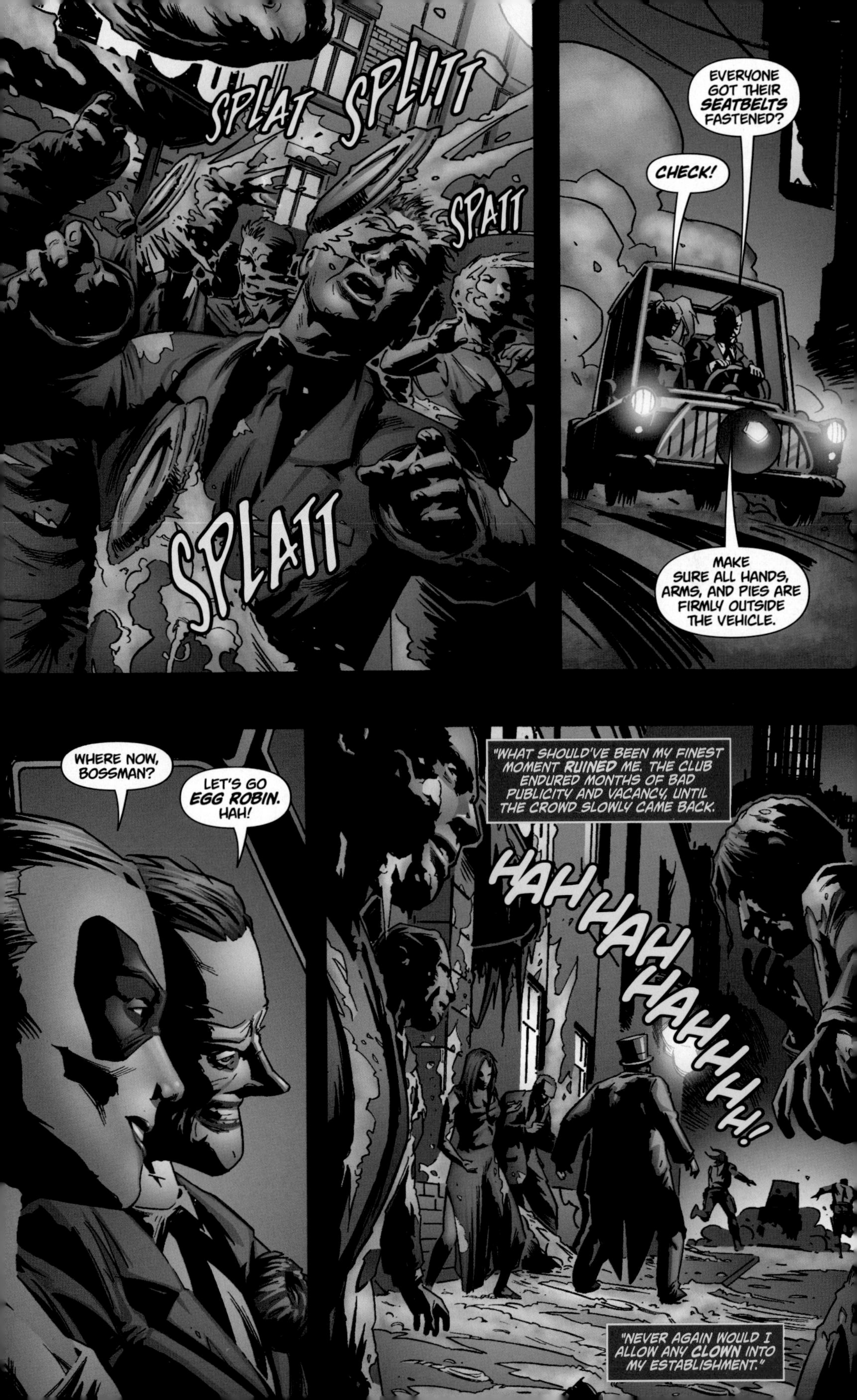
SPLAT
SPLITT
SPATT
SPLATT
EVERYONE GOT THEIR SEATBELTS FASTENED?
CHECK!
MAKE SURE ALL HANDS, ARMS, AND PIES ARE FIRMLY OUTSIDE THE VEHICLE.
WHERE NOW, BOSSMAN?
LET'S GO EGG ROBIN. HAH!
"WHAT SHOULD'VE BEEN MY FINEST MOMENT RUINED ME. THE CLUB ENDURED MONTHS OF BAD PUBLICITY AND VACANCY, UNTIL THE CROWD SLOWLY CAME BACK.
HAH HAH HAHHHHH!
"NEVER AGAIN WOULD I ALLOW ANY CLOWN INTO MY ESTABLISHMENT."

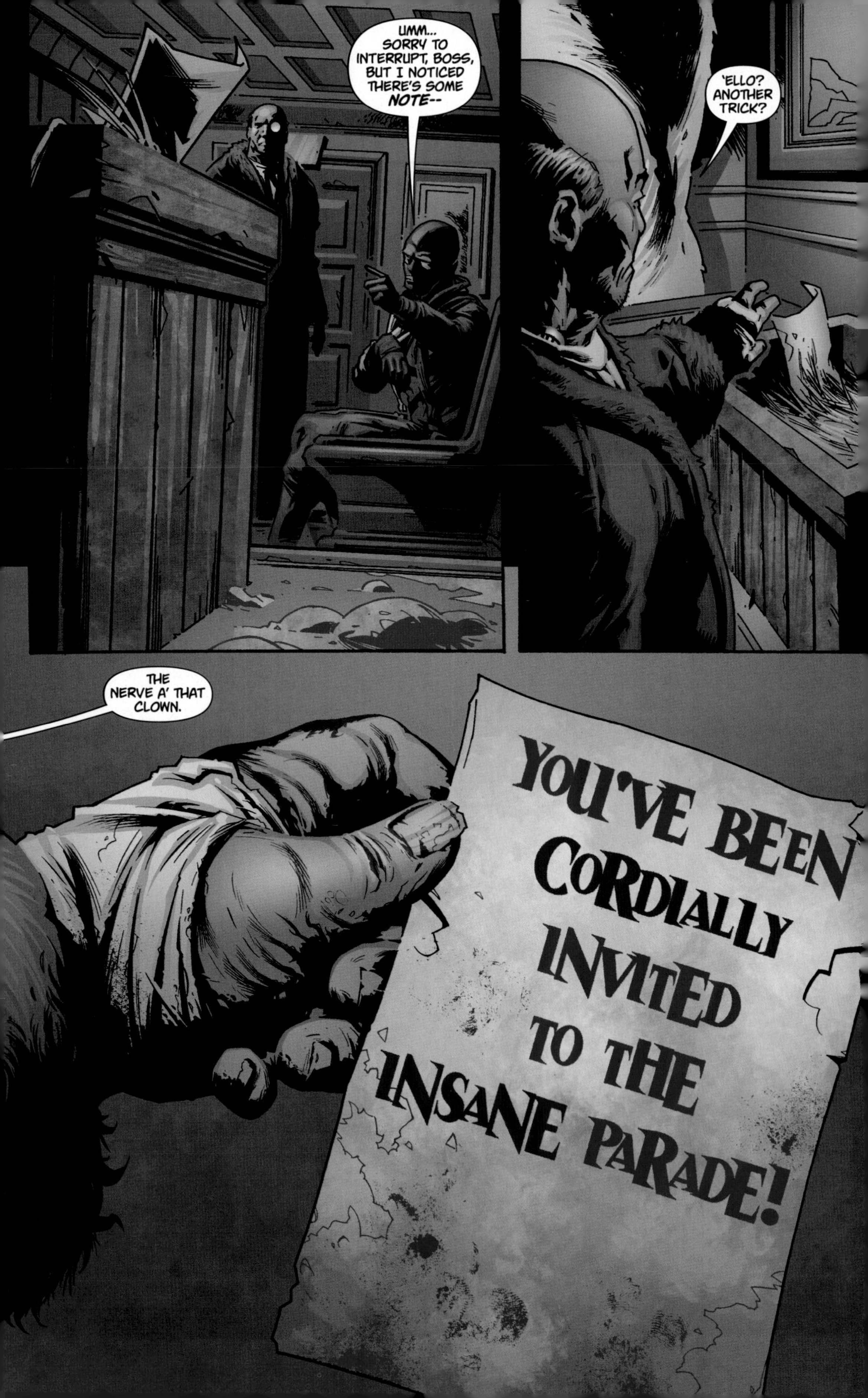
UMM... SORRY TO INTERRUPT, BOSS, BUT I NOTICED THERE'S SOME NOTE--
'ELLO? ANOTHER TRICK?
THE NERVE A' THAT CLOWN.
YOU'VE BEEN CORDIALLY INVITED TO THE INSANE PARADE!

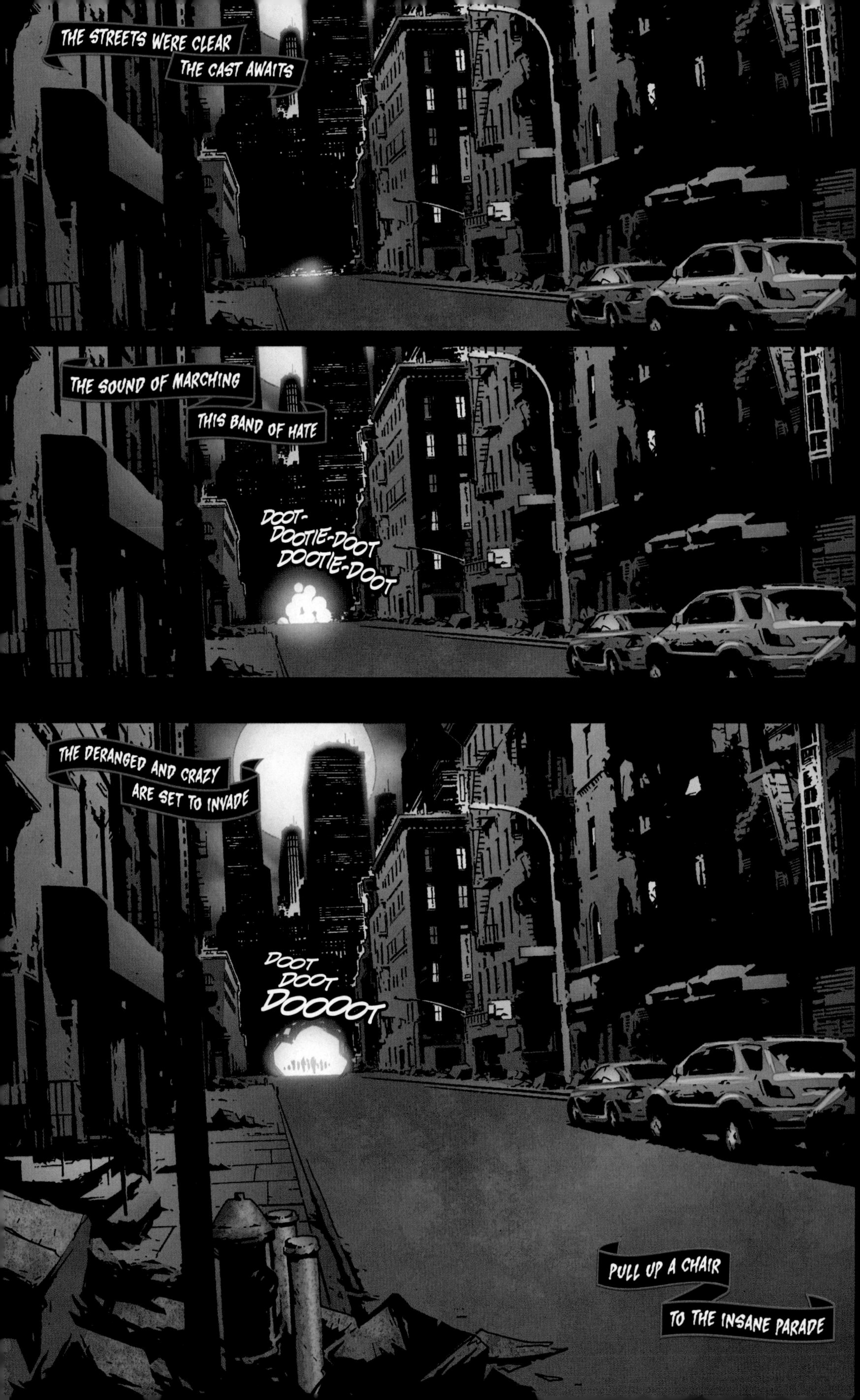
THE STREETS WERE CLEAR
THE CAST AWAITS
THE SOUND OF MARCHING
THIS BAND OF HATE
DOOT-DOOTIE-DOOT DOOTIE-DOOT
THE DERANGED AND CRAZY
ARE SET TO INVADE
DOOT DOOT DOOOOOT
PULL UP A CHAIR
TO THE INSANE PARADE

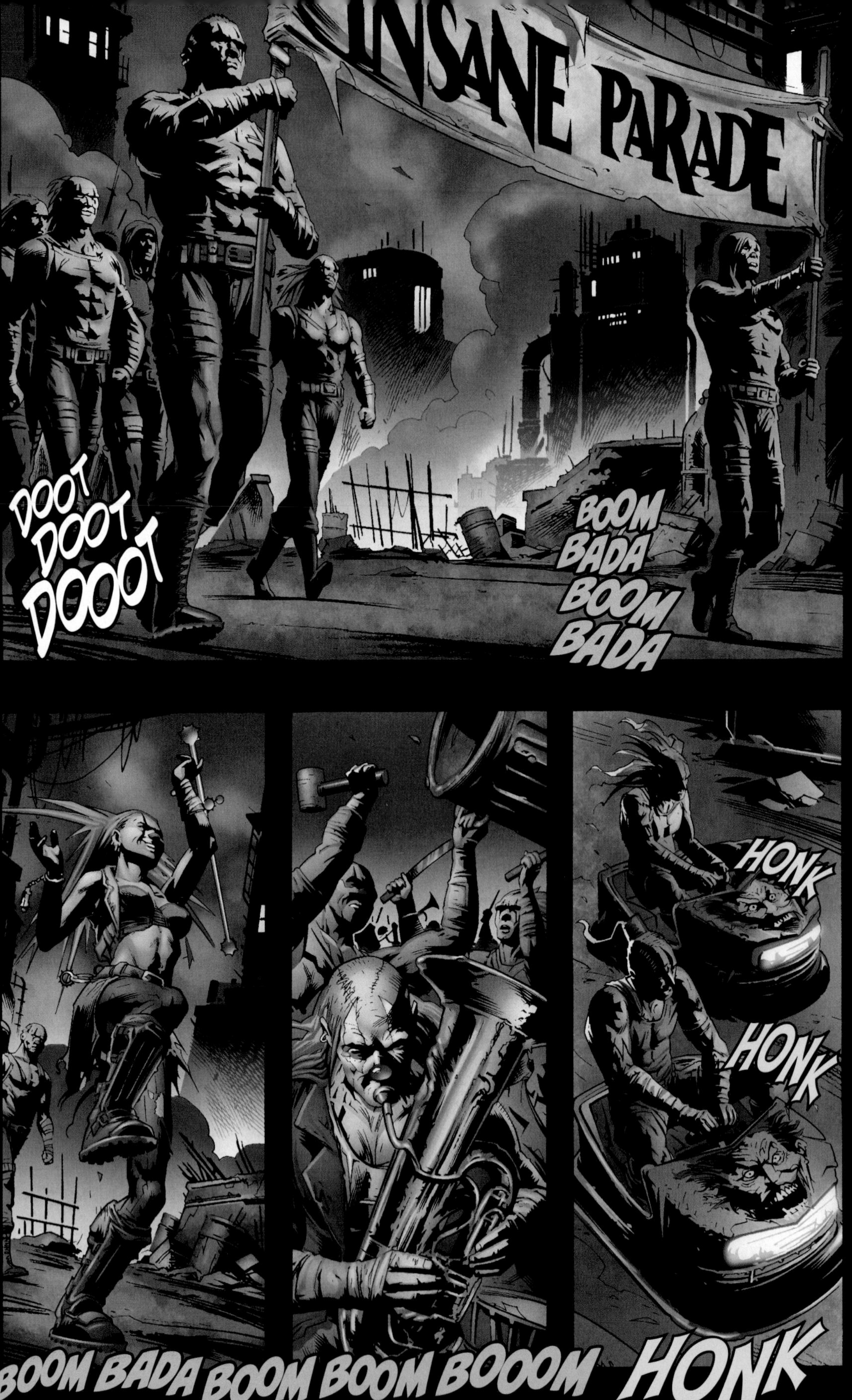
INSANE PARADE
DOOT DOOT DOOOT
BOOM BADA BOOM BADA
HONK
HONK
BOOM BADA BOOM BOOM BOOOM
HONK

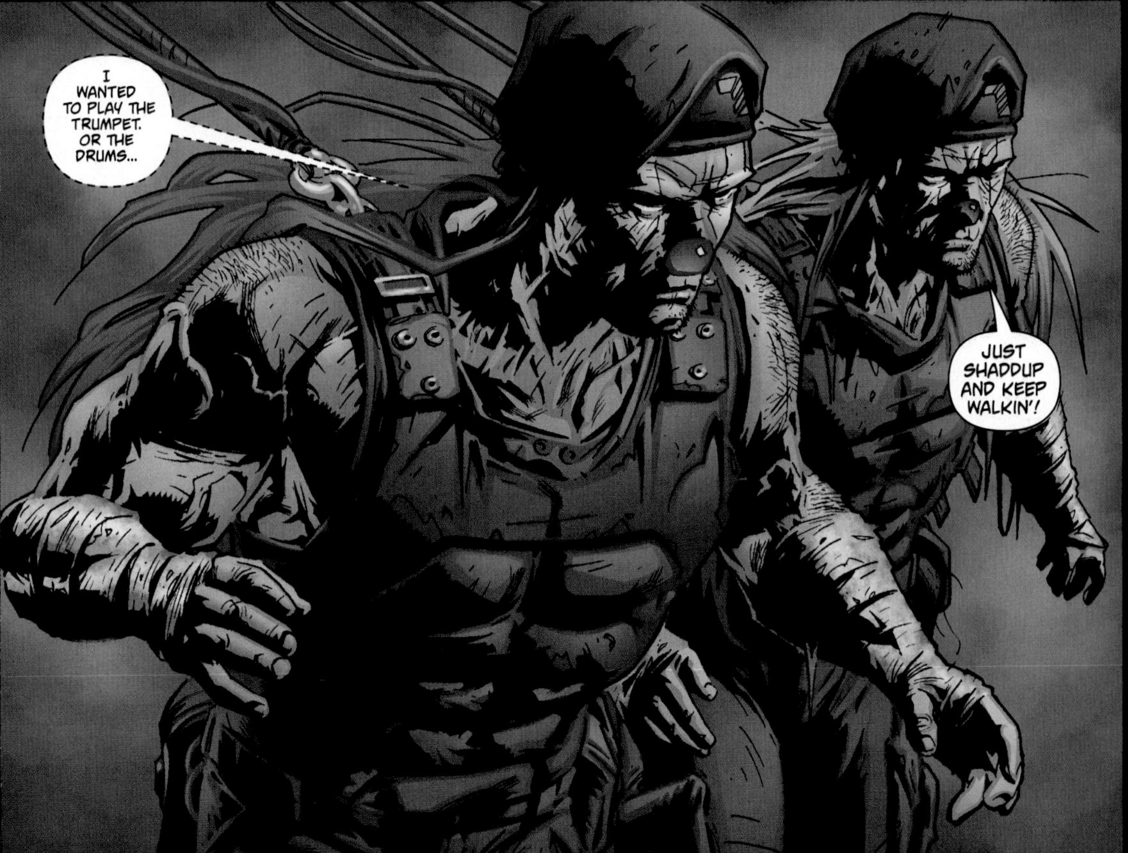
I WANTED TO PLAY THE TRUMPET. OR THE DRUMS...
JUST SHADDUP AND KEEP WALKIN'!

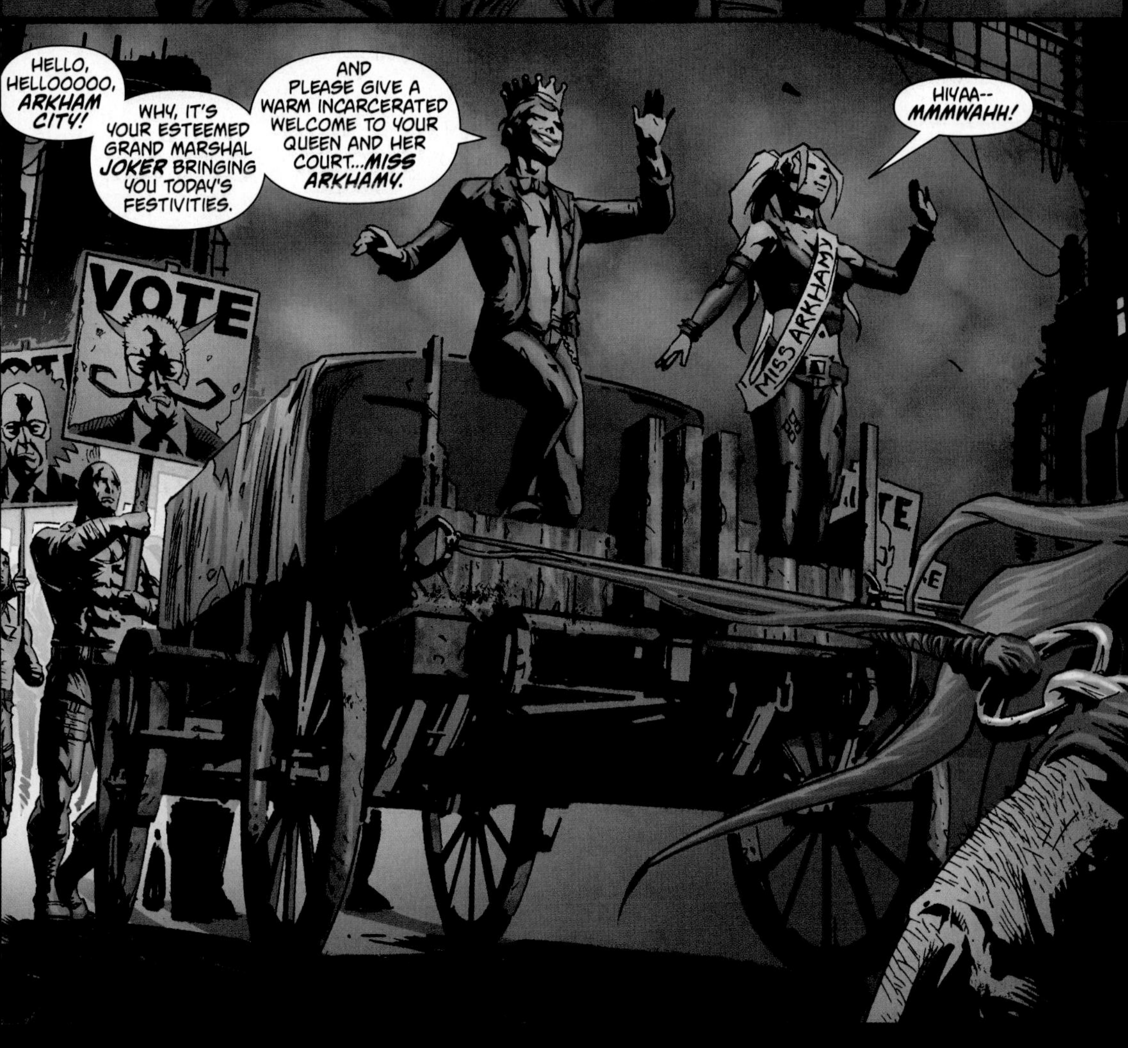
HELLO, HELLOOOOO, ARKHAM CITY!
WHY, IT'S YOUR ESTEEMED GRAND MARSHAL JOKER BRINGING YOU TODAY'S FESTIVITIES.
AND PLEASE GIVE A WARM INCARCERATED WELCOME TO YOUR QUEEN AND HER COURT...MISS ARKHAMY.
HIYAA-- MMMWAHH!
VOTE
MISS ARKHAMY

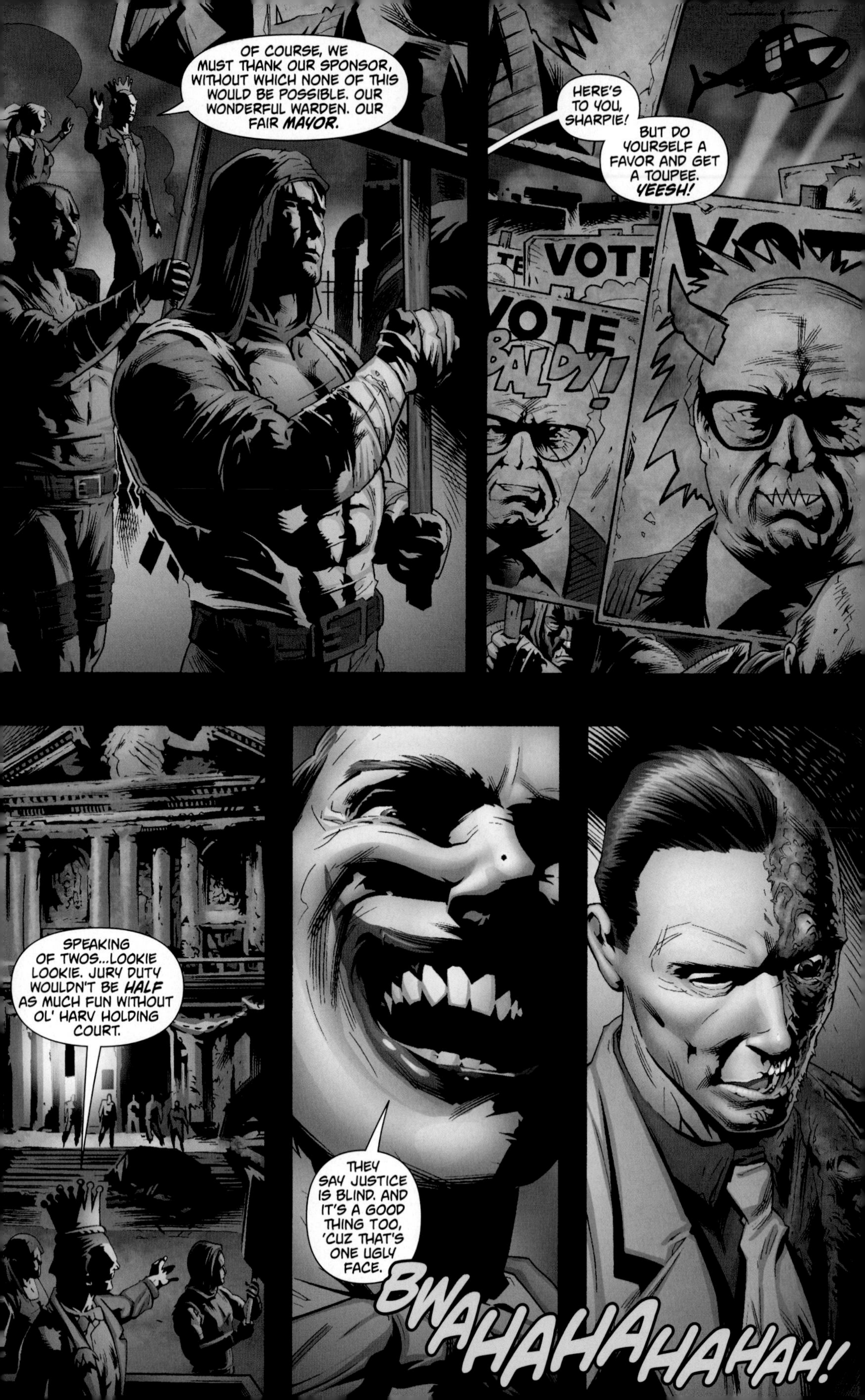

OF COURSE, WE MUST THANK OUR SPONSOR, WITHOUT WHICH NONE OF THIS WOULD BE POSSIBLE. OUR WONDERFUL WARDEN. OUR FAIR *MAYOR*.
HERE'S TO YOU, SHARPIE!
BUT DO YOURSELF A FAVOR AND GET A TOUPEE. *YEESH!*
VOTE
VOTE
VOTE BALDY!
SPEAKING OF TWOS...LOOKIE LOOKIE. JURY DUTY WOULDN'T BE *HALF* AS MUCH FUN WITHOUT OL' HARV HOLDING COURT.
THEY SAY JUSTICE IS BLIND. AND IT'S A GOOD THING TOO, 'CUZ THAT'S ONE UGLY FACE.
BWAHAHAHAHAHAH!

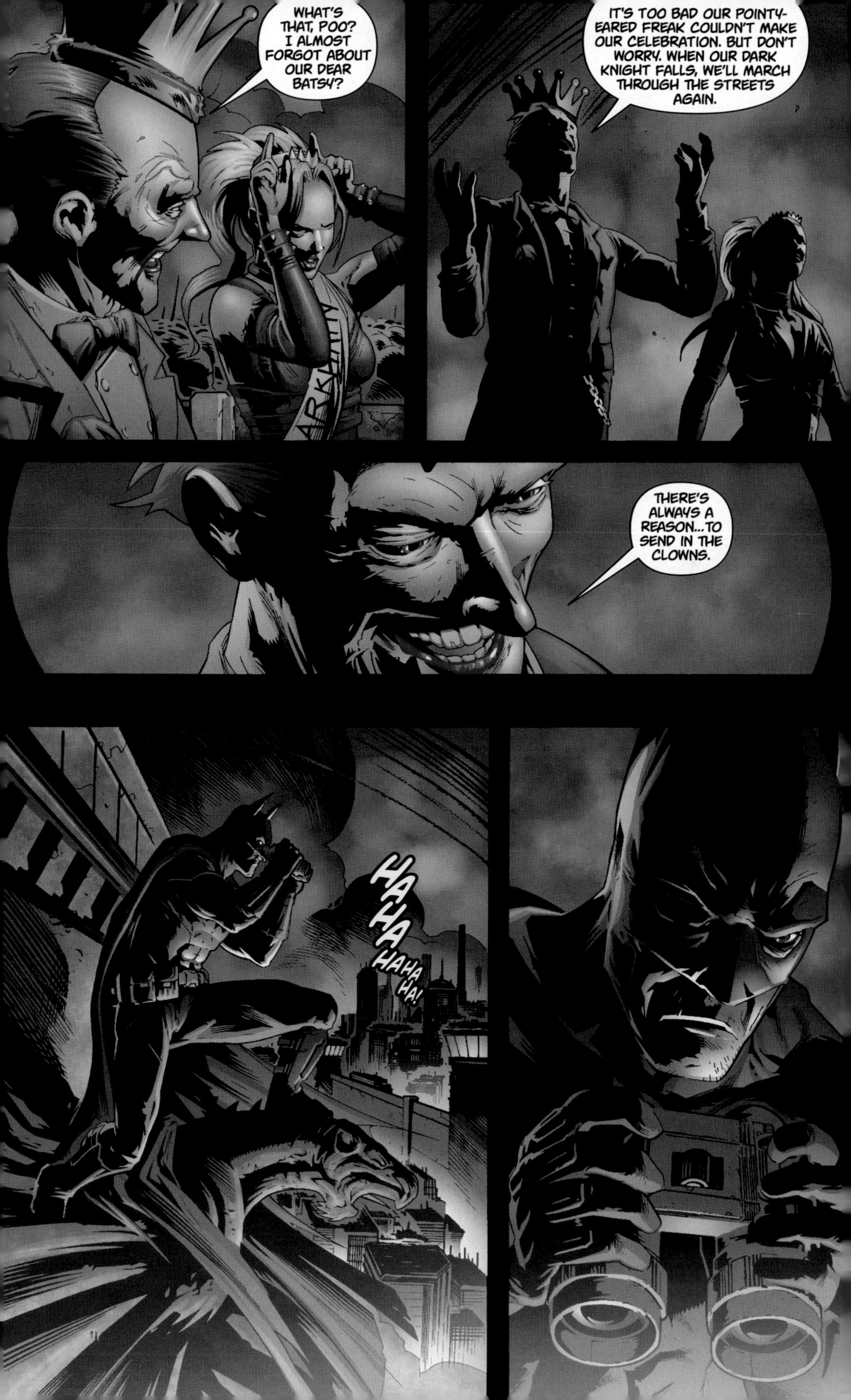
WHAT'S THAT, POO? I ALMOST FORGOT ABOUT OUR DEAR BATSY?
IT'S TOO BAD OUR POINTY-EARED FREAK COULDN'T MAKE OUR CELEBRATION. BUT DON'T WORRY. WHEN OUR DARK KNIGHT FALLS, WE'LL MARCH THROUGH THE STREETS AGAIN.
THERE'S ALWAYS A REASON...TO SEND IN THE CLOWNS.
HA HA HA HAHA HA!

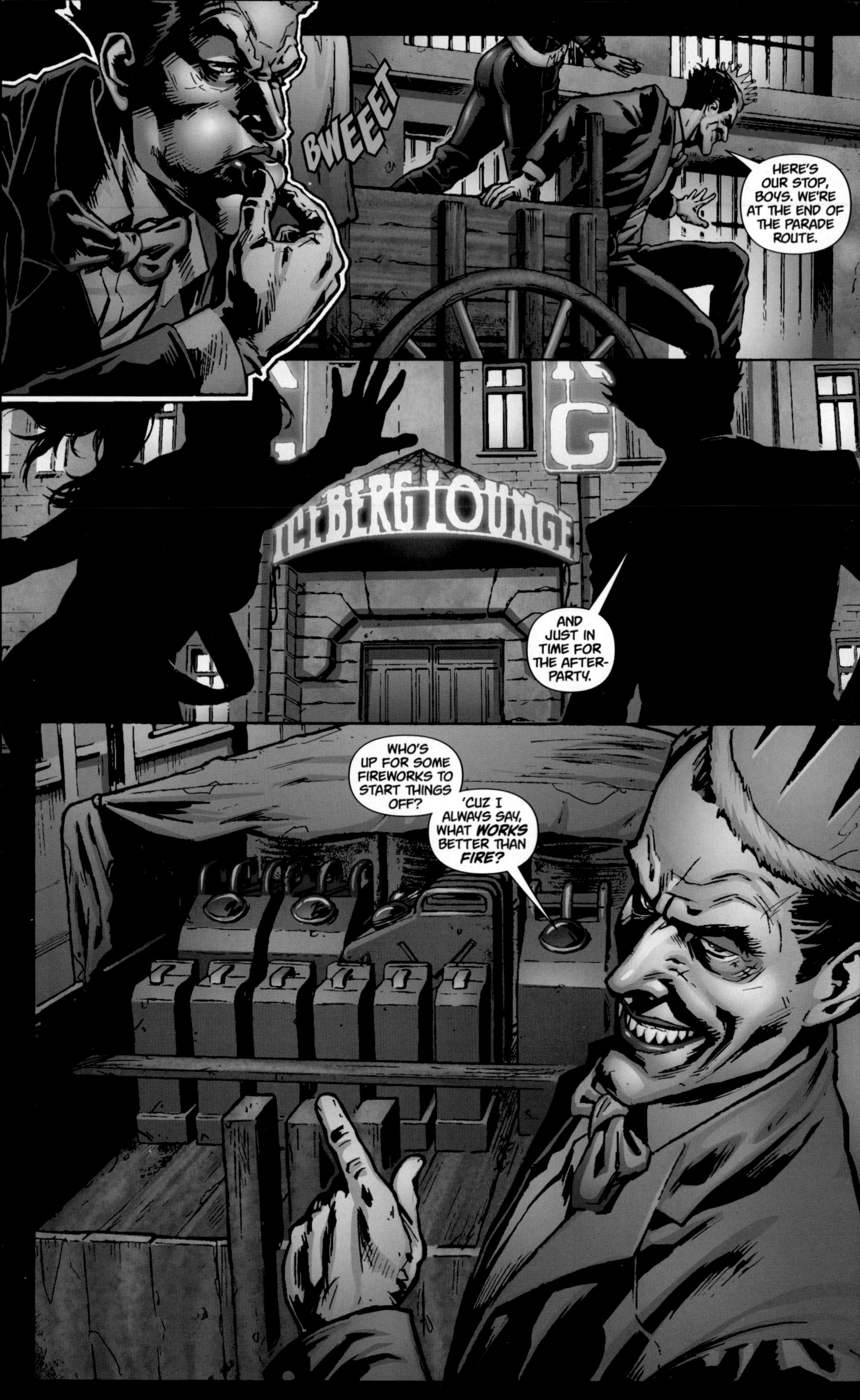
BWEEET
HERE'S OUR STOP, BOYS. WE'RE AT THE END OF THE PARADE ROUTE.
ICEBERG LOUNGE
AND JUST IN TIME FOR THE AFTER-PARTY.
WHO'S UP FOR SOME FIREWORKS TO START THINGS OFF?
'CUZ I ALWAYS SAY, WHAT *WORKS* BETTER THAN *FIRE?*

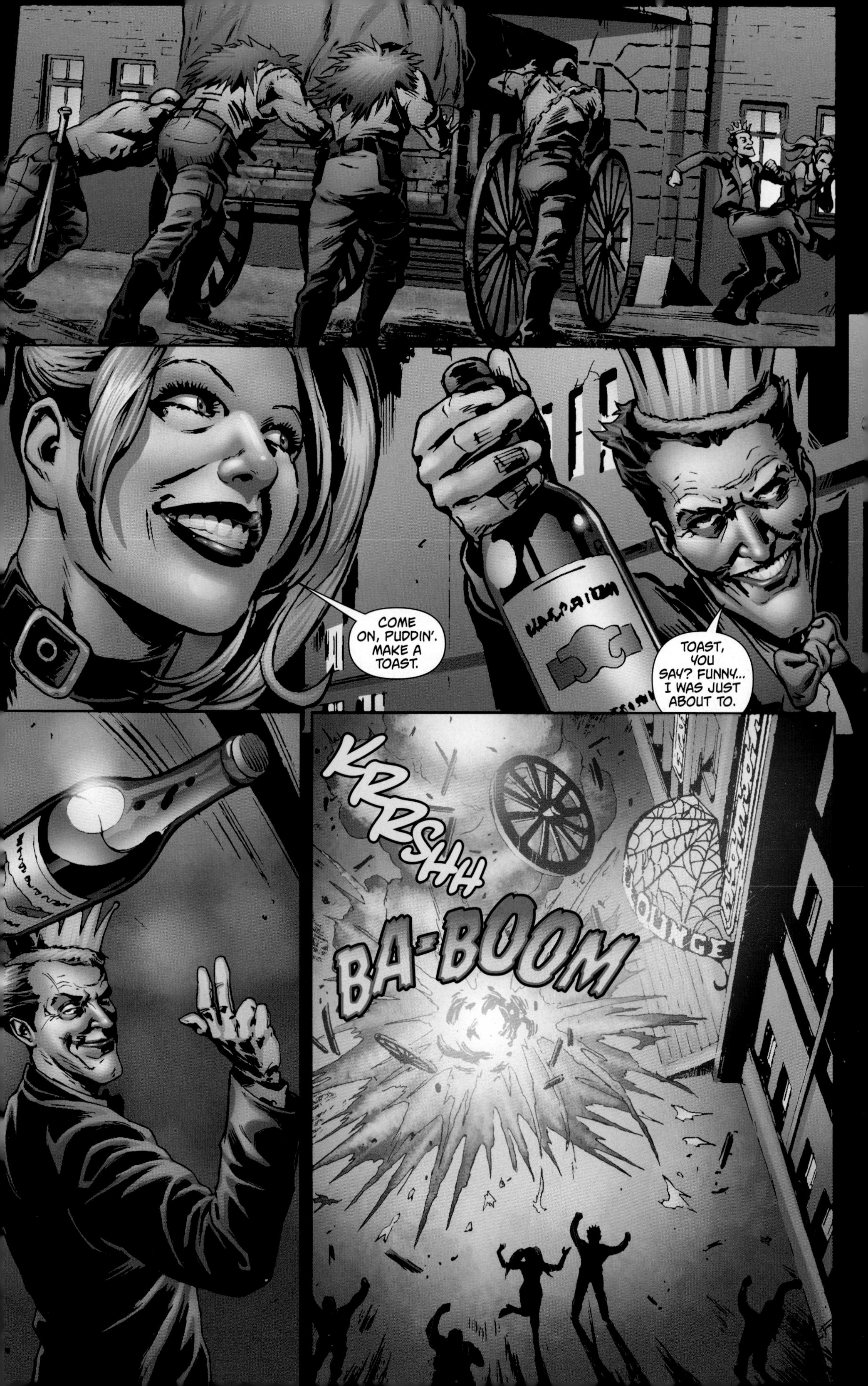

COME ON, PUDDIN'. MAKE A TOAST.
TOAST, YOU SAY? FUNNY... I WAS JUST ABOUT TO.
KRRSHH
BA-BOOM
LOUNGE

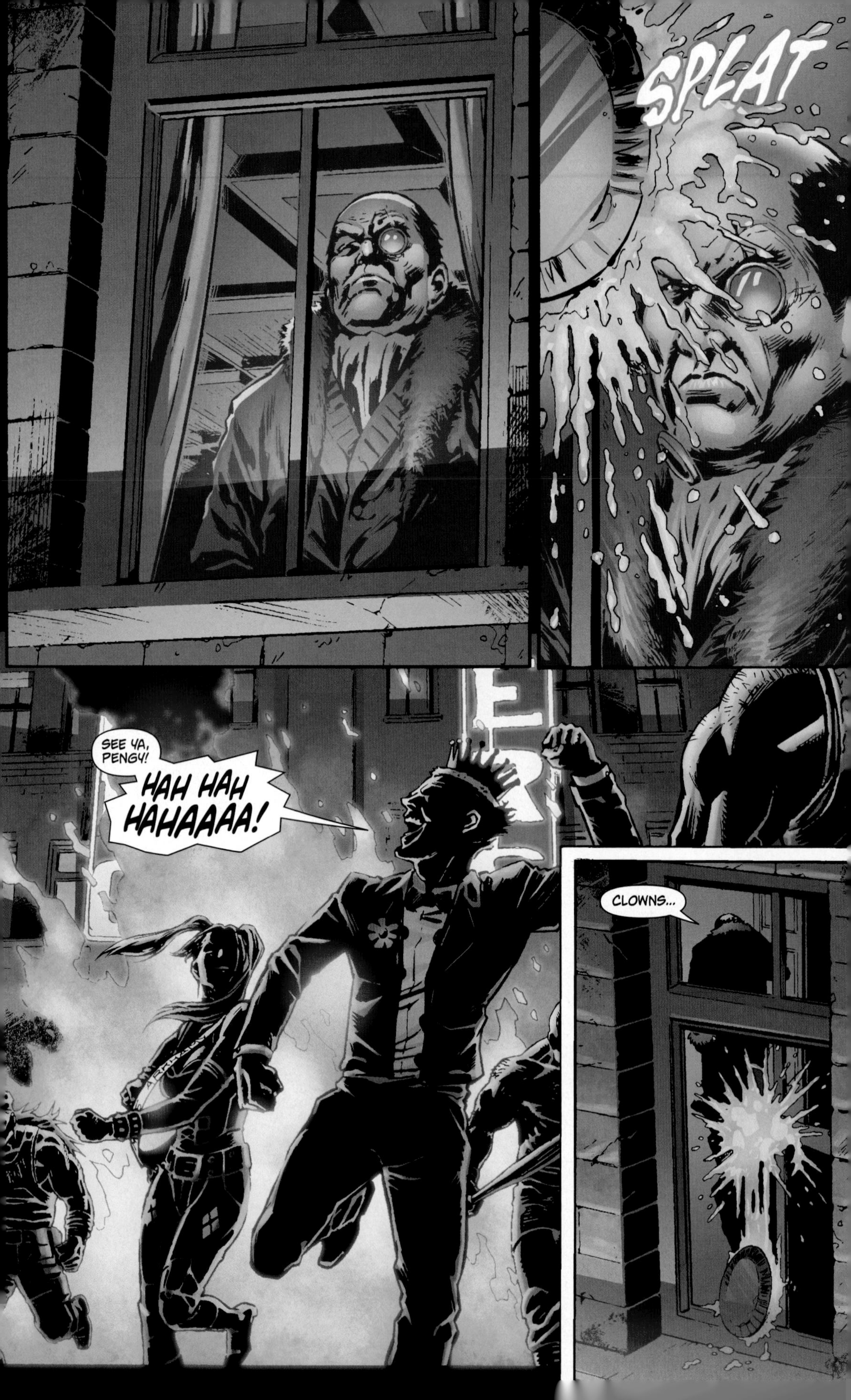
SPLAT
SEE YA, PENGY!
HAH HAH HAHAAAA!
CLOWNS...

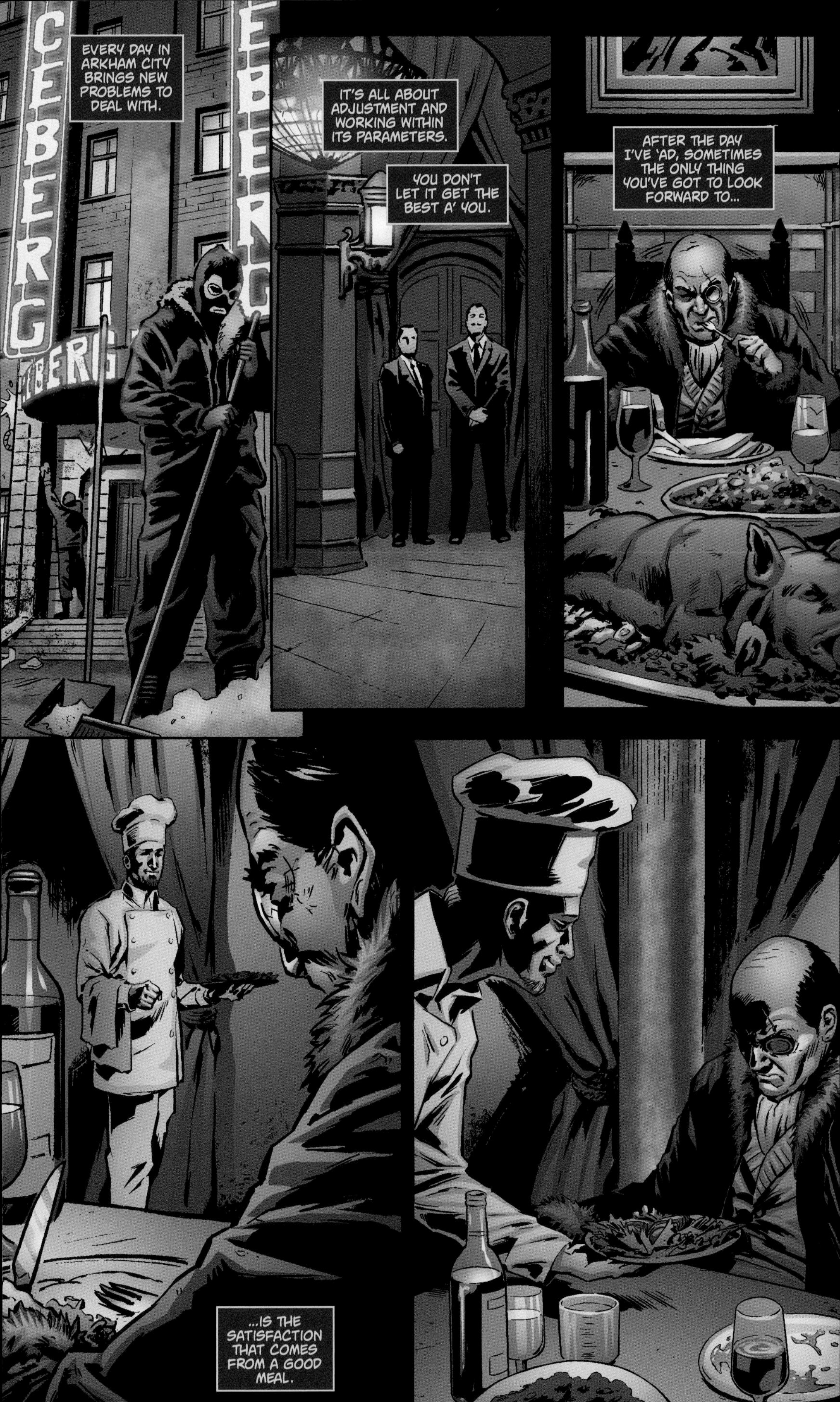
EVERY DAY IN ARKHAM CITY BRINGS NEW PROBLEMS TO DEAL WITH.
IT'S ALL ABOUT ADJUSTMENT AND WORKING WITHIN ITS PARAMETERS.
YOU DON'T LET IT GET THE BEST A' YOU.
AFTER THE DAY I'VE 'AD, SOMETIMES THE ONLY THING YOU'VE GOT TO LOOK FORWARD TO...
...IS THE SATISFACTION THAT COMES FROM A GOOD MEAL.

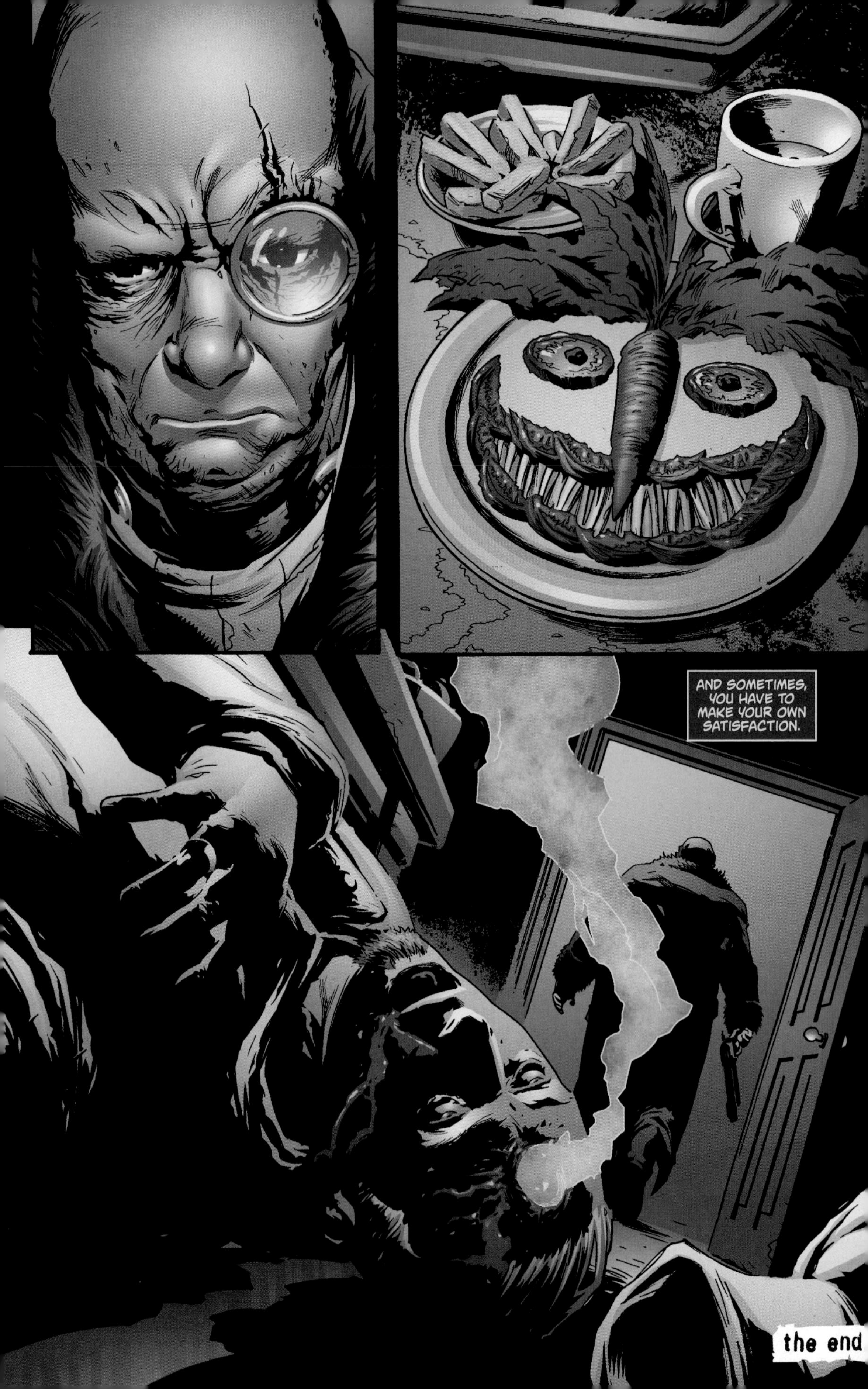
AND SOMETIMES, YOU HAVE TO MAKE YOUR OWN SATISFACTION.
the end

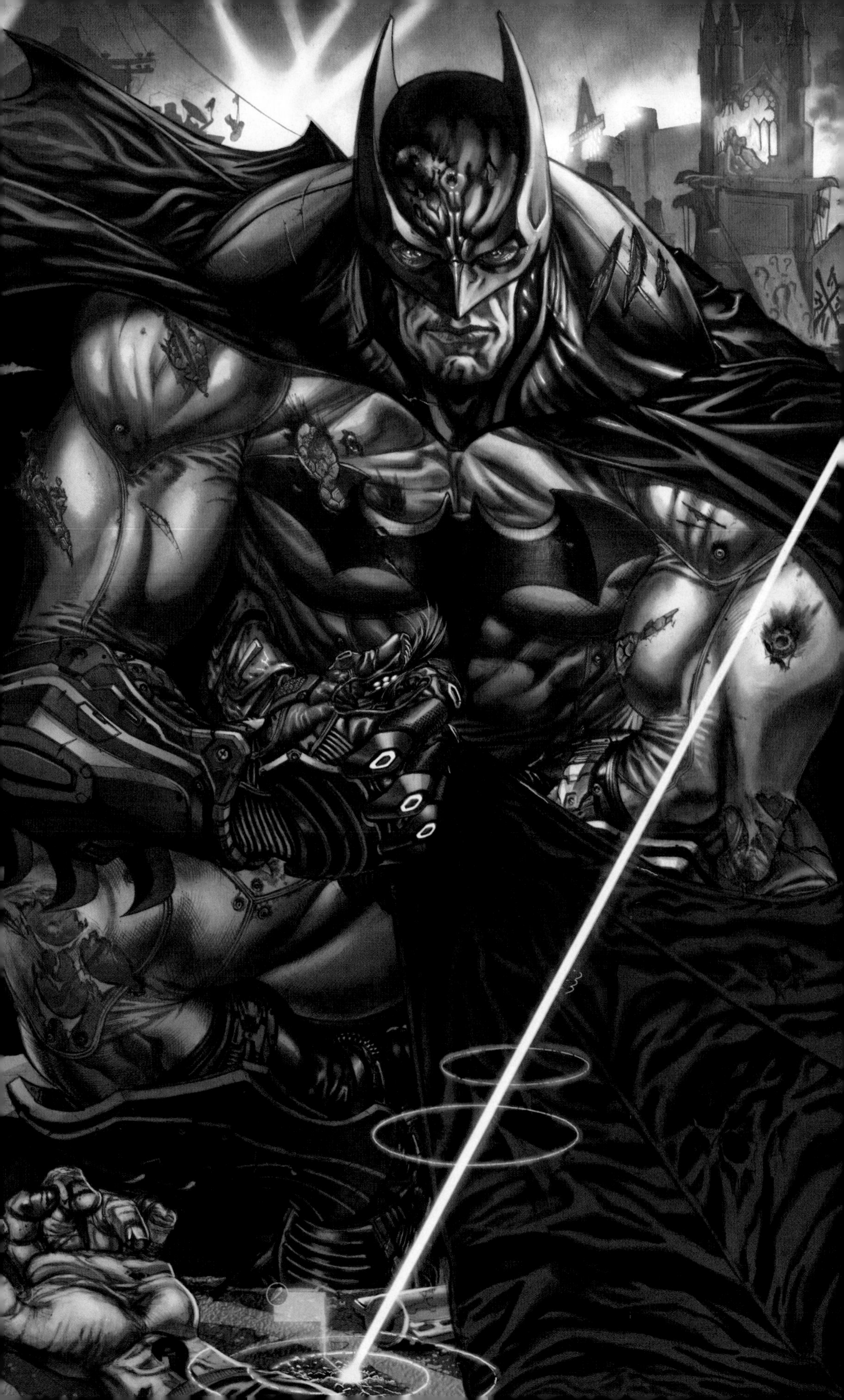

SURGEON'S GENERAL

WRITTEN BY: **DEREK FRIDOLFS**

ART BY: **PETE WOODS**

COLORS BY: **GABE ELTAEB**

LETTERS: **TRAVIS LANHAM**

THREE'S A CROWD

STORY BY: **PAUL DINI**

SCRIPT BY: **DEREK FRIDOLFS**

PENCILS BY: **AL BARRIONUEVO**

INKS BY: **MICHEL LACOMBE**

COLORS BY: **RANDY MAYOR**

LETTERS: **TRAVIS LANHAM**

GLACIAL SPEED

STORY BY: **PAUL DINI**

SCRIPT BY: **DEREK FRIDOLFS**

PENCILS BY: **JIMBO SALGADO**

INKS BY: **JEFFREY HUET**

COLORS BY: **RANDY MAYOR**

LETTERS: **TRAVIS LANHAM**

COVER ART BY: **BRANDON BADEAUX**

COVER COLOR BY: **WES HARTMAN**

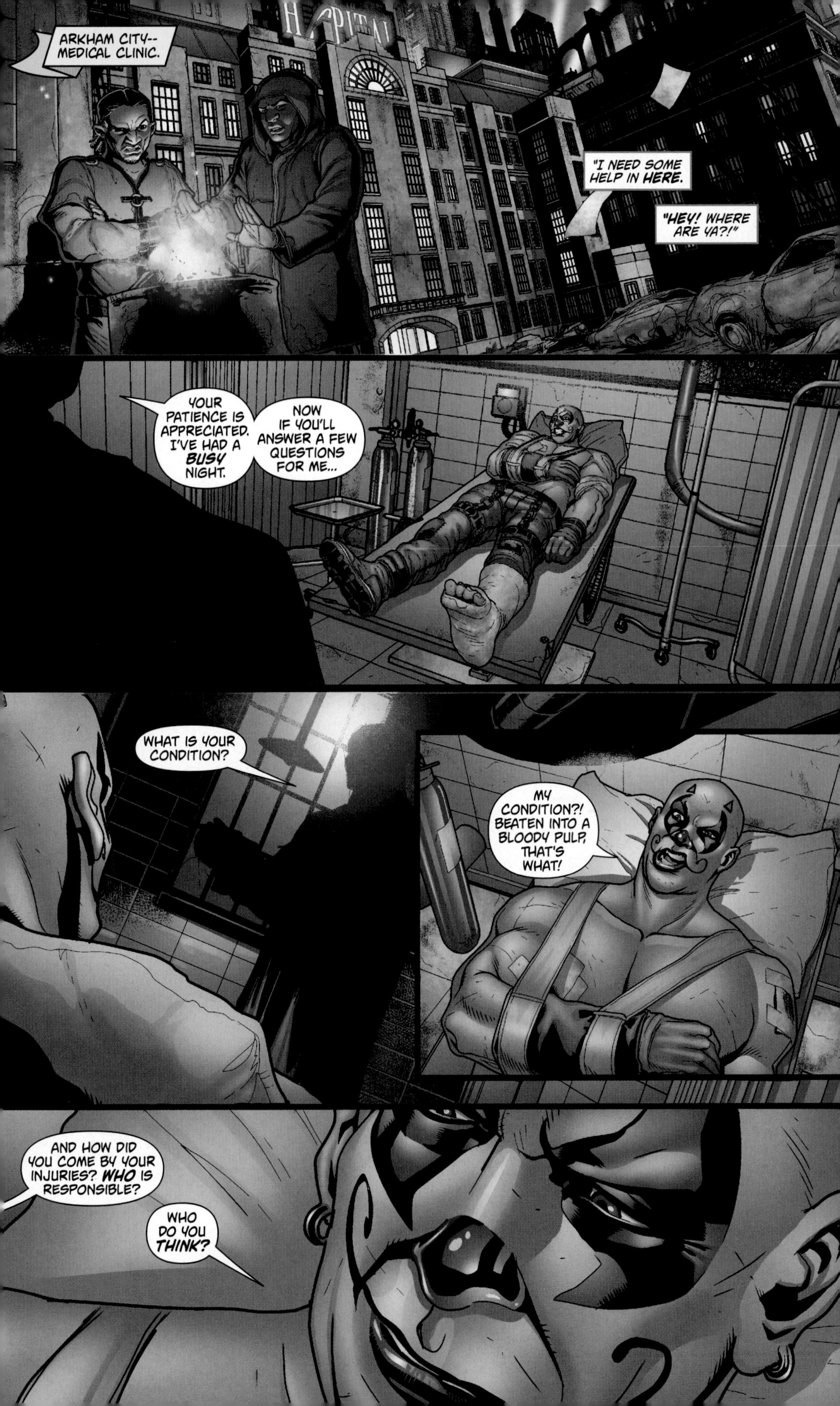
H PITAL
ARKHAM CITY-- MEDICAL CLINIC.
"I NEED SOME HELP IN HERE.
"HEY! WHERE ARE YA?!"
YOUR PATIENCE IS APPRECIATED. I'VE HAD A BUSY NIGHT.
NOW IF YOU'LL ANSWER A FEW QUESTIONS FOR ME...
WHAT IS YOUR CONDITION?
MY CONDITION?! BEATEN INTO A BLOODY PULP, THAT'S WHAT!
AND HOW DID YOU COME BY YOUR INJURIES? WHO IS RESPONSIBLE?
WHO DO YOU THINK?

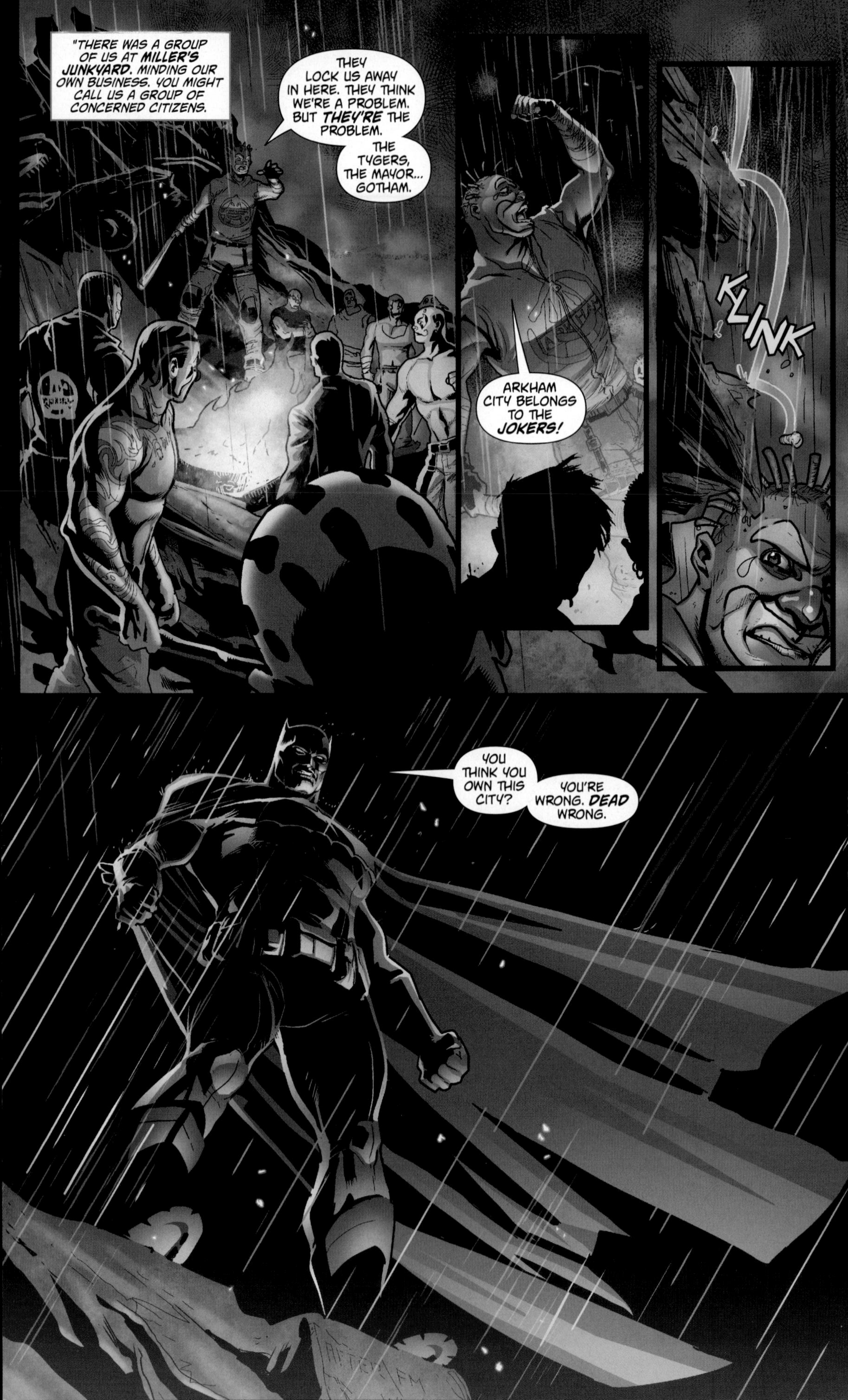
"THERE WAS A GROUP OF US AT MILLER'S JUNKYARD. MINDING OUR OWN BUSINESS. YOU MIGHT CALL US A GROUP OF CONCERNED CITIZENS.
THEY LOCK US AWAY IN HERE. THEY THINK WE'RE A PROBLEM. BUT THEY'RE THE PROBLEM.
THE TYGERS, THE MAYOR... GOTHAM.
ARKHAM CITY BELONGS TO THE JOKERS!
KLINK
YOU THINK YOU OWN THIS CITY?
YOU'RE WRONG. DEAD WRONG.

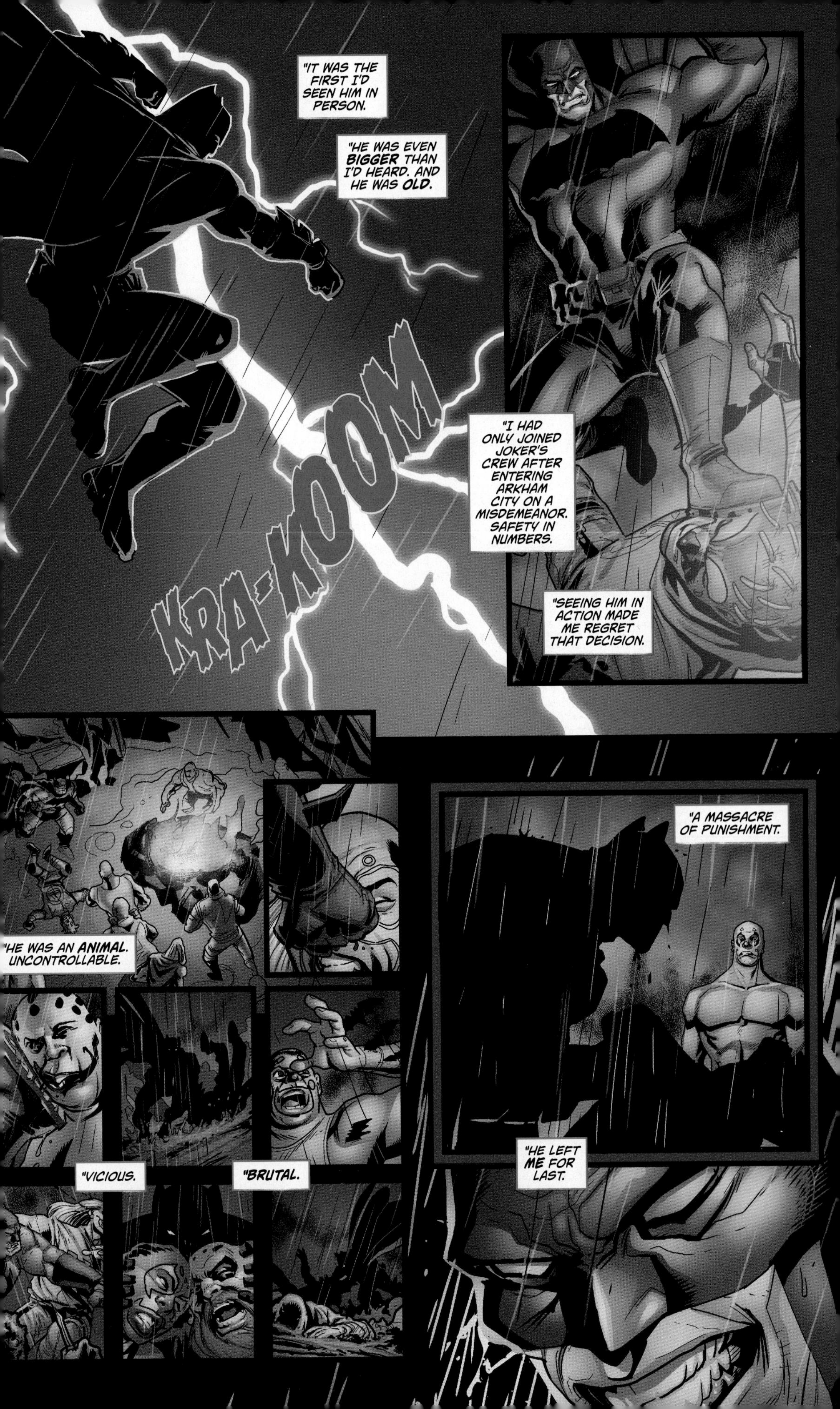
"IT WAS THE FIRST I'D SEEN HIM IN PERSON.
"HE WAS EVEN BIGGER THAN I'D HEARD. AND HE WAS OLD.
KRA-KOOM
"I HAD ONLY JOINED JOKER'S CREW AFTER ENTERING ARKHAM CITY ON A MISDEMEANOR. SAFETY IN NUMBERS.
"SEEING HIM IN ACTION MADE ME REGRET THAT DECISION.
"HE WAS AN ANIMAL. UNCONTROLLABLE.
"VICIOUS.
"BRUTAL.
"A MASSACRE OF PUNISHMENT.
"HE LEFT ME FOR LAST.

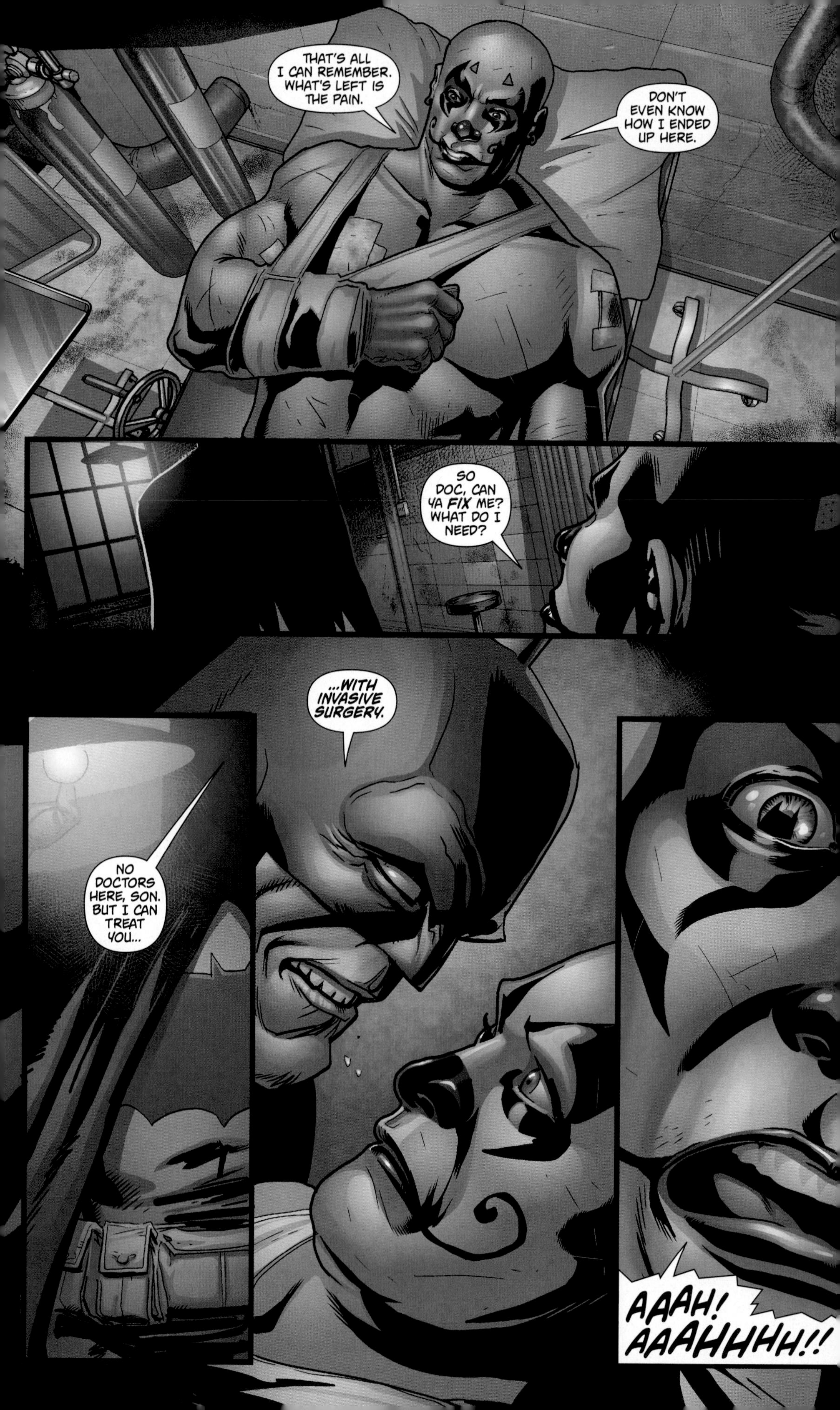
THAT'S ALL I CAN REMEMBER. WHAT'S LEFT IS THE PAIN.
DON'T EVEN KNOW HOW I ENDED UP HERE.
SO DOC, CAN YA FIX ME? WHAT DO I NEED?
NO DOCTORS HERE, SON. BUT I CAN TREAT YOU...
...WITH INVASIVE SURGERY.
AAAH! AAAHHHH!!

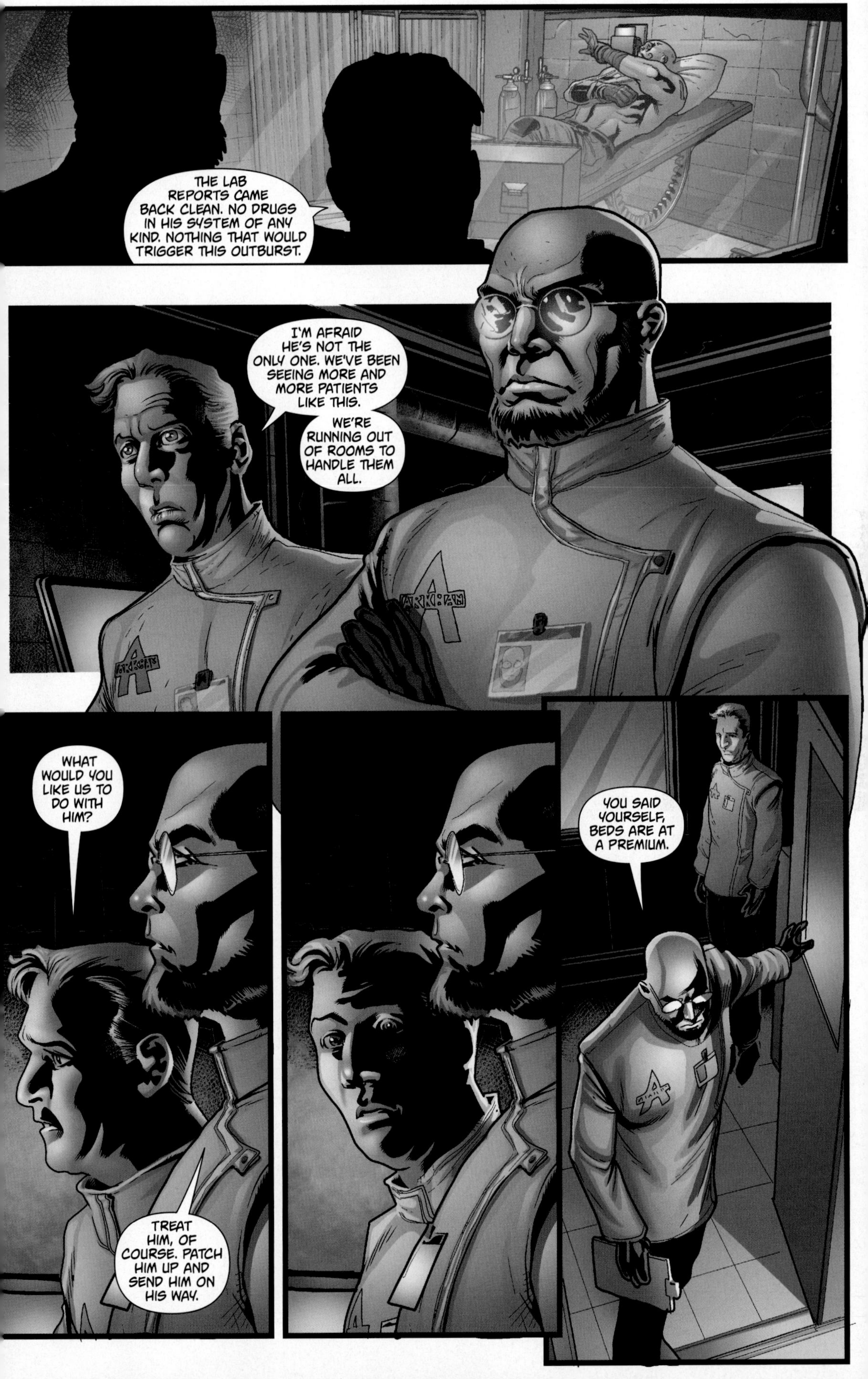
THE LAB REPORTS CAME BACK CLEAN. NO DRUGS IN HIS SYSTEM OF ANY KIND. NOTHING THAT WOULD TRIGGER THIS OUTBURST.
I'M AFRAID HE'S NOT THE ONLY ONE. WE'VE BEEN SEEING MORE AND MORE PATIENTS LIKE THIS.
WE'RE RUNNING OUT OF ROOMS TO HANDLE THEM ALL.
WHAT WOULD YOU LIKE US TO DO WITH HIM?
TREAT HIM, OF COURSE. PATCH HIM UP AND SEND HIM ON HIS WAY.
YOU SAID YOURSELF, BEDS ARE AT A PREMIUM.

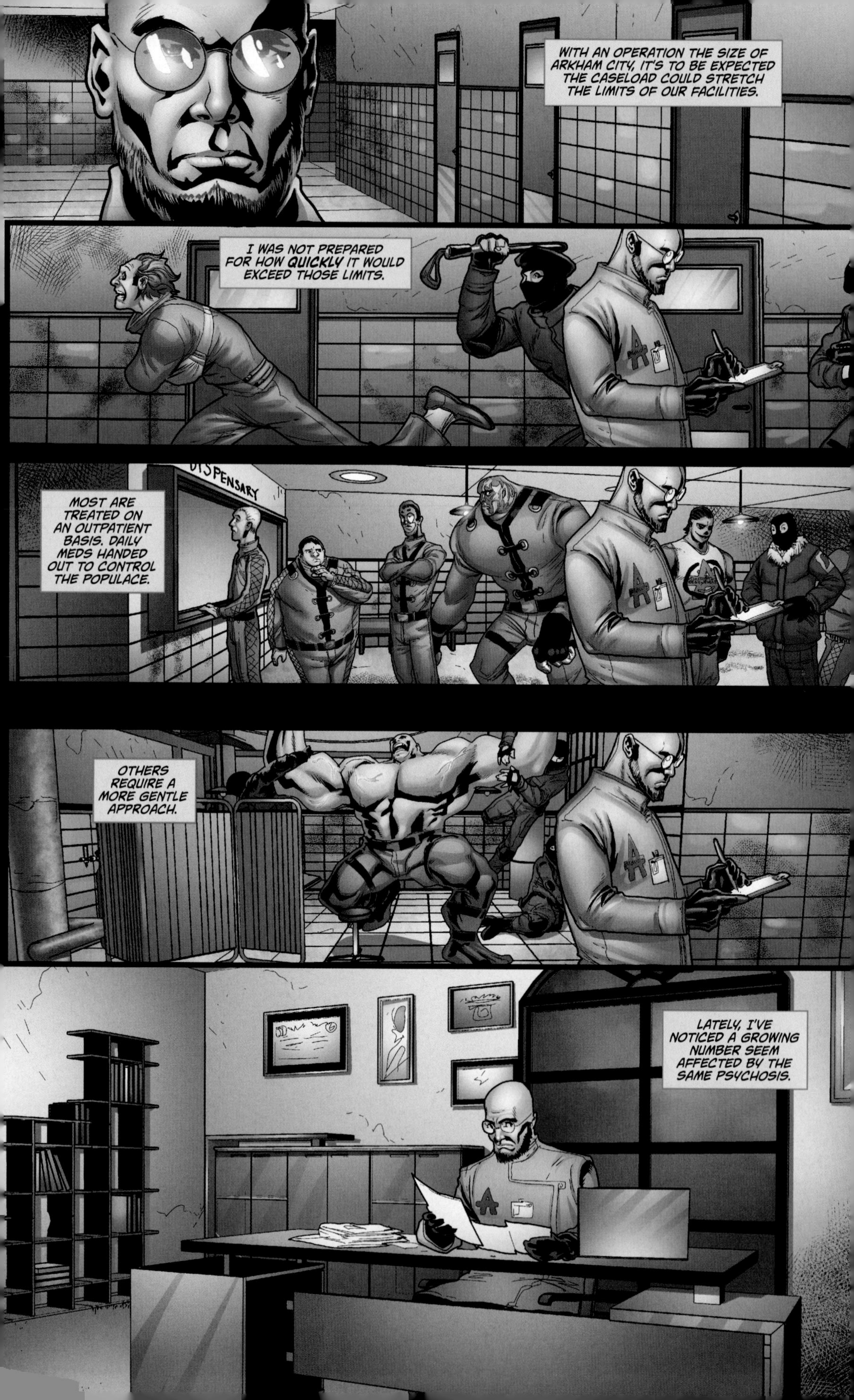
WITH AN OPERATION THE SIZE OF ARKHAM CITY, IT'S TO BE EXPECTED THE CASELOAD COULD STRETCH THE LIMITS OF OUR FACILITIES.
I WAS NOT PREPARED FOR HOW QUICKLY IT WOULD EXCEED THOSE LIMITS.
DISPENSARY
MOST ARE TREATED ON AN OUTPATIENT BASIS. DAILY MEDS HANDED OUT TO CONTROL THE POPULACE.
OTHERS REQUIRE A MORE GENTLE APPROACH.
LATELY, I'VE NOTICED A GROWING NUMBER SEEM AFFECTED BY THE SAME PSYCHOSIS.

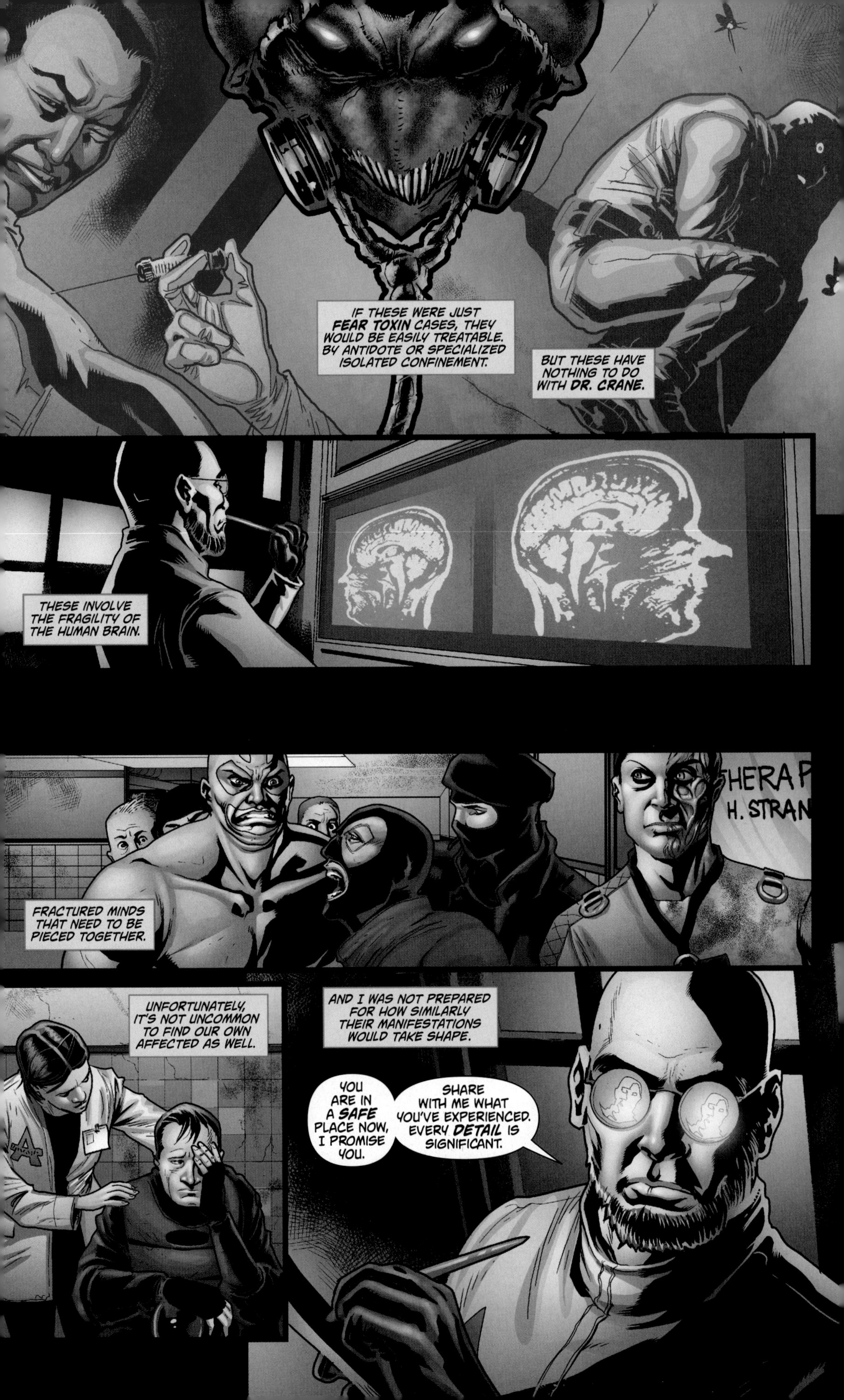
IF THESE WERE JUST FEAR TOXIN CASES, THEY WOULD BE EASILY TREATABLE. BY ANTIDOTE OR SPECIALIZED ISOLATED CONFINEMENT.
BUT THESE HAVE NOTHING TO DO WITH DR. CRANE.
THESE INVOLVE THE FRAGILITY OF THE HUMAN BRAIN.
FRACTURED MINDS THAT NEED TO BE PIECED TOGETHER.
HERA P
H. STRAN
UNFORTUNATELY, IT'S NOT UNCOMMON TO FIND OUR OWN AFFECTED AS WELL.
AND I WAS NOT PREPARED FOR HOW SIMILARLY THEIR MANIFESTATIONS WOULD TAKE SHAPE.
YOU ARE IN A SAFE PLACE NOW, I PROMISE YOU.
SHARE WITH ME WHAT YOU'VE EXPERIENCED. EVERY DETAIL IS SIGNIFICANT.

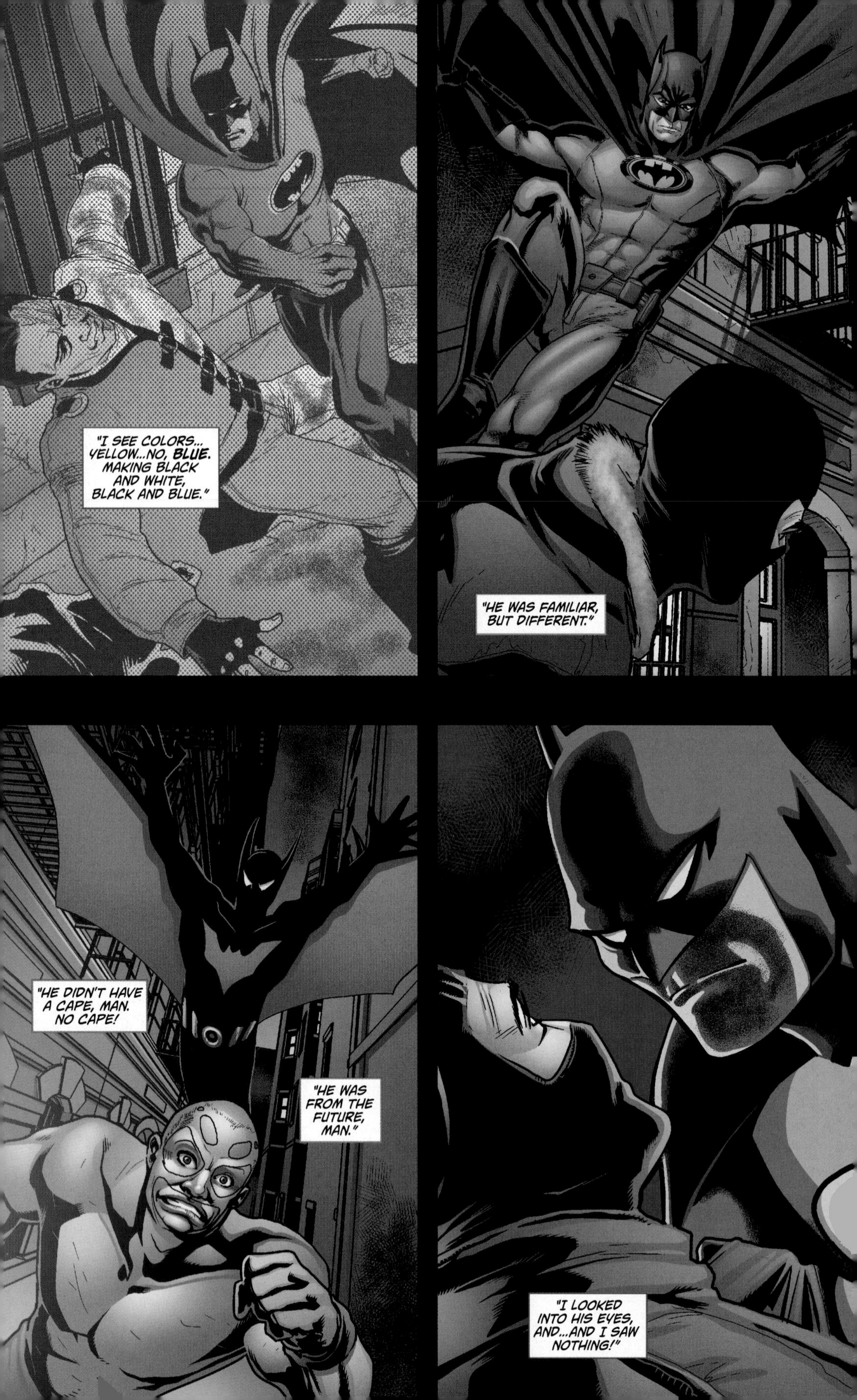
"I SEE COLORS... YELLOW...NO, BLUE. MAKING BLACK AND WHITE, BLACK AND BLUE."
"HE WAS FAMILIAR, BUT DIFFERENT."
"HE DIDN'T HAVE A CAPE, MAN. NO CAPE!
"HE WAS FROM THE FUTURE, MAN."
"I LOOKED INTO HIS EYES, AND...AND I SAW NOTHING!"

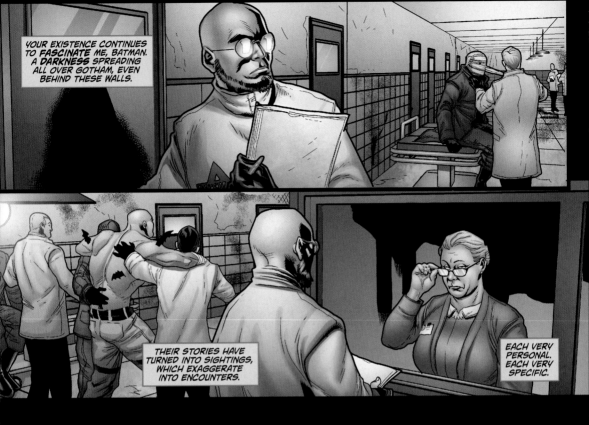

YOUR EXISTENCE CONTINUES TO FASCINATE ME, BATMAN. A DARKNESS SPREADING ALL OVER GOTHAM, EVEN BEHIND THESE WALLS.

THEIR STORIES HAVE TURNED INTO SIGHTINGS, WHICH EXAGGERATE INTO ENCOUNTERS.

EACH VERY PERSONAL. EACH VERY SPECIFIC.

AND ALL OF THEM BAT-RELATED.

DNGG

WHUPWHUPWHUP

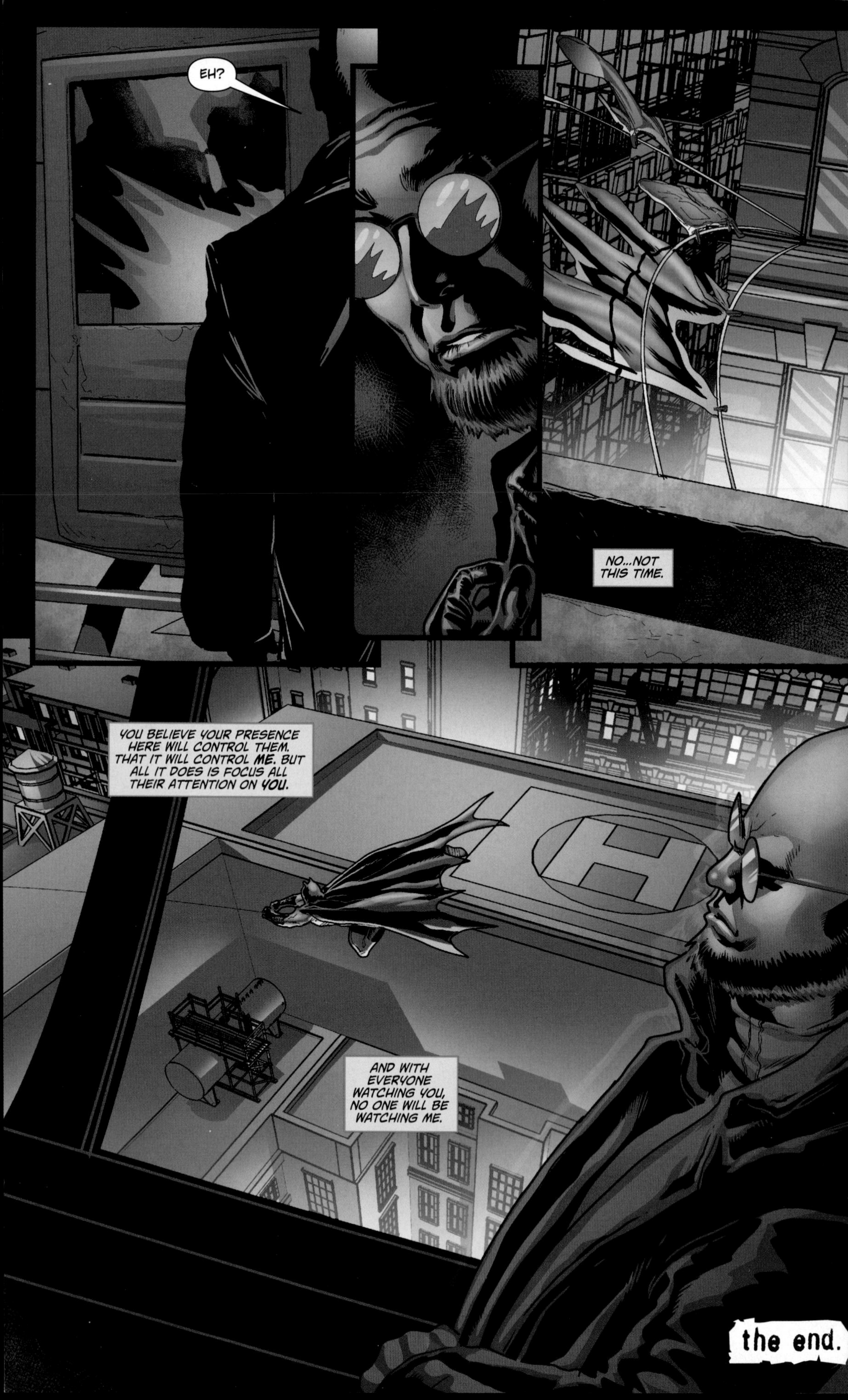
EH?
NO...NOT THIS TIME.
YOU BELIEVE YOUR PRESENCE HERE WILL CONTROL THEM. THAT IT WILL CONTROL ME. BUT ALL IT DOES IS FOCUS ALL THEIR ATTENTION ON YOU.
AND WITH EVERYONE WATCHING YOU, NO ONE WILL BE WATCHING ME.
the end.

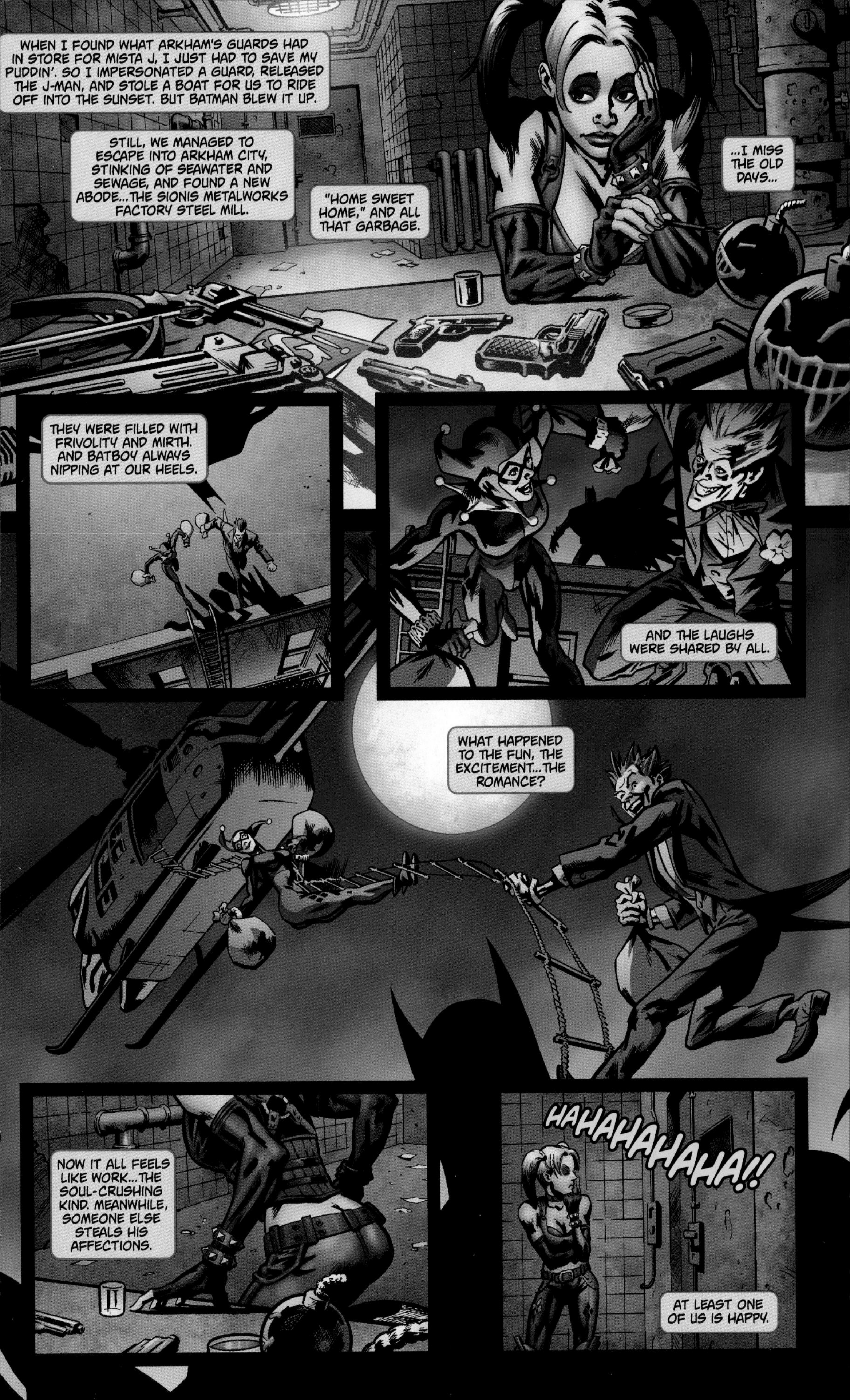
WHEN I FOUND WHAT ARKHAM'S GUARDS HAD IN STORE FOR MISTA J, I JUST HAD TO SAVE MY PUDDIN'. SO I IMPERSONATED A GUARD, RELEASED THE J-MAN, AND STOLE A BOAT FOR US TO RIDE OFF INTO THE SUNSET. BUT BATMAN BLEW IT UP.
STILL, WE MANAGED TO ESCAPE INTO ARKHAM CITY, STINKING OF SEAWATER AND SEWAGE, AND FOUND A NEW ABODE...THE SIONIS METALWORKS FACTORY STEEL MILL.
"HOME SWEET HOME," AND ALL THAT GARBAGE.
...I MISS THE OLD DAYS...
THEY WERE FILLED WITH FRIVOLITY AND MIRTH. AND BATBOY ALWAYS NIPPING AT OUR HEELS.
AND THE LAUGHS WERE SHARED BY ALL.
WHAT HAPPENED TO THE FUN, THE EXCITEMENT...THE ROMANCE?
NOW IT ALL FEELS LIKE WORK...THE SOUL-CRUSHING KIND. MEANWHILE, SOMEONE ELSE STEALS HIS AFFECTIONS.
HAHAHAHAHAHA!!
AT LEAST ONE OF US IS HAPPY.

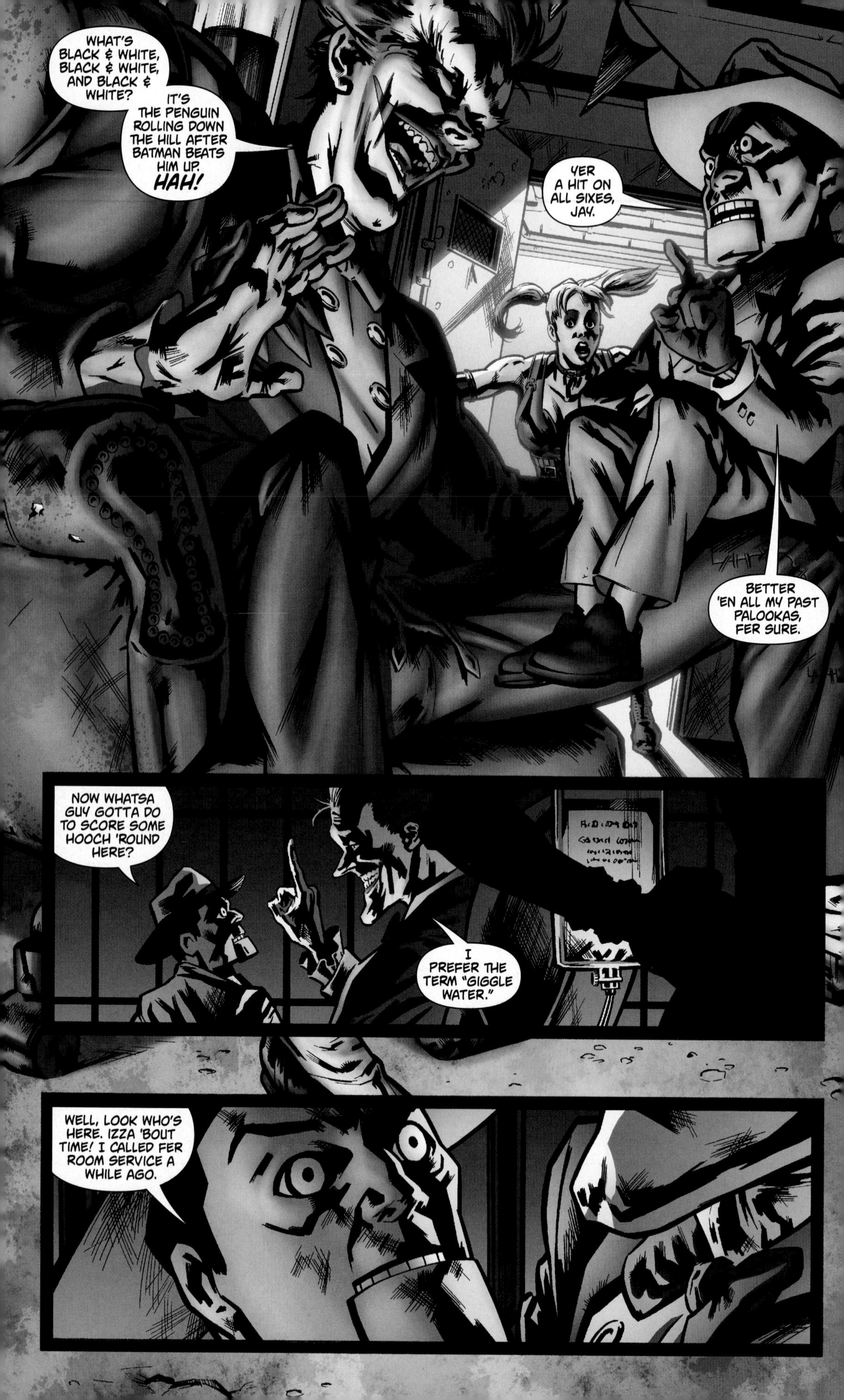
WHAT'S BLACK & WHITE, BLACK & WHITE, AND BLACK & WHITE?
IT'S THE PENGUIN ROLLING DOWN THE HILL AFTER BATMAN BEATS HIM UP. HAH!
YER A HIT ON ALL SIXES, JAY.
BETTER 'EN ALL MY PAST PALOOKAS, FER SURE.
NOW WHATSA GUY GOTTA DO TO SCORE SOME HOOCH 'ROUND HERE?
I PREFER THE TERM "GIGGLE WATER."
WELL, LOOK WHO'S HERE. IZZA 'BOUT TIME! I CALLED FER ROOM SERVICE A WHILE AGO.

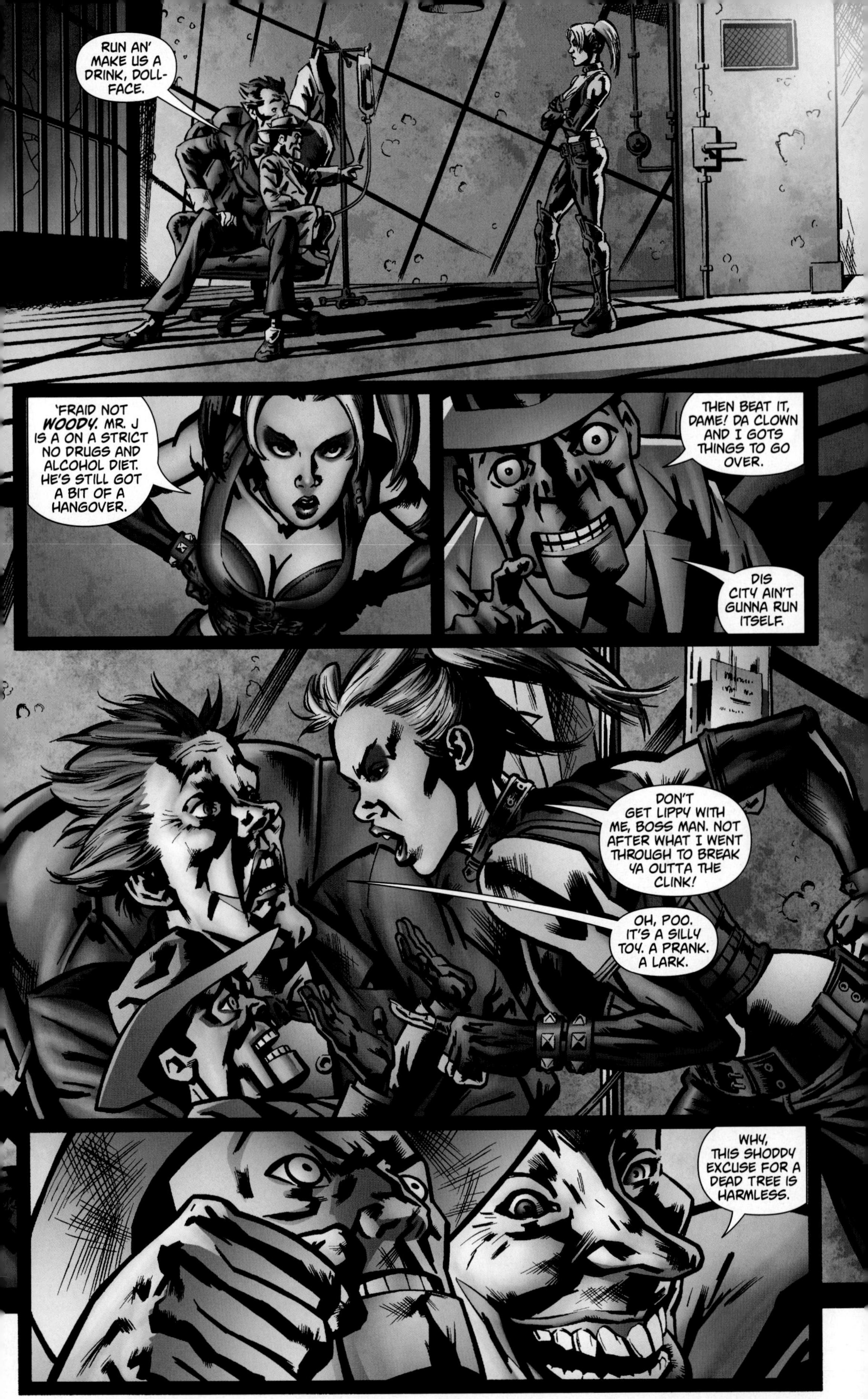
RUN AN' MAKE US A DRINK, DOLL-FACE.
'FRAID NOT WOODY. MR. J IS A ON A STRICT NO DRUGS AND ALCOHOL DIET. HE'S STILL GOT A BIT OF A HANGOVER.
THEN BEAT IT, DAME! DA CLOWN AND I GOTS THINGS TO GO OVER.
DIS CITY AIN'T GUNNA RUN ITSELF.
DON'T GET LIPPY WITH ME, BOSS MAN. NOT AFTER WHAT I WENT THROUGH TO BREAK YA OUTTA THE CLINK!
OH, POO. IT'S A SILLY TOY. A PRANK. A LARK.
WHY, THIS SHODDY EXCUSE FOR A DEAD TREE IS HARMLESS.

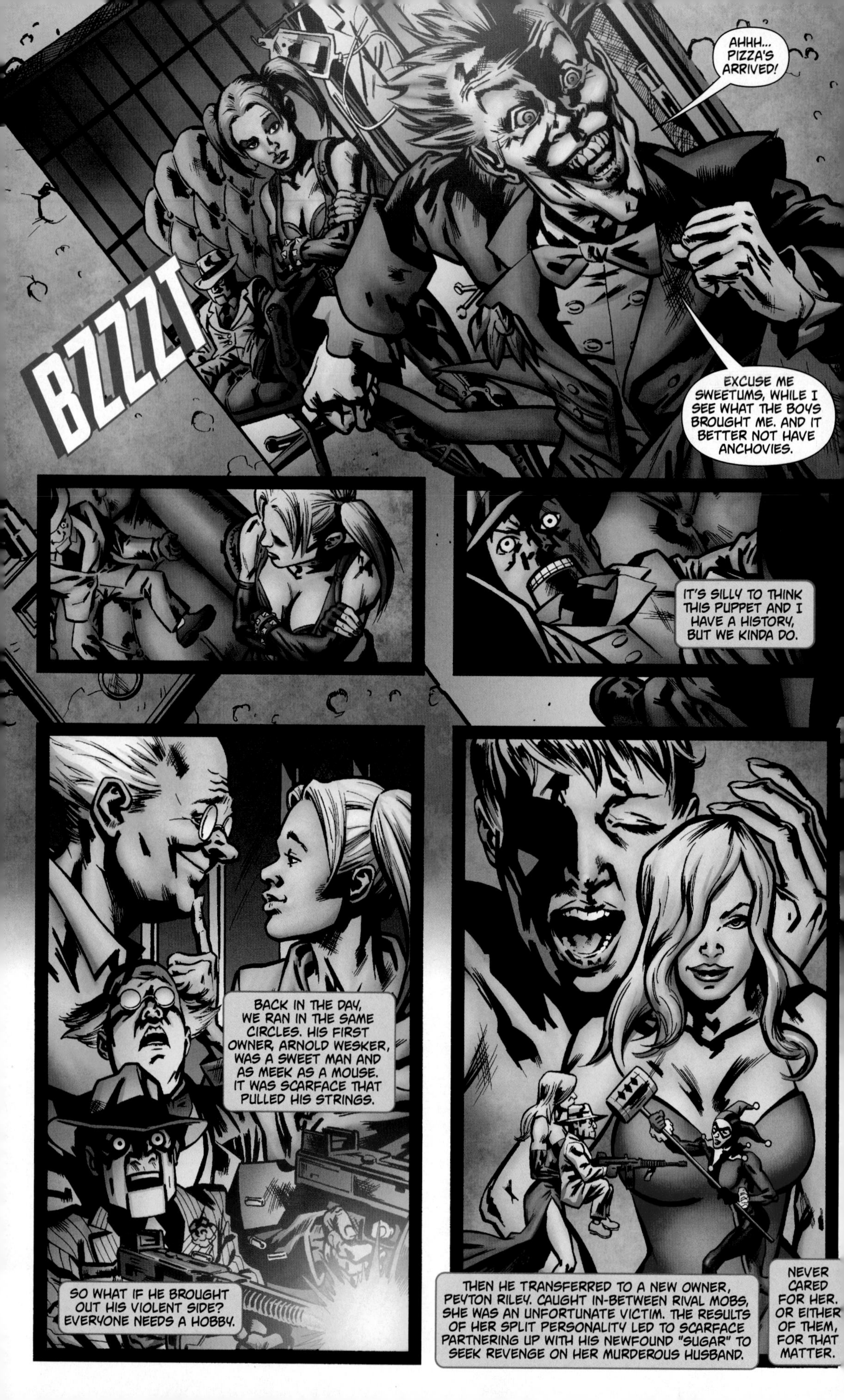
AHHH... PIZZA'S ARRIVED!
BZZZZT
EXCUSE ME SWEETUMS, WHILE I SEE WHAT THE BOYS BROUGHT ME. AND IT BETTER NOT HAVE ANCHOVIES.
IT'S SILLY TO THINK THIS PUPPET AND I HAVE A HISTORY, BUT WE KINDA DO.
BACK IN THE DAY, WE RAN IN THE SAME CIRCLES. HIS FIRST OWNER, ARNOLD WESKER, WAS A SWEET MAN AND AS MEEK AS A MOUSE. IT WAS SCARFACE THAT PULLED HIS STRINGS.
SO WHAT IF HE BROUGHT OUT HIS VIOLENT SIDE? EVERYONE NEEDS A HOBBY.
THEN HE TRANSFERRED TO A NEW OWNER, PEYTON RILEY. CAUGHT IN-BETWEEN RIVAL MOBS, SHE WAS AN UNFORTUNATE VICTIM. THE RESULTS OF HER SPLIT PERSONALITY LED TO SCARFACE PARTNERING UP WITH HIS NEWFOUND "SUGAR" TO SEEK REVENGE ON HER MURDEROUS HUSBAND.
NEVER CARED FOR HER. OR EITHER OF THEM, FOR THAT MATTER.

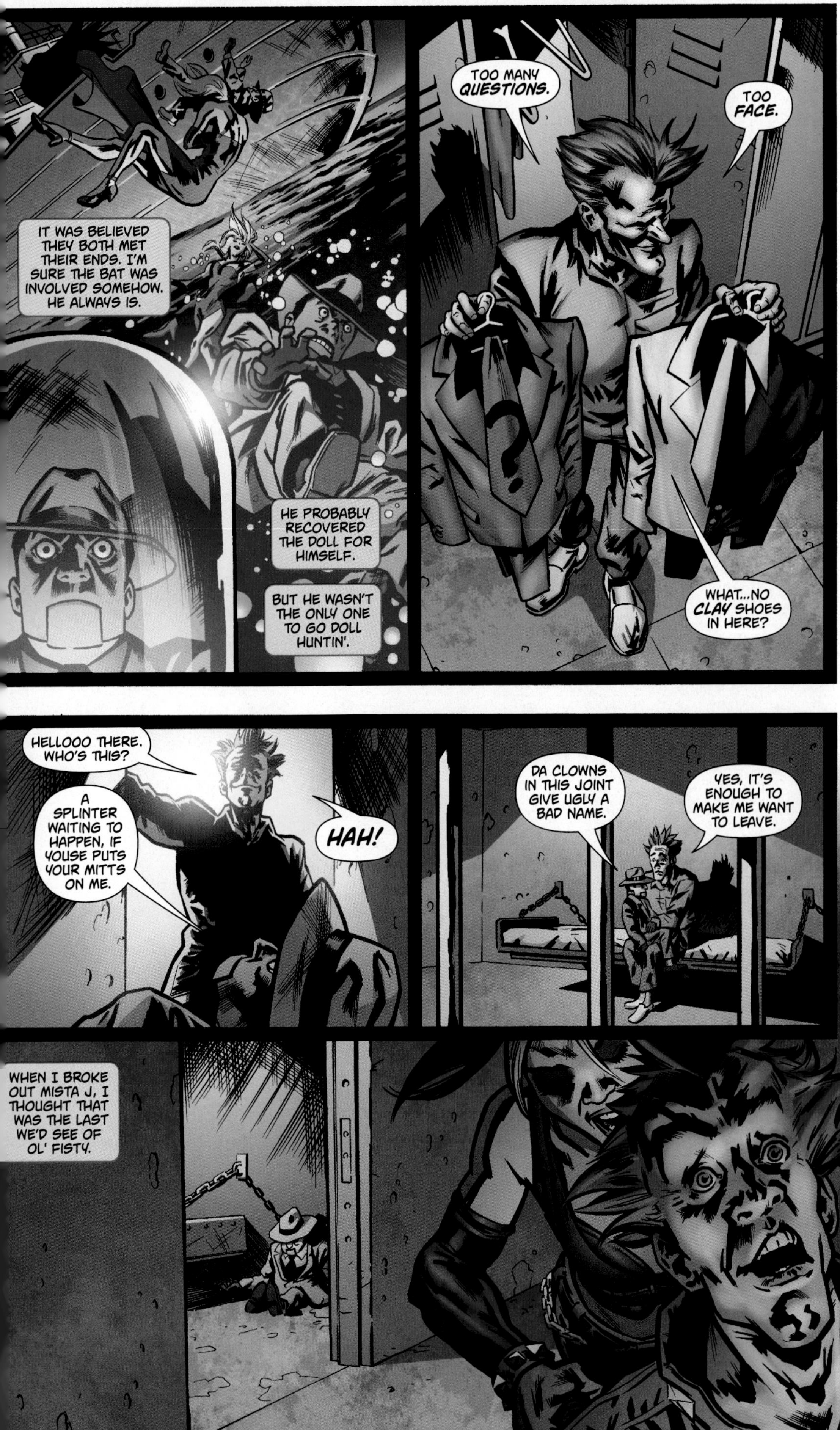
IT WAS BELIEVED THEY BOTH MET THEIR ENDS. I'M SURE THE BAT WAS INVOLVED SOMEHOW. HE ALWAYS IS.
HE PROBABLY RECOVERED THE DOLL FOR HIMSELF.
BUT HE WASN'T THE ONLY ONE TO GO DOLL HUNTIN'.
TOO MANY QUESTIONS.
TOO FACE.
WHAT...NO CLAY SHOES IN HERE?
HELLOOO THERE. WHO'S THIS?
A SPLINTER WAITING TO HAPPEN, IF YOUSE PUTS YOUR MITTS ON ME.
HAH!
DA CLOWNS IN THIS JOINT GIVE UGLY A BAD NAME.
YES, IT'S ENOUGH TO MAKE ME WANT TO LEAVE.
WHEN I BROKE OUT MISTA J, I THOUGHT THAT WAS THE LAST WE'D SEE OF OL' FISTY.

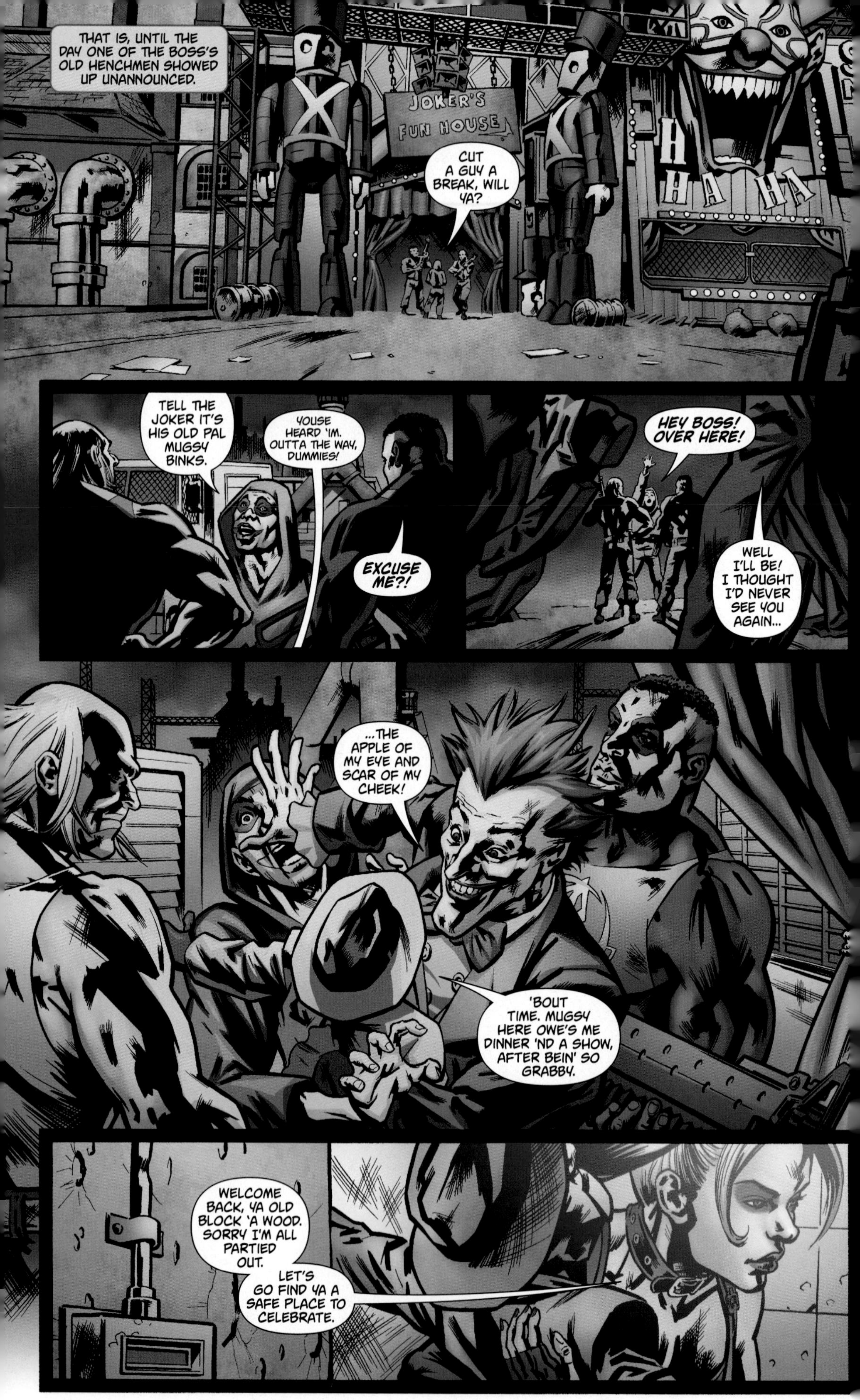
THAT IS, UNTIL THE DAY ONE OF THE BOSS'S OLD HENCHMEN SHOWED UP UNANNOUNCED.
JOKER'S FUN HOUSE
CUT A GUY A BREAK, WILL YA?
HA HA HA
TELL THE JOKER IT'S HIS OLD PAL MUGSY BINKS.
YOUSE HEARD 'IM. OUTTA THE WAY, DUMMIES!
EXCUSE ME?!
HEY BOSS! OVER HERE!
WELL I'LL BE! I THOUGHT I'D NEVER SEE YOU AGAIN...
...THE APPLE OF MY EYE AND SCAR OF MY CHEEK!
'BOUT TIME. MUGSY HERE OWE'S ME DINNER 'ND A SHOW, AFTER BEIN' SO GRABBY.
WELCOME BACK, YA OLD BLOCK 'A WOOD. SORRY I'M ALL PARTIED OUT.
LET'S GO FIND YA A SAFE PLACE TO CELEBRATE.

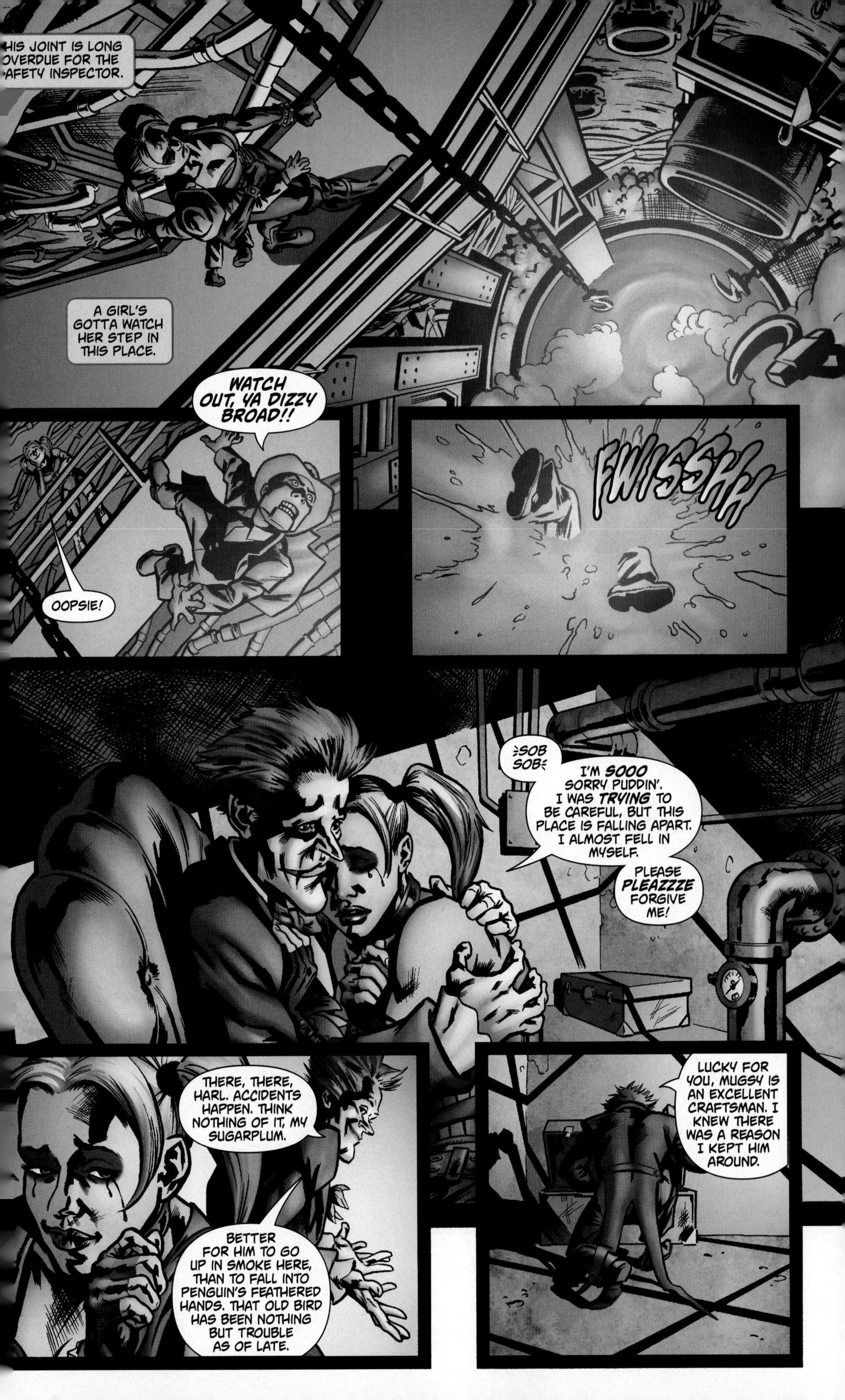
HIS JOINT IS LONG OVERDUE FOR THE AFETY INSPECTOR.
A GIRL'S GOTTA WATCH HER STEP IN THIS PLACE.
WATCH OUT, YA DIZZY BROAD!!
OOPSIE!
FWISSHH
SOB SOB
I'M SOOO SORRY PUDDIN'. I WAS TRYING TO BE CAREFUL, BUT THIS PLACE IS FALLING APART. I ALMOST FELL IN MYSELF.
PLEASE PLEAZZZE FORGIVE ME!
THERE, THERE, HARL. ACCIDENTS HAPPEN. THINK NOTHING OF IT, MY SUGARPLUM.
BETTER FOR HIM TO GO UP IN SMOKE HERE, THAN TO FALL INTO PENGUIN'S FEATHERED HANDS. THAT OLD BIRD HAS BEEN NOTHING BUT TROUBLE AS OF LATE.
LUCKY FOR YOU, MUGSY IS AN EXCELLENT CRAFTSMAN. I KNEW THERE WAS A REASON I KEPT HIM AROUND.

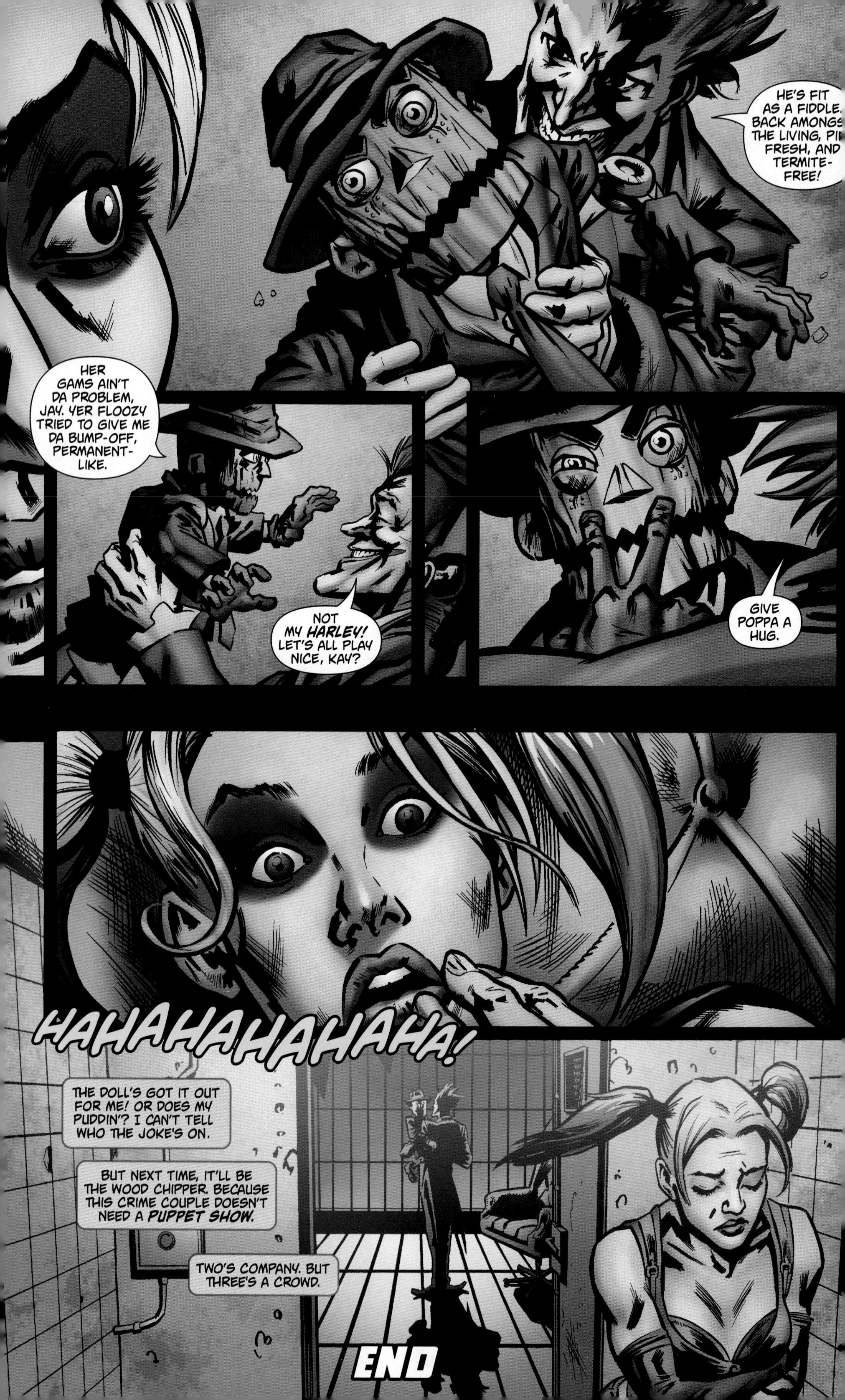
HE'S FIT AS A FIDDLE, BACK AMONGST THE LIVING, PINK FRESH, AND TERMITE-FREE!
HER GAMS AIN'T DA PROBLEM, JAY. YER FLOOZY TRIED TO GIVE ME DA BUMP-OFF, PERMANENT-LIKE.
NOT MY HARLEY! LET'S ALL PLAY NICE, KAY?
GIVE POPPA A HUG.
HAHAHAHAHAHAHA!
THE DOLL'S GOT IT OUT FOR ME! OR DOES MY PUDDIN'? I CAN'T TELL WHO THE JOKE'S ON.
BUT NEXT TIME, IT'LL BE THE WOOD CHIPPER. BECAUSE THIS CRIME COUPLE DOESN'T NEED A PUPPET SHOW.
TWO'S COMPANY. BUT THREE'S A CROWD.
END

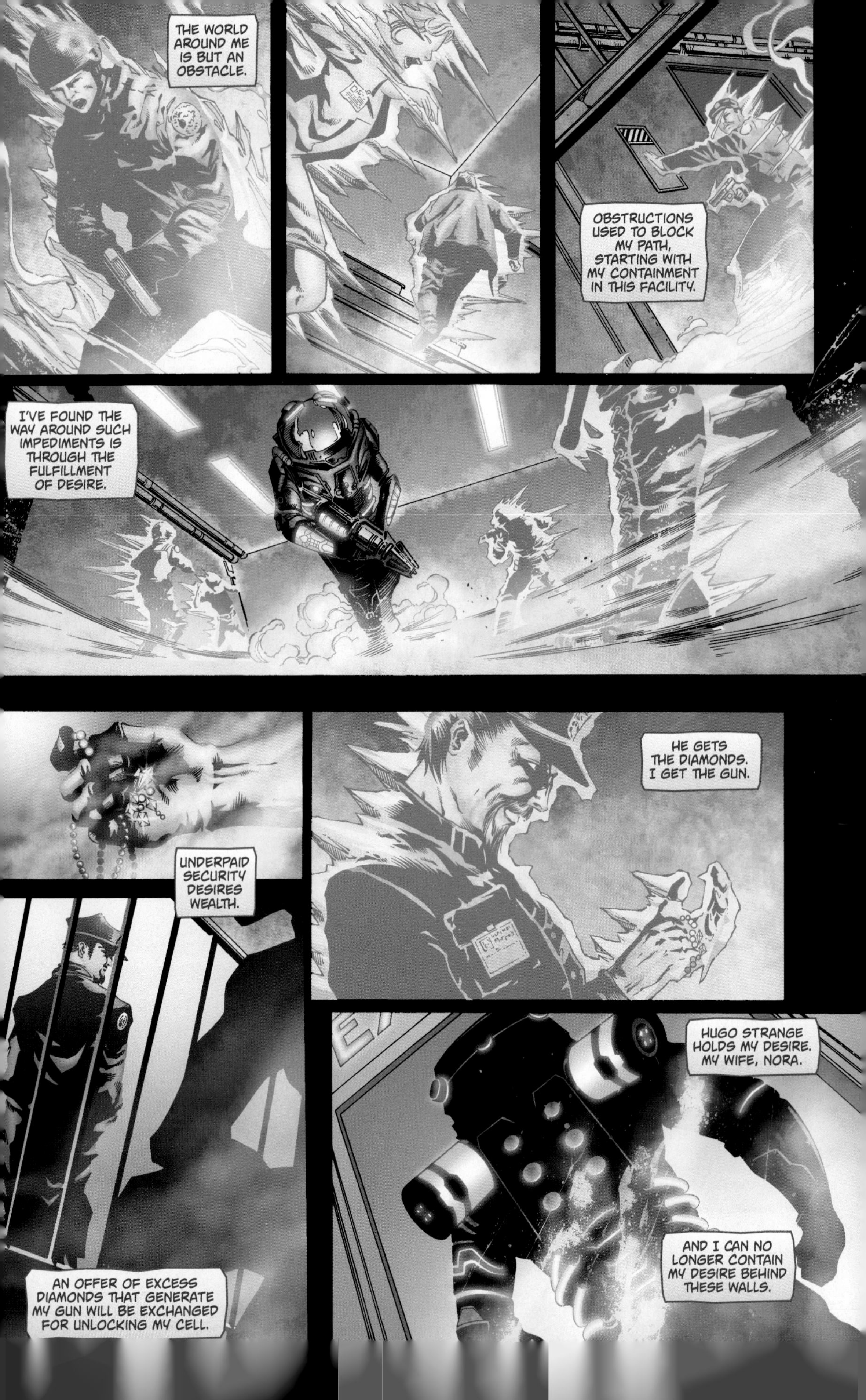
THE WORLD AROUND ME IS BUT AN OBSTACLE.
OBSTRUCTIONS USED TO BLOCK MY PATH, STARTING WITH MY CONTAINMENT IN THIS FACILITY.
I'VE FOUND THE WAY AROUND SUCH IMPEDIMENTS IS THROUGH THE FULFILLMENT OF DESIRE.
UNDERPAID SECURITY DESIRES WEALTH.
AN OFFER OF EXCESS DIAMONDS THAT GENERATE MY GUN WILL BE EXCHANGED FOR UNLOCKING MY CELL.
HE GETS THE DIAMONDS. I GET THE GUN.
HUGO STRANGE HOLDS MY DESIRE. MY WIFE, NORA.
AND I CAN NO LONGER CONTAIN MY DESIRE BEHIND THESE WALLS.

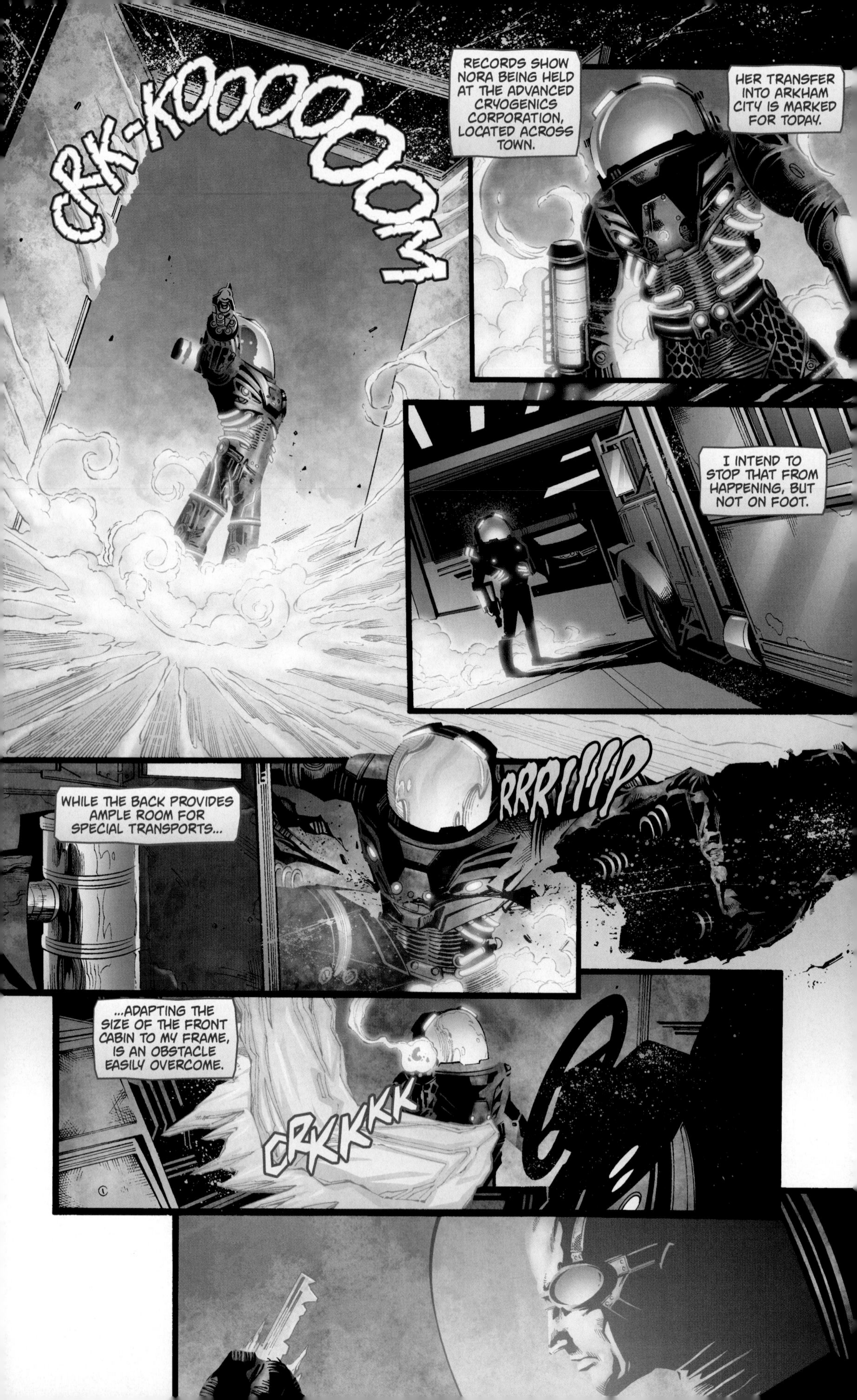
CRK-KOOOOOOOM
RECORDS SHOW NORA BEING HELD AT THE ADVANCED CRYOGENICS CORPORATION, LOCATED ACROSS TOWN.
HER TRANSFER INTO ARKHAM CITY IS MARKED FOR TODAY.
I INTEND TO STOP THAT FROM HAPPENING, BUT NOT ON FOOT.
WHILE THE BACK PROVIDES AMPLE ROOM FOR SPECIAL TRANSPORTS...
RRRIIIIP
...ADAPTING THE SIZE OF THE FRONT CABIN TO MY FRAME, IS AN OBSTACLE EASILY OVERCOME.
CRKKKK

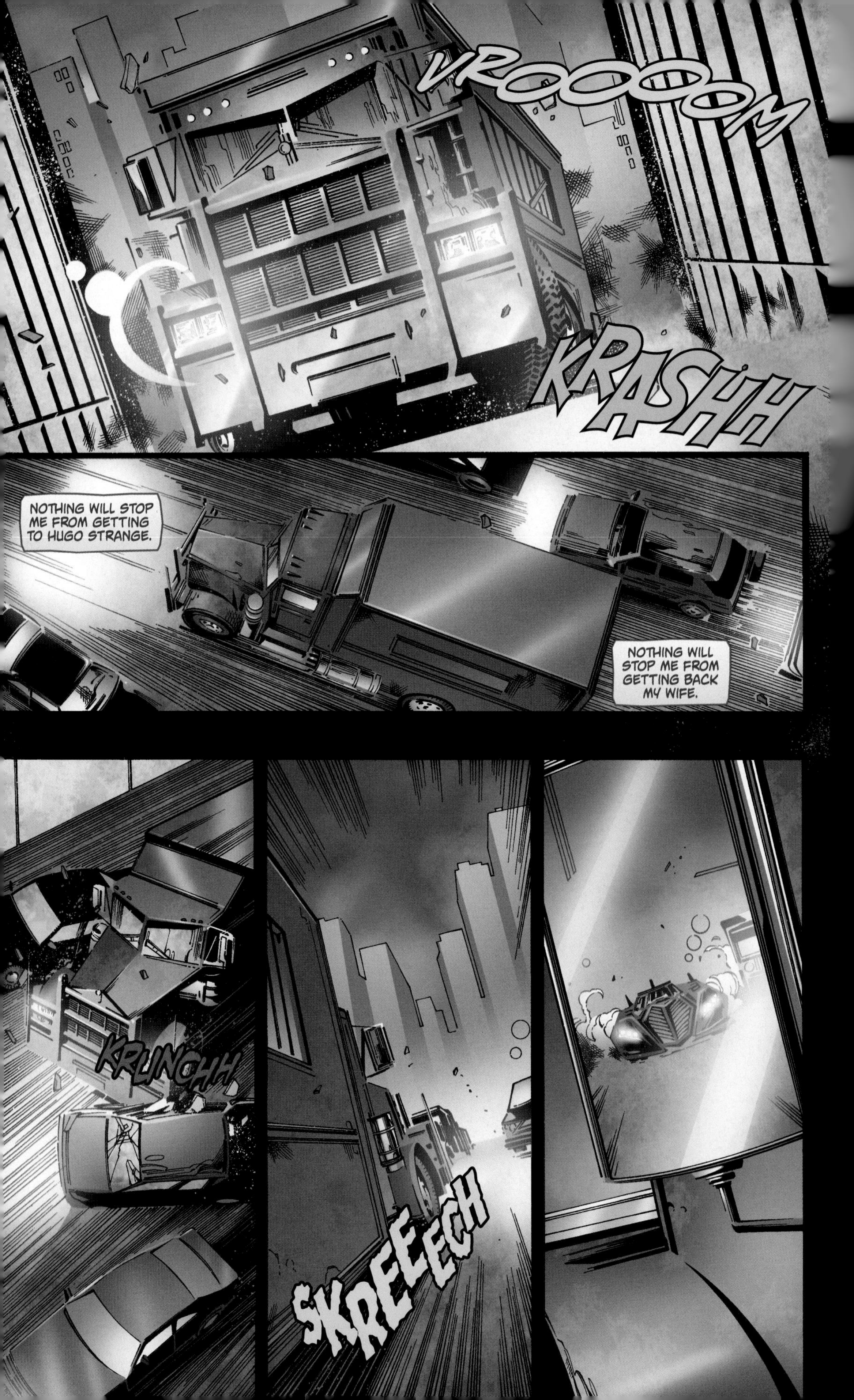
VROOOOOM
KRASHH
NOTHING WILL STOP ME FROM GETTING TO HUGO STRANGE.
NOTHING WILL STOP ME FROM GETTING BACK MY WIFE.
KRUNCHH
SKREEECH

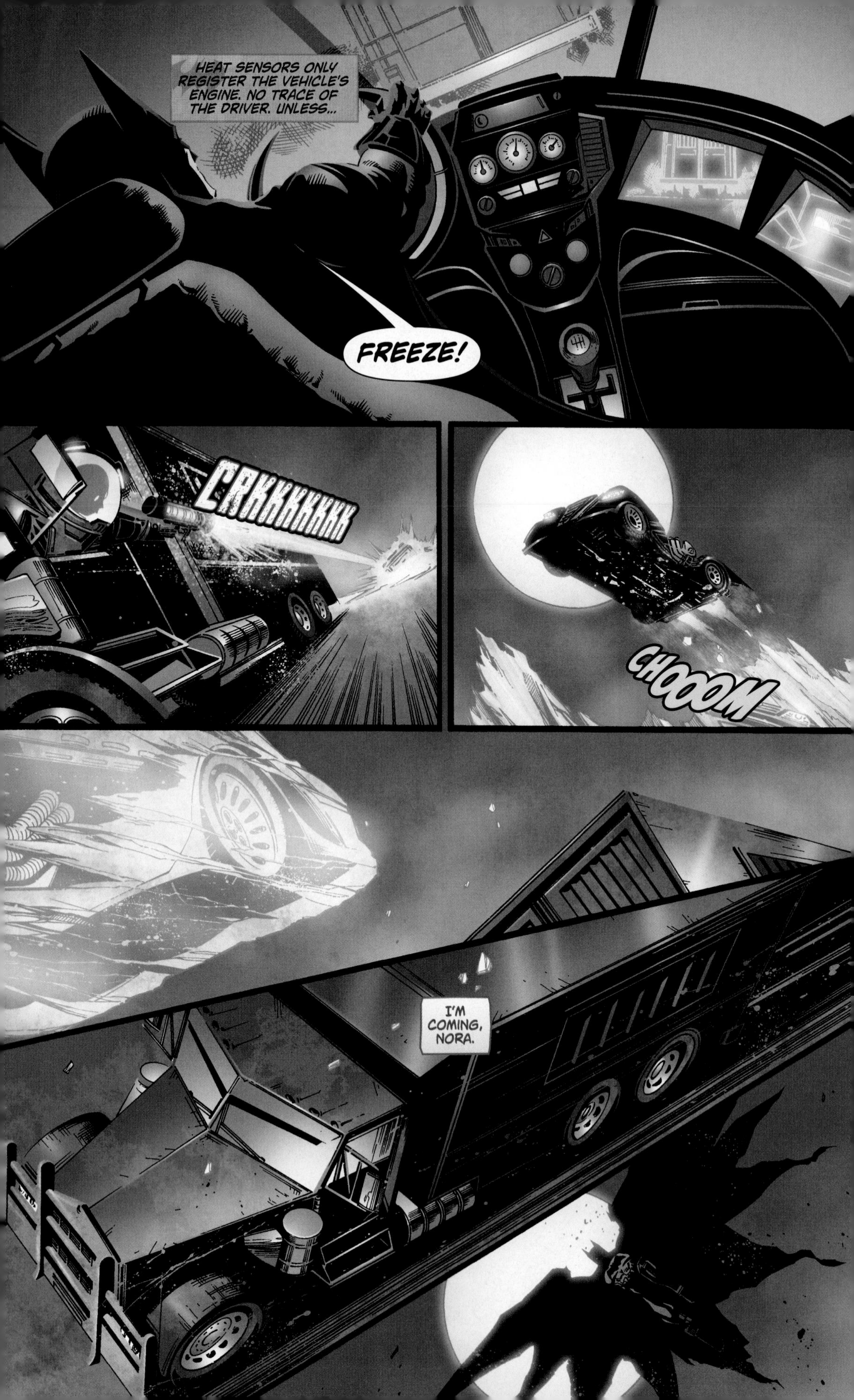
HEAT SENSORS ONLY REGISTER THE VEHICLE'S ENGINE. NO TRACE OF THE DRIVER. UNLESS...
FREEZE!
CRKKKKKKK
CHOOOM
I'M COMING, NORA.

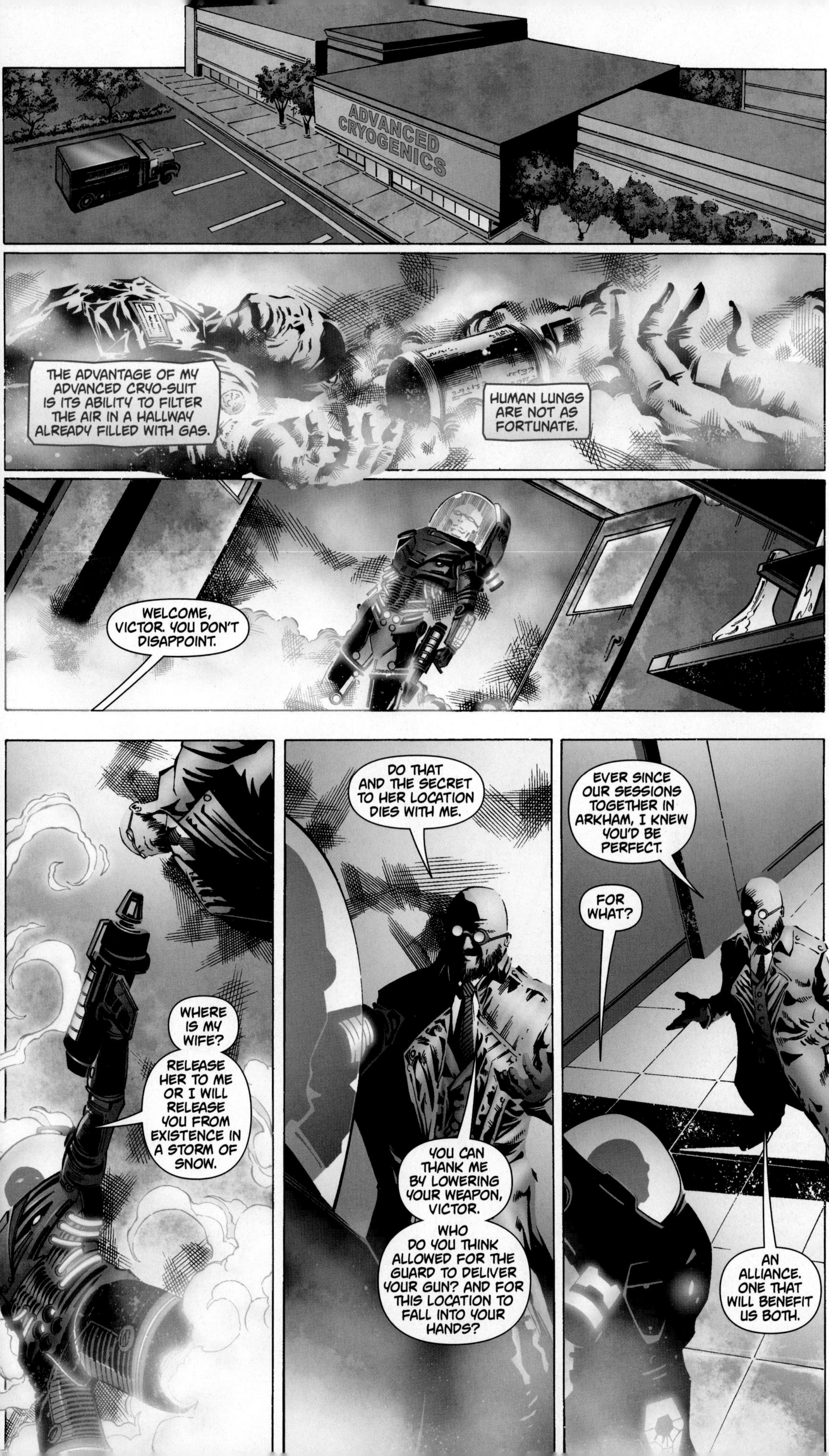
ADVANCED CRYOGENICS
THE ADVANTAGE OF MY ADVANCED CRYO-SUIT IS ITS ABILITY TO FILTER THE AIR IN A HALLWAY ALREADY FILLED WITH GAS.
HUMAN LUNGS ARE NOT AS FORTUNATE.
WELCOME, VICTOR. YOU DON'T DISAPPOINT.
WHERE IS MY WIFE?
RELEASE HER TO ME OR I WILL RELEASE YOU FROM EXISTENCE IN A STORM OF SNOW.
DO THAT AND THE SECRET TO HER LOCATION DIES WITH ME.
YOU CAN THANK ME BY LOWERING YOUR WEAPON, VICTOR.
WHO DO YOU THINK ALLOWED FOR THE GUARD TO DELIVER YOUR GUN? AND FOR THIS LOCATION TO FALL INTO YOUR HANDS?
EVER SINCE OUR SESSIONS TOGETHER IN ARKHAM, I KNEW YOU'D BE PERFECT.
FOR WHAT?
AN ALLIANCE. ONE THAT WILL BENEFIT US BOTH.

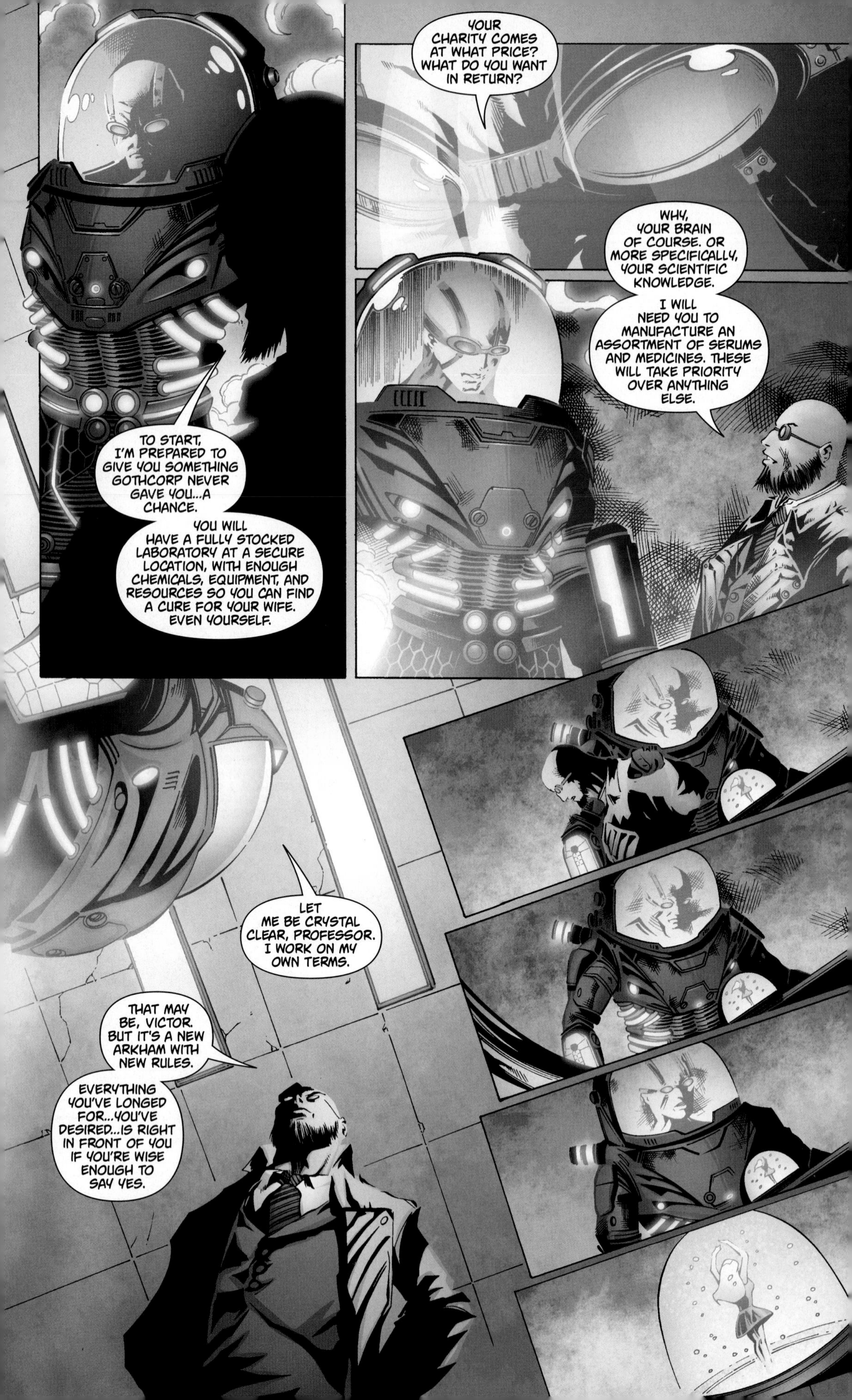
TO START, I'M PREPARED TO GIVE YOU SOMETHING GOTHCORP NEVER GAVE YOU...A CHANCE.
YOU WILL HAVE A FULLY STOCKED LABORATORY AT A SECURE LOCATION, WITH ENOUGH CHEMICALS, EQUIPMENT, AND RESOURCES SO YOU CAN FIND A CURE FOR YOUR WIFE. EVEN YOURSELF.
YOUR CHARITY COMES AT WHAT PRICE? WHAT DO YOU WANT IN RETURN?
WHY, YOUR BRAIN OF COURSE. OR MORE SPECIFICALLY, YOUR SCIENTIFIC KNOWLEDGE.
I WILL NEED YOU TO MANUFACTURE AN ASSORTMENT OF SERUMS AND MEDICINES. THESE WILL TAKE PRIORITY OVER ANYTHING ELSE.
LET ME BE CRYSTAL CLEAR, PROFESSOR. I WORK ON MY OWN TERMS.
THAT MAY BE, VICTOR. BUT IT'S A NEW ARKHAM WITH NEW RULES.
EVERYTHING YOU'VE LONGED FOR...YOU'VE DESIRED...IS RIGHT IN FRONT OF YOU IF YOU'RE WISE ENOUGH TO SAY YES.

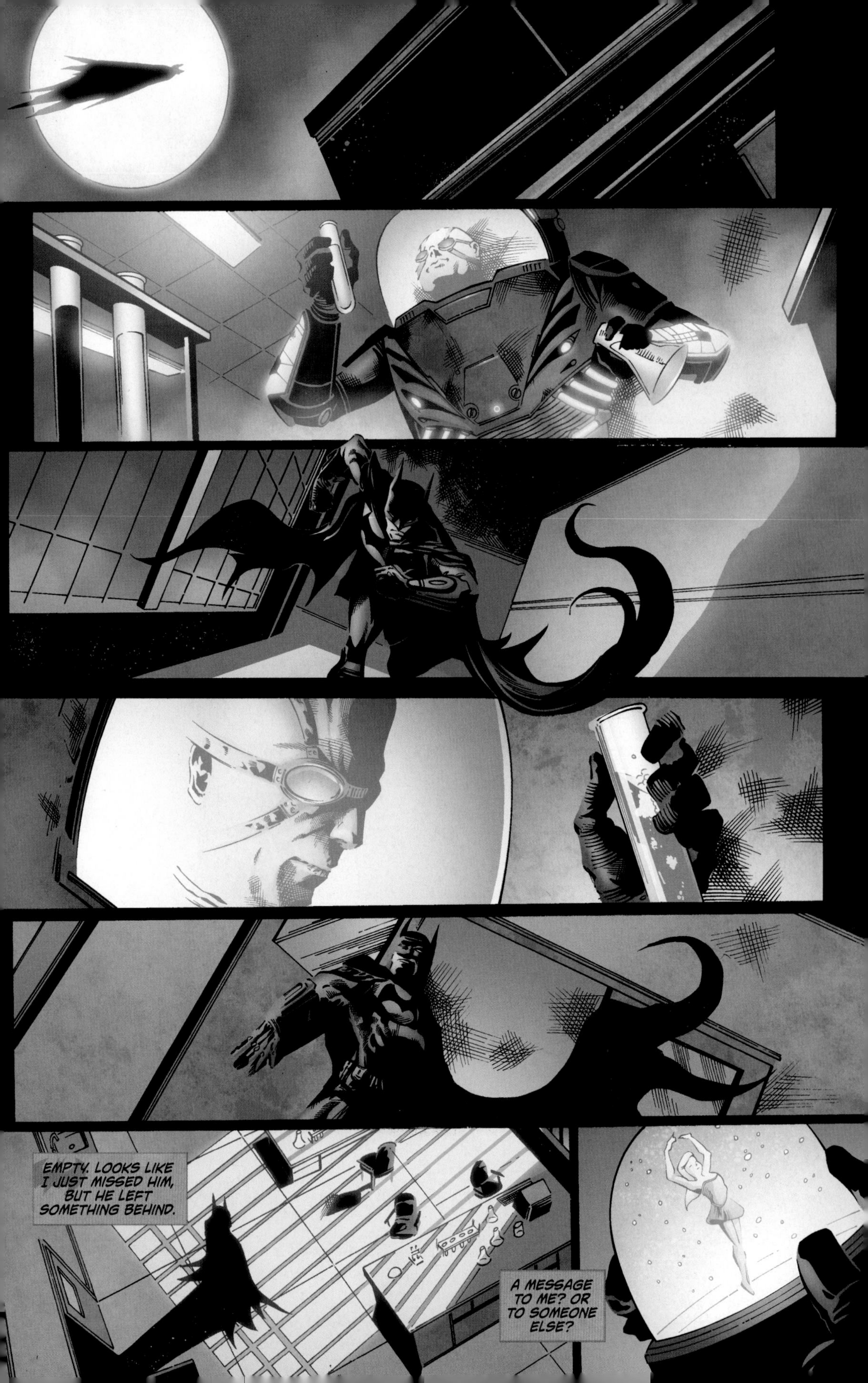
EMPTY. LOOKS LIKE I JUST MISSED HIM, BUT HE LEFT SOMETHING BEHIND.
A MESSAGE TO ME? OR TO SOMEONE ELSE?

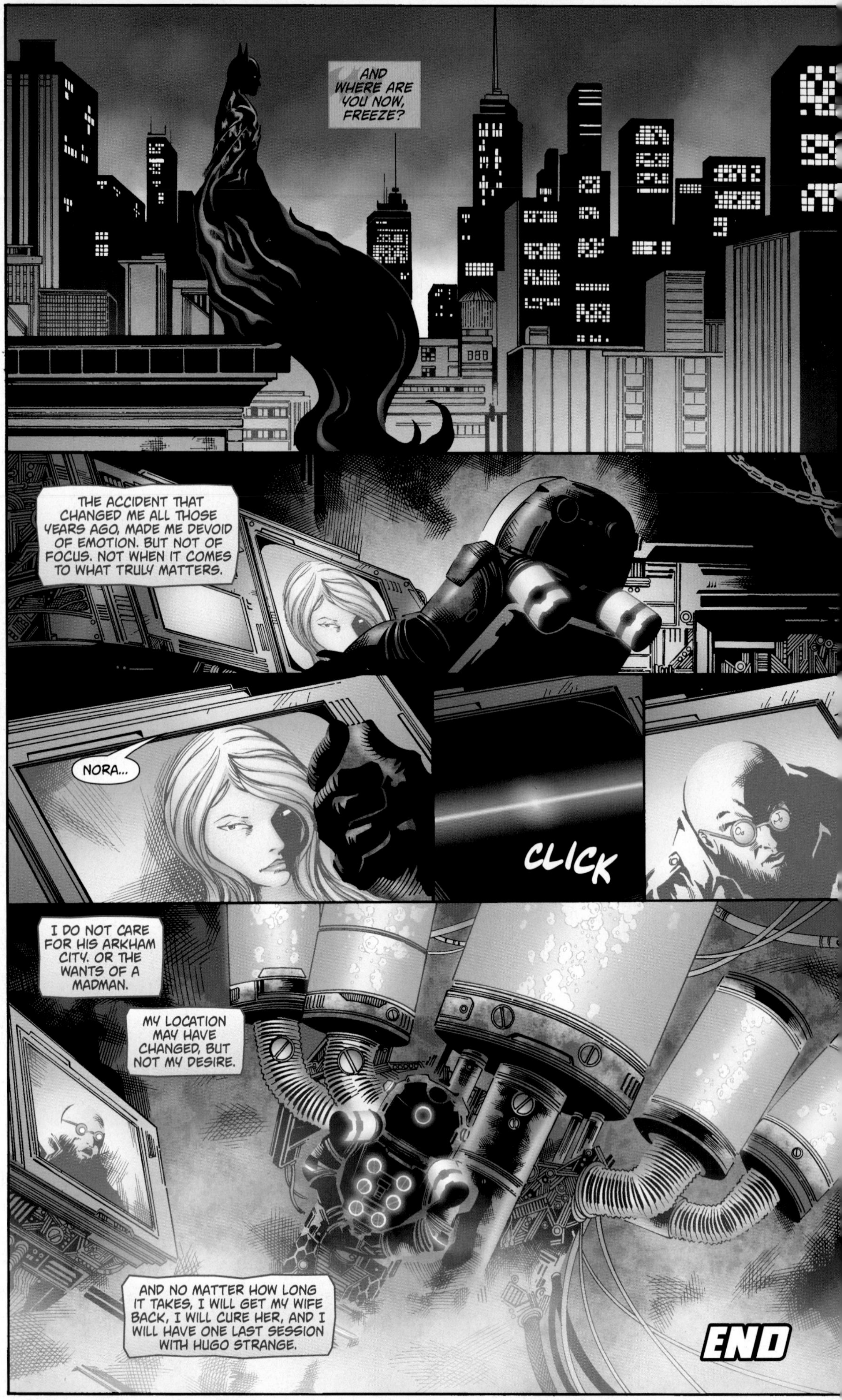
AND WHERE ARE YOU NOW, FREEZE?
THE ACCIDENT THAT CHANGED ME ALL THOSE YEARS AGO, MADE ME DEVOID OF EMOTION. BUT NOT OF FOCUS. NOT WHEN IT COMES TO WHAT TRULY MATTERS.
NORA...
CLICK
I DO NOT CARE FOR HIS ARKHAM CITY. OR THE WANTS OF A MADMAN.
MY LOCATION MAY HAVE CHANGED, BUT NOT MY DESIRE.
AND NO MATTER HOW LONG IT TAKES, I WILL GET MY WIFE BACK, I WILL CURE HER, AND I WILL HAVE ONE LAST SESSION WITH HUGO STRANGE.
END

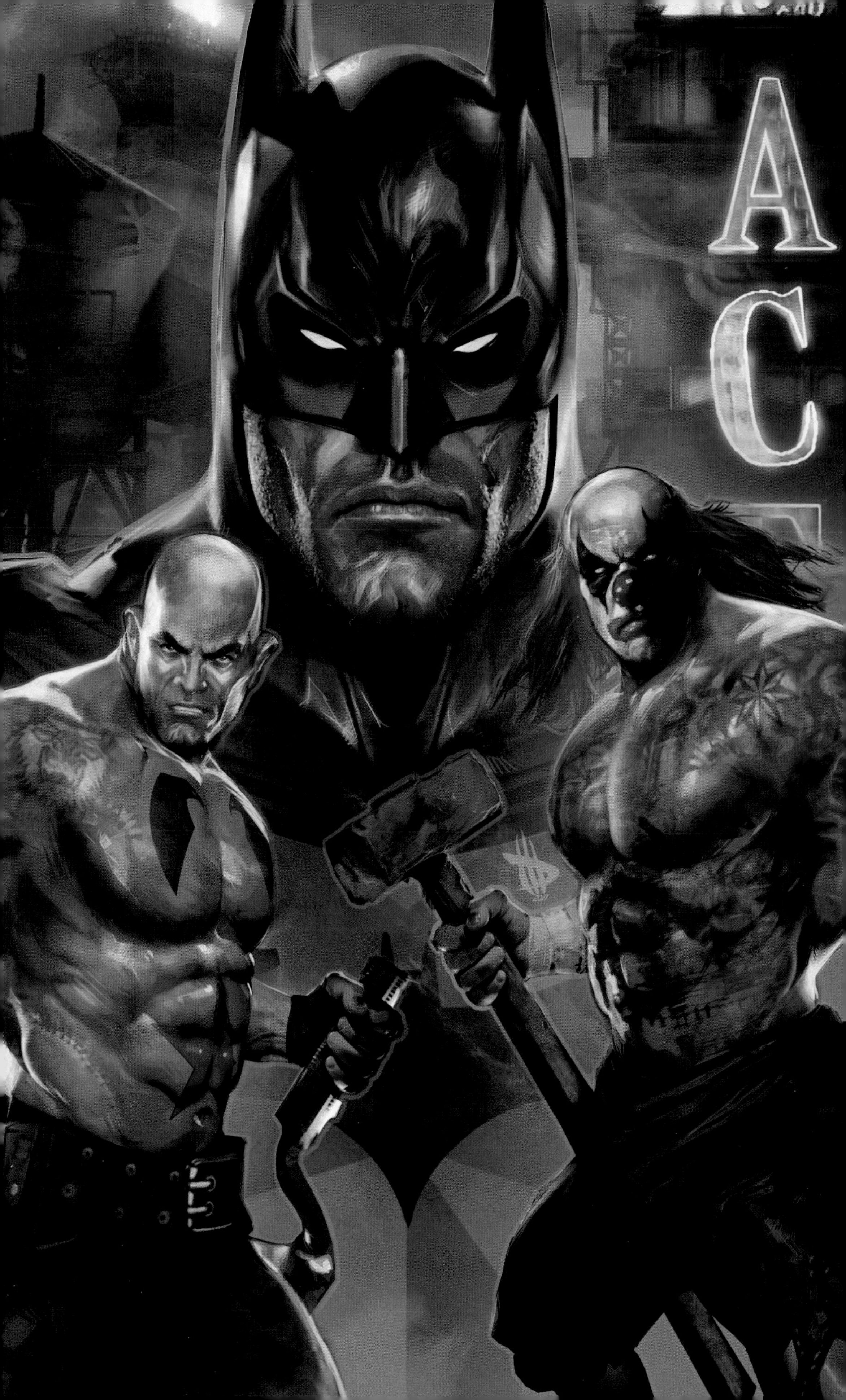
AC

SEPARATION ANXIETY

WRITTEN BY:	**DEREK FRIDOLFS**
ART BY:	**JUAN RYP**
COLORS BY:	**ANDREW ELDER**
LETTERS BY:	**TRAVIS LANHAM**
COVER BY:	**DAVE WILKINS**

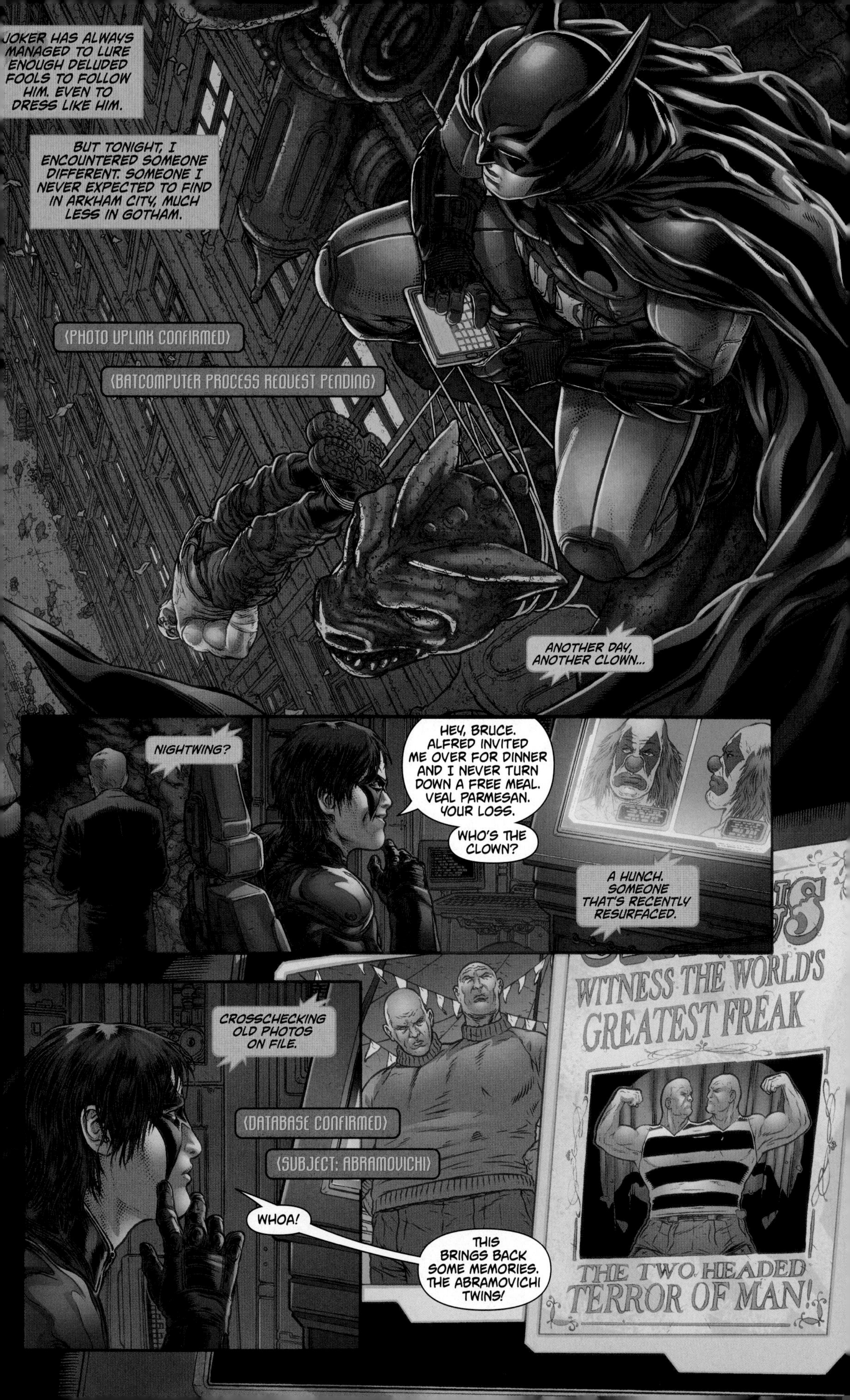
JOKER HAS ALWAYS MANAGED TO LURE ENOUGH DELUDED FOOLS TO FOLLOW HIM. EVEN TO DRESS LIKE HIM.
BUT TONIGHT, I ENCOUNTERED SOMEONE DIFFERENT. SOMEONE I NEVER EXPECTED TO FIND IN ARKHAM CITY, MUCH LESS IN GOTHAM.
(PHOTO UPLINK CONFIRMED)
(BATCOMPUTER PROCESS REQUEST PENDING)
ANOTHER DAY, ANOTHER CLOWN...
NIGHTWING?
HEY, BRUCE. ALFRED INVITED ME OVER FOR DINNER AND I NEVER TURN DOWN A FREE MEAL. VEAL PARMESAN. YOUR LOSS.
WHO'S THE CLOWN?
A HUNCH. SOMEONE THAT'S RECENTLY RESURFACED.
CROSSCHECKING OLD PHOTOS ON FILE.
(DATABASE CONFIRMED)
(SUBJECT: ABRAMOVICHI)
WHOA!
THIS BRINGS BACK SOME MEMORIES. THE ABRAMOVICHI TWINS!
WITNESS THE WORLD'S GREATEST FREAK
THE TWO HEADED TERROR OF MAN!

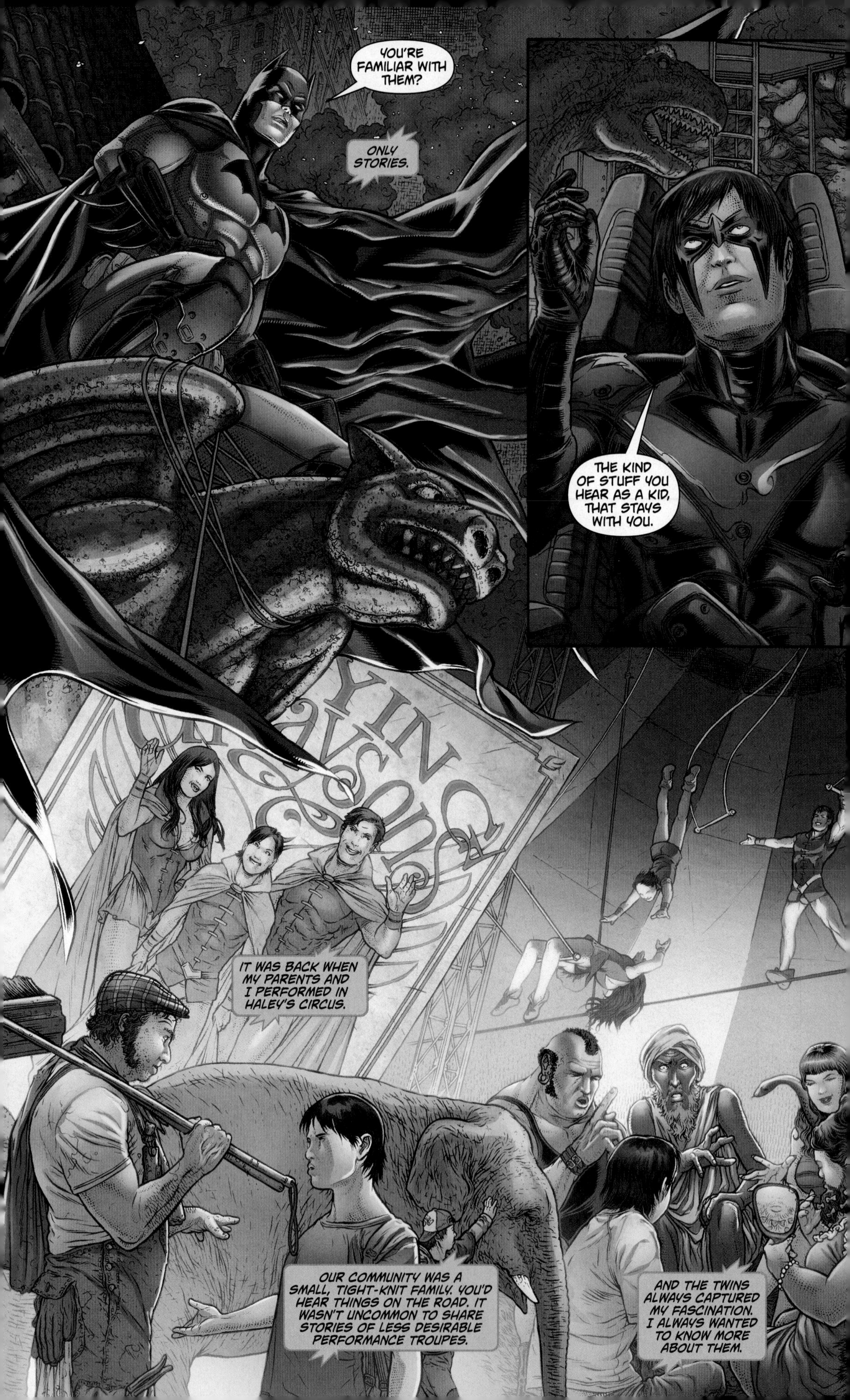
YOU'RE FAMILIAR WITH THEM?
ONLY STORIES.
THE KIND OF STUFF YOU HEAR AS A KID, THAT STAYS WITH YOU.
IT WAS BACK WHEN MY PARENTS AND I PERFORMED IN HALEY'S CIRCUS.
OUR COMMUNITY WAS A SMALL, TIGHT-KNIT FAMILY. YOU'D HEAR THINGS ON THE ROAD. IT WASN'T UNCOMMON TO SHARE STORIES OF LESS DESIRABLE PERFORMANCE TROUPES.
AND THE TWINS ALWAYS CAPTURED MY FASCINATION. I ALWAYS WANTED TO KNOW MORE ABOUT THEM.

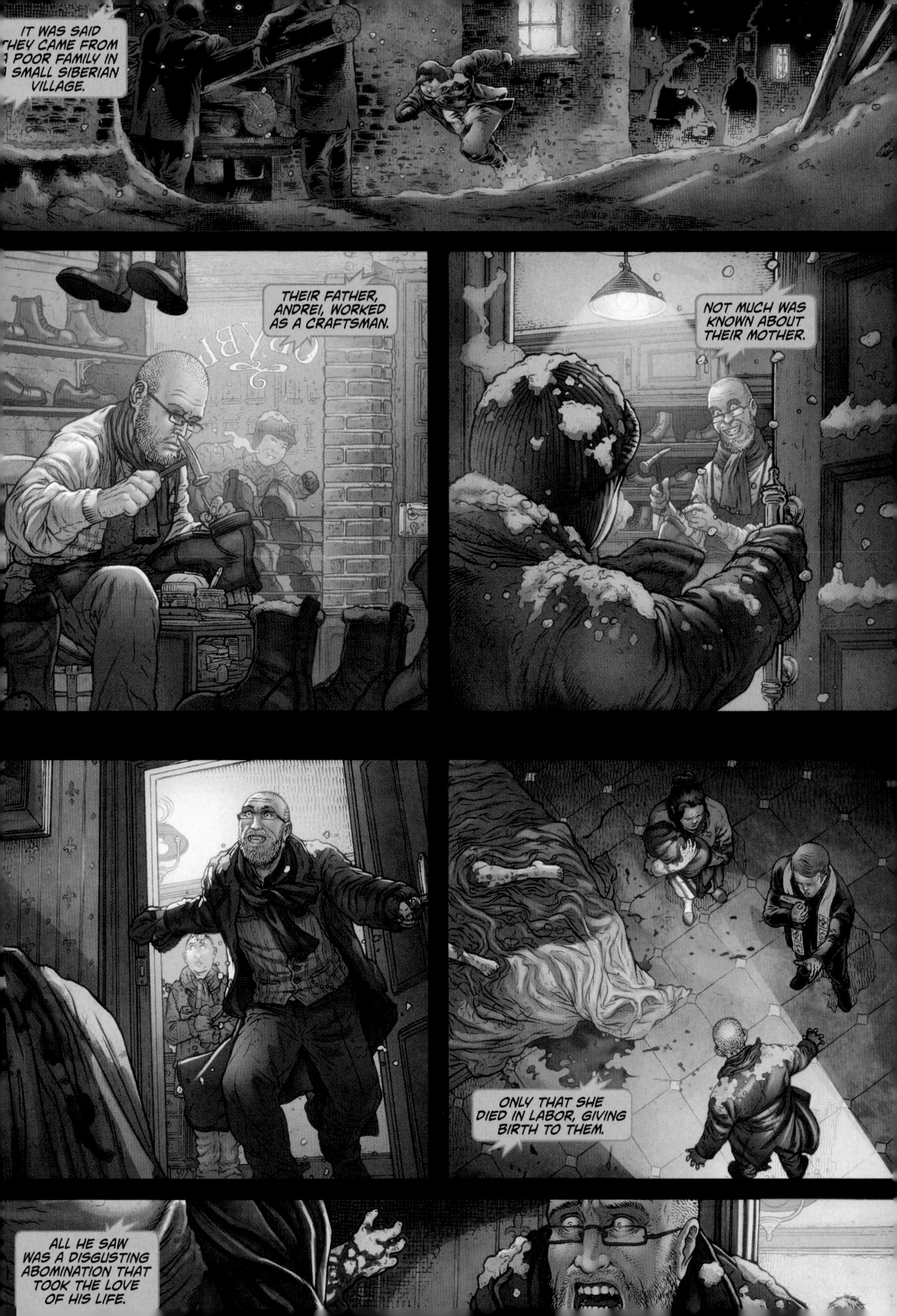
IT WAS SAID THEY CAME FROM A POOR FAMILY IN A SMALL SIBERIAN VILLAGE.
THEIR FATHER, ANDREI, WORKED AS A CRAFTSMAN.
NOT MUCH WAS KNOWN ABOUT THEIR MOTHER.
ONLY THAT SHE DIED IN LABOR, GIVING BIRTH TO THEM.
ALL HE SAW WAS A DISGUSTING ABOMINATION THAT TOOK THE LOVE OF HIS LIFE.

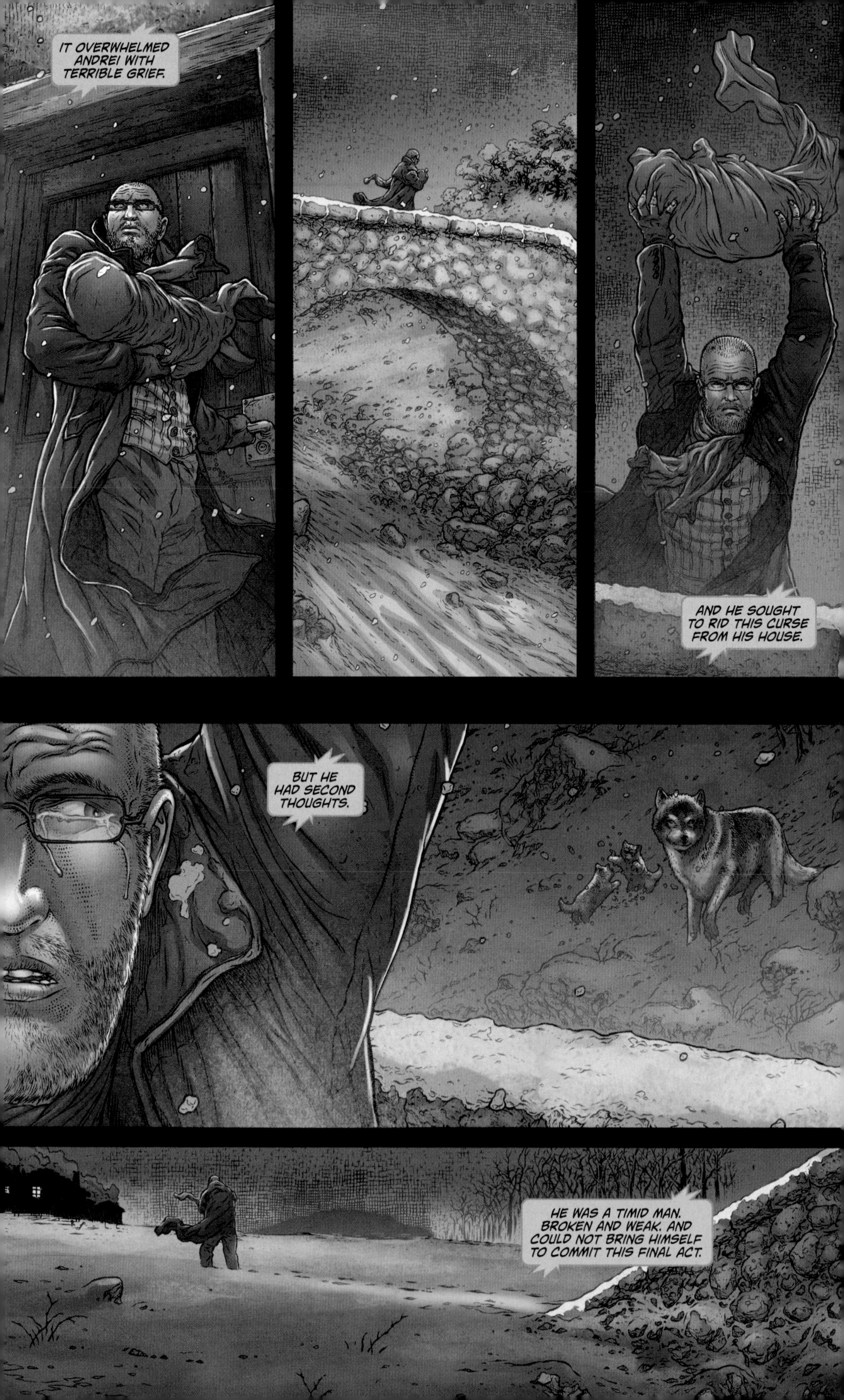
IT OVERWHELMED ANDREI WITH TERRIBLE GRIEF.
AND HE SOUGHT TO RID THIS CURSE FROM HIS HOUSE.
BUT HE HAD SECOND THOUGHTS.
HE WAS A TIMID MAN. BROKEN AND WEAK. AND COULD NOT BRING HIMSELF TO COMMIT THIS FINAL ACT.

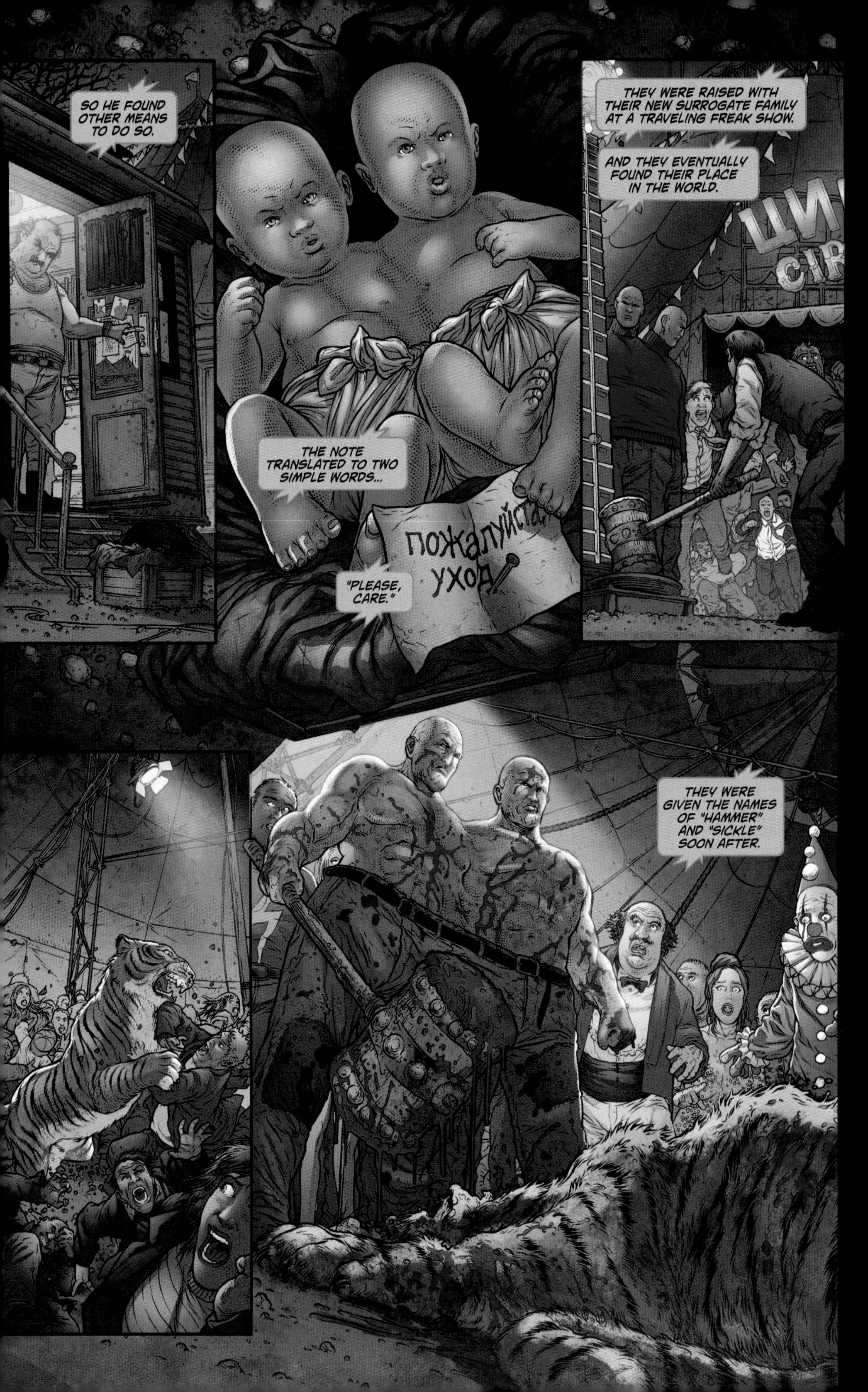
SO HE FOUND OTHER MEANS TO DO SO.
THE NOTE TRANSLATED TO TWO SIMPLE WORDS...
пожалуйста, уход
"PLEASE, CARE."
THEY WERE RAISED WITH THEIR NEW SURROGATE FAMILY AT A TRAVELING FREAK SHOW.
AND THEY EVENTUALLY FOUND THEIR PLACE IN THE WORLD.
THEY WERE GIVEN THE NAMES OF "HAMMER" AND "SICKLE" SOON AFTER.

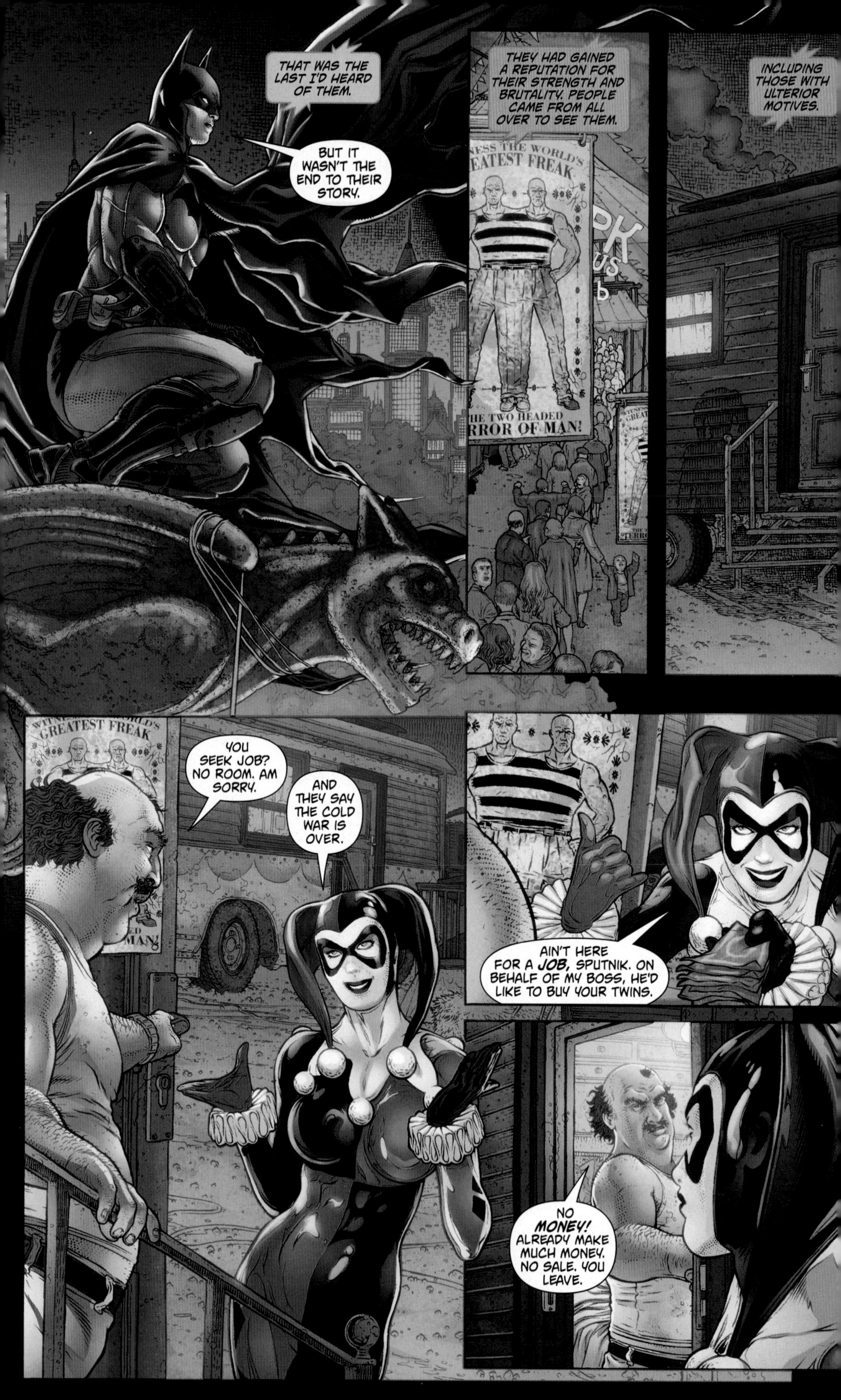
THAT WAS THE LAST I'D HEARD OF THEM.
BUT IT WASN'T THE END TO THEIR STORY.
THEY HAD GAINED A REPUTATION FOR THEIR STRENGTH AND BRUTALITY. PEOPLE CAME FROM ALL OVER TO SEE THEM.
NESS THE WORLD'S GREATEST FREAK
THE TWO HEADED TERROR OF MAN!
INCLUDING THOSE WITH ULTERIOR MOTIVES.
GREATEST FREAK
YOU SEEK JOB? NO ROOM. AM SORRY.
AND THEY SAY THE COLD WAR IS OVER.
AIN'T HERE FOR A JOB, SPUTNIK. ON BEHALF OF MY BOSS, HE'D LIKE TO BUY YOUR TWINS.
NO MONEY! ALREADY MAKE MUCH MONEY. NO SALE. YOU LEAVE.

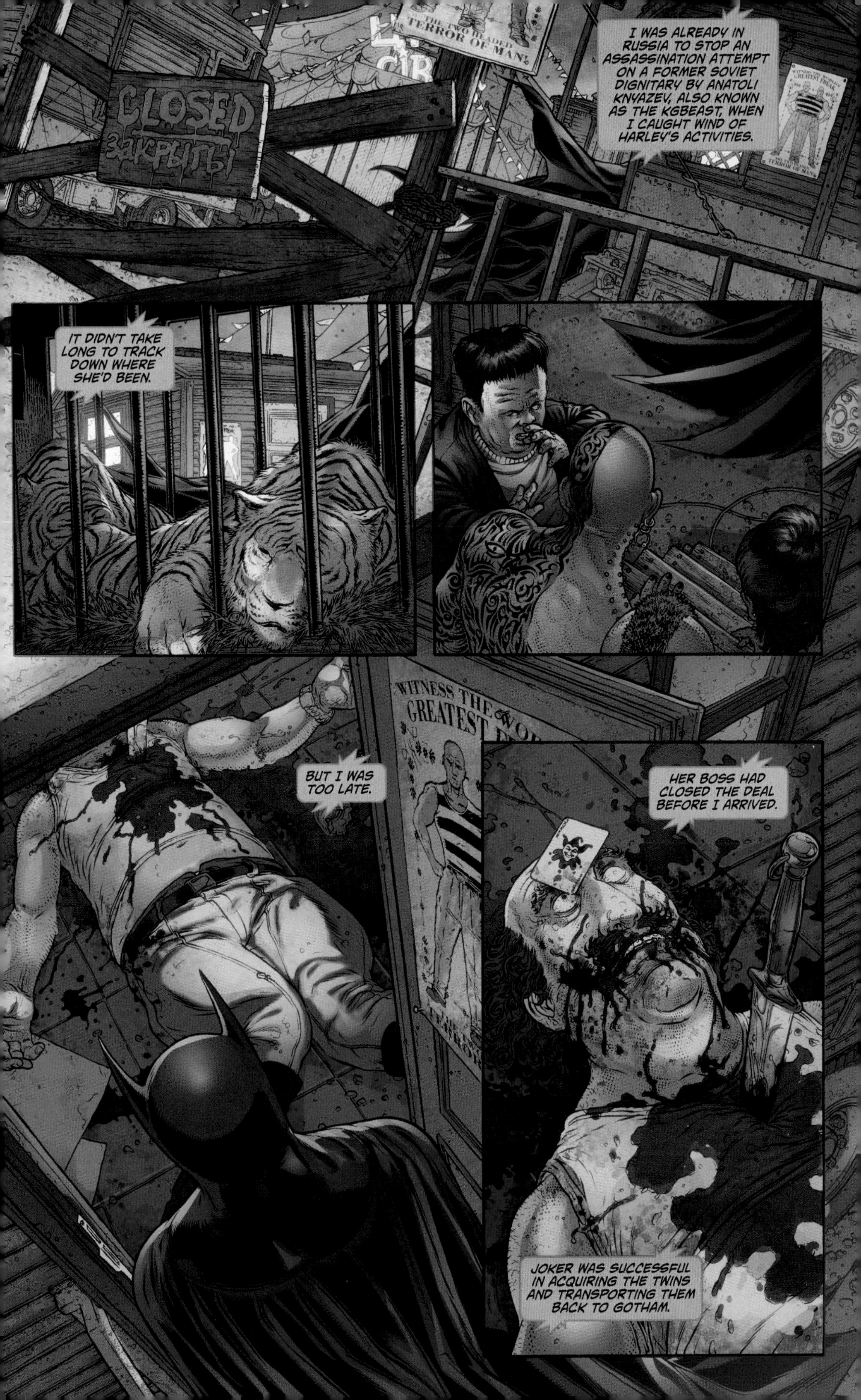
THE TWO HEADED
TERROR OF MAN!
CLOSED
ЗАКРЫТЫ
I WAS ALREADY IN RUSSIA TO STOP AN ASSASSINATION ATTEMPT ON A FORMER SOVIET DIGNITARY BY ANATOLI KNYAZEV, ALSO KNOWN AS THE KGBEAST, WHEN I CAUGHT WIND OF HARLEY'S ACTIVITIES.
IT DIDN'T TAKE LONG TO TRACK DOWN WHERE SHE'D BEEN.
BUT I WAS TOO LATE.
HER BOSS HAD CLOSED THE DEAL BEFORE I ARRIVED.
JOKER WAS SUCCESSFUL IN ACQUIRING THE TWINS AND TRANSPORTING THEM BACK TO GOTHAM.

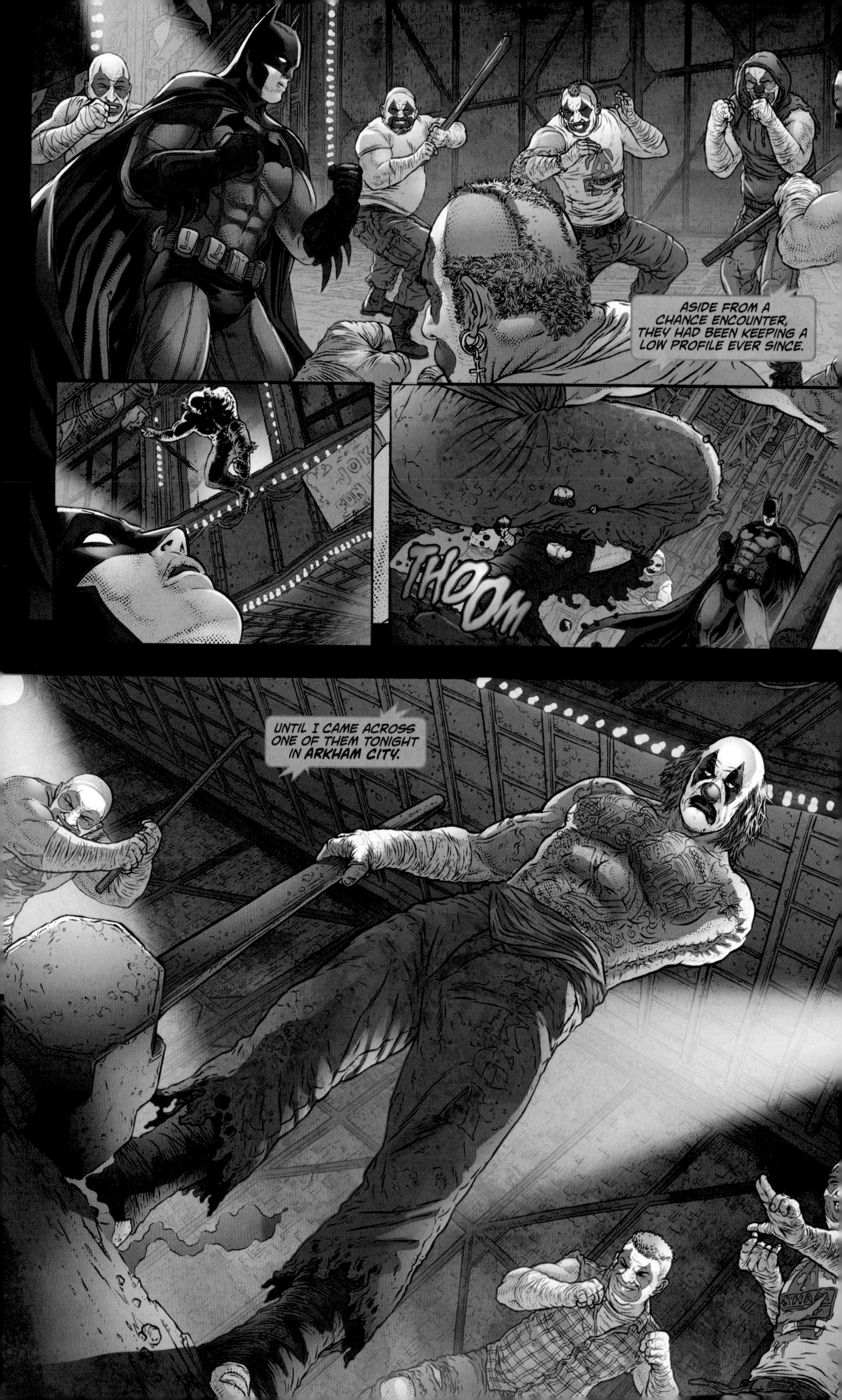
ASIDE FROM A CHANCE ENCOUNTER, THEY HAD BEEN KEEPING A LOW PROFILE EVER SINCE.
THOOM
UNTIL I CAME ACROSS ONE OF THEM TONIGHT IN ARKHAM CITY.

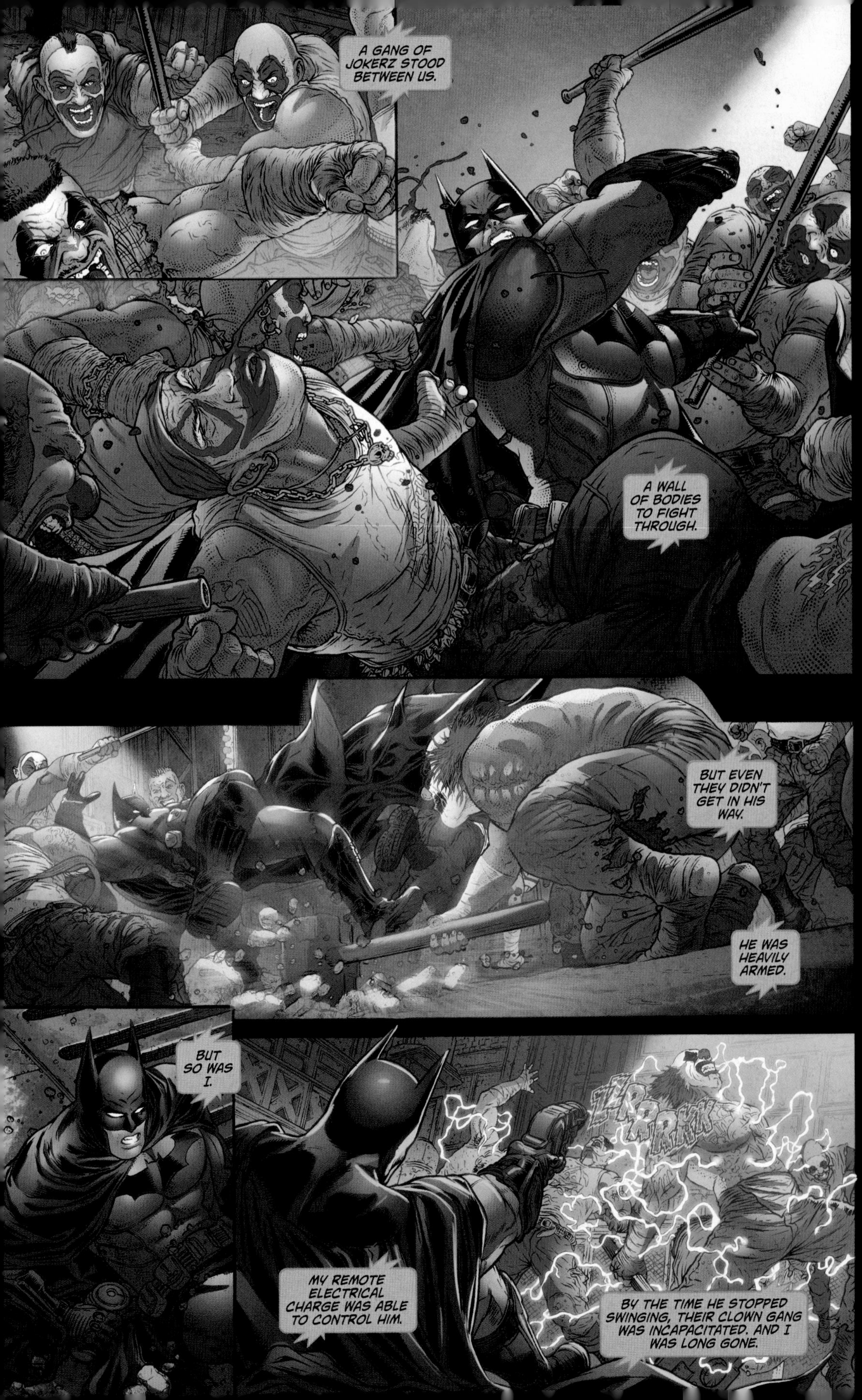
A GANG OF JOKERZ STOOD BETWEEN US.
A WALL OF BODIES TO FIGHT THROUGH.
BUT EVEN THEY DIDN'T GET IN HIS WAY.
HE WAS HEAVILY ARMED.
BUT SO WAS I.
MY REMOTE ELECTRICAL CHARGE WAS ABLE TO CONTROL HIM.
BY THE TIME HE STOPPED SWINGING, THEIR CLOWN GANG WAS INCAPACITATED. AND I WAS LONG GONE.

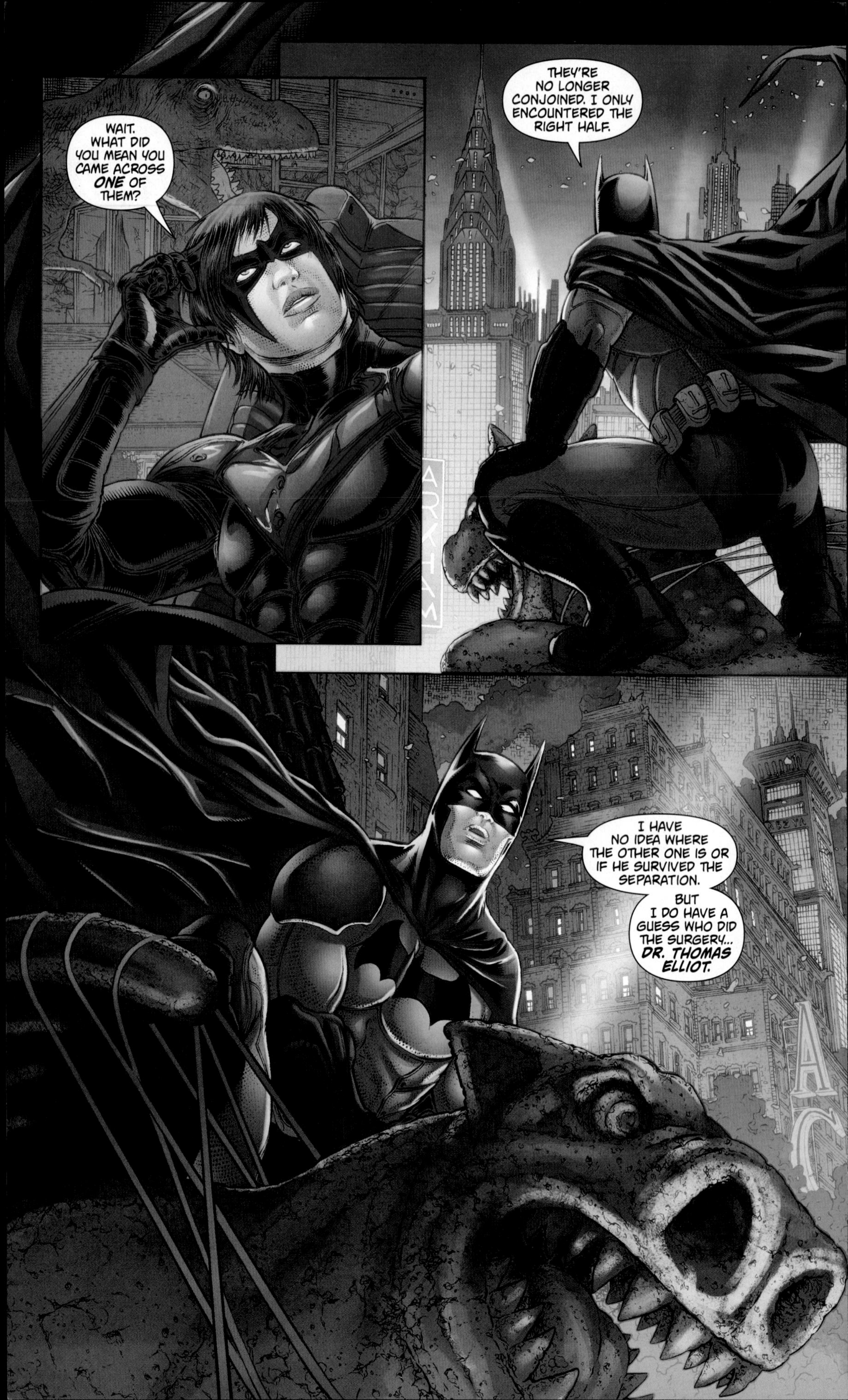
WAIT. WHAT DID YOU MEAN YOU CAME ACROSS ***ONE*** OF THEM?
THEY'RE NO LONGER CONJOINED. I ONLY ENCOUNTERED THE RIGHT HALF.
ARKHAM
I HAVE NO IDEA WHERE THE OTHER ONE IS OR IF HE SURVIVED THE SEPARATION.
BUT I DO HAVE A GUESS WHO DID THE SURGERY... ***DR. THOMAS ELLIOT.***

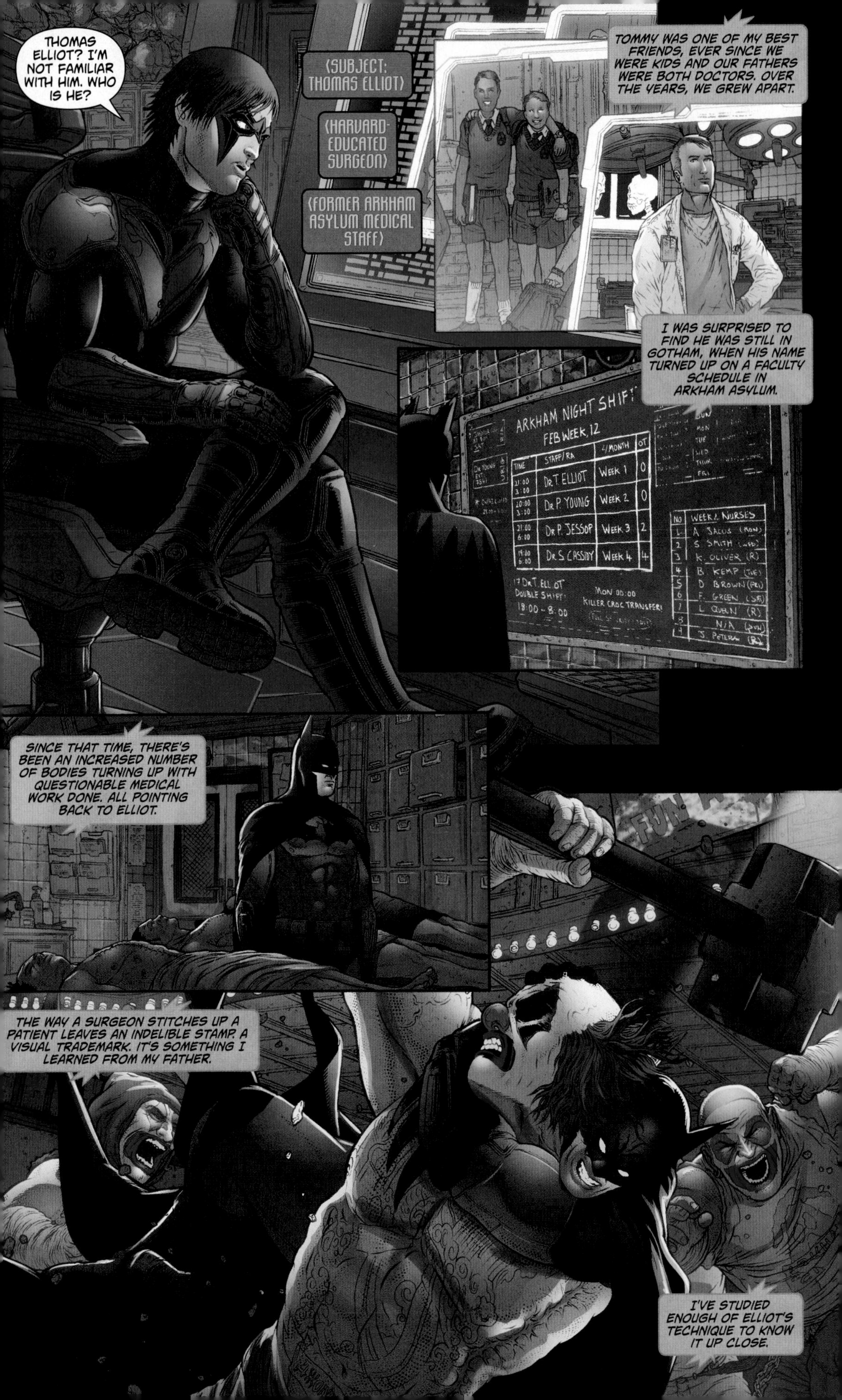
THOMAS ELLIOT? I'M NOT FAMILIAR WITH HIM. WHO IS HE?
(SUBJECT: THOMAS ELLIOT)
(HARVARD-EDUCATED SURGEON)
(FORMER ARKHAM ASYLUM MEDICAL STAFF)
TOMMY WAS ONE OF MY BEST FRIENDS, EVER SINCE WE WERE KIDS AND OUR FATHERS WERE BOTH DOCTORS. OVER THE YEARS, WE GREW APART.
I WAS SURPRISED TO FIND HE WAS STILL IN GOTHAM, WHEN HIS NAME TURNED UP ON A FACULTY SCHEDULE IN ARKHAM ASYLUM.
ARKHAM NIGHT SHIFT
FEB WEEK 12
TIME
STAFF/RA
Dr T. ELLIOT
Dr P. YOUNG
Dr P. JESSOP
Dr S. CASSIDY
Week 1
Week 2
Week 3
Week 4
WEEK NURSES
SINCE THAT TIME, THERE'S BEEN AN INCREASED NUMBER OF BODIES TURNING UP WITH QUESTIONABLE MEDICAL WORK DONE. ALL POINTING BACK TO ELLIOT.
THE WAY A SURGEON STITCHES UP A PATIENT LEAVES AN INDELIBLE STAMP. A VISUAL TRADEMARK. IT'S SOMETHING I LEARNED FROM MY FATHER.
I'VE STUDIED ENOUGH OF ELLIOT'S TECHNIQUE TO KNOW IT UP CLOSE.

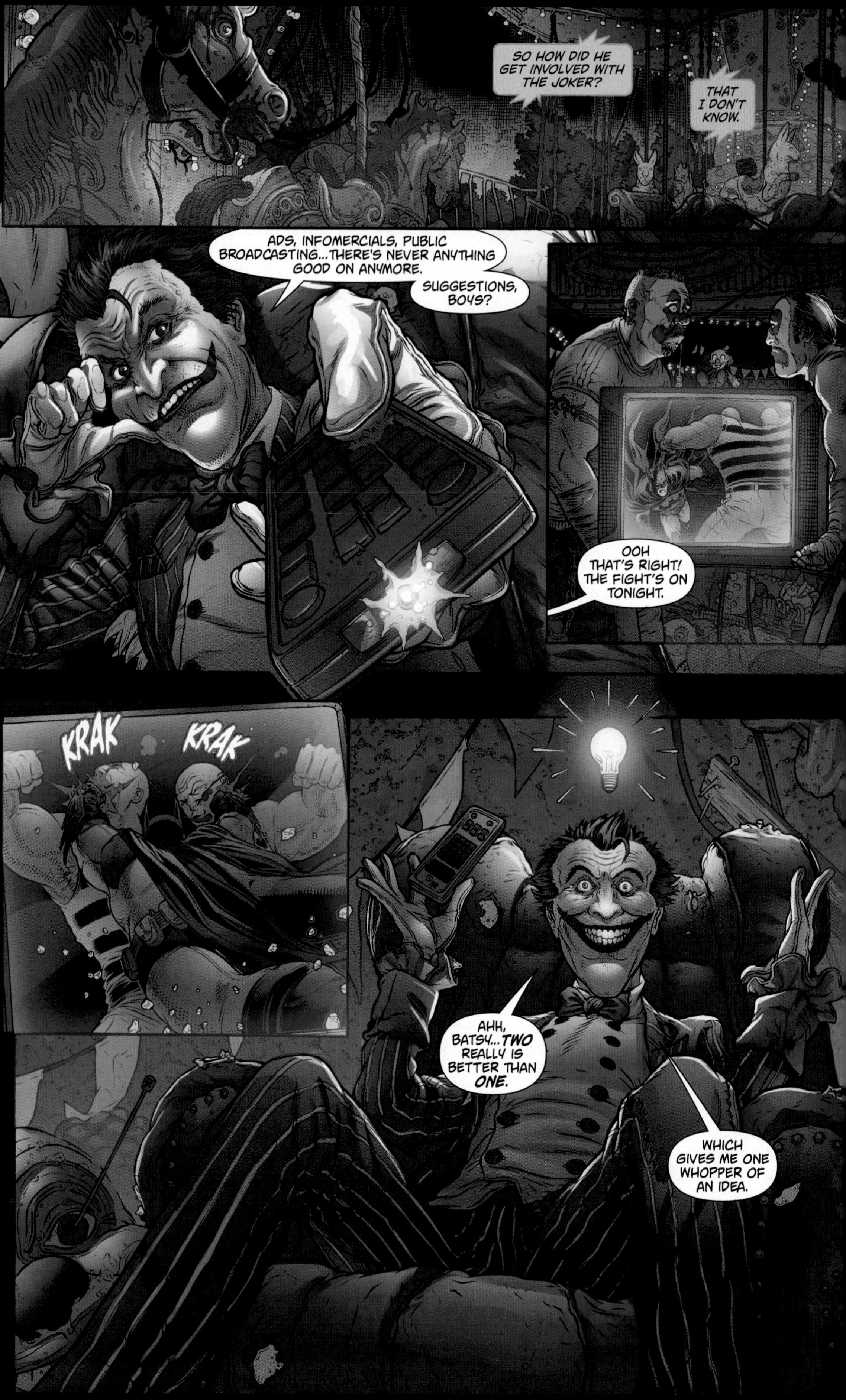
SO HOW DID HE GET INVOLVED WITH THE JOKER?
THAT I DON'T KNOW.
ADS, INFOMERCIALS, PUBLIC BROADCASTING...THERE'S NEVER ANYTHING GOOD ON ANYMORE.
SUGGESTIONS, BOYS?
OOH THAT'S RIGHT! THE FIGHT'S ON TONIGHT.
KRAK
KRAK
AHH, BATSY...**TWO** REALLY IS BETTER THAN **ONE.**
WHICH GIVES ME ONE WHOPPER OF AN IDEA.

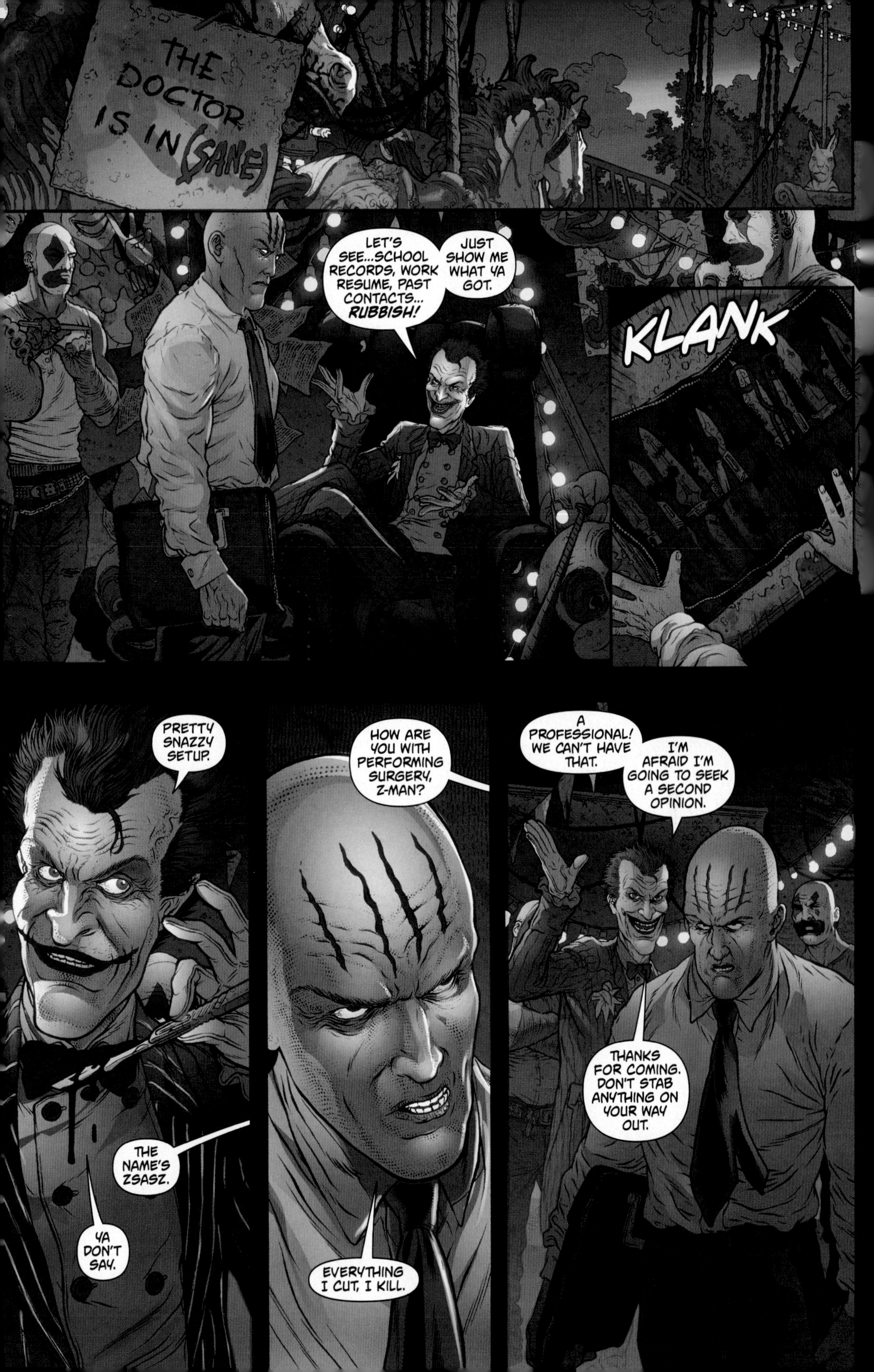
THE DOCTOR IS IN(SANE)
LET'S SEE...SCHOOL RECORDS, WORK RESUME, PAST CONTACTS... RUBBISH!
JUST SHOW ME WHAT YA GOT.
KLANK
PRETTY SNAZZY SETUP.
THE NAME'S ZSASZ.
YA DON'T SAY.
HOW ARE YOU WITH PERFORMING SURGERY, Z-MAN?
EVERYTHING I CUT, I KILL.
A PROFESSIONAL! WE CAN'T HAVE THAT.
I'M AFRAID I'M GOING TO SEEK A SECOND OPINION.
THANKS FOR COMING. DON'T STAB ANYTHING ON YOUR WAY OUT.

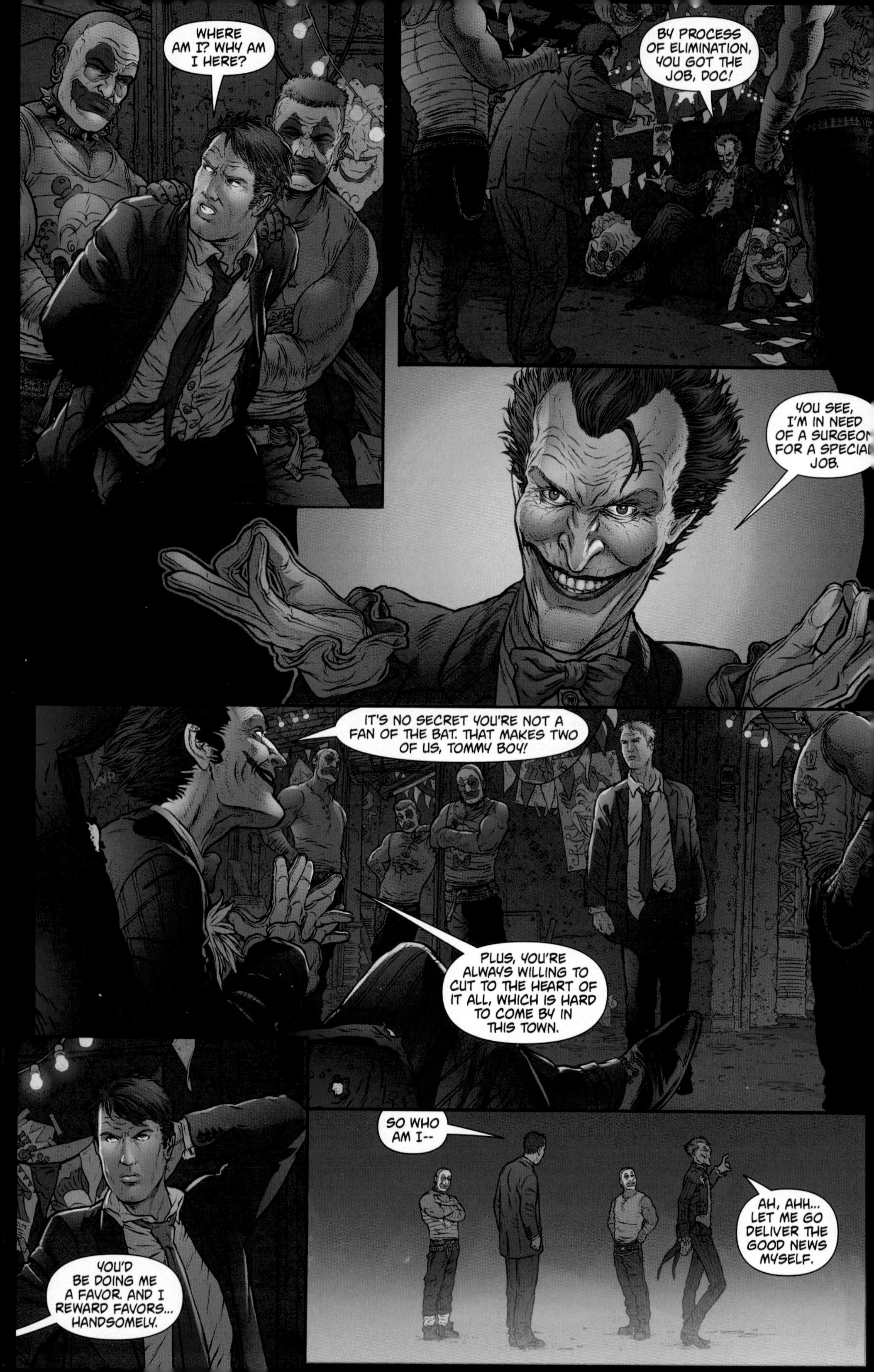
WHERE AM I? WHY AM I HERE?
BY PROCESS OF ELIMINATION, YOU GOT THE JOB, DOC!
YOU SEE, I'M IN NEED OF A SURGEON FOR A SPECIAL JOB.
IT'S NO SECRET YOU'RE NOT A FAN OF THE BAT. THAT MAKES TWO OF US, TOMMY BOY!
PLUS, YOU'RE ALWAYS WILLING TO CUT TO THE HEART OF IT ALL, WHICH IS HARD TO COME BY IN THIS TOWN.
YOU'D BE DOING ME A FAVOR. AND I REWARD FAVORS... HANDSOMELY.
SO WHO AM I--
AH, AHH... LET ME GO DELIVER THE GOOD NEWS MYSELF.

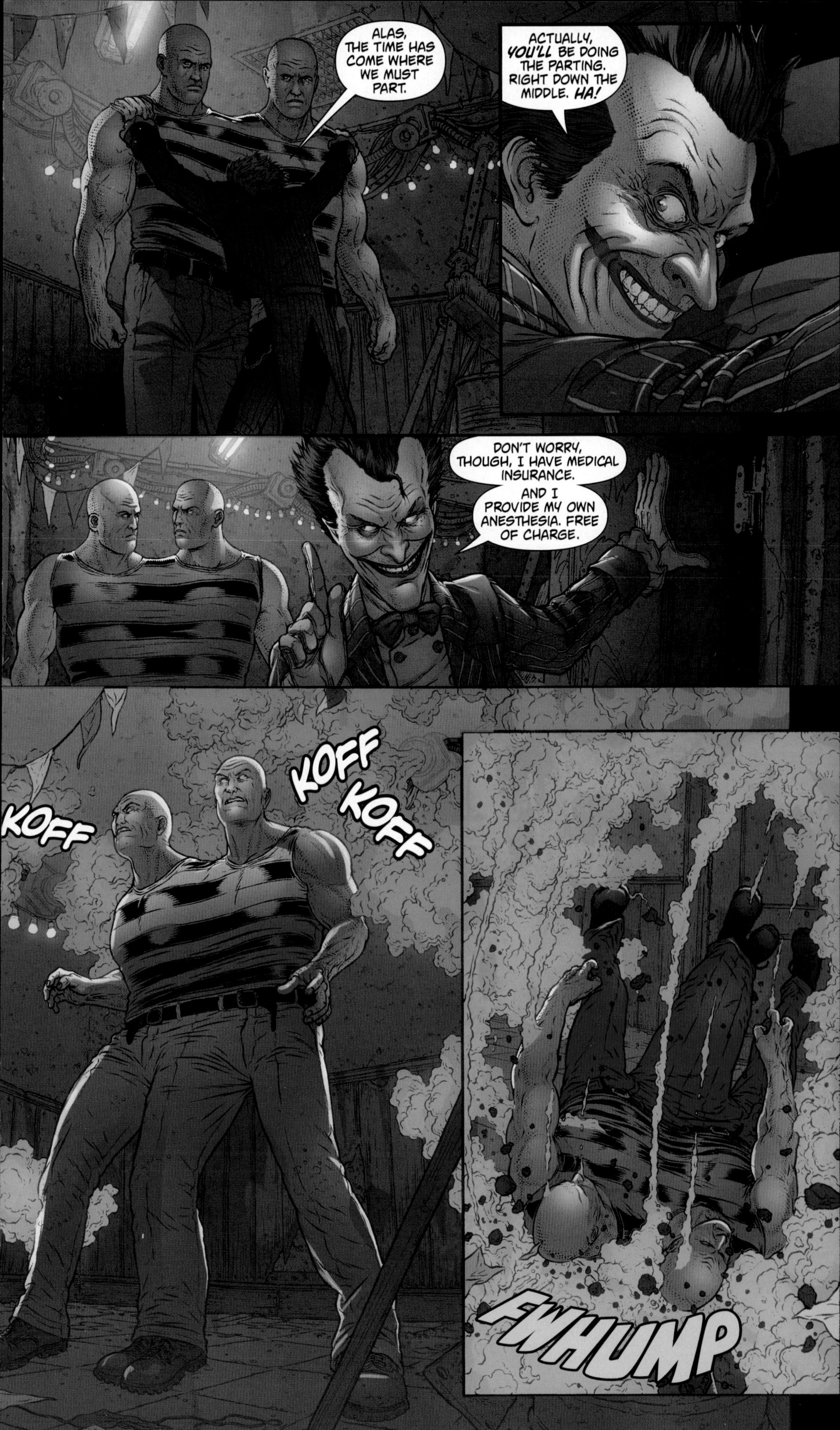
ALAS, THE TIME HAS COME WHERE WE MUST PART.
ACTUALLY, *YOU'LL* BE DOING THE PARTING. RIGHT DOWN THE MIDDLE. *HA!*
DON'T WORRY, THOUGH, I HAVE MEDICAL INSURANCE.
AND I PROVIDE MY OWN ANESTHESIA. FREE OF CHARGE.
KOFF
KOFF KOFF
FWHUMP

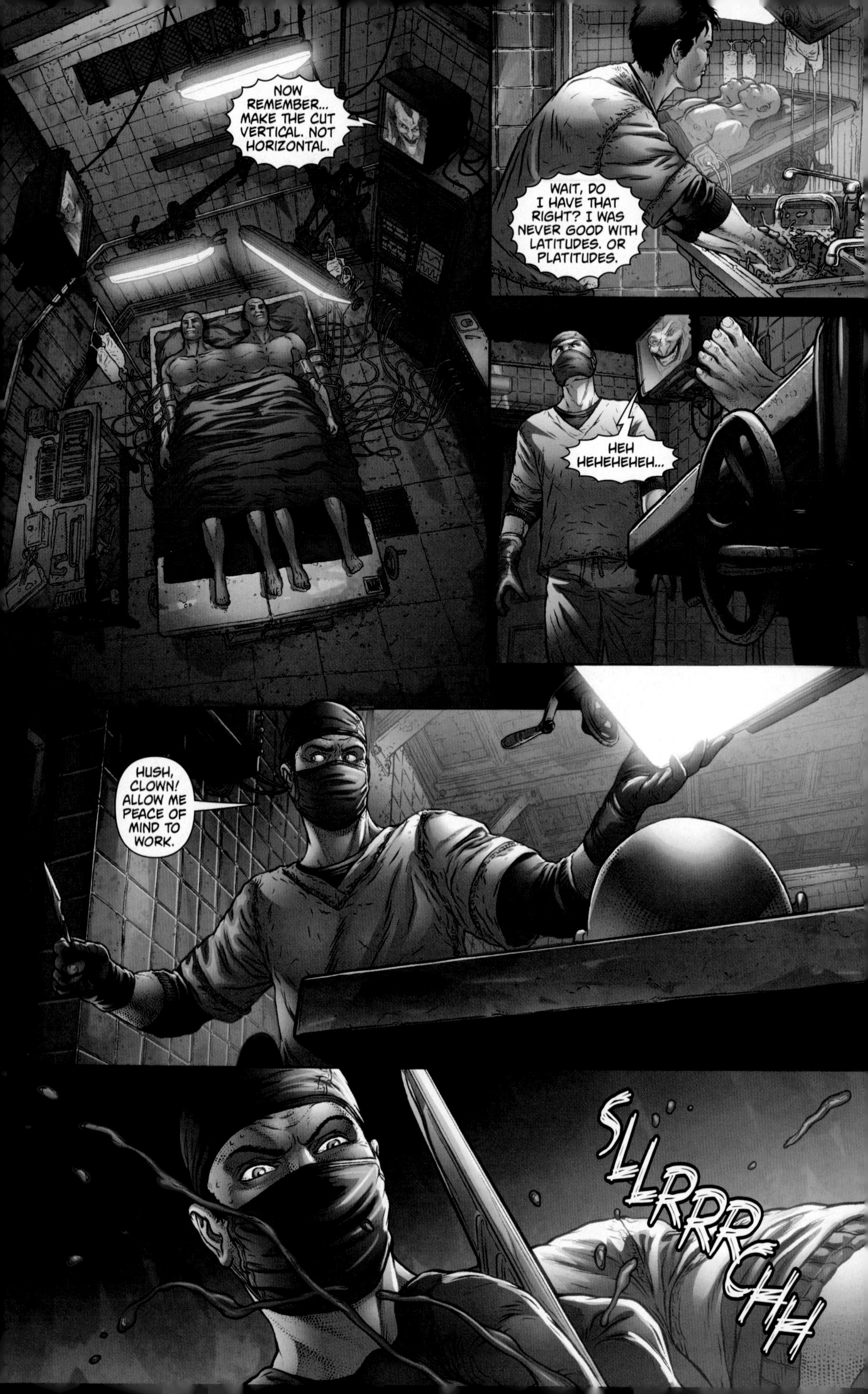
NOW REMEMBER... MAKE THE CUT VERTICAL. NOT HORIZONTAL.
WAIT, DO I HAVE THAT RIGHT? I WAS NEVER GOOD WITH LATITUDES. OR PLATITUDES.
HEH HEHEHEHEH...
HUSH, CLOWN! ALLOW ME PEACE OF MIND TO WORK.
SLLRRRCHH

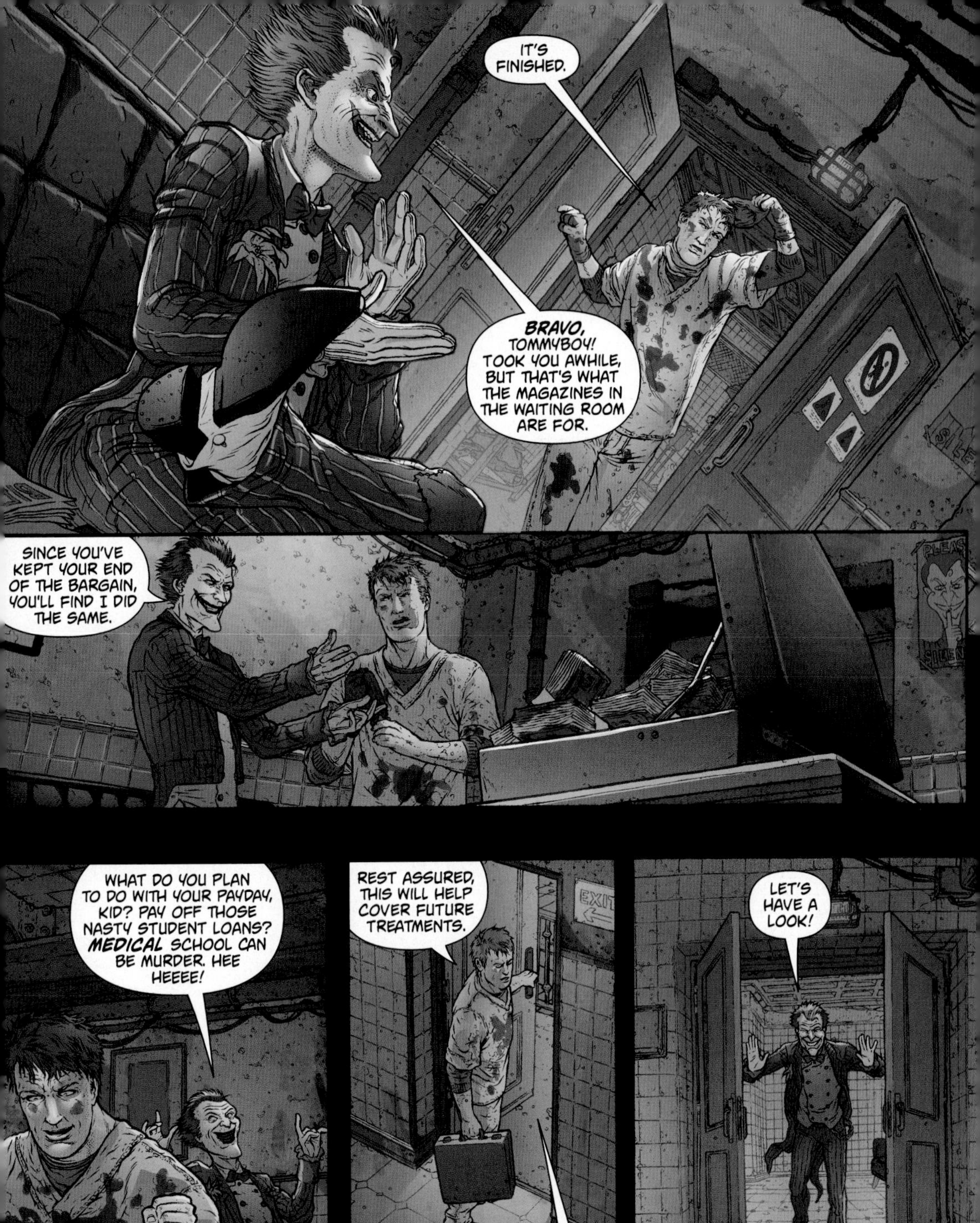
IT'S FINISHED.
BRAVO, TOMMYBOY! TOOK YOU AWHILE, BUT THAT'S WHAT THE MAGAZINES IN THE WAITING ROOM ARE FOR.
SINCE YOU'VE KEPT YOUR END OF THE BARGAIN, YOU'LL FIND I DID THE SAME.
WHAT DO YOU PLAN TO DO WITH YOUR PAYDAY, KID? PAY OFF THOSE NASTY STUDENT LOANS? MEDICAL SCHOOL CAN BE MURDER. HEE HEEEE!
REST ASSURED, THIS WILL HELP COVER FUTURE TREATMENTS.
EXIT
PLASTIC SURGERY CAN BE AN... EXPENSIVE HOBBY.
LET'S HAVE A LOOK!

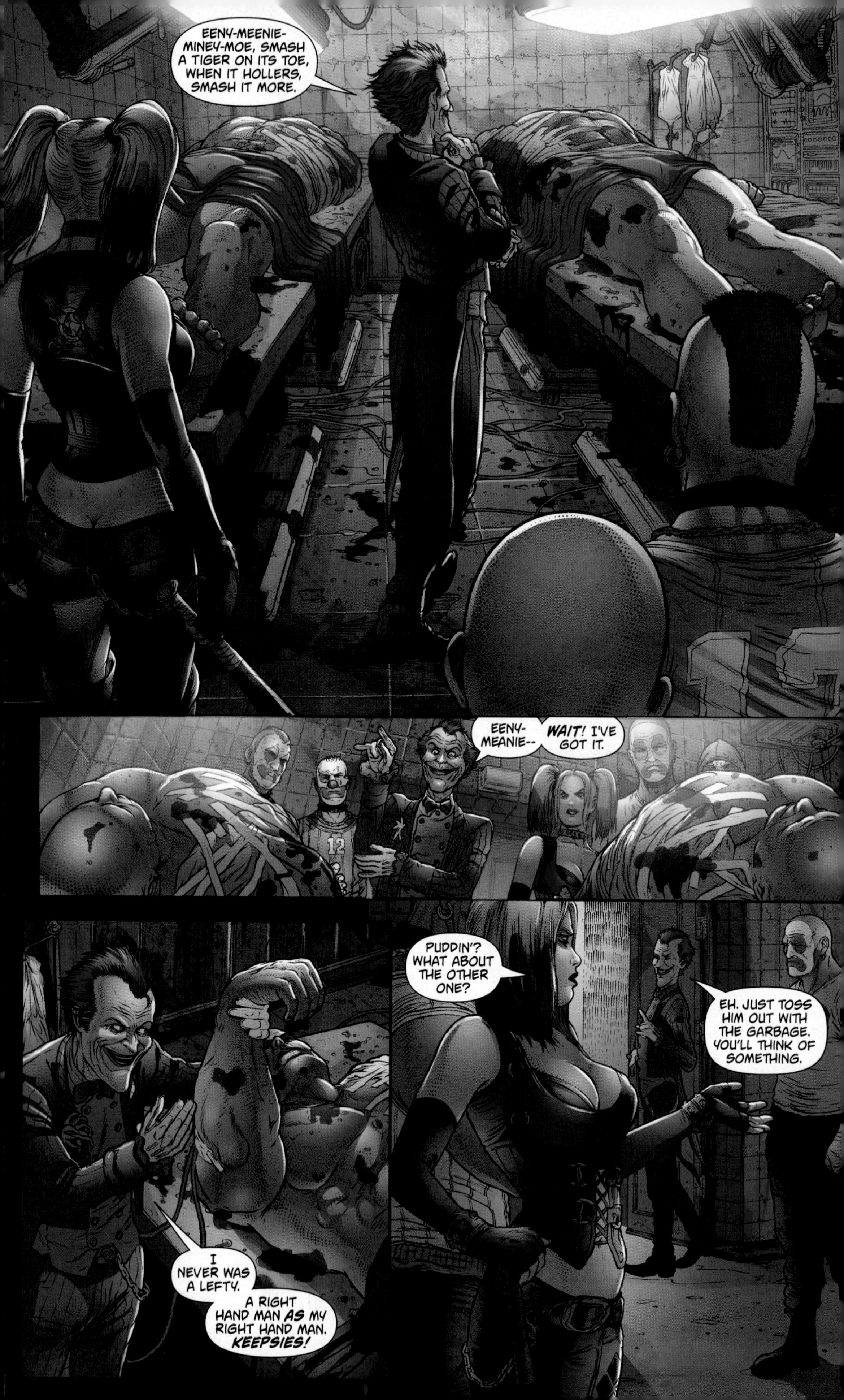
EENY-MEENIE-MINEY-MOE, SMASH A TIGER ON ITS TOE, WHEN IT HOLLERS, SMASH IT MORE.
EENY-MEANIE--
WAIT! I'VE GOT IT.
I NEVER WAS A LEFTY.
A RIGHT HAND MAN **AS** MY RIGHT HAND MAN. **KEEPSIES!**
PUDDIN'? WHAT ABOUT THE OTHER ONE?
EH. JUST TOSS HIM OUT WITH THE GARBAGE. YOU'LL THINK OF SOMETHING.

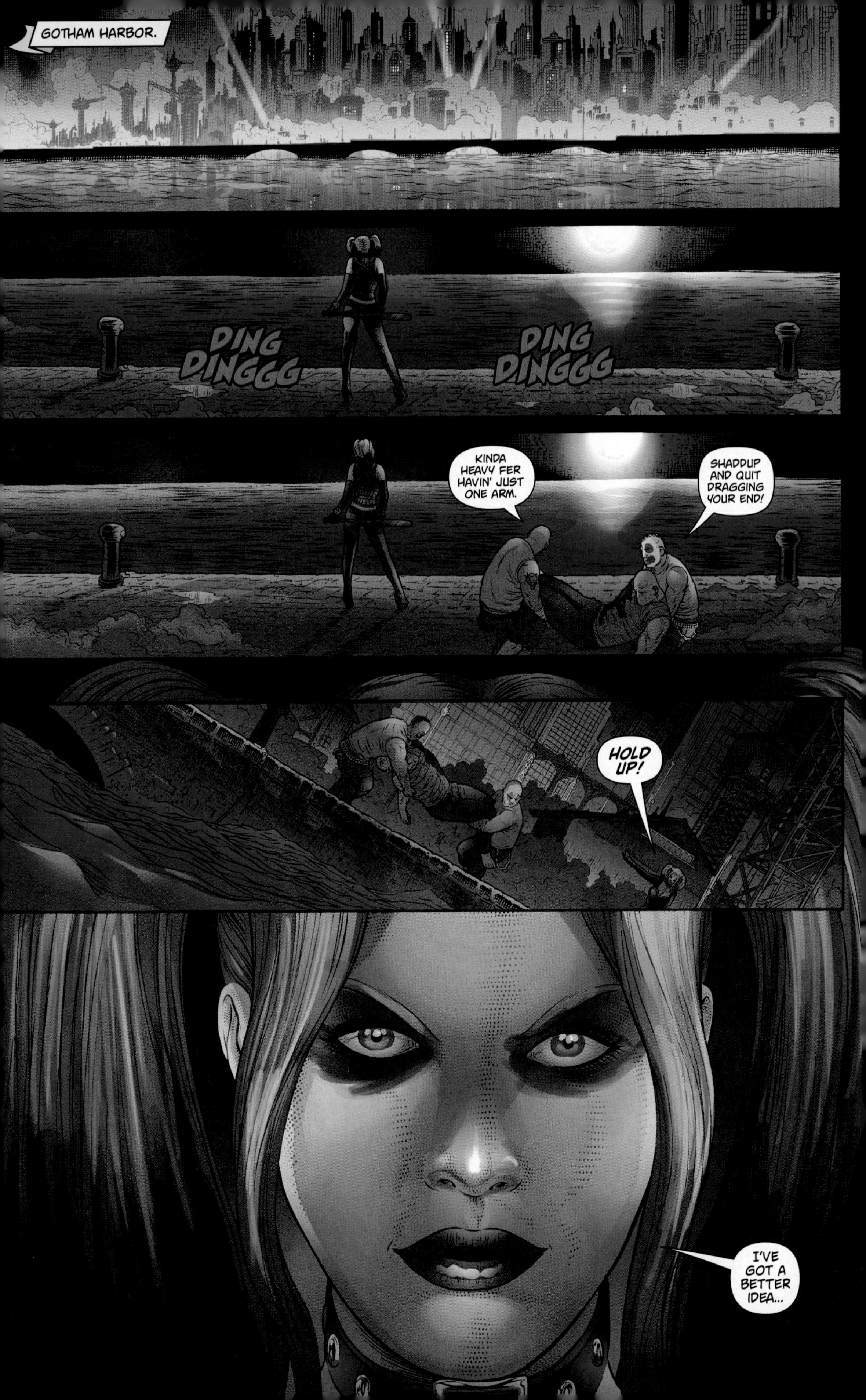
GOTHAM HARBOR.
DING DINGGG
DING DINGGG
KINDA HEAVY FER HAVIN' JUST ONE ARM.
SHADDUP AND QUIT DRAGGING YOUR END!
HOLD UP!
I'VE GOT A BETTER IDEA...

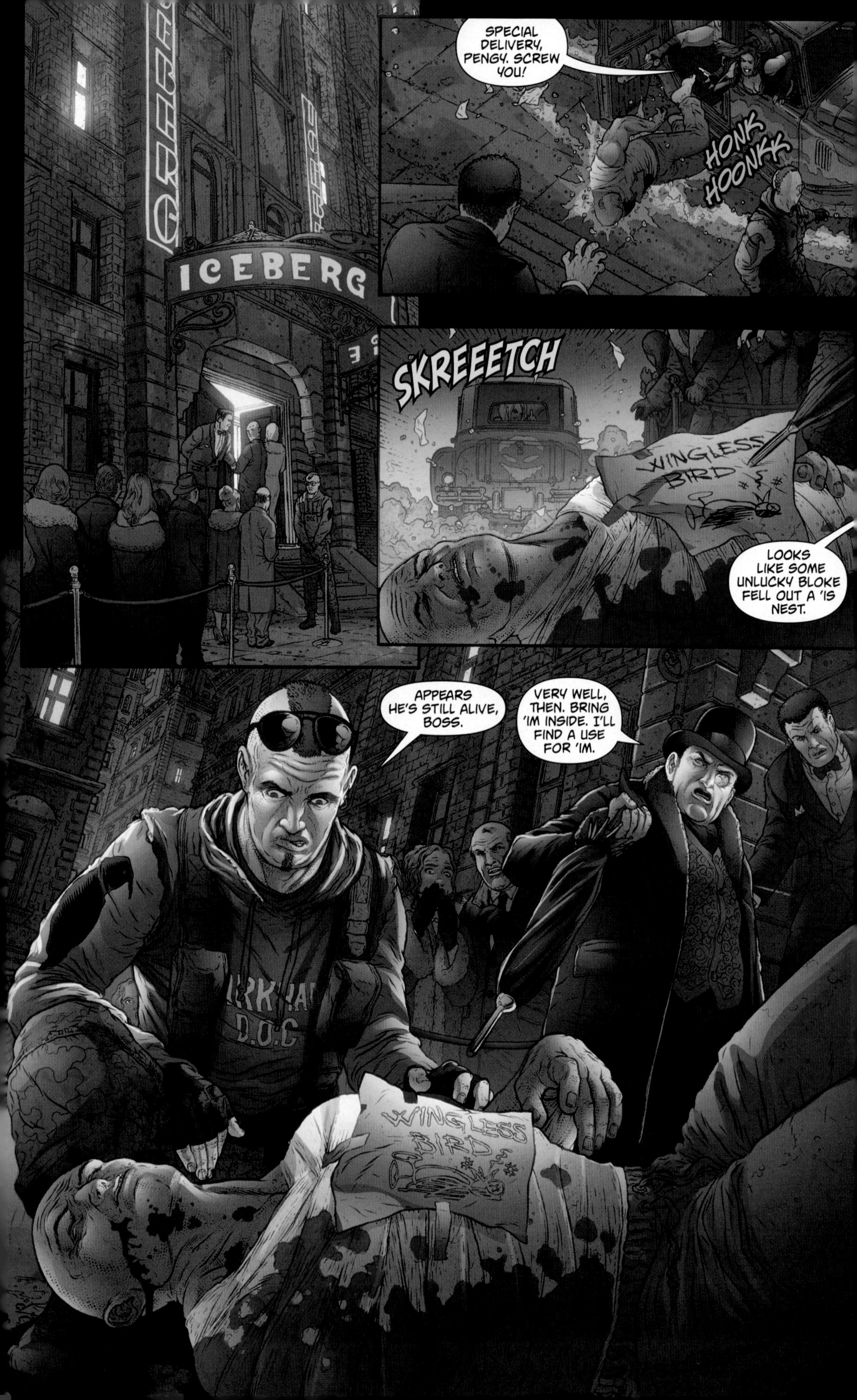
ICEBERG
SPECIAL DELIVERY, PENGY. SCREW YOU!
HONK HOONKK
SKREEETCH
WINGLESS BIRD
LOOKS LIKE SOME UNLUCKY BLOKE FELL OUT A 'IS NEST.
APPEARS HE'S STILL ALIVE, BOSS.
VERY WELL, THEN. BRING 'IM INSIDE. I'LL FIND A USE FOR 'IM.
D.O.C
WINGLESS BIRD

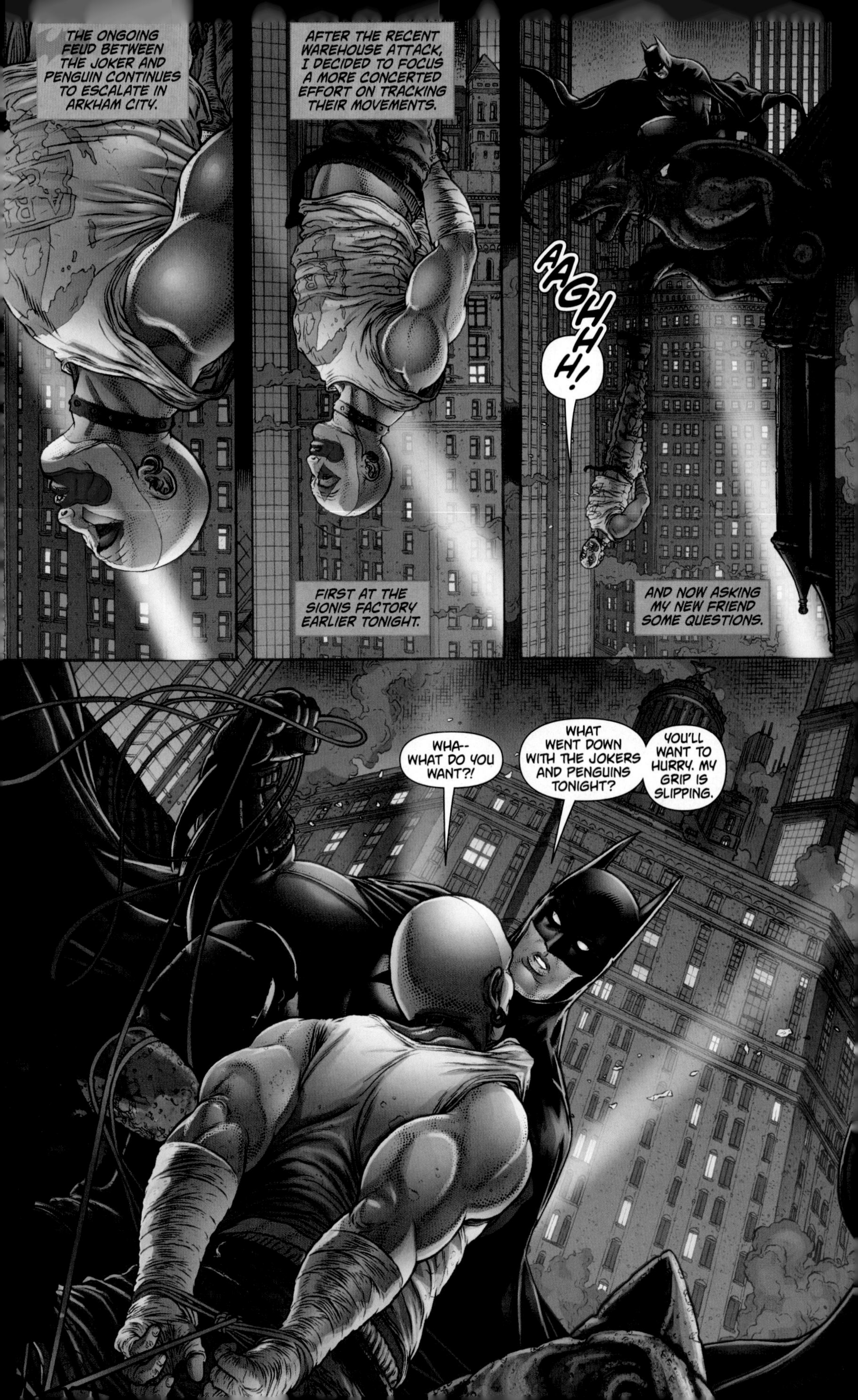
THE ONGOING FEUD BETWEEN THE JOKER AND PENGUIN CONTINUES TO ESCALATE IN ARKHAM CITY.
AFTER THE RECENT WAREHOUSE ATTACK, I DECIDED TO FOCUS A MORE CONCERTED EFFORT ON TRACKING THEIR MOVEMENTS.
FIRST AT THE SIONIS FACTORY EARLIER TONIGHT.
AAGHHH!
AND NOW ASKING MY NEW FRIEND SOME QUESTIONS.
WHA-- WHAT DO YOU WANT?!
WHAT WENT DOWN WITH THE JOKERS AND PENGUINS TONIGHT?
YOU'LL WANT TO HURRY. MY GRIP IS SLIPPING.

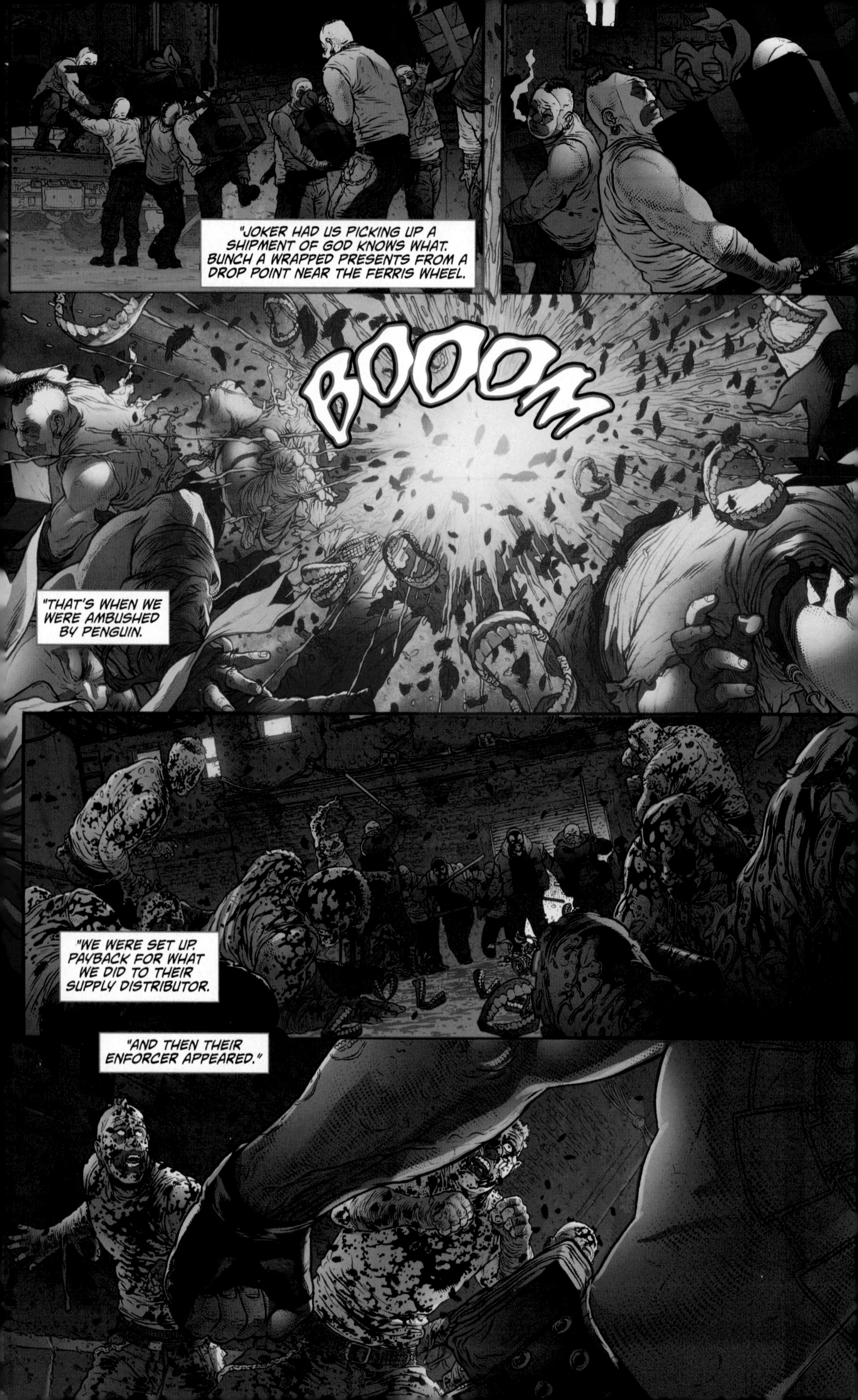
"JOKER HAD US PICKING UP A SHIPMENT OF GOD KNOWS WHAT. BUNCH A WRAPPED PRESENTS FROM A DROP POINT NEAR THE FERRIS WHEEL.
BOOOM
"THAT'S WHEN WE WERE AMBUSHED BY PENGUIN.
"WE WERE SET UP. PAYBACK FOR WHAT WE DID TO THEIR SUPPLY DISTRIBUTOR.
"AND THEN THEIR ENFORCER APPEARED."

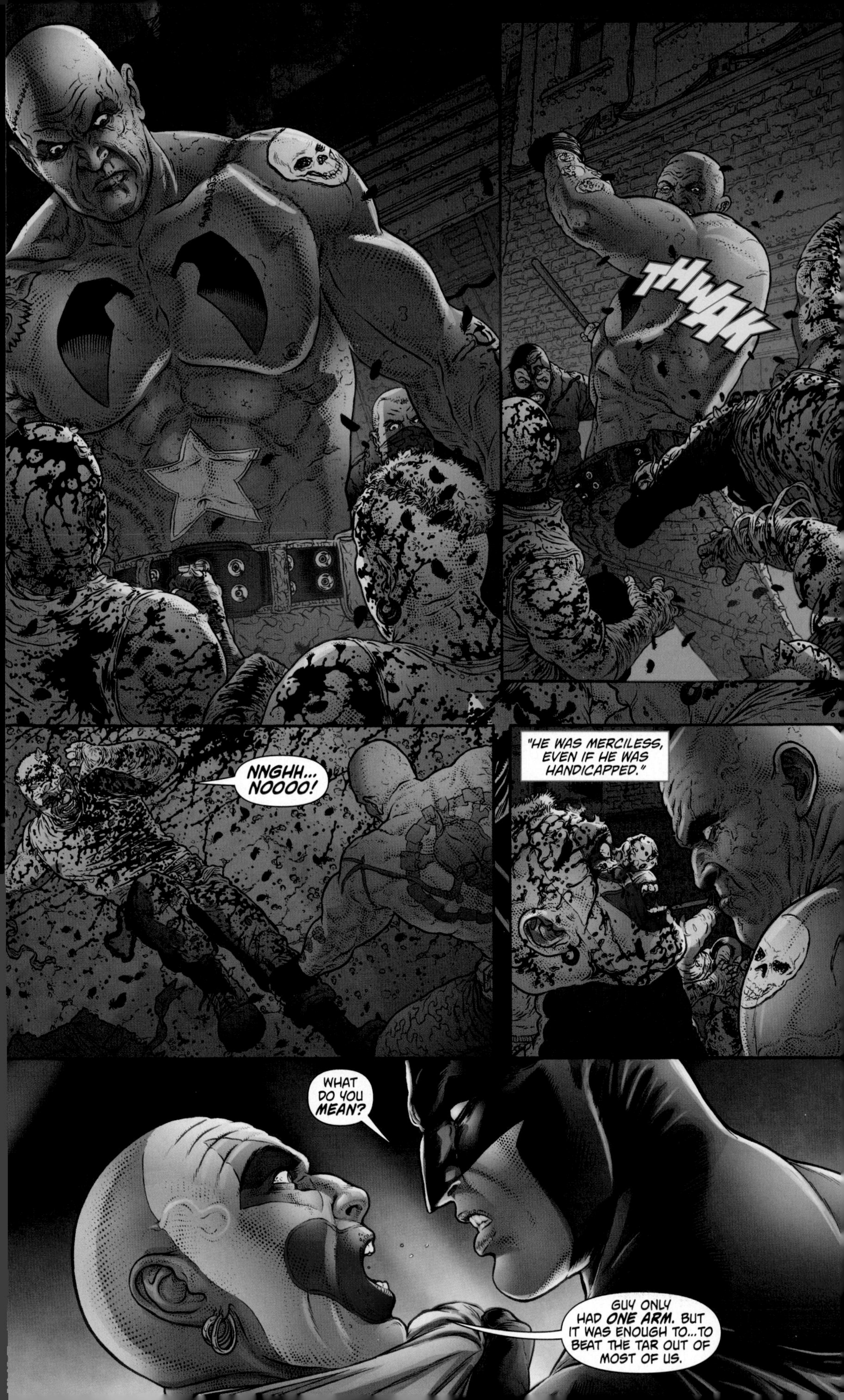
THWAK
NNGHH... NOOOO!
"HE WAS MERCILESS, EVEN IF HE WAS HANDICAPPED."
WHAT DO YOU MEAN?
GUY ONLY HAD ONE ARM. BUT IT WAS ENOUGH TO...TO BEAT THE TAR OUT OF MOST OF US.

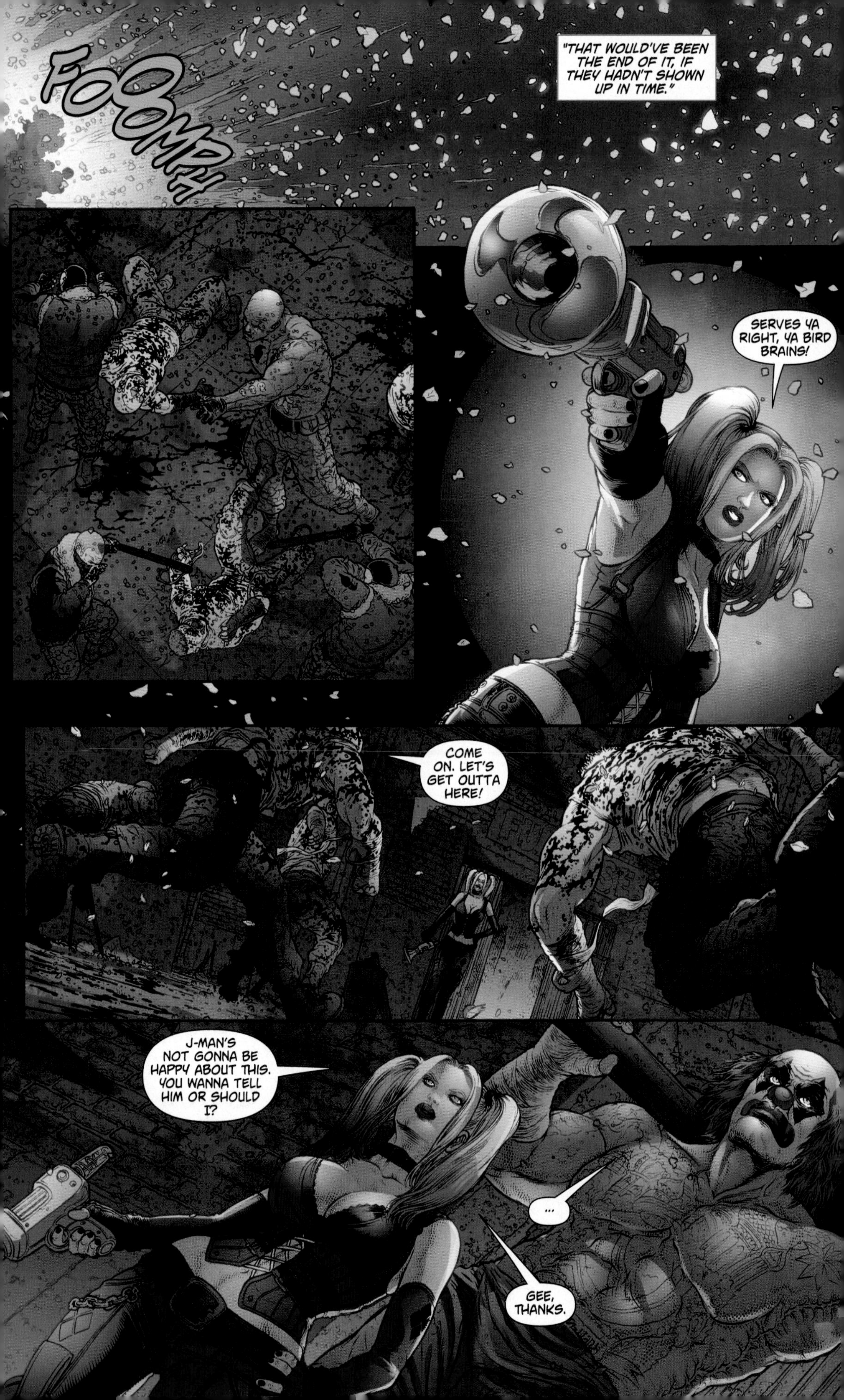
FOOOMPH
"THAT WOULD'VE BEEN THE END OF IT, IF THEY HADN'T SHOWN UP IN TIME."
SERVES YA RIGHT, YA BIRD BRAINS!
COME ON. LET'S GET OUTTA HERE!
J-MAN'S NOT GONNA BE HAPPY ABOUT THIS. YOU WANNA TELL HIM OR SHOULD I?
...
GEE, THANKS.

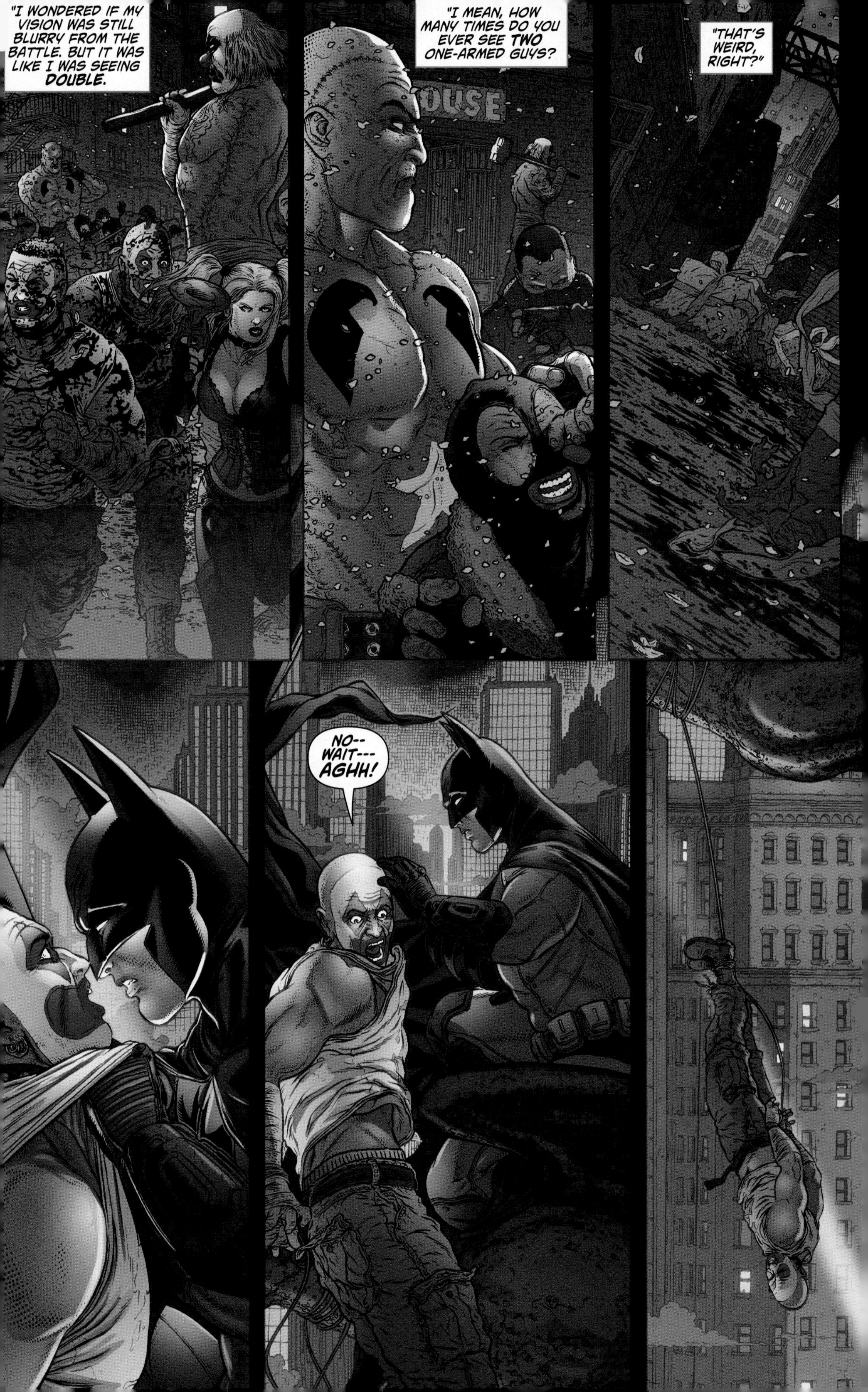
"I WONDERED IF MY VISION WAS STILL BLURRY FROM THE BATTLE. BUT IT WAS LIKE I WAS SEEING **DOUBLE.**
"I MEAN, HOW MANY TIMES DO YOU EVER SEE **TWO** ONE-ARMED GUYS?
"THAT'S WEIRD, RIGHT?"
OUSE
NO-- WAIT--- AGHH!

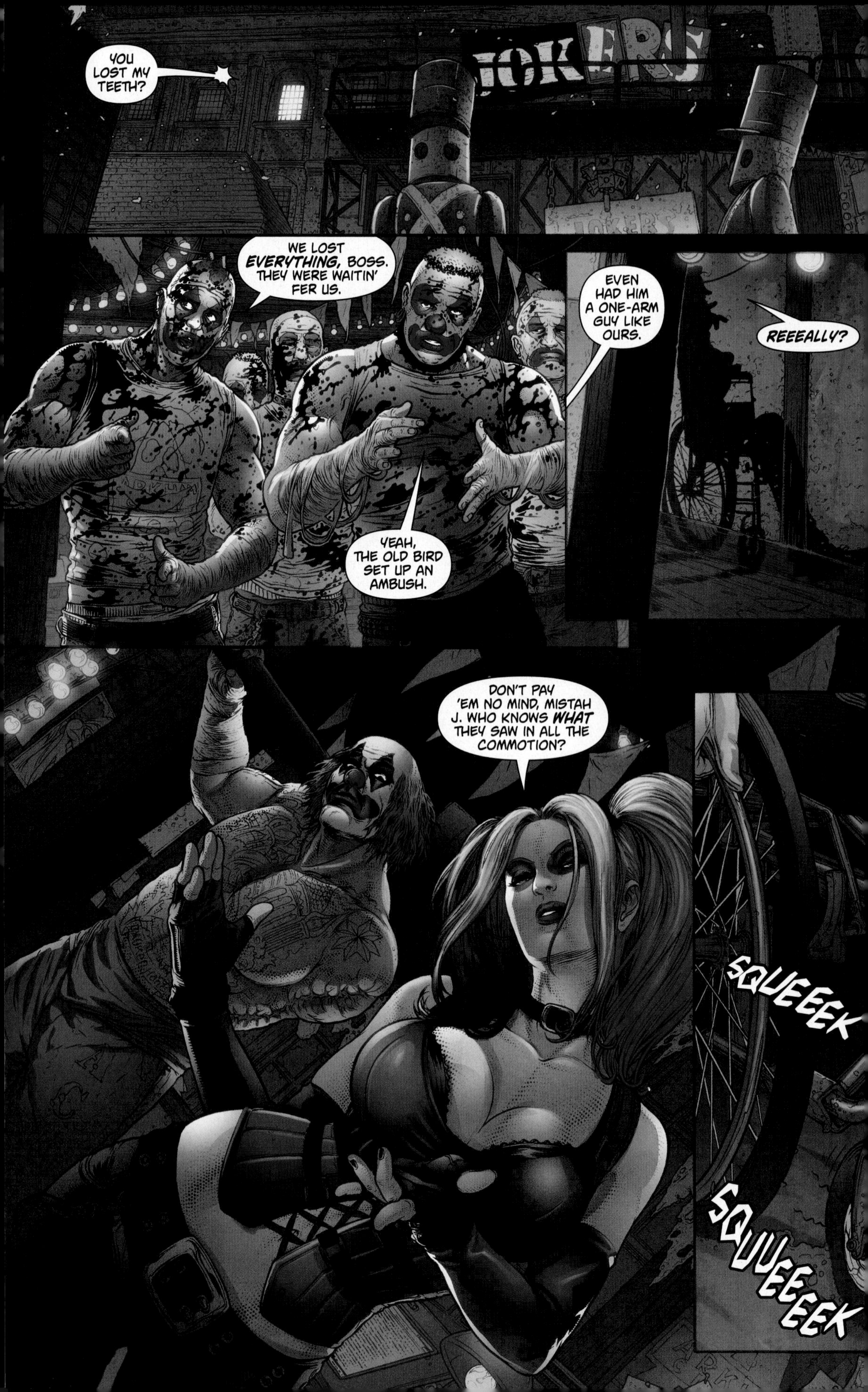
YOU LOST MY TEETH?
WE LOST EVERYTHING, BOSS. THEY WERE WAITIN' FER US.
YEAH, THE OLD BIRD SET UP AN AMBUSH.
EVEN HAD HIM A ONE-ARM GUY LIKE OURS.
REEEALLY?
DON'T PAY 'EM NO MIND, MISTAH J. WHO KNOWS WHAT THEY SAW IN ALL THE COMMOTION?
SQUEEEK
SQUUEEEEEK

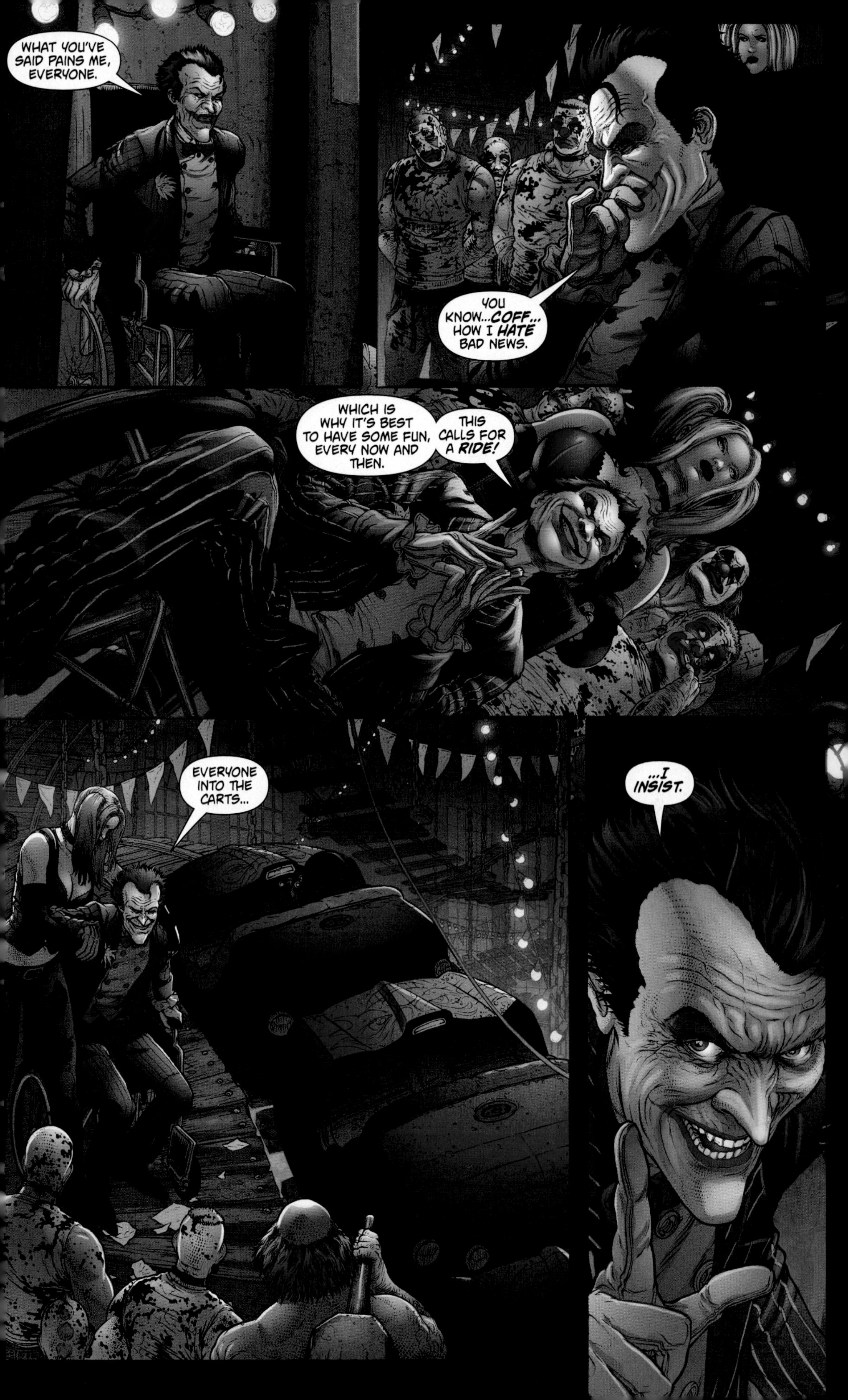
WHAT YOU'VE SAID PAINS ME, EVERYONE.
YOU KNOW...COFF... HOW I HATE BAD NEWS.
WHICH IS WHY IT'S BEST TO HAVE SOME FUN, EVERY NOW AND THEN.
THIS CALLS FOR A RIDE!
EVERYONE INTO THE CARTS...
...I INSIST.

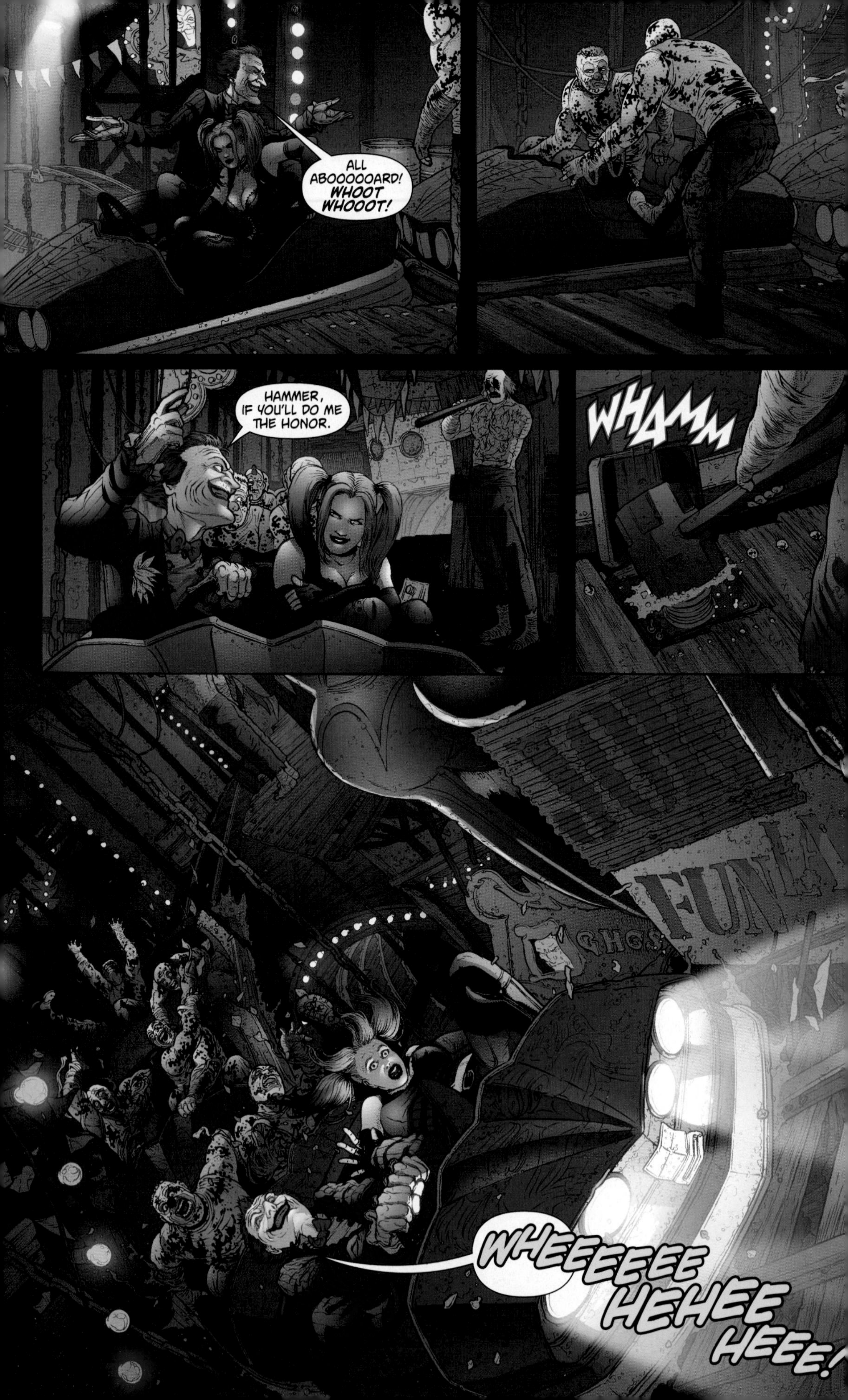
ALL ABOOOOOARD! WHOOT WHOOOT!
HAMMER, IF YOU'LL DO ME THE HONOR.
WHAMM
FUN
WHEEEEEEE HEHEE HEEE!

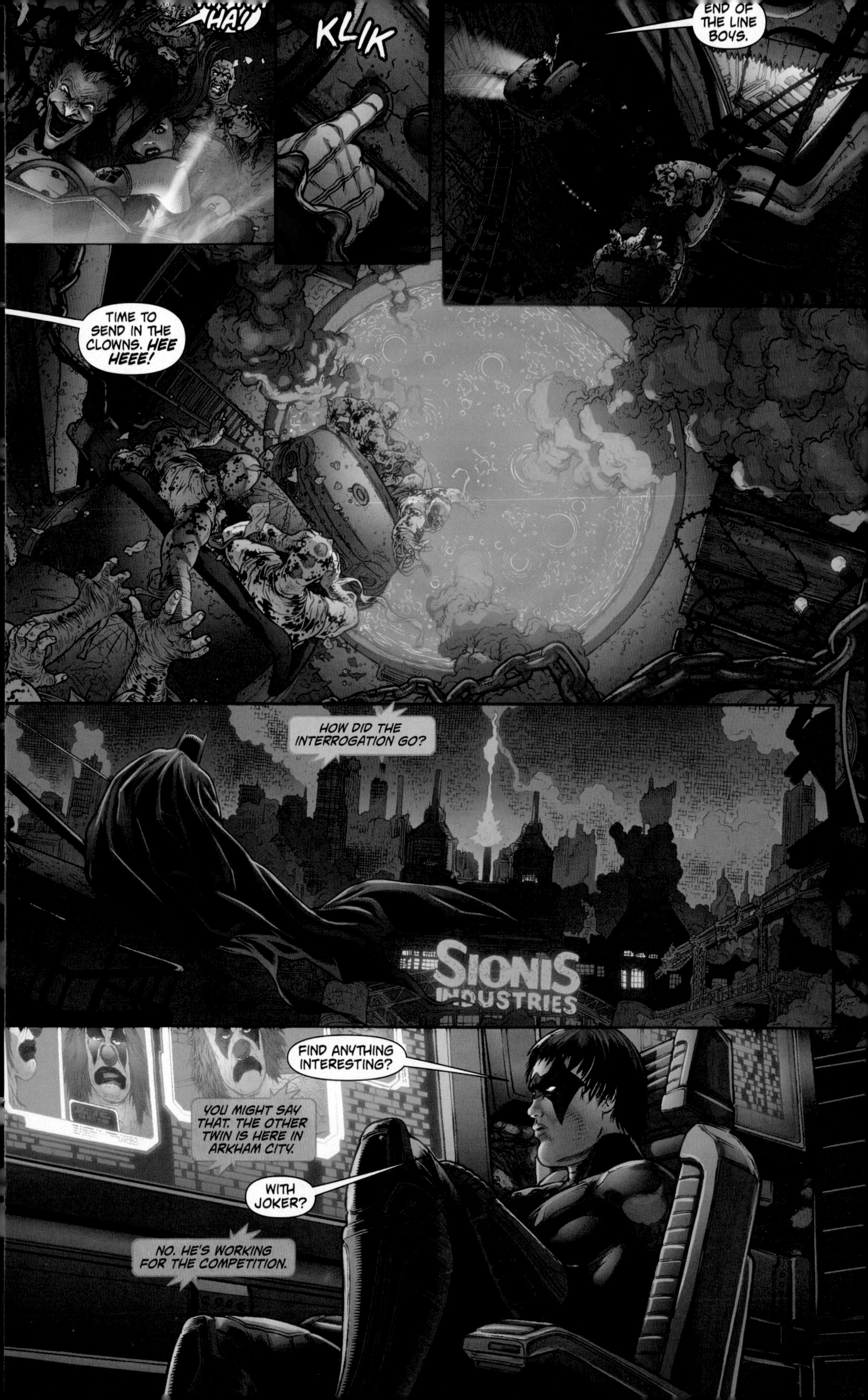
HA!!
KLIK
END OF THE LINE BOYS.
TIME TO SEND IN THE CLOWNS. HEE HEEE!
HOW DID THE INTERROGATION GO?
SIONIS INDUSTRIES
FIND ANYTHING INTERESTING?
YOU MIGHT SAY THAT. THE OTHER TWIN IS HERE IN ARKHAM CITY.
WITH JOKER?
NO. HE'S WORKING FOR THE COMPETITION.

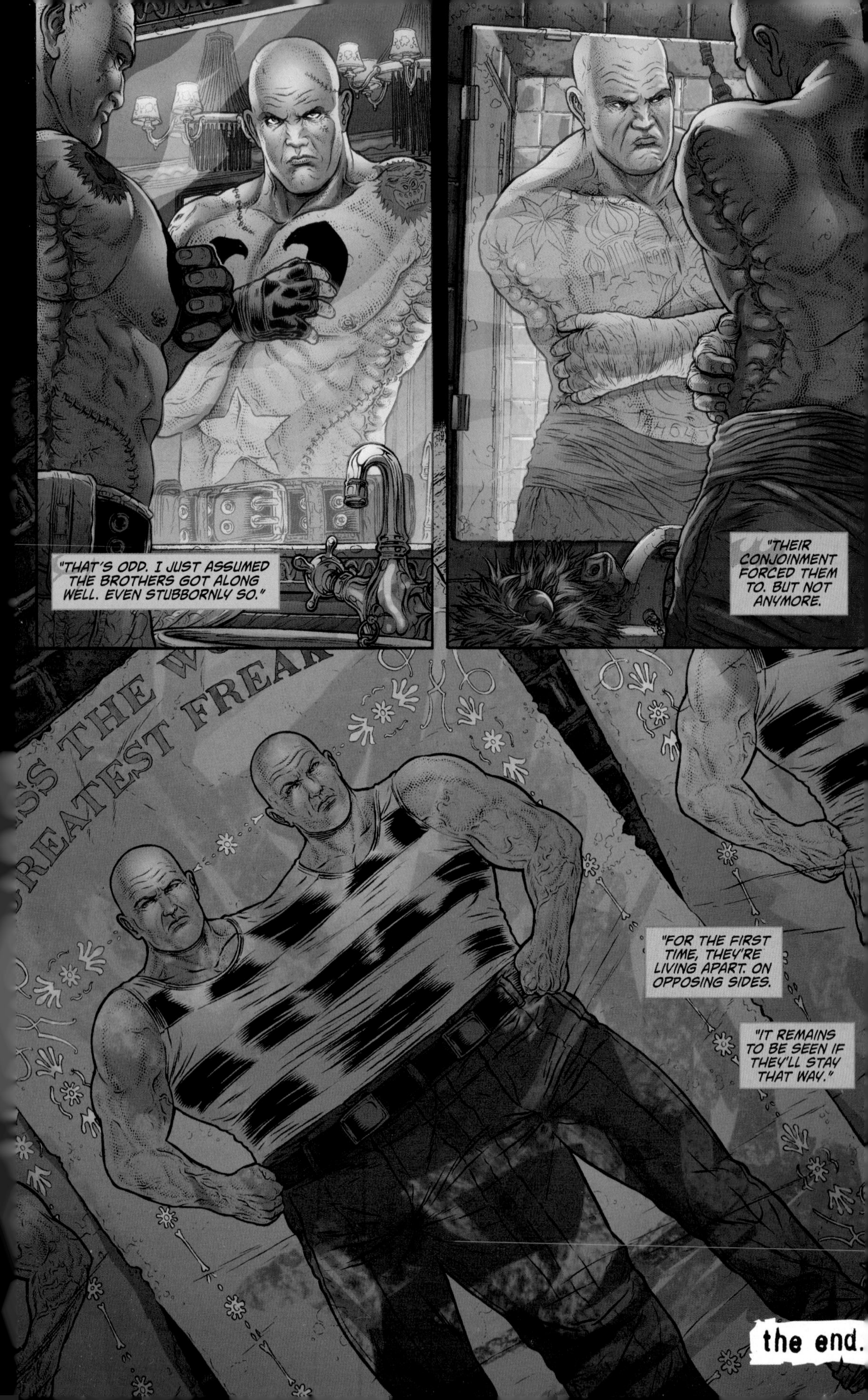
"THAT'S ODD. I JUST ASSUMED THE BROTHERS GOT ALONG WELL. EVEN STUBBORNLY SO."
"THEIR CONJOINMENT FORCED THEM TO. BUT NOT ANYMORE.
GREATEST FREAK
"FOR THE FIRST TIME, THEY'RE LIVING APART. ON OPPOSING SIDES.
"IT REMAINS TO BE SEEN IF THEY'LL STAY THAT WAY."
the end.